$2

D0160913

The
Allyn & Bacon
Workbook
Fifth Edition

Kathleen Shine Cain

Merrimack College

New York Boston San Francisco
London Toronto Sydney Tokyo Singapore Madrid
Mexico City Munich Paris Cape Town Hong Kong Montreal

Credits
Page 1: Excerpt from "Zealot of God" by Joe Treen in *People Weekly*.
Page 2: Excerpt from "In the Grip of a Psychopath" by Richard Lacayo, in *Time*.
Copyright © 1993 Time Inc. Reprinted with permission.
Pages 16-17: Excerpt from "A Botched Mission in Waco, Texas" by James Popkin and
Jeannye Thornton, in *U.S. News & World Report*. Copyright © March 15, 1993, *U.S.
News & World Report*. Reprinted with permission.
Pages 17-18: Excerpt from "Cult of Death" by Richard Lacayo, in *Time*. Copyright ©
1993, Time Inc. Reprinted with permission.
Pages 20-21: Excerpt form "Senseless" by Rick Telander is reprinted courtesy of *Sports
Illustrated* from the May 14, 1990 issue. Copyright © 1990, Time Inc. All rights
reserved.
Page 107: Excerpt from "Salvation" from *The Big Sea* by Langston Hughes. Copyright ©
1940, Langston Hughes. Renewal copyright © 1968, Arna Bontemps and George
Houston Bass. Reprinted by permission of Hill and Wang, a division of Farrar, Straus &
Giroux, Inc.

Cover Design Manager: Wendy Ann Fredericks
Cover Design: Silvers Design and Wendy Ann Fredericks
Cover Art: © Digital Vision/Creatas

Kathleen Shine Cain, *The Allyn & Bacon Workbook, Fifth Edition*

Copyright ©2003 Pearson Education, Inc.

All rights reserved. Printed in the United States of America. Instructors may reproduce
portions of this book for classroom use only. All other reproductions are strictly
prohibited without prior permission of the publisher, except in the case of brief quotations
embodied in critical articles and reviews.

Please visit our Web site at http://www.ablongman.com

ISBN: 0-321-10816-7

1 2 3 4 5 6 7 8 9 10–BMP–05 04 03 02

CONTENTS

PART III   UNDERSTANDING GRAMMAR

PART V   WRITING EFFECTIVE SENTENCES

PART VII   USING PUNCTUATION

PART XII   ENGLISH AS A SECOND LANGUAGE

PREFACE

As in the previous editions of this workbook, this edition follows the same organizational pattern as *The Allyn & Bacon Handbook.* The workbook features extensive additional exercises to help students master the reading and writing processes. Written with a basic writing student in mind, the workbook retains the four mutually reinforcing themes of the handbook: **critical thinking, writing as a process, argumentation,** and **writing across the curriculum.** This edition also includes a section on **English as a second language (ESL),** complete with exercises. Features from the previous editions of *The Allyn & Bacon Workbook* that have been retained include:

- Content for exercises is drawn from various disciplines, making reading more interesting and relevant to students.

- Exercises include both discrete sentences and connected discourse, depending on the nature of the material under discussion.

- Appropriate chapters end with review exercises for students to practice individual skills mastered within the chapter.

- Appropriate chapters include exercises that refer students to textbooks in other courses, reinforcing the interdisciplinary theme of the handbook.

- Appropriate chapters include exercises that call for students to work with their own writing, making it clear to students that the material is designed to facilitate the writing process.

In addition, this edition includes:

- Revised content and exercises for Parts I and II.

- Extensive treatment of ESL issues, with exercises.

- **Critical Decisions** boxes based on those in the handbook.

ACKNOWLEDGMENTS

I wish to thank Len Rosen and Larry Behrens for offering me the opportunity to contribute to a handbook package of the highest quality. The editorial staff at Allyn and Bacon, including Joe Opiela and Allen Workman provided invaluable assistance and advice—as did Susan McIntyre of the production staff. On the home front, my husband Jim was both supportive and understanding during the entire writing process. Finally, I want to thank my daughter Shannon not only for her patience with a preoccupied mom, but also for doing a masterful job of preparing the manuscript.

Kathleen Shine Cain
Merrimack College

CHAPTER 1

Critical Thinking and Reading

Most of your college and career writing will begin with thinking about what you have read. This chapter will prepare you to think critically by suggesting both general habits of mind and specific strategies for understanding and responding to sources (also called *source materials* and *texts*).

ACTIVE, CRITICAL HABITS OF MIND

In order to work successfully with source materials, you will need to be alert to differences and discrepancies, to challenge source materials and be challenged by them, to set issues in broader contexts, and to form and support opinions.

 Active, critical thinkers are alert to differences and discrepancies.

As an active, critical thinker, you are alert to differences and discrepancies. Think of a difference as a disagreement between what you expect to see and what you see, or as a discrepancy between what different people say about a given subject, issue, or problem. Consider the differences and discrepancies between the following two passages on the same subject:

People Weekly
Zealot of God

For someone who claimed to believe he was Jesus, David Koresh was a twisted representation of Christian ideals. Rather than practice the forgiveness of sinners, he frequently punished children as young as 8 months old by beating them till they were bruised and bloody. Instead of putting temptation behind him, he had a harem of as many as 19 "wives" and slept with girls 12 and 13 years old. And unlike the Prince of Peace, Koresh packed a Glock 9-mm pistol and kept a deadly arsenal he was willing to use. Despite all this, he had a passionate following—his own religious cult of several hundred members—who believed that to get to heaven they had to go through hell.

—Joe Treen

Time
In the Grip of a Psychopath

Equipped with both a creamy charm and a cold-blooded willingness to manipulate those drawn to him, [David] Koresh was a type well known to students of cult practices: the charismatic leader with a pathological edge. He was the most spectacular example since Jim Jones, who committed suicide in 1978 with more than 900 of his followers at the People's Temple in Guyana. Like Jones, Koresh fashioned a tight-knit community that saw itself at desperate odds with the world outside. He plucked sexual partners as he pleased from among his followers and formed an élite guard of lieutenants to enforce his will. And like Jones, he led his followers to their doom.

—Richard Lacayo

Differences lead to questions

A reader trained to be alert to differences and discrepancies would notice that these two passages offer different perspectives on Koresh. One expresses disbelief that anyone could follow such a man, while the other explains why he had so many followers. Noticing differences and discrepancies should lead you to ask the question *why?* Here is a set of techniques for being alert to differences:

Be Alert to Differences

Before reading:

- Skim a text and identify its topic.
- Make a note, mental or written, on what you know about the topic or what you can remember others have written about it.

During reading:

- Compare what the author has written with your notes.
- Identify differences
- Complete your reading by returning to each point of difference and using it to generate questions.

After reading:

- Option: Begin an investigation or create an action plan for doing so, guided by your questions.

Pose questions based on a difference between sources.

Some questions you may ask after reading these two passages include:

What, exactly, was Koresh's message?
How did Koresh gather his following?
Where did his followers come from?

Pose questions based on a difference between a text and your experience.

You may also discover differences between what you read and what you know to be true or likely, based on your experience. For example, you may have taken a psychology course in which cult behavior was discussed, you may be familiar with the Bible, or you may be familiar with non-mainstream religions. This knowledge could lead to further questions about the passages:

How do Koresh's teachings fit with those of other Christian religions?
What would make someone join his cult?
How did this cult emerge from a more mainstream religion?

Option: Generate an action plan

Your questions may well lead to some research. For example, you may decide to investigate the history of the Branch Davidians or some other cult. While not all of your questions will lead to research, be prepared to follow up on those questions that intrigue you.

1b Active, critical thinkers challenge, and are challenged by, sources.

Questions are the doors that lead you inside a text. The more questions you pose, the deeper you delve into the text.

1 Asking questions of the text

You can pose the following questions as you read a text critically:

- What central problem, issue, or subject does the text explore? What are the reasons for this problem? What are the effects of this problem?

- What is the most important, or the most striking, statement the author makes? Why is it important or striking?

- Who is the author, and what are the author's credentials for writing on this topic? What is the author's stake in writing this? What does the author have to gain?

- How can I use this selection? What can I learn from it?

2   Asking questions of yourself, based on the text

As you read a text, you should question your own experience, values, and opinions until you understand your views on the topic. Pose the following questions to yourself in order to let a text challenge you:

- What can I learn from this text? Will this knowledge change me?

- What is my background on this topic? How will my experience affect my reading?

- What is the origin of my views on the topic?

- What new interests, or what new question or observation, does this text spark in me?

- If I turned the topic of this selection into a question on which people voted, how would I vote—and why?

1c   Active, critical thinkers set issues in a broader context.

Every issue, concern, or problem that you read about exists in a larger context—in a larger cluster of related issues, concerns, or problems. The following techniques should help you discover the context:

Setting Issues in Their Broader Context

- Begin by identifying one or more issues you feel are important to a text.
- Assume that each issue is an instance, or example, of something larger. Your job is to speculate on this larger something.
- Write the name of the issue at the top of a page, or on the computer screen. Below this, write a question: "What's this a part of?" Then write a one-paragraph response.
- Reread your response, and briefly state the broader context.

- Use this broader context to stimulate more thought on the reading selection and to generate questions about issues of interest.
- Option: Begin an investigation or create an action plan for doing so, guided by your questions (optional).

Option: Generate an action plan

Identifying broader contexts will allow you to generate further questions, possibly leading to further research.

1d Active, critical thinkers will form, and support, opinions.

If you know how to ask questions, you will be able to form and support your own opinions. Use the following questions as you develop your opinions:

- Has the author explained things clearly?

- In what ways does this topic confuse me?

- Has the author convinced me of his or her main argument?

- What is my view on this topic?

- Would I recommend this source to others?

Although you won't be asked to compose a formal response to everything you read, you should be prepared to offer reasons for your opinions. Techniques for reading to evaluate a source appear on page 10; techniques for writing formal evaluations appear in chapter 2 (pages 29–33).

In order to have an informed discussion with others who have opinions different from yours, you must have read the material, questioned both the text and yourself, thought about broader contexts, and developed a response that can be supported with evidence from the text. An informed reader should be able to write a formal response, if called upon. (See chapter 6 for a discussion on stating and supporting opinions.)

COMPONENTS OF A CLOSE, CRITICAL READING

The first part of this chapter prepares you in a general way for thinking critically about what you see and hear. In some situations, however, you will need to formalize and systematize your critical thinking skills. In this section you will learn how to understand, respond to, evaluate, and synthesize what you read. The forms of writing associated with close reading—summary, evaluation, analysis, and synthesis—are discussed in chapter 2.

Reading and *re*reading

Most experienced critical readers find that it is necessary to read a text two or more times. Although four types of close, critical reading are discussed here, ordinarily it is not necessary to read a selection four times.

1e   Critical reading (1): Reading to understand

The first goal of the critical reader is to understand the material.

1   Setting goals for reading to understand

The steps in reading to understand can be summarized as follows:

- *Identify the author's purpose.* This will likely be to inform or to argue.

- *Identify the author's intended audience.* The text will be written with particular readers in mind. Determine if you are the intended audience.

- *Locate the author's main point.* Every competently written text has a main point that you should be able to express in your own words.

- *Understand the structure of the text.* If the author is arguing, locate the main point and supporting points; if the author is presenting information, locate the main point and identify the stages into which the presentation has been divided.

- *Identify as carefully as possible what you do not understand.*

2   Applying techniques for reading to understand

Most systems for reading to understand involve three stages.

PREVIEW   Skim the text, reading quickly both to identify the author's purpose and to recall what you know about the topic.

READ   Read with pen in hand, making notes on separate sheets or on photocopied pages about the content and the structure of the text. Stop periodically to monitor your progress.

REVIEW   Skim the text a second time to consolidate your notes: jot down questions and highlight especially important passages.

What follows are techniques for highlighting information important to understanding a source.

Preview

Preview the Text

- Read titles, openings, and closings in full.
- Skim the rest of the text.
- Recall what you know about the topic.
- Predict what you will learn from reading.

- *Read titles, openings, and closings in full*. This preview will give you a sense of topic, audience, purpose, and main point. Read the title and guess the relationship between the title and text. If you are reading an article or a chapter of a book, read the opening and closing paragraphs in full. If you are reading a book, read the preface along with the first and last chapters.

- *Skim the rest of the text*. A brief look at the text will help you to understand the structure, or layout, of the source. When skimming an article, read all headings along with a few sentences from every second or third paragraph. When skimming a book, review the table of contents and then read the opening and closing paragraphs of each chapter.

- *Recall what you know about the topic*. A review of your previous exposure to a topic will prepare you to be interested and ready with questions as you begin reading. After skimming a text, think about the topic: reflect on your personal history with it.

- *Predict what you will learn from reading*. Based on your quick review of the text and on your knowledge of the topic, predict what you will learn. Predictions form an important part of a close, critical reading by keeping you focused on the content and alert to potential difficulties.

Read

Read the Text

- Identify the author's purpose.
- Underline important phrases and sentences.
- Write notes that summarize your underlining.
- Identify sections.
- Identify difficult passages.
- Periodically ask: Am I understanding?

Read with a pen or pencil in hand and make notes that will help you understand.

- *Identify the author's purpose.* The author's purpose will likely be to inform or to argue. Locate passages that illustrate this purpose.

- *Underline important phrases and sentences.* Your underlining or highlighting of important information should work with your notes (see below) so that you can return to the text and spot the author's main topic at a glance.

- *Write notes that summarize your underlining.* You can summarize important points of an explanation or an argument by writing brief phrases in the margins; this will help you to understand as you read and to recall important information as you reread.

- *Identify sections.* A section of a text is a grouping of related paragraphs (see 5a). Sometimes, an author will provide section headings; at other times, you will need to write them. In either case, your awareness of sections will help you understand the structure of a text.

- *Identify difficult passages.* You can use a question mark to identify passages that confuse you, and circle unfamiliar words. Unless a particular word is repeated often and seems central to the meaning of a text, postpone using a dictionary until you complete your reading. Frequent interruptions to check the meaning of words will fragment your reading and disrupt your understanding (see 22e).

- *Periodically ask: Am I understanding?* You should stop at least once during your reading to ask yourself this question. If you are having trouble, change your plan for reading. For especially difficult selections, try dividing the text into small sections and reading one section at a sitting. Read until you understand each section, or until you can identify what you do not understand.

Review

Review the Text

- Consolidate information.
- Organize your questions.

After you have read and made notes, you will integrate what the author has said with how the material has been presented. This activity will help you later on when you are asked to recall the selection.

- *Consolidate information.* Skim the passage and reread your notes. Clarify them, if necessary, so that they accurately represent the selection. Reread and highlight (with boxes or stars) what you consider to be the author's significant sentences or paragraphs.

- *Organize your questions.* Review the various terms and concepts you have had trouble understanding. Organize your questions concerning vocabulary and content. Use dictionaries; seek out fellow students or a professor to clarify especially difficult points. Even if you do not pursue these questions immediately, you should clarify what you do not understand. Your questions, gathered into one place, such as a journal, will be an excellent place to begin reviewing for an exam.

1f Critical reading (2): Reading to respond

Once you understand what you have read, focus on your personal response.

1 Setting goals for reading to respond

The goals of reading to respond are as follows:

- Reflect on your experience and associations with the topic of a text.

- Know what you feel about a text—know your emotional response.

- Let the text challenge you.

- Use a text to spark new, imaginative thinking.

2 Applying techniques for reading to respond

Ask questions like the following to focus on *you* and *your* reactions to a text:

Questions that promote a personal response

- *Which one or two sentences did I respond to most strongly in this text? What was my response?* Usually, you will read one or two sentences that will prompt reactions. Name these reactions. Explore your reasons for being excited, angry, thoughtful, surprised, or threatened. Keep the focus on you.

- *What is the origin of my views on this topic? Who else shares my views?* If you are reading on a controversial topic, explore where and under what circumstances you learned about the topic. For the sake of developing a response, criticize the views of people who believe as you do. Apply this criticism to yourself. What do you discover?

- *If I turned the subject of this text into a question on which people would vote, how would I vote—and why?* This question can help involve you with the text, since casting a vote requires some interest, if only self-interest, in a topic. Try getting involved with the text by locating a debate in the text and by taking sides.

- *What new interest, question, or observation does this text spark in me?* Use a text to spark your own thinking. Let the text help you pose new questions or make new observations. Use the text as a basis for speculation.

1g Critical reading (3): Reading to evaluate

Having understood and responded to a text, you will determine how effective the author has been in presenting the material.

1 Setting goals for reading to evaluate

The goals in reading to evaluate are to:

- Distinguish between an author's use of facts and opinions.

- Distinguish between an author's assumptions (fundamental beliefs about the world) and your own.

- Judge the effectiveness of an explanation.

- Judge the effectiveness of an argument.

2 | Applying techniques for reading to evaluate

When you are reading to evaluate, you should recognize an author's use of *facts, opinions, definitions,* and his or her *assumed views of the world.* You should also try to determine whether the author intends to inform or to argue.

Distinguish facts from opinions

A fact is any statement that can be verified. While you can—and should—question some of the facts you read, it is always possible to determine whether or not a fact is true or false. An opinion, on the other hand, is a statement of interpretation and judgment. Evaluating an opinion involves analyzing the foundation of that opinion. As you read, you should make note of opinions and your response to them.

Distinguishing Fact from Opinion

Fact: A statement, the accuracy of which can be checked

Ask: Is this fact dependable?
How could I check the accuracy of this fact?

Opinion: An interpretation judgment

Ask: Is this opinion well supported?
If so, do I agree or disagree? Why?

Distinguish your assumptions from those of an author

An assumption is a fundamental belief that shapes the way people see. The concept of beauty, for example, is not the same for all people. Some assumptions are based on clearly defined reasons, while others are based on ill-defined feelings. To understand an author's opinions, it is often necessary to identify the assumptions on which they are based. (Sometimes an opinion is a direct expression of an assumption.)

CONSIDER TWO SETS OF ASSUMPTIONS

In evaluating what you read, you need to understand both the author's assumptions and your own. To do so, you must perform two related tasks: identify an author's opinions, and determine whether each opinion is based on some other opinion or assumed view.

IDENTIFY DIRECT AND INDIRECT ASSUMPTIONS

The following assumption is stated directly: "Every United States citizen has a right to quality health care." An indirect assumption might read as follows: "Because such a large percentage of the population is without it, a plan must be implemented to provide quality health care for all." The second assumption implies the first, that quality health care is a right. If you can show that an author's assumed views are flawed or that you disagree with them, you can challenge all opinions based on those assumptions.

Distinguish your definitions of terms from an author's

In evaluating a source, you must determine how the author defines important words. If your definition differs from the author's, then you will probably disagree with the author's ideas.

Question sources that explain and sources that argue

A critical reader must pose questions based on the author's intent: to inform or to argue.

SOURCES THAT EXPLAIN

When a selection asks you to accept an explanation, a description, or a procedure as accurate, pose—and respond to—these questions:

- For whom has the author intended the description, explanation, or procedure? The general public—non-experts? Someone involved in the same business or process? An observer, such as an evaluator or a supervisor?

- What does the text define and explain? How successful is the presentation, given its intended audience?

- How trustworthy is the author's information? How current it it? If it is not current, are the points being made still applicable, assuming more recent information could be obtained?

- If the author presents a procedure, what is its purpose or outcome? Who would carry out this procedure? When? For what reasons? Does the author present the stages of the procedure?

SOURCES THAT ARGUE

When a selection asks you to accept an argument, pose—and respond to—these questions:

- What conclusion am I being asked to accept?

- What reasons and evidence has the author offered for me to accept this conclusion? Are the reasons logical? Is the evidence fair? Has the author acknowledged and responded to other points of view?

- To what extent is the author appealing to logic? to my emotions? to my respect for authorities?[1]

1h Critical reading (4): Reading to synthesize

Having understood, responded to, and evaluated a text, you can synthesize, or link, that text with others.

1 Setting goals for reading to synthesize

Your goals for reading to synthesize are to:

- Read to understand, respond to, and evaluate multiple sources on a subject, problem, or issue

- Understand your own views on the subject, problem, or issue. Be able to state these views in a sentence or two.

- Forge relationships among source materials, according to your purpose. In a synthesis, *your* views should predominate. Use the work of various authors to support what you think.

- Generally, try to create a conversation among sources. Be sure that yours is the major voice in the conversation.

2 Applying techniques for reading to synthesize

As you seek out relationships among sources, make sure that you consider yourself a source as well.

---

[1]See 6h for a full discussion of evaluating arguments.

A Strategy for Synthesizing Sources

1. *Read, respond to, and evaluate multiple sources on one topic.* It is very likely that the authors will have different observations to make. Because you are working with the different sources, you are in a unique position to draw relationships among them.

2. *Subdivide the topic into parts and give each a brief title.* Call the topic that the several authors discuss X. What are all the parts, or the subdivisions, of X that the authors discuss? List the separate parts, giving each a brief title.

3. *Write cross-references for each part.* For each subdivision of the topic, list *specific* page references to whichever sources discuss that part. This is called **cross-referencing.** Once you have cross-referenced each of the topic's parts, you will have created an index to your reading selections.

4. *Summarize author's information or ideas about each part.* Now that you have generated cross-references that show you which authors discuss which parts of topic X, take up one part at a time and reread all passages you have cross-referenced. Summarize what each author has written on particular parts of the topic.

5. *Forge relationships among reading selections.* Study your notes and try to link sources. Here are several relationships that you might establish:

    Comparison: One author *agrees* with another.

    Contrast: One author *disagrees* with another.

    Example: Material in one source *illustrates* a statement in another.

    Definition: Material from several sources, considered together, may help you *define* or redefine a term.

    Cause and effect: Material from one source may allow you to *explain directly* why certain events occur in other sources.

    Personal response: You find yourself agreeing or disagreeing with points made in one or more sources. Ask yourself *why* and then develop an answer by referring to specific passages.

Read multiple sources on a topic

When you identify relationships among sources, look at *specific parts* of these works. If you divide a topic into parts, you will find it easier to make cross-references, a key to developing a synthesis.

Divide the topic into parts

You will be able to divide a topic into parts and relate sources to one another if your have read closely and critically.

Cross-reference each part and summarize

After you have identified parts of your topic, list page numbers from your sources that relate to each part and write a brief note summarizing the author's information or ideas.

Forge relationships among your sources

Five general questions should help you establish relationships among your sources.

1. Which authors agree?
2. Which authors disagree?
3. Are there examples in one source of statements or ideas expressed in another?
4. What definitions can you offer, based on the readings?
5. Do you detect a cause and effect relationship in any of the readings?

EXERCISE 1-1   Becoming alert to differences

Read the following two excerpts from accounts of the raid on the Branch Davidian compound in Waco, Texas, on February 28, 1993. Both appeared on March 15, 1993. Following the guidelines in 1a, observe differences and discrepancies between the two excerpts or between anything in the excerpts and your own experience. Pose questions based on these differences. Finally, outline a plan for potential research based on your questions.

A botched mission in Waco, Texas

Critics have tried to abolish it. Much of its mission involves hohum chores like preventing the sale of contraband cigarettes. It doesn't even have its own TV show.

But the Bureau of Alcohol, Tobacco and Firearms is a low-profile agency no more. After a Sunday-morning firefight at the 77-acre Branch Davidian compound outside Waco, Texas, that left four agents dead, 15 injured and an undetermined number of cult members dead or wounded, the ATF faces its own judgment day. Its bosses in the Treasury Department, Congress and the public are all aching to know how such a delicate mission could go so disastrously awry. "I think this was a very ineptly planned operation. It was carried out with the same unfortunate ineptitude," says Tony Cooper, a former Justice Department terrorism expert who now teaches courses in terrorism and conflict resolution at the University of Texas at Dallas. Among the questions he and others ask:

- Why wasn't a less aggressive approach tried first? In 1988, when Branch Davidian leader David Koresh was charged in a shooting incident, he was taken into custody peacefully. The charges were eventually dismissed.

- Why weren't the compound's phones tapped? If they had been, authorities would have learned that a tipster had told Koresh about the raid.

- If officials feared Koresh's firepower and were counting on the element of surprise, why didn't they raid before dawn when most of the 100 or so sect members would have been sleeping?

- Why wasn't the undercover agent who had infiltrated the group ordered to stay in the compound to face arrest with the others? That would have kept his cover and, if the raid failed, would have allowed better monitoring of the sect.

"Ambushed." Bureau officials argue that such second-guessing is unfair. Cult leader Koresh was "sworn to resistance," says bureau spokesman Jack Killorin, who contends it was only prudent to plan a raid backed by serious firepower. The *Houston Chronicle* reported late last week that Koresh met agents just before the gunfire began. "One of our guys said, 'Federal agents—put your hands up,' " one agent told the newspaper. "Koresh smiled, backed up and slammed the door. Almost immediately, within seconds, we were ambushed."

Although a wiretap might have helped prevent the slaughter, ATF spokesman Tom Hill says court officials would have rejected the request because the bureau could just as easily have received the wiretap information from its undercover agent. Bureau commanders also decided it was safe for its infiltrator to leave the compound, ATF Deputy Director Dan Hartnett says, because when he left "everything was normal." And Hill says ATF commanders decided to storm the ranch in the late morning because "that was the time when the children would come out to play and would be separated from the adults."

Despite such justifications, questions about the botched raid are fueling broader attacks on the ATF.

—James Popkin and Jeannye Thornton
U.S. News and World Report, March 15, 1993 (page 24)

Cult of Death

Planning for last week's raid began months ago, when federal and state law-enforcement officials concluded that cult members were stockpiling guns and preparing to make legal semiautomatics into illegal automatic weapons. ATF agents acquired a house near the compound, pretending to be neighbors and potential recruits. Search warrant in hand, more than 100 agents charged the buildings early Sunday morning, only to be met by an explosion of gunfire. "From the moment we stepped out of the trailer we were under fire from everywhere," says one agent who was pinned to the ground for 45 minutes.

The failure of the assault led to criticisms that ATF had fatally underestimated its adversary—or overestimated its own capabilities in a bid for the media spotlight. Treasury Secretary Lloyd Bentsen, whose department includes the bureau, promised a full inquiry. ATF officials claim that the raid failed largely because Koresh was tipped off. About 45 minutes before the shooting began, an agent who had infiltrated the cult's worship services saw Koresh get a phone call that he believes warned him that attackers were on their way.

Among the questions that remain is why ATF agents did not try to nab Koresh on the frequent occasions when he left the compound to jog, shop or eat in local restaurants. And with children in the buildings, why didn't they treat the whole operation as a delicate hostage situation? "When these groups are confronted by law enforcement they should be handled gingerly," said Marc Galanter, a professor of psychiatry at the New York University School of Medicine, who has studied cults. "You should establish communication rather than confront them head on."

ATF spokesman Jack Killorin said that his bureau decided to move because it believed that during a long siege—or even if Koresh were seized alone outside—cult members would opt for suicide, taking the children with them. And almost all show-downs with determined and fanatical groups have led to casualties, he insisted, no matter how they were handled. "We've gone about them in a number of different ways—ruse, ambush, siege and talk," said Killorin. "In almost every one we lose law-enforcement officers."

After two days of negotiation that followed the shootout, Koresh promised to surrender himself peacefully if he could deliver a statement on radio. But after his rambling 58-minute address was broadcast on Christian stations around the country, he reneged, saying he was still awaiting "further instructions from God." With Biblical scholars on hand to help them fathom Koresh's thinking, three negotiating teams headed by the FBI remained in periodic phone contact with him and other Davidians. "The constant theme is, 'When are you coming out?' " said Jeffrey Jamar, the FBI agent in charge of the operation.

The cult has stockpiled enough water, canned goods, grain and ready-to-eat meals to last several months. Even if electricity is cut off, the group may have its own emergency generators. Koresh is telling negotiators that he is annoyed by reports that he has claimed to be Christ, despite the stories of ex-cult members that he often did so. Though he is reported to have urged his flock last Easter to prepare for mass suicide, he now insists that they will not turn their guns upon themselves. But people who know them well are not reassured. Say the worried Lisa and Bruce Gent: "They will kill for him." And Koresh, a man caught up in a dream of the Apocalypse, may be ready to die as well.

—Richard Lacayo
Time, March 15, 1993 (page 39)

EXERCISE 1-2   Challenging sources

Read either the two passages on David Koresh in 1a or the two accounts of the raid in Exercise 1-1. Following the guidelines in 1b, pose questions that challenge each piece. Then pose questions to challenge yourself based on one of the selections.

EXERCISE 1-3   Setting issues in a broader context

Return to the selections you used for Exercise 1-2. Following the guidelines in 1c, create a phrase that summarizes an issue, subject, or problem found in the selections. Then write a response to the question "What's this a part of?" in order to place the selection in a broader context. Finally, generate an action plan to further research the issue.

Phrase:

"What's this a part of?"

Action plan:

EXERCISE 1-4   Forming and supporting opinions

Following guidelines in 1d, develop an opinion based on one of the selections and write a paragraph in support of that opinion. After completing your paragraph, meet in groups of three or four and compare your opinions and support with fellow students. Does each member offer sufficient support for his or her opinion? If not, how might the opinion be better supported?

EXERCISE 1-5   Reading to understand

Using the guidelines in 1f, conduct a close reading to understand the following section from Rick Telander's essay, "Senseless." After completing your reading, meet in groups of three or four and compare your notes and observations with fellow students. Are there any significant differences? How do you account for them? Do other students note anything you missed (or vice versa)?

1
. . . In a country that has long been hung up on style over substance, flash over depth, the athletic shoe and sportswear industries (a projected 5.5 billion dollars in domestic sales of name-brand shoes in 1990; more than $2 billion in sweatpants, sweatshirts, and warmup suits) suddenly have come to represent the pinnacle of consumer exploitation. In recent months the industries, which include heavyweights Nike and Reebok as well as smaller players Adidas, Asics, British Knights, Brooks, Converse, Ellesse, Etonic, Fila, L.A. Gear, New Balance, Pony, Puma, Starter, and numerous other makers of sports shoes, caps, and jackets, have been accused of creating a fantasy-fueled market for luxury items in the economically blasted inner cities and willingly tapping into the flow of drug and gang money. This has led to a frightening outbreak of crimes among poor black kids trying to make their mark by "busting fresh," or dressing at the height of fashion.

2
In some cities muggings for sportswear are commonplace—Atlanta police, for instance, estimate they have handled more than fifty such robberies in the last four months. Yet it is not only the number of violent acts but also the seeming triviality of the booty that has stunned the public. In February, nineteen-year-old Calvin Wash was about to cross Central Park Avenue on Chicago's West Side when, according to police, two youths drove up in a van and demanded that he give them the Cincinnati Bengal jacket he was wearing. When Wash resisted, one of the youths is alleged to have fatally shot him in the back—through the A in BENGALS.

3
Chicago police sergeant Michael Chasen, who works in the violent crimes division in Area Four, which covers four of Chicago's twenty-five police districts, says his districts have about fifty reported incidents involving jackets and about a dozen involving gym shoes each month. "When you really think about the crime itself—taking someone's clothes off their body—you can't get much more basic," he says.

4
But of course, these assailants aren't simply taking clothes from their victims. They're taking status. Something is very wrong with a society that has created an underclass that is slipping into economic and moral oblivion, an underclass in which pieces of rubber and plastic held together by shoelaces are sometimes worth more than a human life. The shoe companies have played a direct role in this. With their million-dollar advertising campaigns, superstar spokesmen, and overdesigned, high-priced products aimed at impressionable young people, they are creating status from thin air to feed those who are starving for self-esteem. "No one person is responsible for this type of violence," says Patricia Graham, principal of Chicago's Simeon High, one of the city's perennial basketball powers. "It's a combination of circumstances. It's about values and training. Society's values are out of sync, which is why these things have become important."

"The classic explanation in sociology is that these people are driven by peer pressure," says Mervin Daniel, a sociology professor at Morgan State. "What is advertised on TV and whatever your peers are doing, you do it too." Most assuredly, the shoe industry relies heavily on advertising; it spends more than two hundred million dollars annually to promote and advertise its products, churning out a blizzard of images and words that make its shoes seem preternaturally hip, cool, and necessary. Nike alone will spend sixty million dollars in 1990 on TV and print ads that have built such slogans as "Bo knows," and "Just do it," and "Do you know? Do you know? Do you know?" into mantras of consumerism.

5

What is baffling, however, is the strength of certain sporting products as icons for drug dealers and gangs. In Boston the Greenwood Street gang wears Green Bay Packer garb, the Vamp Hill Kings wear Los Angeles Kings and Raider gear, and the Castlegate gang wears Cincinnati Reds clothes. "The Intervale gang uses all Adidas stuff exclusively—hats, jackets, sweatpants, shoes," says Bill Stewart III, the probation officer at the Dorchester District Court in Boston, one of the busiest criminal courts in the nation. "They even have an Adidas handshake, copying the three stripes on the product. They extend three fingers when they shake hands."

6

Stewart knows how certain young drug dealers feverishly load up on the latest models of sneakers, tossing out any old ones that are scuffed or even slightly worn and replacing them with new pairs. "I was in a kid's apartment recently and there were about fifty pairs of brand-new sneakers, all top-of-the-line stuff—Adidas, Reebok, and so forth," he says. "I asked the kid's mother how he came into all this stuff. She said she didn't know."

7

The use of Major League Baseball hats by gangs has prompted some high schools around the nation to ban them from school grounds, and expensive gold chains, major league or major college team jackets, and other ostentatious, potentially troublesome items have also been prohibited. "When I look around sometimes, I think I'm in spring training in Florida," says Stewart.

8

When informed that baseball caps are being used by gangs as part of their uniforms, Major League Baseball public relations director Richard Levin seemed shocked. "I'm not aware of it at all, nor would I understand why," he said. "Obviously, we don't support it in any way."

9

Could any respectable U.S. corporation support the use of its products in this way? Absolutely not, said most shoe company executives contacted for this article. You better believe it, said a number of sports apparel retailers, as well as some of the more candid shoe execs.

10

EXERCISE 1-6   **Reading to respond**

Return to the Telander selection in Exercise 1-5, this time reading to respond. When making notes and underlining, use a different color pen or pencil than the one you used while reading to understand. After completing your reading, meet in groups of three or four and compare your responses.

EXERCISE 1-7   **Reading to evaluate**

Return to the Telander selection in Exercise 1-5, this time reading to evaluate. When making notes and underlining, use a different color pen or pencil than the ones you used while reading to understand and to respond. After completing your reading, meet in groups of three or four and compare your evaluations. Are there any significant differences? How do you account for them? Do other students' evaluations cause you to rethink your own?

EXERCISE 1-8   **Reading to synthesize: Read, respond to, and evaluate**

Read the following four passages, following the guidelines in 1f, g, and h.

A measure of critical dissent emanating from universities can help to keep national institutions flexible and growing, but if this reaches the point at which university discipline or social order is threatened the fruitful balance will have been broken. The pursuit of truth is usually held to require a certain detachment from immediate political and social problems; yet if institutions are not deeply involved with the life of the region and the nation, they will fail to produce the well-trained talent that both need. Institutions of higher education are involved in the transmission of a cultural heritage, or perhaps in the revival of a failing national culture, and yet they are drawn by other loyalties into an international community of scholarship transcending national and regional differences. If a balance is not held, nationalism easily deteriorates from a desirable dynamic of political unity into the isolation of group hatred. By the same token, when a university teacher uses his position as a base from which to exert pressures toward purely political objectives, or when a government official uses his power to prevent a university from achieving its intrinsic aims, the desirable framework of balance is weakened.

—*The New Encyclopaedia Brittanica*

The white kids were going to have a chance to become Galileos and Madame Curies and Edisons and Gauguins, and our boys (the girls weren't even in on it) would try to be Jesse Owenses and Joe Louises.

Owens and the Brown Bomber were great heroes in our world, but what school official in the white-goddom of Little Rock had the right to decide that those two men must be our only heroes? Who decided that for Henry Reed to become a scientist he had to work like George Washington Carver, as a boot-black, to buy a lousy microscope? Bailey was obviously always going to be too small to be an athlete, so which concrete angel glued to what country seat had decided that if my brother wanted to become a lawyer he had to first pay penance for his skin by picking cotton and hoeing corn and studying correspondence books at night for twenty years?

—Maya Angelou

The academic and cultural revolution on campus . . . is conducted in the name of those who suffer from the effects of race and gender discrimination in America, or from the effects of Western colonialism in the Third World. It is a revolution in behalf of minority victims. Its mission is to put an end to bigoted attitudes that permit perceived social injustice to continue, to rectify past and present inequities, and to advance the interests of the previously disenfranchised—unobjectionable aims, to be sure. But because the revolutionaries view xenophobia, racism, sexism, and other prejudices to be endemic and culturally sanctioned, their project seeks a fundamental restructuring of American society. It involves basic changes in the way economic rewards are distributed, and in the way cultural and political power is exercised.

—Dinesh D'Souza

The world is full of multicultural, multiethnic, multilingual nations, so there are plenty of models around. Indeed, [academic Allan] Bloom, [former Secretary of Education William] Bennett, [author Saul] Bellow, and the rest (known by now in some quarters as the Killer B's) are advocating one of them: to create a narrowly specific cultural capital that will be the normative *referent* for everyone, but will remain the *property* of a small and powerful caste that is linguistically and ethnically unified. . . . Few doubt that behind the Bennett-Bloom program is a desire to close not the American mind, but the American university, to all but a narrow and highly uniform elite with no commitment to either multiculturalism or educational democracy. Thus while the Killer B's . . . depict themselves as returning to the orthodoxies of yesteryear, their project must not be reduced to nostalgia or conservatism. Neither of these explain the blanket contempt they express for the country's universities. They are fueled not by reverence for the past, but by an aggressive desire to lay hold of the present and future. . . .

—Mary Louise Pratt

Today, education is perhaps the most important function of state and local governments. Compulsory school attendance laws and the great expenditures for education both demonstrate our recognition of the importance of education to our democratic society. It is required in the performance of our most basic public responsibilities, even service in the armed forces. It is the very foundation of good citizenship. Today it is a principal instrument in awakening the child to cultural values, in preparing him for later professional training, and in helping him to adjust normally to his environment. In these days, it is doubtful that any child may reasonably be expected to succeed in life if he is denied the opportunity of an education. Such an opportunity, where the state has undertaken to provide it, is a right which must be made available to all on equal terms.

—Earl Warren

EXERCISE 1-9   **Cross-referencing sources**

Based on your close reading of the selections in Exercise 1-8, complete the
note-making started here. If you find that notes you wish to make are appropriate for
more than one category, make two entries.

The social responsibility of education

Britannica: higher education must balance responsibility to the nation with
                    responsibility to scholarship

Angelou:

D'Souza:

Pratt:

Warren:

Education and racial discrimination

Angelou: segregation prevents blacks from achieving their potential

D'Souza:

Pratt:

Warren:

EXERCISE 1-10   Forging relationships among sources

Based on your close reading of the selections in Exercise 1-8 and on your cross-references and notes, respond to the following questions.

1. Which authors agree?

    How do Angelou and Warren agree on the impact of segregation?

    How do Britannica and Warren agree on the social impact of education?

2. Which authors disagree?

    How do D'Souza and Pratt disagree on the role of education in combating prejudice?

3. Are there any examples in one source of statements made in another?

    How do D'Souza and Pratt illustrate the point made in Britannica about the delicate balance in educational responsibilities?

CHAPTER 2

Critical Thinking and Writing

Four patterns of writing and thinking will recur throughout your academic career: summary, evaluation, analysis, and synthesis.

Forms of writing that build on reading

- **Summary**   When you summarize, you briefly—and neutrally—restate the main points of a text. Summary draws on your skills of reading to understand (see 1f).

- **Evaluation**   When you evaluate, you judge the effectiveness of an author's presentation and explain your agreement or disagreement. Evaluation draws on your skills of reading to understand (1f), reading to respond (1g), and reading to evaluate (1h).

- **Analysis**   When you analyze, you use the clearly defined principles set out by one or more authors to investigate the work of other authors (or to investigate various situations in the world). Analysis draws on your skills of reading to understand (1f), reading to respond (1g), and reading to evaluate (1h).

- **Synthesis**   When you synthesize texts, you gather the work of various authors according to your purpose. Synthesis draws on your skills of reading to understand (1f), reading to respond (1g), reading to evaluate (1h), and reading to synthesize (1i).

The cumulative layers of writing

While summary, evaluation, analysis, and synthesis are treated here as distinct forms of writing, they are interrelated: evaluations often contain summaries; analyses and syntheses contain both summaries and evaluations.

2a   Writing a summary

A summary is a brief, neutral restatement of a text. In order to write a good summary, you must understand the material you are reading on its own terms.

1   Setting goals for writing a summary

A summary focuses on what the author says rather than on what you think of the topic. In writing a summary, you should aim to meet these goals:

- Understand the author's purpose for writing—for instance, to inform, explain, argue, justify, defend, compare, contrast, or illustrate. Most often, the author will have a single purpose; at times, an author may have two closely related purposes, such as to explain and justify.

- State the author's thesis in relation to this purpose.

- Identify the sections of the text and understand the ways in which these work together to support, or explain, the thesis.

- Distinguish information needed to explain the author's thesis from examples and less important information.

- Write the summary using your own words; avoid phrase-by-phrase "translations" from the original.

2   Understanding the techniques for writing a summary

Your summary is built directly from the material you have underlined and the notes you have made on the original source. For a complete discussion of reading to understand, see 1f.

Techniques for summarizing an especially difficult text

When attempting to summarize particularly difficult texts, use these strategies:

1. Identify every example in the text and ask: what point is being illustrated here? Make a list of these points. Considered together, they will reveal the author's thesis.
2. Look for repeated terms or phrases. Define them, consulting specialized dictionaries or encyclopedias, if necessary.
3. Read and reread the opening and closing paragraphs of the text. Look for a sentence or two—the thesis—that seems to summarize the whole. "Interrogate" that sentence, following advice in 3d-4. Link specific parts of the sentence to different parts (or sections) of the text. Understand what you can; identify what you cannot understand—and then take *specific* questions to a fellow student or your professor.

Writing a Summary

- Read your source with care, putting into practice strategies discussed in 1f.
- Determine the purpose of the source—for instance, to inform, explain, argue, justify, defend, compare, contrast, or illustrate.
- Summarize the thesis. Based on the notes you have made and the phrases or sentences you have highlighted while reading, restate the author's main point in your own words. In this statement, refer to the author by name; indicate the author's purpose (e.g., to argue or inform); and refer to the title.
- Summarize the body of the text. STRATEGY 1: Write a one- or two-sentence summary of every paragraph. Summarize points important to supporting the author's thesis. Omit minor points and omit illustrations. Avoid the temptation to translate phrase for phrase from sentences in the text. STRATEGY 2: Identify sections (groupings of related paragraphs) and write a two- or three-sentence summary of each section.
- Study your paragraph or section summaries. Determine the ways in which the paragraphs or sections work together to support the thesis.
- Write the summary. Join your paragraph or section summaries with your summary of the thesis, emphasizing the relationship between the parts of the text and the thesis.
- Revise for clarity and for style. Quote sparingly. Provide transitions where needed.

 2b Writing an evaluation

In evaluating a source, you ask how effective and reliable it is and whether or not you agree with the author. Writing an evaluation formalizes the process of reading to evaluate (see 1g, 1h, 1f). Before you begin to evaluate a source, you must be able to summarize it (see 2a).

1 Setting goals for writing an evaluation

The two primary goals when writing an evaluation both depend on a critical, comprehensive reading:

- Judge the effectiveness of the author's presentation. Your concern is on the quality of the presentation, not (for the moment) on your agreement or disagreement with the author.

- Agree and/or disagree with the author, and explain your responses.

2 | Understanding techniques for writing an evaluation

The basic pattern of evaluation is: (1) offer a judgment about the text; (2) refer to a specific passage—summarize, quote, or paraphrase; and (3) explain your judgment in light of the passage referred to.

Prepare: Make notes on the effectiveness of the presentation

When evaluating the effectiveness and reliability of a text, your criteria (standards of judgment) depend on whether the author is arguing a position or informing. Certain criteria, however, are suitable for evaluating any text. Whatever criteria you use, always remember to support your evaluation by referring to and discussing a specific passage.

CRITERIA FOR TEXTS THAT INFORM *OR* PERSUADE

ACCURACY	Are the author's facts accurate?
DEFINITIONS	Have terms important to the discussion been clearly defined—and if not, has lack of definition confused matters?
DEVELOPMENT	Does each part of the presentation seem well developed, satisfying to you in the extent of its treatment? Is each main point adequately illustrated and supported with evidence?

CRITERIA FOR TEXTS THAT INFORM

AUDIENCE	Is the author writing for a clearly defined audience who will know what to do with the information presented? Is the author consistent in presenting information to one audience?
CLARITY	How clear has the author been in defining and explaining? Is information presented in a way that is useful? Will readers be able to understand an explanation or follow a procedure?
PROCEDURE	Has the author presented the stages of a process? Is the reader clear about the purpose of the process, about who does it and why?

CRITERIA FOR TEXTS THAT PERSUADE

FAIRNESS   If the issue being discussed is controversial, has the author presented opposing points of view? Has the author seriously considered and responded to these points? (See 6e.)

LOGIC   Has the author adhered to standards of logic? Has the author avoided, for instance, fallacies such as personal attacks and faulty generalization? (See 6h.)

EVIDENCE   Do facts and examples fairly represent the available data on the topic? Are the author's facts and examples current? Has the author included negative examples? (See 6h.)

AUTHORITY   Are the experts that the author refers to qualified to speak on the topic? Are the experts neutral? (See 6d-3 and 6h.)

Prepare: Make notes on your agreement and disagreement with the author

Whether or not you agree with the author, in preparing an evaluation you should (1) identify an author's views, pointing out particular passages where these views are apparent; (2) identify your own views; and (3) examine the basis on which you and the author agree or disagree. Filling in the following chart will help you identify both assumptions:

Author's view on topic X:

My view:

Author's assumption:

My assumption:

CRITICAL DECISIONS

CHALLENGE AND BE CHALLENGED: WRITING EVALUATIONS

When you evaluate a text and particularly when you respond to the text, you can choose to have a moment of real contact with an author—or not. What distinguishes real contact from a pat, uninvolved response?

- Real contact with an author invites you to "suspend disbelief." You allow yourself for a moment to accept what the author is saying as true, probable, or desirable. For a moment, at least, you believe. Then you respond.

- In your moment of belief, what did you feel? How did the author's views affect you? Investigate your response, especially the more volatile ones—these suggest that the author has touched a nerve.
- Reconsider your response. Might you allow the author's views to change yours? When you can entertain this question seriously, you are letting the text challenge you.
- Form your response into a challenge, and direct that challenge at the author. How do you imagine the author responding?

Devise an action plan: Accept a moment of real contact with an author whose work you are evaluating. Let your evaluation reflect this encounter.

Prepare: Organize your notes and gain a general impression

Since you cannot respond to everything in a selection, review your notes to determine several points that will best support your overall impression of the selection. Present your evaluation in a well planned, clearly organized fashion, and support the points you make. A typical evaluation will consist of five parts (as presented in the box), which will vary in length depending on your occasion for writing.

Writing an Evaluation

- Introduce the topic and author: one paragraph.
  One sentence in the introduction should hint at your general impression of the piece.

- Summarize the author's work: one to three paragraphs.
  If brief, the summary can be joined to the introduction.

- Briefly preview the key point(s) in the author's work that you will evaluate: one paragraph.*

- Identify key points in the author's presentation; discuss each in detail: three to six paragraphs.

  If you are evaluating the quality of the author's presentation, state your criteria for evaluation explicitly; if you are agreeing or

---

*The order of parts in the written evaluation may not match the actual order of writing. You may be unable to write this third section of the evaluation without first having evaluated the author's key points—the next section.

disagreeing with opinions, try to identify assumptions (yours and the author's) underlying these.

- Conclude with your overall assessment of the author's work.

 Applying techniques for writing evaluations

Two questions will help to organize your thinking for an evaluation: (1) How effective and reliable is the author's presentation? (2) Do I agree with the author?

 Writing an analysis

An **analysis** as demonstrated here is an investigation conducted by applying a principle or definition to an activity or to an object. The purpose of an analysis is to see how that activity or object works, what it might mean, or why it might be significant. An analysis should reflect not only your understanding of the material presented, but also your ability to think—to analyze—according to principles and definitions important to your coursework. Analysis builds on the skills of reading to understand (1f) and writing summaries (2a).

 Setting goals for writing an analysis

The specific goals of analysis are to:

- Understand a principle or definition and demonstrate your understanding by using it to study an activity or an object.

- Thoroughly apply this principle or definition to all significant parts of the activity or object under study.

- Create for the reader a sense that your analysis makes the activity or object being studied understandable—if not for the first time, then at least in a new way.

Different analyses lead to different interpretations

Interpretations will differ depending on the principles applied to the activity or object under study. For example, an analysis of the *Star Wars* films from the perspective of myth will produce a very different vision from an analysis focusing on social issues such as race, violence, and gender. Regardless of the principles used, an analysis is useful or authoritative to the extent that a writer (1) clearly defines a principle or definition to be applied; (2) applies this principle or definition thoroughly and systematically; and, in so doing (3) reveals new and convincing insights into the activity or object being analyzed.

2 | Understanding the techniques for writing and analysis

Prepare: Turn elements of a principle or definition into questions—and *probe*

You can prepare for an analysis by developing questions based on the definition or principle you are going to apply, and then by directing these questions to the activity or object under study. Your written analysis will develop from your notes from these activities.

A strategy for writing analyses

The guidelines in the box will help you prepare to analyze material in any discipline.

Writing an Analysis

- Introduce and summarize the activity or object to be analyzed. Whatever parts of this activity or object you intend to analyze should be mentioned here.
- Introduce and summarize key definition or principle that will form the basis of your analysis.
- Analyze. Systematically apply elements of this definition or principle to parts of the activity or object under study. Part by part, discuss what you find.
- Conclude by reviewing all the parts you have analyzed. To what extent has your application of the definition or principle helped you to explain how the object works, what it might mean, or why it is significant?

▕3▏ Applying techniques for writing analyses

Be sure to summarize the object or activity you are examining and the principle or definition with which you are working, if this is not known to your readers. Then be sure to *apply* the principle or definition, using it as an investigative tool.

▕2d▏ Writing a synthesis

A **synthesis** is a written discussion in which you gather and present source materials according to a well-defined purpose. In the process of writing a synthesis you answer these questions: (1) Which authors have written on my topic? (2) In what ways can I link the work of these authors to one another and to my own thinking? (3) How can I best use the material I've gathered to create a discussion that supports *my* views? A synthesis goes beyond merely stringing together a series of summaries; it must include *your* assessment of the sources.

Your chances of producing a meaningful synthesis depend on your ability to read sources to understand (1f), respond (1g), evaluate (1h), and synthesize (1i). Synthesis uses all of the critical reading and writing skills discussed in this and the previous chapter.

Ensuring that your voice is heard

Although a synthesis makes use of a number of sources, ultimately it is *your* paper. You must have a point to make, a purpose which governs your choice of material and organization. If your paper is organized around sources rather than your own ideas, then you will disappear from the paper. Remember that in a synthesis, your insights predominate.

Do Not Become Invisible in Your Papers

The danger signs:
1. Your paragraphs are devoted wholly to the work of the authors you are synthesizing.
2. Virtually every sentence introduces someone else's ideas.
3. The impulse to use the first-person *I* never arises.

Setting goals for writing a synthesis

In writing a synthesis, you want to do the following:

- Understand your purpose for writing.

- Define your topic and your thesis (see 3d).

- Locate the work of others who have written on this topic and read to understand, respond to, and evaluate.

- Forge relationships among sources; link the thinking of others to your own thinking.

- Create a discussion governed by your views; draw on sources as contributors to a discussion that you design and control.

2 **Understanding the techniques for writing a synthesis**

Although synthesis makes use of summaries, evaluations, and analyses, it moves beyond these forms by merging sources and looking for larger patterns of relation.

Cross-referencing ideas

In order to develop a synthesis organized around *ideas* rather than simply summaries of each selection, use as key ideas the component parts of the topic as discussed by the authors. When you have cross-referenced those ideas (see 1d), you are almost ready to write.

A Strategy for Forging Relationships among Sources

1. Read multiple sources on a topic.
2. Subdivide the topic into parts and give each a brief title.
3. Cross-reference your sources for each part.
4. Summarize author's information or ideas about each part.
5. Identify connections among readings, which may be related by comparison, contrast, example, definition, cause and effect—or by the extent of your agreement or disagreement with particular selections.

Clarifying relationships among authors

After you have cross-referenced what several authors say about a topic, you are ready to forge relationships among the authors' discussions. The following questions will help you identify patterns of relationships:

Which authors agree?

Which disagree?

Are there any examples in one source of statements made in another?

Can you offer any definitions?

Are any readings related by cause and effect?

CRITICAL DECISIONS

SET ISSUES IN A BROADER CONTEXT: FORGING RELATIONSHIPS

When forging relationships among sources, look for authors who provide a broad context in which to situate the topic you are studying.

- Be alert to historical backgrounds.

    Example: A labor dispute in the garment industry, read about in one source, might be viewed differently when seen in light of a general history of the garment industry, discussed in another source.

- Be alert to broader sets of problems.

    Example: The difficulties that some children have in adjusting to school, presented in one source, might be viewed differently when seen in the context of children who have alcoholic parents, discussed in another source.

- Be alert to broader cultural views.

    Example: The discussion of sex-role identity in America discussed in one source can be viewed differently when set in the context of cross-cultural studies.

Devise an action plan: Devote an hour or two of concentrated research to seeking out broader contexts in which to view your topic. Understanding broader contexts helps you to place the topic in relation to other topics—which you may or may not choose to investigate. This knowledge is always helpful, if only to let you know the boundaries of the topic you are researching.

A strategy for writing syntheses

Before writing a synthesis, consider how the ideas in the sources you have chosen will relate to your ideas. Consider also the relationships you have forged among sources. The following guidelines should help you write your synthesis.

Synthesis: Writing a Paper Based on Sources

- Read sources on the topic; subdivide the topic into parts and infer relationships among parts, cross-referencing sources when possible.
- Clarify relationships among authors by posing these questions:
  Which authors agree?
  Which authors disagree?
  Are there any examples in one source of statements made in another?
  Can I offer any definitions?
  Are any readings related by cause and effect?
- Write a thesis (see 3d) that ensures your voice is heard and that allows you to develop sections of the paper in which you refer to sources.
- Sketch an outline of your paper, organizing your discussion by *idea*, not by summary. Enter the names of authors into your outline along with notes indicating how these authors will contribute to your discussion.
- Write a draft of your paper and revise, following strategies discussed in chapter 4.

The importance of the writer's views

What you do with the relationships you forge among source materials will depend on your purpose and your opinions. Even though you may agree with others writing from the same sources, each paper will be unique because each writer is guided by different purposes and different theses.

EXERCISE 2-1   Writing summaries

What follows is the final section of Rick Telander's essay, the first section of which appears in Exercise 1-5. Using the guidelines provided in 2a, write a summary of both sections.

But can promoting athletic shoes possibly be wrong in a capitalist society? Reebok chairman Paul Fireman was recently quoted as describing the Pump as "a product that's aspirational to a young person"—that is, something to be desired. He added, if prospective buyers couldn't afford the shoes, "that's the place for a kid to get a job after school." What, indeed, is the point of ads if not to inform the public of products that it may or may not need, but that it may wish to buy? Should we demand that the sports shoe industry be held to a higher standard than, say, the junk food industry? The advertising community itself thought so highly of Nike's "Bo knows" spot with Bo Jackson and Bo Diddley that *Advertising Age* named Jackson its Star Presenter of 1989.   11

What are we looking for here, anyway?   12

"Responsibility," says [Wally] Grigo, the New Haven store owner. "Have Spike Lee and Michael Jordan look at the camera and say, 'Drug dealers, don't you dare wear my shoes!' Put antidrug labels on the box. I already do at my stores."   13

"Everybody wants us to do everything," says Nike's Dolan. "It's naive to think an antidrug message on the shoe box is going to change anyone's behavior. Our theme is 'Just do it!' because we want people playing sports, because they'll need more shoes. The healthier people are, the more shoes we'll sell."   14

Trouble is, young black males—a significant portion of the market—are not healthy right now. In fact, 23 percent of black males between the ages of twenty and twenty-nine are under the supervision of the criminal justice system—incarcerated, paroled, or on probation. According to a 1989 study in the *Journal of the American Medical Association*, a black male is six times more likely to be a homicide victim than a white male. Writes *Washington Post* columnist William Raspberry: "The inability of so many young black men to see themselves as providers, or even as necessary to their families, may be one explanation for their irresponsible behavior." Marc Mauer, of the Sentencing Project, a nonprofit group concerned with disparities in the administration of criminal justice, says, "We now risk the possibility of writing off an entire generation of black men."   15

Obviously we are talking about something bigger than shoes here. . . .   16

Of course drug money is, to a troubling extent, supporting [Air Jordans], as well as other brands of sneakers and sports apparel. And kids are being killed for them. So what should the shoe companies, the schools, the advertising industry, the endorsers, the media, parents—all of us—do about it?   17

Do you know? Do you know? Do you know?   18

EXERCISE 2-2   Writing evaluations

Using the guidelines in 2b, write an evaluation of the Telander selection from Exercises 1-5 and 2-1, identifying facts and opinions, and distinguishing between the author's assumptions and your own.

EXERCISE 2-3   **Preparing an analysis**

Telander's theory about the influence of athletic-wear advertising on inner-city youth is one of many that attempt to explain one type of violent crime. Think of two or three other perspectives from which to approach the problem (political, sociological, psychological, religious). Choose one that you can state clearly, and briefly explain (1) how that theory would account for the high crime rate among inner-city youth, and (2) how you respond to the theory. Use the guidelines in 2c.

EXAMPLE

THEORY: The civil rights movement played a role in the demise of the inner city.

EXPLANATION: As middle-class blacks moved into suburban areas, valuable role models for inner-city youth were eliminated. The remaining poor, uneducated people lost all hope for upward mobility, turning to crime.

RESPONSE: While upwardly mobile blacks were able to leave the inner cities as a result of the civil rights movement, this theory blames inner-city problems on the blacks who left. That reasoning is not only unfair, but it also assumes that blacks should not be part of the American Dream of upward mobility.

THEORY:

EXPLANATION:

RESPONSE:

EXERCISE 2-4   Writing a synthesis

Using the five statements on education from Exercise 1-8, prepare a synthesis according to the guidelines in 2d. You may use one of the following thesis statements, or compose your own.

The role of the university is to promote the common cultural heritage.

American education is a bastion of elitism, designed to keep out minorities.

The government has a responsibility to monitor public education.

CHAPTER 3

Planning, Developing, and Writing a Draft

As you write and rewrite a draft, your ideas about the topic will become clearer to you and to your readers.

An Overview of the Writing Process

Preparing to write

3a   **Discovering your topic, purpose, and audience.** Know your topic and, if necessary, research it. Know your purpose for writing and use this to generate and organize ideas. Keep specific readers in mind as you write.

3b   **Generating ideas and information.** Use strategies like freewriting or reading to generate the ideas and information on the basis of which you will write your draft.

3c   **Reviewing and categorizing ideas and information.** Review the material you have generated and group like ideas and information into categories.

3d   **Writing a thesis and sketching your paper.** Study the material you have assembled and write a working thesis, a statement that will give your draft a single, controlling idea. Based on your thesis, sketch your draft.

Writing

3e   **Writing a draft.** Prepare a draft of your document by adopting a strategy suited to your temperament. As you write, expect to depart from your sketch.

Revising

4a   **Early revision: Rediscovering your main idea.** Refine your thesis; use it to revise for unity, coherence, and development. Be sure that the broad sections of your document and the sentences within your paragraphs are coherent and lead logically from one to the next.

4b   **Later revision: Bringing your main idea into focus.** Read and clarify individual sentences. Correct problems with grammar, usage, punctuation, and spelling.

The three stages of writing—preparing to write, writing, and revising—are distinct. However, you will find yourself generating ideas, evaluating your work, and revising your work at almost every stage of the writing process. The process of writing is *recursive:* it bends and it circles, and it is illustrated well with a wheel.

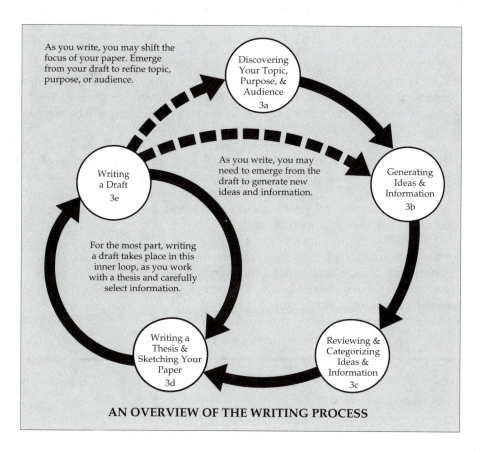

AN OVERVIEW OF THE WRITING PROCESS

3a   Discovering your topic, purpose, and audience

1   Understanding your topic

When choosing a topic or responding to an assigned topic, follow three rules: write about what you know or can learn about in a reasonably brief period of time; make the topic your own; and narrow a topic so that you can develop it fully in a given number of pages.

Know your topic

Because of the nature of college and business writing, knowing your topic will usually require some investigation on your part.

Know Your Topic

Read: If you do not know a topic well, read sources and gather information: letters, photographs, articles, lecture notes—whatever is pertinent. Read until you understand all the aspects of your topic that you will be writing about.

Interview: Locate people who are knowledgeable about your topic and interview them. Read sufficiently before the interview so that you do not pose questions that can be answered with basic research. Develop pointed questions that yield information and ideas unique to this source. (See 1b for help on generating good questions.)

Reflect: Investigate your personal commitment to the topic. What experiences have you had that influence your thinking? How has your point of view been shaped by these experiences? Issues on which you might write may require that you take a stand. Know your position. (See 1b for strategies that can aid reflection.)

Own your topic

Your interest in a topic will engage your readers' interest. Here are a few suggestions for making a topic your own:

Own Your Topic

Stretch the topic to fit your interests. Redefine the assignment in such a way that it touches on your experience and at the same time is acceptable to your professor.

Identify a debate concerning the topic and choose sides. Try to understand why the topic is debatable (if it is) and whom the topic affects, as well as the merits and limitations of each side of the debate. To stimulate interest, personalize the debate. Imagine yourself affected by it and take a position.

Talk with friends. Sometimes informal conversations will help you to identify elements of a topic that interest you. Get a conversation going, listen, and participate. What aspects of the topic interest other people? Become engaged yourself.

Narrow your topic

Using topics that are too broad for brief papers results in superficial products.

Narrow Your Topic

- *Divide the topic into constituent parts.* Ask yourself: What are the component parts of this topic? What parts (or subtopics) do I know most about? Can I link subtopics together in meaningful ways? In which subtopic am I most interested?

- *Ask a journalist's questions.* Narrow a topic to a subtopic that interests you by posing questions, as appropriate: who, what, where, when, why, how? Often, a response to one or more of these questions can become the focus for a paper.

2 Identifying your purpose

There are four basic purposes for writing: to *inform,* to *persuade,* to *express,* and to *entertain.* Most of your writing in college will be informative and/or persuasive.

Informative writing

Informative writing explains, defines, or describes a topic; the language and level of difficulty of the paper depends on your audience's knowledge of the topic.

Persuasive writing

Persuasive writing seeks to convince a reader that your view on a topic is valid. As with informative writing, assessing your audience's knowledge is important.

Expressive writing and writing to entertain

Expressive writing explores your ideas and emotions about a topic. Entertaining writing usually takes the form of poetry, fiction, or drama.

Although purposes for writing may overlap, each essay should have a primary purpose.

3 Defining your audience

Whenever you write for an audience other than yourself, you must consider your audience before you begin writing a first draft. The following guidelines will help you analyze your audience.

Audience Needs Analysis

Pose these general questions, regardless of your purpose:
- Who is the reader? What is the reader's age, sex, religious background, educational background, and ethnic heritage?
- What is my relationship with the reader?
- What impact on my presentation—on choice of words, level of complexity, and choice of examples—will the reader have?
- Why will the reader be interested in my paper? How can I best spark the reader's interest?

If you are writing to inform, pose these questions as well:
- What does the reader know about the topic's history?
- How well does the reader understand the topic's technical details?
- What does the reader need to know? want to know?
- What level of language will I use in discussing the topic, given the reader's understanding?

- At what level (beginner? expert?) should I treat the content of this paper, given the reader's understanding?

If you are writing to persuade, pose both sets of questions as well as the following:

- What are the reader's views on the topic? Given what I know about the reader (from the preceding questions), is the reader likely to agree with my view on the topic? to disagree? to be neutral?
- What factors are likely to affect the reader's beliefs about the topic? What special circumstances (work, religious conviction, political views, etc.) should I be aware of that will affect the reader's views?
- How can I shape my argument to encourage the reader's support, given his or her present level of interest, level of understanding, and beliefs?

Writing for an unspecified audience

Your primary audience in college will often be your professor. Consider your professor an editor whose job it is to evaluate your paper before passing it on to an audience of non-experts. Assume that this audience is willing to accept a position that is clearly stated and developed.

 4   **Analyzing topic, purpose, audience—and the writing occasion**

For each paper you write, topic, purpose, and audience constitute a specific **occasion for writing**. The tone and register you adopt depends on the writing occasion.

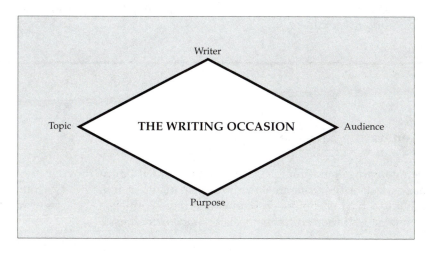

Tone refers to a writer's attitude toward the reader and the subject. How you present your material indicates your level of interest in the topic, your preparation, and your commitment to the topic. Tone must be appropriate to the topic. **Register** refers to the degrees of formality in your writing. **Formal register** adheres to conventions of standard written English. **Informal register** is freer in structure and language. **Popular register** combines adherence to conventions with more conversational style. See 21e for advice on matching tone and register to the writing occasion.

When Does Your Audience Need to Know More?

Consider these points when deciding whether your audience needs to know more about a key term or person.

- Major personalities referred to in textbooks or in lectures will help constitute the general, shared knowledge of a discipline. In all cases, *refer to people in your papers either by their* last *names or by their first* and *last names.* Do not identify "giants of a field" with explanatory tags like *who was an important inventor in the early part of the 20th century.*
- Terms that have been defined at length in a textbook or lecture also constitute the general, shared knowledge of a discipline. Once you have understood these terms, use them in your papers—but do not define them. Demonstrate your understanding by using the terms accurately.
- The same people and terms not requiring definition in an academic context may well need to be defined in a nonacademic one. Base decisions about what information to include in a paper on a careful audience analysis.

3b   Generating ideas and information

When you are generating ideas for a paper, you will draw on your own experience as well as on research—in a library, in a lab, or in the field. While generating ideas, try to keep the critic in you at bay—in the early stages of writing, exploration is more important than precision and correctness.

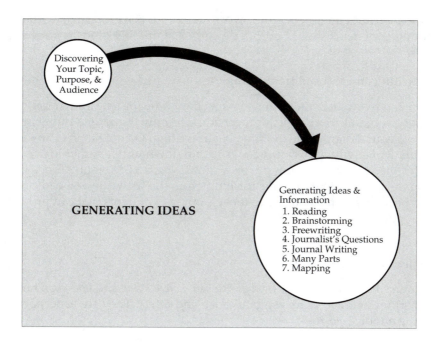

As you review the following strategies for generating ideas, bear in mind the "User's Manual" for generating information:

- No one method will work for all topics.
- Some methods may not suit your style of discovery.
- Some methods work well when paired.
- Move quickly to a new strategy if one does not work.
- Tell your critic to take a vacation.

1 Reading

Regardless of whether or not your assignment calls for research, reading can help you generate ideas. As you jot down notes from your reading, you will begin to see your topic more clearly.

2 Brainstorming

When you brainstorm, you think on paper. Place your topic at the top of a page, and then list any related phrase or word that comes to mind in a five- or ten-minute span. Brainstorming in groups can be accomplished with the aid of a board or easel. As each member of the group offers words or phrases, other members build on those ideas. Once the list is generated, group words together. The groupings with the greatest number of items should produce a sufficient number of ideas for a paper.

3   Freewriting and focused freewriting

When you freewrite, you write for a specified time (or length) without giving any thought to organization, style, or mechanics. Simply think for a moment about the subject of your assignment, and then begin writing. Do not stop for any reason. If you can't think of anything to say, then write that down until another idea comes up.

In a focused freewrite, you write on a specific topic. The result of focused freewriting is similar to that of brainstorming: from the freewrite you can circle words and phrases and make notes to form groupings of items that can produce ideas for a paper.

4   The journalist's questions

The journalist's questions (*who, what, when, where, why,* and *how*) can help you define, compare, contrast, or investigate cause-and-effect. They are especially useful in narrowing a topic (see 3b-3).

5   Journal writing

In a journal you reflect, in your own words, on anything relevant to what you have been studying. The journal allows you to explore what you know about a topic and to discover what you don't know. You can discover topics for papers by looking through your journal.[1]

6   The "many parts" strategy[2]

In order to begin thinking in more specific terms about your topic, number the items on your list and ask yourself, "What are the uses of Number 1? Number 2?" and so on. Or ask what the consequences are for each item. Follow up on this strategy with a focused freewrite on one or two of the most promising responses.

7   Mapping

People who are good at visualizing frequently use mapping. Begin by writing your topic as briefly as possible. Circle the topic and draw several short spokes from

---

[1]Discussion of journal writing here is based on Toby Fulwiler, ed. *The Journal Book* (Portsmouth, N.H.: Boynton/Cook-Heinemann, 1987), 1–7.

[2]This strategy is adapted from John C. Bean and John D. Ramage, *Form and Surprise in Composition: Writing and Thinking Across the Curriculum* (New York: Macmillan, 1986), 170–171.

the circle. At each end of the circle place one of the journalist's questions, making a major branch off the spoke for every answer to a question. Now pose one of the journalist's questions for each answer. Once you have finished, you will have a page that looks like a map. (You can also use the "many parts" strategy for mapping.) Mapping can help you begin to outline your paper.

3c   Reviewing and categorizing ideas and information

After you have generated enough information, you must begin to determine which ideas look most promising. Because the value of ideas will only become clear as you write, the decisions you make at this stage are somewhat tentative.

1   Reviewing ideas and making meaningful categories

Create categories in order to make sense of the information you have generated. A category is like a file drawer in which you group related items. On a clean sheet of paper, look over your notes and put your ideas into groups. Then assign categories to the groups. This technique will help you arrive at a core idea for your paper.

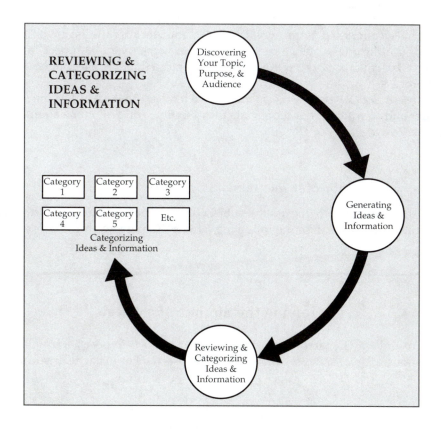

2 Organizing information *within* categories

Organizing information within categories helps you clarify your ideas and their relation to each other. Within each category, identify main (general) points and the subordinate (specific) points that support them. Use an informal outline or a tree diagram to organize major and supporting points within a category.

3 Expanding information: Filling in gaps

Try to determine which of your main points needs further development, or more support. You may need to read sources to fill in gaps. Identifying and correcting weak support at this stage will help later when you draft the paper.

3d Writing a thesis and sketching your paper

A thesis is a general statement that you make about your topic, a one-sentence summary of the controlling idea of your paper. Before writing a first draft, you can devise a **working thesis:** a statement that, based on everything you know of the topic, should prove to be a reasonably accurate summary of what you will write. After you have completed a draft you can revise the working thesis into a **final thesis:** the accurate one-sentence summary of your work that will appear in your final draft. Expect your working thesis to change more than once throughout the drafting process.

Because it is a sentence, a thesis must have a *subject* that identifies the subject of your paper and a *predicate* that represents the assertion you will make about that subject (see 7a-1).

1 Narrowing the subject of your thesis

You should be able to discuss the subject of your thesis statement within the allotted number of pages. Use the following strategy to narrow your thesis.

Narrowing the Subject of a Thesis

One useful way to narrow the subject of your thesis is to pose a journalist's questions: *who, what, when, where,* and *which aspects.* For instance, if you were planning to write a paper on the topic of *the wilderness* or *voter registration drives*, you would want to narrow your focus considerably (assuming a five-page paper).

Subject (too broad): voter registration drives

Limiting questions: where, when, who?

Narrowed subject: voter registration drives among the urban poor in the 1993 elections

Subject (too broad): wilderness

Limiting questions: which aspects?

Narrowed subject: wilderness camping

Critical Decisions

Devise an action plan: Theses that lead to *informative* papers

A thesis is an action plan for the paper you intend to write. The predicate part of a thesis establishes a relationship that you believe brings meaning to the material you are working with. Once you determine this relationship, your goal is to demonstrate it in your paper.

Certain relationships—sequential order, definition, classification, comparison, and contrast—lead to an informational thesis that says, in effect: "Here's how X works. Here are its distinctive features. Here are its parts. Here are its uses." This type of thesis results in a paper that informs. In the examples that follow, the key, informational relationship of each thesis is italicized.

Sequential order: You place your information and ideas in a logical order, or sequence—a pattern of first, second, third. . . .

> A creative thinker *will study a problem, arrive at a solution, and then delay accepting that solution until she has explored alternatives.*

Definition: Your information, considered as a whole, allows you to define a term.

> Creativity *is the act of recognizing problems and finding solutions.*

Classification: You find enough examples of something that you can recognize varieties.

> The four types of creativity *are visual, verbal, musical, and mathematical.*

Comparison: After studying two or more people, places, things, or ideas, you are able to demonstrate similarities.

> Of the four types of creativity, musical and mathematical *are most alike.*

Contrast: After studying two or more people, places, things, or ideas, you are able to demonstrate differences.

> Of the four types of creativity, visual and verbal *differ the most.*

---

2 Basing your thesis on a relationship you want to clarify

A subject alone, no matter how carefully narrowed, is not a thesis. You must make an assertion about your subject. As you study your notes and research, you begin to make logical connections among ideas. It is through this process that you develop a complete thesis. Ask yourself what new statement you can make about the material, and think of how all (or part) of the material ties together. This relationship will become the predicate part of your thesis.

CRITICAL DECISIONS

DEVISE AN ACTION PLAN: THESES THAT LEAD TO *ARGUMENTATIVE* PAPERS

A thesis is an action plan for a paper you intend to write. The predicate part of a thesis establishes a relationship that you believe brings meaning to the material you are working with. Once you determine this relationship, you set yourself the goal of demonstrating it in your paper.

Certain relationships—generalization, causation, sign, and analogy—lead to an argumentative thesis that says, in effect: "Here is my opinion on X. Here is my support and here are my reasons for thinking this way. I want you to agree with me." This type of thesis results in a paper that argues. In the examples that follow, the key, argumentative relationship of each thesis is italicized.

Generalization: Representative examples of a group allow you to infer a general principle that is true for all members of that group.

> Creative students *are essential to the success of any classroom.*

Causation: You can show that certain actions lead to certain effects or that certain effects follow from certain actions or conditions.

> The causes of creativity *are complex and involve a rich mixture of inheritance and learning.*

Sign: You can establish that one thing tends to occur in the presence of (and therefore is a sign of) another.

> Risk taking *is a sign of creativity.*

Analogy: You compare your topic to another topic, apparently unrelated, and can show an illuminating relation.

> In the same way that athletes who train vigorously for one sport may be out of shape for others, people who are creative in one sphere—visually, verbally, musically, or mathematically—*will not necessarily be creative in others.*

---

3 The thesis and your ambitions for a paper

Regardless of the subject part of your thesis, the predicate part can be more or less ambitious. The legal scholar and Supreme Court justice Oliver Wendell Holmes (1841-1935) described intellectual ambition in terms of the stories in a building: "One-story intellects" are those who do no more than collect facts, "two-story

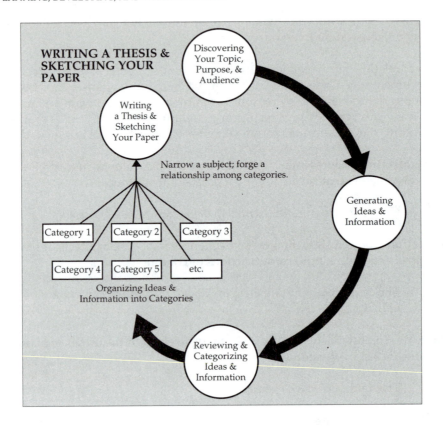

intellects" use facts to make generalizations and infer relationships, and "three-story intellects with skylights" make predictions by using their creativity and imagination. Holmes's characterization of intellects can be applied to thesis statements as well.[3]

One-story thesis

A one-story thesis leads to informative writing and demonstrates that you can gather and report facts. Essay exams occasionally call for one-story thesis statements. A one-story thesis might read: "Tornadoes occur most frequently in the midwestern United States."

Two-story thesis

A one-story thesis calls for you to do little more than summarize; a two-story thesis calls for you to look at facts in relation to one another, to make inferences, and

---

[3]Oliver Wendell Holmes, cited in Esther Fusco, "Cognitive Levels Matching and Curriculum Analysis," ed. Arthur L. Costa, *Developing Minds: A Resource Book for Teaching Thinking* (Alexandria, VA: ASCD, 1985), 81.

to see implications. A two-story thesis might read: "The paucity of funding for meteorological research on tornadoes may reflect the relative lack of political power in areas where tornadoes are most prevalent."

Three-story thesis

A three-story thesis calls for you to take an intellectual risk, to expand your paper by creating tension among its parts. This tension motivates readers.[4] The writer of a three-story thesis has opened up his or her mind to the "skylight" that Holmes talks about, and frequently goes on to learn, to question, and finally to argue a point. A three-story thesis might read: "If tornadoes were prevalent in the powerful northeast section of the United States, funding to study them would be far greater." Note that this thesis draws upon the inferences made in the two-story thesis and speculates on the implications of the statement.

What sort of paper you are writing?

Simply because a three-story thesis (and paper) reflects a greater intellectual exercise, do not assume that you should avoid one- and two-story papers. Certain assignments call for certain levels of inquiry. The important point to remember is that you should be aware of the commitment you make in your thesis. If you can't follow through on your promise, you should alter your thesis. As you revise your paper, you should be able to determine the complexity of your final thesis and the shape of your final paper.

Generating a Working Thesis

1. Narrow your subject so that you will be able to write specifically on it in the number of pages allotted.
2. Assemble the notes—arranged in categories—that you have generated for your paper.
3. Forge a relationship that clarifies the material you have assembled.
4. Devise a sentence—a working thesis—that links the relationship you have forged with your narrowed subject.
5. Determine how ambitious you will be with your thesis—and in your paper.

---

4 Sketching your paper, or developing a formal outline

In an academic paper, you must develop all directly stated or implied ideas in the thesis. It may help to consider the thesis of the final draft as a contract between

---

[4]The term *tension,* as it relates to the thesis statement, is borrowed from Bean and Ramage, 168-169.

you and the reader; you are obliged to make good on the promises in your thesis. The working thesis is a draft of the contract that you will alter depending on what promises you are prepared to keep.

CRITICAL DECISIONS

CHALLENGE AND BE CHALLENGED: QUIZZING YOUR WORKING THESIS TO DETERMINE MAJOR SECTIONS OF YOUR PAPER

In writing a thesis, you compress a great deal of information into a single sentence; in writing a paper based on this thesis, you will need to "unpack" and discuss this information. Use the following technique as an aid to unpacking: challenge, or quiz, your thesis with questions (see box on p. 59). The technique will lead to a sketch of your paper.

Thesis

define   *what are the key features?*   *why?*

Though belonging to a group has its benefits, the price of membership is steep : the loss of individual conscience — *how does this happen?*

Sketching the paper
- —Define group identity
- —Discuss key benefits of belonging to a group
- —Define individual conscience
- —Review the process of how an individual sacrifices in order to belong to a group
- —Explain the paradox: reasons that the strength of a group comes at the expense of an individual's integrity

Thesis   *review the reasoning*

define "students' behalf" from student's - administration's point of view

By instituting a curfew and acting on what it believed was the students behalf, the administration undermined the moral and educational principles it wanted to uphold.   *how?*   *define both*

Sketching the paper
- —Review the reasoning: in setting a curfew, the administration said it was acting in the best interest of students
- —Define "students' behalf" from student and administrative perspectives
- —Define moral issues and educational principles at issue

—Explain the paradox: in mandating morality through a curfew, the administration denied students a chance to grapple with moral issues and reach mature decisions on their own. The administration undermined its own educational aims.

Devise an action plan: A sketch based on your thesis is an action plan, a paper to be written. Depending on your preference, you can fill in the sketch, converting it to a detailed outline, or you can work with it as a sketch. In either case, this plan—closely connected to your thesis—sets an agenda for the paper to follow.

Identifying significant parts of your thesis

If you write your working thesis at the top of a page and circle its significant words, you can determine how to develop your paper.

Question or Make Comments about Your Thesis in Order to Identify Major Sections of Your Paper

Questions

how does/will it happen?
how to describe?
what are some examples?
what are the reasons for?
what is my view?
compared to what?
what is the cause?
any stories to tell?
how?
when?

what has/will prevent it from
   happening?
who is involved?
what are the key features?
what are the reasons against?
how often?
possible to classify types or parts?
what is the effect of this?
which ones?

Comments

define
review the facts

review the reasoning
explain the contrast or paradox

Option: Preparing a formal outline of your paper

Many writers—especially those collaborating with others on a single
project—prefer to use a formal outline with clearly delineated major and minor
points. Even formal outlines are subject to change, however. Outlines help you unify
papers by keeping to the point. They also help you develop the significant points of
the thesis, and they help you achieve coherence, making sure that each part of the
paper leads to the next.

An outline should be arranged logically by dividing a topic into parts and
discussing each separately. Order can be either chronological (time sequence) or
spatial (location of parts). Regardless of arrangement, an outline will change as you
draft and revise your paper.

Illustration: Formal outline

Thesis: Of the five theories of tornado formation, the general vortex theory is the
most plausible.

I.   Description of tornadoes
   A. Origin of word
   B. Characteristics
     1. Shape
     2. Speed
II.   Description of five theories
   A. Downward development
     1. Rotation of clouds
     2. Movement of funnel
   B. Vortex-contraction
     1. Use of radar
     2. "Hook echo" theory
   C. Severe local-storm
     1. Warm, moist updraft
     2. Leading downdraft
     3. Radar echo
     4. "Vault" region
     5. Hook-shaped echo
   D. Electricity
     1. Lightning transfers
     2. Results of laboratory experiments
   E. General vortex
     1. Unstable stratification
     2. Vorticity
     3. Mathematical equations
       a. Two-cell solution
       b. Other solutions

III.   Reasons for preference for general vortex
      1. Limitations of other theories
      2. Flexibility of general vortex theory

A formal outline makes clear the major sections and subsections of your paper, along with the support for each section and subsection. Standard outline form is as follows: uppercase Roman numerals for general headings (major sections), uppercase letters for major points within each heading, Arabic numbers for supporting points, and lowercase letters for further subordination. Note that the entries at each level are grammatically parallel, that each level has at least two entries, and that only the first letter of an entry is capitalized. A formal outline need not show plans for your introduction or conclusion. Outlining a draft can help you see whether or not your paper is unified and coherent.

Illustration: Formal outline with sentences

A formal outline can also be presented in complete sentences, as the section below illustrates:

I.   Tornadoes can be described in both descriptive and scientific terms.
   A. The word *tornado* originates from the Spanish *tronada* (for thunderstorm), which itself derived from the Latin *tornare* (meaning to make round by turning).
   B. A tornado is characterized by its shape and speed.
      1. A tornado is shaped like a flexible funnel, the top of which is lost in cumulonimbus thunderstorm clouds.
      2. Both the forward speed and the speed of rotation in tornadoes vary drastically.

3e   Writing a draft

As you move from sketch or outline through drafting, you will alter your original plans considerably. You must be alert to changes as you write your draft.

A first draft is designed to get ideas on paper, to explore them, and to establish the shape of your paper. Remember that you will be revising extensively; free yourself to write first drafts quickly—and imperfectly.

Strategies for Drafting

Working yourself through the draft

1. Write *one* section of the paper at a time: write a general statement that supports some part of your thesis, then provide details about

the supporting statement. Once you have finished a section, take a break. Then return to write another section, working incrementally in this fashion until you have completed the draft.

Alternately, write one section of the paper and take a break. Then reread and revise that one section before moving to the next. Continue to work in this fashion, one section at a time, until you complete the draft.

2. Accept *two* drafts, minimum, as the standard for writing any formal paper. In this way, you give yourself permission to write a first draft that is not perfect.

3. If you have prepared adequately for writing, then trust that you will discover what to write *as* you write.

4. Save for later substantial revisions concerning grammar, punctuation, usage, and spelling. In your first drafts, focus on content.

---

1 Beating writer's block

Everyone who writes avoids writing at some point. If you have prepared yourself to write according to the guidelines in Chapter 3, you will minimize the danger of writer's block. Consider the following strategies for getting started with the paper itself.

stuck	*I cannot get started.* Even though I have ideas, I am afraid of the blank page—or screen.
unstuck	*Prepare yourself mentally to write* one *section of the paper, not the entire paper.* Take a break after writing each section, and you will recognize your progress.
stuck	*I want my writing to be perfect.* If it doesn't sound right as I'm writing, I'm convinced that it will sound terrible in final draft.
unstuck	*Accept* two *drafts, minimum, as the standard for writing any formal paper.* If you know that you have three drafts, you will be more willing to let the first draft look messy.
stuck	*Why advertise my problems?* I don't want to embarrass myself publicly.
unstuck	*Use a writer's reference tools.* So long as you can use a dictionary and a handbook, you can look up rules that pose problems for you.

2 Working with your sketch or outline

Choose one of the following strategies for writing based on what works best for you. No single strategy is inherently better than others.

Adhering closely to your outline

When you write from the "outside-in," you follow your outline closely.

Advantages

You will have a sense of progress, and confidence in where you're headed.

Disadvantages

You may be reluctant to stray from the outline, preventing you from moving in other directions.

Adhering loosely to your outline

When you write from the "inside-out," you use the outline solely for preparation, and generate a new outline as you draft your paper.

Advantages

You will be able to discover material as you see where your writing takes you.

Disadvantages

You may produce a draft that lacks unity and coherence.

Combining strategies

Some writers review their outline for each section of the paper, but then write the section without further reference to the outline. They constantly revise outline or draft, depending on the direction in which their writing takes them.

 Writing one section of your paper at a sitting

Papers are divided into **sections:** typically groupings of three, four, or five related paragraphs. After writing each section of your paper, take a break. Make sure that each section has a controlling focus—a **section thesis**—that addresses the major point of the section. The section thesis will help you write your draft and will help readers to follow your discussion in the final paper.

 Recalling the key relationships in your thesis

Once you express a relationship in the predicate part of your thesis, you must support it. *The types of paragraphs you write in a paper are tied directly to the relationships that you express in your thesis.* As you write your draft, you should keep in mind the key relationship established in your thesis.

How to Write One Section of a Paper

1. **Prepare to write.** Identify purpose and define audience; generate and organize ideas and information; and devise a working thesis.

2. **Identify sections of the paper.** Ask of your thesis: What parts must I develop in order to deliver on the promise of this statement? Your answer of perhaps three or four points will identify the sections you need to write to complete that statement.

3. **Plan to write one section of your paper at a sitting.** If a section is long, divide it into manageable parts and write one part at a sitting.

4. **Write individual paragraphs.** Each paragraph will be related to others in the section. As you begin a second paragraph, clearly relate it to the first; relate the third paragraph to the second, and so on until you finish writing the section. Then take a break.

5. **Write other sections, one at a time.** Continue writing, building one section incrementally on the next, until you complete your first draft.

---

5 | **Identifying and resolving problems in mid-draft**

At some point, you will probably encounter that vague sense that a section isn't right. At this point, step back and ask yourself where the trouble stems from.

Potential obstacles in writing a draft

1. You do not have enough information to write. You have not gathered the information or, if you have, you may not understand it well enough to write.
2. You do not understand the point you planned to make or its relation to the rest of your paper.
3. The point you planned to make no longer seems relevant or correct, given what you have discovered about your subject in the draft thus far.

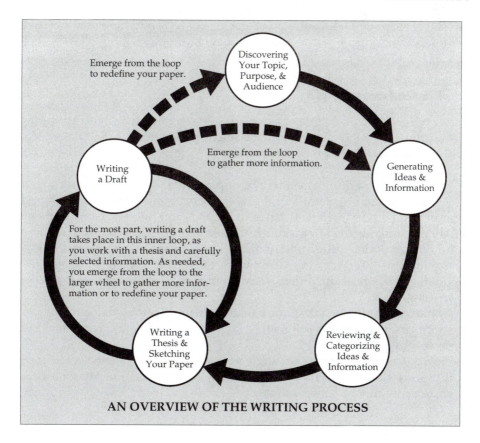

AN OVERVIEW OF THE WRITING PROCESS

4. You recognize a gap in the structure of your paper, and you suddenly see the need to expand an existing section or to write an entirely new section. In either case, your decision will affect the writing of the section that is giving you trouble.
5. The material in the section seems inappropriate for your audience.
6. You have said everything you need to in a page, but the assignment calls for six to ten pages.
7. At the moment, you do not have the attention span to write.

If you encounter one or more of these obstacles, rely on your own sense of your writing. If you are honestly frustrated, then identify the problem and find a solution.

The writing circle

The preceding diagram shows how drafting is a recursive process, looping back on itself as you discover new things about your topic. The inner loop represents the drafting stage; when you encounter an obstacle, you return to the outer loop to find the solution before returning once again to the inner loop.

 6 **Working collaboratively**

Some professors ask students to work collaboratively on a single assignment. When you produce a paper as a group, you must make sure that the final version reads as though it were written by one person.

- To minimize rewriting, meet with group members before any writing takes place. Agree on a structure for the overall document and then assign parts to individual group members. Agree on a consistent point of view for the paper.
- At a second meeting after writing has just begun, ask each group member to outline his or her section and to discuss its structure. As a group, think specifically of the ways in which one section will build from and lead to another. Also raise and address any problems encountered thus far in the writing.
- At the completion of a first draft, distribute the assembled document to the entire group and have each member revise for content and consistency of perspective.
- Incorporate all revisions in a single version of the document. *One* member of the group should then take responsibility for rewriting the paper so as to ensure continuity of style and voice.

EXERCISE 3-1   Narrowing a topic

Using the boxes in section 3a-1, come to know and own one of the following topics. Then produce two appropriately narrow topics for your topic. When you finish, discuss your responses with your classmates, trying to determine whether or not your topics are appropriately narrow.

1. popular music

2. environmental problems

3. women in business

4. parent-child relationships

EXERCISE 3-2   Recognizing purposes for writing

Identify the purpose of each of the following statements (informative, persuasive, expressive, or writing to entertain).

1. My seat on the subway is like a theater seat, from
    which I watch a pageant that changes daily. _____   _____

2. The neglect of public transportation by government
    officials is a direct cause of traffic congestion and its
    accompanying pollution.   _____

3. Moving from the New York City subway to the
    Atlanta underground is like moving from darkest
    night into brightest day.   _____

4. If drivers of public transport were given random
    drug tests, then the entire system would be safer
    and more efficient.   _____   _____

5. As Charlie passed through the turnstile on that
    fateful morning, he never realized that he was
    embarking on the journey of a lifetime.   _____

EXERCISE 3-3   **Understanding audience/Recognizing tone**

Choose a magazine with which you are familiar, and after perusing several issues, write an analysis of the magazine's intended audience. (Possible choices: *The Atlantic, Forbes, GQ, Mademoiselle, Ms., Road & Track.*) For assistance, refer to the questions in the box in section 3a-2.

Magazine:

Audience:

EXERCISE 3-4   Generating ideas

Generate ideas for your topic from Exercise 3-2, using two different methods of invention. After you finish, compare your responses. Did one of the methods yield better results than the other? Were you more comfortable with one of the methods? (Use the space below for your response.)

TOPIC _____ METHOD _____

EXERCISE 3-5   Selecting, organizing, and expanding information

Return to the topic you chose for Exercise 3-2. Define several categories from the information you gathered; organize each category into major points and supporting points; expand information by filling in gaps and/or using source materials. (Use the space below for your response.)

EXERCISE 3-6   Recognizing classes of thesis statements

Identify each of the following thesis statements as a one-, two-, or three-story thesis, and explain the reasons for your decision.

1. A subway system is a microcosm of the city
    itself.   _____

2. The Atlanta subway system is the result of
    years of careful planning, exhaustive research,
    and imaginative development.   _____

3. If Los Angeles is the city of the future, then its
    failure to implement a comprehensive public
    transportation system indicates that the
    United States is headed for an era of isolation
    and tension.   _____

EXERCISE 3-7   Clarifying purpose and thesis

In order to understand more fully the notion of a thesis as a contract, explain what you would expect the writer to address, given the following thesis statements:

1. The fall of communist governments in Eastern Europe has made it necessary for capitalist economies to reassess their values.

2. In bringing Alice Walker's *The Color Purple* to the screen, Steven Spielberg abandoned the essence of Celie's conversations with God.

3. When contemplating a shutdown, the managers of a major plant must acknowledge responsibilities not only to employees facing layoffs but to the entire community as well.

4. While they eliminate many of the environmental problems caused by disposable diapers, cloth diapers themselves carry a great environmental cost.

EXERCISE 3-8   Developing a thesis and an outline

Return to the topic you organized in Exercise 3-6. Using the guidelines in section 3d, develop a two- or three-story thesis on the topic, and prepare a formal outline.

Thesis:_____

_____

_____

Outline:

EXERCISE 3-9   Drafting

Using the guidelines in section 3e, compose a draft of the paper you outlined in Exercise 3-8.

CHAPTER 4

The Process of Revision

When you write a first draft, your primary consideration should be to give the paper potential; your goal is to establish a controlling idea. In later drafts, you will make significant changes in your first draft in order to make your ideas clear to both yourself and your readers.

The Process of Revision

Think of revision as occurring in three stages: early, later, and final:

4a   **Early revision:** Reread your first draft and rediscover your main idea. What you *intended* to write is not always, or even usually, what you *in fact* have written.

4b   **Later revision:** Make all significant parts of your document work together in support of your main idea.

4c   **Final revision (editing):** Correct errors at the sentence level that divert attention from your main point.

4a   Early revision: Rediscovering your main idea

Whether or not you revise successfully depends on the commitment you are willing to make. In the early stages of revision, you will add, alter, or delete entire paragraphs in order to make your main idea clearer. The quality of your final draft will reflect the commitment you have made to revision.

Strategies for Early Revision

Pose three questions to get started on early revision. Your goal is to rediscover and clarify what you have written in a first draft. Here are some tactics to help discover a main idea:

- What I *intended* to write in my first draft may not be what I have *in fact* written. What is the main idea of this first draft?

  Underline one sentence in your draft in answer to this question; if you cannot find such a sentence, write one.

  Choose a title for your second draft. The title will help you to clarify your main idea.

- Does what I have written in this draft satisfy my original purpose for writing?

  Review the assignment or set of instructions that began your writing project. Restate the purpose of that assignment. Reread your draft to determine the extent to which you have met this purpose. To the degree you have not, plan to revise.

- Does my writing communicate clearly to my audience?

  Think of your audience (see p. 46) and reread your draft with this audience clearly in mind. If need be, revise your level of language, your choice of illustrations, and your general treatment of the topic in order to help your audience understand.

---

1 Choosing a revision strategy that suits you

Some writers revise each paragraph in a draft before they write the next paragraph. Others revise each section before moving on. The approach advised here is to write a complete first draft before beginning revision. After writing an entire draft, first revise sections, then paragraphs, and finally individual sentences. If you do not already have a revision strategy that suits you, use the advice given here as your strategy.

2   Strategies for clarifying and developing your main idea

Your first revision should clarify your main idea. As you begin to revise, check to see if you have written what you intended to write. Here are some techniques for evaluating your first draft.

Get some distance from your writing

If at all possible, put your first draft away for a day before rereading it.

Study your working thesis and ask questions

Underline your working thesis. As you reread the draft, ask yourself if you have answered every development question and comment you posed when planning the draft. (See 3d-4.) If so, go on to 4b-1.

Search for a competing thesis

Sometimes you will have to alter your thesis after a first draft. Try to find a sentence other than your working thesis that may describe more accurately what you have written. Chances are the "competing thesis" will appear toward the end of your paper. You may need to alter your working thesis, regardless of whether or not you find a competing thesis.

Use your new thesis to direct further revision of your first draft. Quiz your new thesis with development questions and comments, and determine what material from your first draft can be revised to fit the new thesis. (See 3d.)

Outline the sections of a revised paper

A *section* of your paper is a group of related paragraphs. (See 3e-3 and 5a-2.) Normally, you will devote at least one section of your final paper to each development question or comment. Outline the sections to make sure that you have done this.

Incorporate sections of your first draft into your revised outline

After studying your new outline, cut and paste from your first draft sections that can be used in your new draft. Make sure that every sentence you keep contributes to your revised thesis. (This task is easier if you are working on a computer.)

Write new sections of the final outline, as needed

You should now have a detailed outline, along with some nearly completed sections from your first draft and ideas for sections yet to be written. Before beginning each of these new sections, write a section thesis to help you focus your ideas. (See 3e-3 and 5a-2.)

CRITICAL DECISIONS

CHALLENGE AND BE CHALLENGED: EARLY REVISION

Early revision is a crucial stage in the writing process; in some ways it is as important as generating a first draft, for in early revision you make a unified, coherent presentation out of your work and give it the shape readers will see. You can help the process by challenging key elements of your paper.

- **Challenge your thesis.** You began your first draft with a working thesis. The thesis that organized your actual draft may differ from this. Try two strategies for identifying the sentence that will become your final thesis.

  Underline the sentence you intended to be your thesis in the first draft. Ask: "Is this the sentence I wrote about?" For a moment, play a doubting game. Provisionally answer with a *no* and search for a competing thesis. Reread the draft's final paragraphs with special care. If you find no alternate thesis, return to the original.

  Study the sentence you now know to be your thesis and revise repeatedly until it is both precise and concise: make the sentence say what it must in as few words as possible. Base all subsequent revisions of your paper on this new, leaner version of your thesis.

- **Challenge your paper's structure.** What often changes most from first draft to second is the structure of a paper. A first draft is *yours* in the sense that you are writing it, at least partly, to discover what you think about a topic. The second draft is more the *reader's* in the sense that you must consider how others will regard your work and how you might best present it to secure approval and understanding. Rethink the structure of your paper in light of the reader's needs. Challenge the structure of your draft in two ways:

  Consider locating your revised thesis in some different part of the paper. How would this change the order of presentation? Are there advantages to be gained?

Consider beginning your paper not with your present first paragraph, but with some paragraph from the middle of the draft. How does the paper present itself differently, based on this change? What further changes would be needed to ensure coherence?

Devise an action plan: Based on your challenges to the paper's thesis and structure, set yourself a "to do" list. A new thesis may require that you write new sections. A revised structure will require careful attention to coherence and at least several new sentences of transition.

---

3   Reconsidering purpose and audience

Purpose

As you revise your draft, make sure that your paper conforms to the assignment or to your original purpose for writing.

- Identify the key verb in the assignment and define that verb with reference to your topic. (See 41b.)

- If you have trouble understanding the purpose, seek out your professor or your professor's assistant. Bring your draft to a conference and explain the direction you've taken.

- Once you identify the parts of a paper that will achieve a stated purpose, incorporate those parts into your plans for a revised draft.

Audience

In a first draft, you may have written to clarify thoughts for yourself. As you revise, you must keep your audience in mind. Look at your audience analysis (see 3a-3) and ask the following questions:

- How will this subject appeal to my readers?

- Is the level of difficulty with which I have treated this subject appropriate for my readers?

- Is my choice of language, in both its tone (see 3a-4) and its level of difficulty, appropriate for my readers?

- Are my examples appropriate in interest and complexity for my readers?

4 Choosing and using a title

On the basis of your final thesis, devise a title for your paper. A *descriptive* title directly announces the content of a paper. An *evocative* title is playful, intriguing, or indirect in some other way. Both types of titles should be brief (no longer than ten words).

4b Later revision: Bringing your main idea into focus

While the first revision involves major reworking of your paper, later revisions are not so far-reaching. Your purpose in later revisions is to ensure unity, coherence, and balance in your paper.

1 Focusing the paper through unity

In a unified paper, every section and paragraph discusses only those topics implied by your thesis. A unified section is a discussion of those topics implied by your section thesis (see 3d-3 and 5a-2). Discussion of any topics beyond those implied by the thesis and section thesis results in a paper that is not unified.

Unity at the Level of the Essay, the Section, and the Paragraph

Unity is a principle of logic that applies equally to the whole paper, to sections, and to individual paragraphs. A unified discussion will not stray from the sentence that organizes and focuses any one of these principle parts of a paper. Recall that a *thesis* announces and controls the content of an entire essay, and that a *section thesis* announces and controls the content of a section. Just so, a *topic sentence* announces and controls the content of sentences in a single paragraph. Think of the topic sentence as a paragraph-level *thesis,* and you will see the principle of unity at work at *all* levels of the paper. At each level of the essay, a general statement is used to guide you in assembling specific, supporting parts.

Essay-level unity	The thesis (the most general statement in the essay) governs your choice of sections in a paper.
Section-level unity	Section theses (the second-most general statements in the essay) govern your choice of paragraphs in a section.
Paragraph-level unity	Topic sentences (the third-most general statements in the essay) govern your choice of sentences in a paragraph.

Focusing the paper through coherence

Coherence is a principle of logic that applies to all levels of writing in a paper. In a coherent essay, each section follows the last in a reasonable order. In a coherent section, each paragraph follows reasonably. In a coherent paragraph, sentences follow reasonably. Coherence is established through the use of **transitions**, which highlight relationships between sentences, paragraphs, and sections. Transitions can be single words (such as *however* or *thus*), sentences, or brief paragraphs. (See 5d-3 for a detailed discussion of transitions.)

Make the whole paper cohere

A coherent paper is made up of sections that follow logically one after the other. To achieve coherence, generate a list of topics by quizzing your thesis. That list comprises the parts of your paper. Then determine the best arrangement of those parts, paying close attention to how each part relates to the others.

 Focusing the paper through balance

As you revise, you must decide whether or not your development of each topic is appropriate to its importance. Sometimes you will need to expand, adding material from your notes or doing more research. Sometimes you will need to condense, reducing the coverage of some topics. And sometimes you will need to cut sentences that are no longer relevant to your thesis.

Revise for Balance: Expand, Condense, and Cut

1. In conjunction with your revision for unity and coherence, reread your paper to determine how evenly you have developed each section.
2. Expand discussions that are underdeveloped, relative to other discussions in the paper.
3. Condense discussions that are overdeveloped, relative to other sections of the paper.
4. Cut any material that does not directly add to the development of your thesis.

4c   Final revision

 Editing

While most writers do a little tinkering with editing—revising for style, grammar, punctuation, and word choice—as they draft and revise, it is best to save editing until the major issues of content, unity, coherence, and balance are dealt with. However, if you have trouble wording a sentence that is important to your thesis, then you should probably stick with it until you get it right. While you don't have to memorzie all of the rules, it's a good idea to familiarize yourself with particular problems so that you know where to look for solutions.

 Proofreading

Before turning in a paper, check for such annoying errors as misspellings, omitted words, unintentionally repeated words, missing punctuation, and homonyms. Either ask a friend to read a copy of your paper aloud while you check the original, or read each sentence backwards to force you to look at one word at a time. When you have finished proofreading, prepare the final manuscript.

 Determining when a final draft is *final*

When you are no longer making changes that improve the paper, then you should stop revising and editing. To consider a draft final, you should be satisfied that your paper has met these standards:

- The paper has a clearly stated main point to communicate.
- It has met all requirements of unity and coherence at the levels of the paper, section, and paragraph.
- It is punctuated correctly and is free of errors in grammar and usage.

 4d   Responding to editorial advice from peers or professors

There are two basic ground rules for giving and receiving editorial advice: the first concerns ego and the second, honesty.

 Receiving advice

While it is always difficult to accept criticism of your writing, remember that it is the paper and not you personally that the student or instructor is criticizing. Try to distance yourself from the review in order to see it more objectively. When you consider criticism, remember that it is *your* paper under consideration, and you have the right to decide how to revise. Discuss points of disagreement thoughtfully with your critics, and then decide how you wish to proceed.

 2   **Giving advice**

As an editor, you must remember that the paper belongs to the writer, who may have a different perspective and a different style from yours. Be respectful and tactful in offering comments, making sure to offer specific praise as well as criticism. But by all means be honest; you do nobody a favor by refraining from criticism.

Guidelines for Peer Editing

1. Understand your role as an editor. Disinvest your ego and work to improve the paper according to the author's needs, not your own.
2. Ask the writer to identify elements of the paper to which you should pay special attention.
3. Questions you might consider as you are reading:
   Is the writer helping me to become interested in this topic?
   Do all the parts of this paper seem to be present? Are general points backed up with specific examples?
   Is the writing at the sentence level sharp?
   How much help does the writer need with the nuts and bolts of grammar and punctuation?
4. Begin with the positive. Whether you are writing your editorial comments or are delivering them in conference, begin with the parts of the paper that you like. If at all possible, find *something* that is worthy of a compliment.
5. Be specific with criticism. Identify sections or sentences that you particularly like and state why you like them. When you see room for improvement, identify specific words, sentences, or paragraphs, and state specifically what you think needs changing and why. If possible, build your constructive criticisms on earlier strengths:
   Avoid statements like "This is vague."
   Strive for statements like "Your sentences in this section don't have the same vivid detail as your earlier sentences."
6. End your editorial advice with a summary of what you have observed. Then suggest a point-by-point action plan for the writer. That is, advise the writer on specific steps to take that will lead to an improved paper.

EXERCISE 4-1   Understanding the writing process

Using the box on page 42 as a model, describe in as much detail as possible the process you use when writing a paper. Then try to imagine a visual representation, diagram, or flowchart for your process. How would it look? Like a wheel? A line? Something else? When you finish, compare your responses with your classmates: How many different processes are there? Do any resemble the process in the book more than others? Then discuss how well your process works for you.

EXERCISE 4-2   Understanding your writing process

Having recorded observations on your writing process in Exercise 4-1, try to "plug in" your own process on the writing and thinking wheel below. Using the labels provided in the diagram, offer more specific descriptions of what you do at each of the "loops" on the wheel. Compare your diagram to those of a few of your classmates. What similarities can you find? Differences?

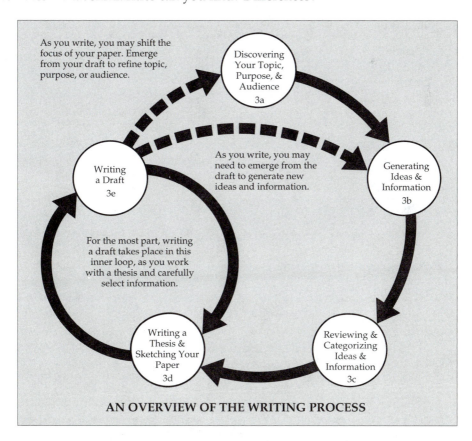

AN OVERVIEW OF THE WRITING PROCESS

EXERCISE 4-3   Revising, editing, and proofreading

A. Revising

Using the guidelines in section 4a, revise your draft.

B. Editing and proofreading

Using the guidelines in section 4c, edit and proofread your draft.

C. Analysis

In the space below, write a brief paragraph analyzing the process you went through to produce your final draft. Focus on the differences between what you did here and what you have done previously when writing papers.

EXERCISE 4-4   Recognizing unity and coherence

Sometimes it's helpful to look at short essays and paragraphs written by professionals in order to better understand the concepts of unity and coherence. Photocopy a brief (1–2 page) self-contained section in one of your textbooks, and analyze it for unity and coherence. Use strategies such as the following: find the thesis; outline the selection; relate sections or paragraphs to the thesis; identify the logic that underlies the arrangement of paragraphs; and identify transitional words, phrases, sentences, and paragraphs. After making notes on the photocopy, outline the section below and comment on its unity and coherence.

EXERCISE 4-5   Practicing peer editing

Assume that the following draft has been presented to you for peer editing. Using the guidelines in section 4d, respond to the draft. (Use a separate sheet of paper.) When you finish, compare your responses with your classmates. How are they similar? Different? Do different readers have different expectations?

I will never forget my old dance teacher, Frau Brandt. She was in her fifties when I began taking lessons, but she was still very agile and could leap higher than most of the students. She is memorable to me because she had to overcome incredible hardships in order to be happy. She was also a very good dance teacher.

When I first walked into Frau Brandt's studio, I was very frightened. It had been a bad week anyway, since my pet turtle had died and I had failed an arithmetic test at school. I was a little late, and Frau Brandt was standing in front of the mirrors reading off the names of the children in the class. There were four Frau Brandt's in that room—one standing on the floor, and one in each of the wall mirrors. It was a terrifying sight, especially when she looked up and angrily told me to take my place. I had to tell everyone in the class who I was and promise not to be late again. I never wanted so much to disappear as I did that morning.

As the class progressed, I got to know Frau Brandt better. She was very strict, of course, but she could also be helpful and kind, especially if a student was having trouble learning a step. She also told great stories about her girlhood in Germany.

It was years later, at her funeral, that I found out about Frau Brandt's difficult life. She was in her early teens when World War II broke out, and her father was drafted into the German army. She never saw him again. When she was fifteen, her home city of Dresden was firebombed, killing most of her family. She moved to Berlin after the war, and when the Communists erected the wall she was cut off from her remaining family. In 1966 she escaped to the West, strapped to the underside of a van. The ordeal was harrowing. She came to the United States in 1972, and had lived here ever since, teaching children to dance.

My initial judgment of Frau Brandt was a harsh one. I couldn't understand her impatience with our behavior, especially when I thought of how infinitely patient she was with the problems we encountered in learning to dance. As I left her funeral, I began to realize that life had taught her to be intense in everything she did. When you have undergone the trials and traumas that someone like Frau Brandt had, you learn to value every moment of life, and you become intolerant of the kind of silly behavior exhibited by many grade-school girls. But if you cling to something you love, as Frau Brandt clung to dance, you can find joy in life.

CHAPTER 5

The Paragraph and the Paper

A paragraph is a group of related sentences organized by a single, controlling idea. In this chapter paragraphs will be discussed in terms of their individual features as well as their relationship to the paper as a whole.

5a The relationship of single paragraphs to a whole paper

If you learn the techniques involved in writing paragraphs, you will be better able to compose entire essays.

1 The relationship of paragraphs to sections

Most paragraphs are part of **sections** of a larger document. Except for introductions and conclusions, each paragraph you write is involved directly with the paragraphs immediately preceding and following it. If you concentrate on writing one section of your paper at a time, you will find the task of producing an entire paper much more manageable.

2 The relationship of sections to the whole paper

You learned in chapter 3 that a **thesis** announces the topic of your paper and suggests points you will make about that topic. Because each section of your paper will probably be devoted to one point in your thesis, each section will have a **section thesis** that announces the topic of the section and suggests what you will discuss in relation to this point. Each section will be organized in paragraphs. Each section and the paragraphs in it will be **unified, well developed,** and **coherent** if they fulfill the requirements outlined in the accompanying box.

Unity, Coherence, and Development

Each **PARAGRAPH** of a paper consists of **SENTENCES** that are

Unified: sentences are all concerned with a central, controlling idea;

Coherent: sentences are arranged in a clear order, according to a definite plan;

Well developed: sentences provide details that explain and illustrate the paragraph's controlling idea.

Each **SECTION** of a paper consists of **PARAGRAPHS** that are

Unified: groups of paragraphs are devoted to one controlling idea, a section thesis that develops some part of the thesis;

Coherent: groups of paragraphs within a section are arranged in a clear order, according to a definite plan;

Well developed: groups of paragraphs provide details that explain and illustrate the section's controlling idea.

Every **PAPER** consists of **SECTIONS** (groups of related paragraphs) that are

Unified: each section is devoted to developing one part of the thesis, the central organizing idea of the paper;

Coherent: sections are arranged in a clear order, according to some definite plan;

Well developed: each section of the paper provides details important for developing the thesis.

5b | The paragraph: Essential features

Sentences in a paragraph are like paragraphs in an essay: they contribute to **unity** by focusing on a central idea, to **development** by explaining or defending the main point or thesis, and to **coherence** by being arranged according to some clear progression or plan. Organizing paragraphs will help you organize an entire essay. A paragraph is unified when each sentence relates to the controlling idea, it is well developed when each sentence explains the controlling idea, and it is coherent when the sentences are arranged according to a clear progression of ideas.

5c   Writing and revising to achieve paragraph unity

The **topic sentence** of the paragraph, like the **thesis** of the essay and the **section thesis** of the section, announces and controls the content of sentences in the paragraph. Thus the entire essay is unified as a whole and in its parts:

Essay-level unity	The thesis (the most general statement in the essay) governs your choice of sections in a paper.
Section-level unity	Section theses (the second-most general statements in the essay) govern your choice of paragraphs in a section.
Paragraph-level unity	Topic sentences (the third-most general statements in the essay) govern your choice of sentences in a paragraph.

Topic sentences, as illustrated by the paragraphs presented so far, can appear anywhere in a paragraph. You will find reference to some of these paragraphs by number throughout the remainder of this chapter.

1 Placing the topic sentence at the beginning of a paragraph

Writers who want to inform or persuade as directly as possible place the topic sentence first in a paragraph.

> The New England witch was a human being with superhuman powers. Foremost among these was her ability to perform *maleficium,* that is, to cause harm to others by supernatural means. The motive most commonly ascribed was malice, stimulated, ministers argued, by pride, discontent, greed, or envy. Although the witch's powers could bring harm to anyone, her victims tended to be her close neighbors or other people who knew her well enough to anger her. Witchcraft accusations often emerged out of the context of personal disputes, with one of the parties attributing some personal adversity to the diabolically supported malevolence of the other.   1
>
> —Carol F. Karlsen, *The Devil in the Shape of a Woman*

2 Placing the topic sentence in the middle of a paragraph

The topic sentence appears in the middle of some paragraphs, either because of the need to provide readers with background information or because of the writer's desire to build momentum.

[In 1945 English philosopher Bertrand] Russell and others, including Albert Einstein, urged full, global disarmament, but the advice was disregarded. Instead, the world set about building the arsenals that we possess today. <u>The period of grace we had in which to ward off the nuclear peril before it became a reality—the time between the moment of the invention of the weapons and the construction of the full-scale machinery for extinction— was squandered, and now the peril that Russell foresaw is upon us.</u> Indeed, if we are to be honest with ourselves we have to admit that unless we rid ourselves of our nuclear arsenals a holocaust not only *might* occur but *will* occur—if not today, then tomorrow; if not this year, then the next. We have come to live on borrowed time: every year of continued human life on earth is a borrowed year, every day a borrowed day.

2

—Jonathan Schell, *The Fate of the Earth*

3 Placing the topic sentence at the end of a paragraph

By delaying the topic sentence until the end of a paragraph, you can create atmosphere or suspense in a narrative, and you can establish common ground between reader and writer before presenting a debatable statement. Paragraph 28 by Langston Hughes (Exercise 5-1) illustrates this strategy.

4 Omitting the topic sentence from the paragraph

In narrative and descriptive papers, a topic sentence is often **implied**, because to state it explicitly would be either redundant or heavy handed. Such paragraphs, however, must still be developed with the implied topic sentence in mind.

I write this in the most recent of my many studies—a pine shed on Cape Cod. The pine lumber is unfinished inside the study; the pines outside are finished trees. I see the pines from my two windows. Nuthatches spiral around their long, coarse trunks. Sometimes in June a feeding colony of mixed warblers flies through the pines; the warblers make a racket that draws me out the door. The warblers drift loosely through the stiff pine branches, and I follow through the thin long grass between the trunks.

3

—Annie Dillard, *The Writing Life*

5d Writing and revising to achieve paragraph coherence

When you revise your drafts, you must make sure that the sentences within your paragraphs are arranged according to a logical plan. When a reader can detect the logical arrangement of your sentences, your paragraph is **coherent.**

1   Arranging sentences to achieve coherence

Paragraphs are arranged according to several standard patterns; space, time, and importance are the most common. As you write and revise, it is useful to keep these patterns in mind.

Arrangement by space

Physical descriptions are often arranged by space. The careful writer establishes a perspective and then moves on through the description. Paragraph 3 by Annie Dillard illustrates arrangement by space.

Arrangement by time

Moving a reader through a paragraph arranged by time requires that signals be given to emphasize the direction of the movement.

> One day, full of such thoughts, I tried to work and failed. After eight hours of watching helplessly while my own inane, manneristic doodles overstepped their margins and covered the pages I was supposed to be writing, I gave up. I decided to hate myself, to make popcorn and read. I had just sunk into the couch, the bowl of popcorn beside me, when I heard footsteps outside. It was two little neighborhood boys, Brad and Brian, who were seven and six. "Smells good in here," Brian said. So we ate the bowl of popcorn on the floor and talked. They played the harmonica; they played the recorder; they played the ukelele.

> —Annie Dillard, *The Writing Life*

4

Arrangement by importance

The sentences that relate to your topic sentence can be arranged according to importance, focusing on general to specific concerns, specific to general to specific, and specific to general.

General to specific: When the topic sentence begins the paragraph

In the most common arrangement of sentences in a paragraph, the topic sentence appears first, and the writer is obliged to discuss that topic throughout the paragraph.

> <u>To the young man confronting life the world lies wide. Such powers as he has he may use, must use.</u> If he chooses wrong at first, he may choose again, and yet again. Not effective or successful in one channel, he may do better in another. The growing, varied needs of all mankind call on him for

5

the varied service in which he finds his growth. What he wants to be, he
may strive to be. What he wants to get, he may strive to get. Wealth, power,   5
social distinction, fame—what he wants he can try for.

—Charlotte Perkins Gilman, *Women and Economics*

Specific to general: When the topic sentence ends the paragraph

If the writer's intent is to build momentum, the topic sentence appears at the
end of the paragraph.

What do the following have in common: dioxin in Missouri; chemical
seepage at Love Canal; radioactive contamination at Three Mile Island;
saccharin; hairdyes; formaldehyde; coffee; Red Dye #2? All of these topics   6
have been extensively, and emotionally, covered by the media in recent
years. All have been indicted as possible causes of cancer, birth defects, and
other human maladies.

—Elizabeth M. Whelan, "Big Business vs.
Public Health: The Cigarette Dilemma"

2   Achieving coherence with cues

Readers are helped through a paragraph by careful arrangement and by **cue
words**: words and phrases that remind readers as they move from sentence to
sentence that (1) they continue to read about the same topic and (2) that ideas are
unfolding logically. As you revise your paragraphs, consider using the following
types of cue words: pronouns, repetition, parallel structures, and transitions.

Pronouns

Pronouns allow the reader to understand that the writer is still referring to the
same topic without endlessly repeating nouns. Charlotte Perkins Gilman uses
pronouns *he* and *him* to refer to *the young man* in paragraph 5.

CRITICAL DECISIONS

SET ISSUES IN A BROADER CONTEXT: REVISING PARAGRAPHS FOR COHERENCE

A sentence gains meaning from the sentences that come before and after it in a
paragraph. A paragraph similarly gains meaning from the paragraphs that come

before and after it in a paper. As a writer, you probably have too much to do in a first draft to monitor the relationship among sentences and paragraphs or to develop coherence: the smooth flow of ideas. In a second or third draft, however, once you are settled on your final thesis and on the structure of your paper, you should evaluate your sentences in the broader context of paragraphs, and paragraphs in the broader context of sections (groupings of related paragraphs).

- **Revise every paragraph within its section.** To revise an individual paragraph, examine it in relation to the ones that come before and after. Develop the habit of including transitional words at the beginning or end of paragraphs to help readers move from one paragraph to the next. If you have difficulty writing a particular transition, rethink the logical connection between paragraphs. Transitions highlight a logic already present. A rough transition, always a disruption to the smooth flow of ideas, is a sign of faulty logic.

- **Revise every sentence within its paragraph.** Once you are sure of a paragraph's place in your paper, revise its component sentences to ensure coherence. Evaluate each sentence in relation to the sentences that come before and after. Use cues—pronouns, parallelism, repetition, and transitions—to help move the reader from one sentence to the next through a paragraph.

Repetition

Repetition of key words helps readers understand the importance of the paragraph. In paragraph 1 Carol F. Karlsen repeats words relating to the evil powers of witchcraft (e.g., *superhuman powers, malice, diabolically*) eight times.

Parallelism

Parallel structures, like those used by Jonathan Schell in paragraph 2 (e.g., "the time between the moment . . . and the construction," "not only *might* occur but *will* occur," "if not today, then tomorrow"), help the reader understand the importance of the ideas in the paragraph. (See chapter 18 for a complete discussion of parallelism.)

In the following section the fourth type of cue word, the transition, is discussed.

 Highlighting coherence with transitions

Transitions, words that establish logical relationships between sentences, between paragraphs, and between whole sections of an essay, cause the reader to look back on previous material and to look forward to material that will follow.

Transitions *within* paragraphs

Within paragraphs, single words or phrases usually serve as transitions.

> Those of us who have to spend a great deal of time in crowded conditions become gradually better able to adjust, but no one can ever become completely immune to invasions of Personal Space. This is because they remain forever associated with either powerful hostile or equally powerful loving feelings. All through our childhood we will have been held to be loved and held to be hurt, and anyone who invades our Personal Space when we are adults is, in effect, threatening to extend his behavior into one of these two highly charged areas of human interaction. Even if his motives are clearly neither hostile nor sexual, we still find it hard to suppress our reactions to his close approach. Unfortunately, different countries have different ideas about exactly how close is close. It is easy enough to test your own "space reaction": when you are talking to someone in the street or in any open space, reach out with your arm and see where the nearest point on his body comes. If you hail from western Europe, you will find that he is roughly fingertip distance from you. In other words, as you reach out, your fingertips will just about make contact with his shoulder. If you come from eastern Europe you will find you are standing at "wrist distance." If you come from the Mediterranean region you will find that you are much closer to your companion, at a little more than "elbow distance."

7

> —Desmond Morris, *Manwatching*

Transitions *between* paragraphs

Transitions between paragraphs can also be entire sentences.

> <u>So affluence was not just an economic fact but a demographic one, and the demographic bulge matched the affluent state of mind.</u> The idea of America had long been shaped by the promise of opportunity in a land of plenty, but at long last the dream seemed to be coming true. . . .

8

> —Todd Gitlin,
> *The Sixties: Years of Hope, Days of Rage*

At times, especially in a long or complex section, a paragraph-length transition is necessary. The essay from which the following paragraph is taken discusses three theories attempting to explain the extinction of dinosaurs. After discussing the theories, the author moves on to analyzing their plausibility. Because the essay is long and complex, a transitional paragraph is necessary.

All three theories, testicular malfunction, psychoactive overdosing, and asteroidal zapping, grab our attention mightily. As pure phenomenology, they rank about equally high on any hit parade of primal fascination. Yet one represents expansive science, the others restrictive and untestable speculation. The proper criterion lies in evidence and methodology; we must probe behind the superficial fascination of particular claims.

9

—Stephen Jay Gould,
"Sex, Drugs, and the Extinction of the Dinosaurs"

Providing transitions between sentences, paragraphs, and sections helps readers follow your line of thought clearly. Among the transitions you can expect to use are the following:

Transitional Expressions

To show addition
> additionally, again, also, and, as well, besides, equally important, further, furthermore, in addition, moreover, then

To show similarity
> also, in the same way, just as . . . so too, likewise, similarly

To show an exception
> but, however, in spite of, on the one hand . . . on the other hand, nevertheless, nonetheless, notwithstanding, in contrast, on the contrary, still, yet

To indicate a sequence
> first, second, third . . . , next, then, finally

To show time
> after, afterwards, at last, before, currently, during, earlier, immediately, later, meanwhile, now, recently, simultaneously, subsequently, then

To provide an example
> for example, for instance, namely, specifically, to illustrate

To emphasize a point
> even, indeed, in fact, of course, truly

To indicate place
> above, adjacent, below, beyond, here, in front, in back, nearby, there

To show cause and effect
> accordingly, consequently, hence, so, therefore, thus

To conclude or repeat
> finally, in a word, in brief, in conclusion, in the end, on the whole, thus, to conclude, to summarize

---

4   Combining techniques to achieve coherence

When some or all of the techniques discussed above are combined, the result is a clear, easy-to-follow paragraph. Paragraph 7 by Desmond Morris illustrates the effectiveness of combining techniques: The words *space* and *distance* are repeated, as are the pronouns *he* and *you*. Parallel structure appears several times, including "either powerful hostile or equally powerful loving feelings," "different countries have different ideas," and "If you hail from . . . If you come from . . . If you come from. . . ." He also uses transitions mentioned in 5d-3.

5e   Writing and revising to achieve well-developed paragraphs

To **develop** a paragraph means to devote a block of sentences to discussing its core idea.

Developing Paragraphs: Essential Features

In determining whether a paragraph is well or even adequately developed, you should be able to answer three questions without hesitation:

- **What's the main point of the paragraph?**

- **Why should readers accept this main point?** (That is, what reasons or information have you provided that would convince a reader that your main point is accurate or reasonable?)

- **Why should readers *care* about the main point of this paragraph?**

As you revise your papers, you should begin to think about the methods you employ in developing your paragraphs. The most common method of development involves stating the topic and then dividing it into several parts; this method is called **topical**.

> It seems a pity that the world should throw away so many good things merely because they are unwholesome. I doubt if God has given us any refreshment which, taken in moderation, is unwholesome, except microbes. Yet there are people who strictly deprive themselves of each and every 10
> eatable, drinkable and smokable which has in anyway acquired a shady reputation. They pay this price for health. And health is all they get for it. How strange it is. It is like paying out our whole fortune for a cow that has gone dry.
>
> —Samuel Clemens,
> *Mark Twain's Autobiography*

Within any given paper you will employ many patterns of development. In addition to topical, other patterns include: **narration, description, example, definition, comparison/contrast, process, cause and effect,** and **analysis/classification.** As you revise your papers, you will choose patterns of development based on the inferences that underlie the paper's thesis (see chapter 3).

1   Narration and description

In a narrative, the writer seeks to keep the reader's attention by relating incidents that illustrate the point of the paper. The entire section by Langston Hughes (Exercise 5-1), especially paragraph 33, illustrates narration that works effectively.

Writers who employ description effectively evoke a sense of sight, feeling, smell, hearing, or taste.

> She was seeing Cambridge at its loveliest. The sky was an infinity of blue from whose pellucid depths the sun shone in unclouded but gentle radiance. The trees in the college gardens and the avenues leading to the Backs, as yet untouched by the heaviness of high summer, lifted their green 11
> tracery against stone and river and sky. Punts shot and curtsied under the bridges, scattering the gaudy water fowl, and by the rise of the new Garret Hostel bridge the willows trailed their pale, laden boughs in the darker green of the Cam.
>
> —P. D. James,
> *An Unsuitable Job for a Woman*

2 Example

Sometimes a topic is developed entirely by example, while at other times examples are used in conjunction with other methods.

> At the Lovelace Foundation, Albuquerque, New Mexico, experimenters forced sixty-four beagles to inhale radioactive strontium 90 as part of a larger "Fission Product Inhalation Program" which began in 1961 and has been paid for by the US Atomic Energy Commission. In this particular experiment twenty-five of the dogs eventually died. One of the deaths occurred during an epileptic seizure; another from a brain hemorrhage. Other dogs, before death, became feverish and anemic, lost their appetites, had hemorrhages and bloody diarrhea.

12

> —Peter Singer, "Is Animal Experimentation Harming Society?"

3 Sequential order/process

In a process paragraph, steps must be delineated clearly.

> The next step is to have at Mr. Jones with a thing called a trocar. This is a long, hollow needle attached to a tube. It is jabbed into the abdomen, poked around the entrails and chest cavity, the contents of which are pumped out and replaced with "cavity fluid." This done, and the hole in the abdomen sewn up, Mr. Jones's face is heavily creamed (to protect the skin from burns which may be caused by leakage of the chemicals), and he is covered with a sheet and left unmolested for a while. But not for long—there is more, much more, in store for him. He has been embalmed, but not yet restored, and the best time to start the restorative work is eight to ten hours after embalming, when the tissues have become firm and dry.

13

> —Jessica Mitford, *The American Way of Death*

4 Definition

Paragraphs of definition can serve two different purposes: they can *inform* the reader of the meanings of essential terms, and they can *argue* that a particular definition is preferable over others.

> Cellulitis is a skin infection that sometimes accompanies damage to the skin, poor circulation, or diabetes. The skin becomes red and swollen and is both warm and painful to the touch, and is sometimes accompanied by

14

fever, malaise, chills, and headache. If antibiotics are not given, the condition may progress to abscesses and tissue damage.

14

—Robert R. Walther, M.D., "Skin Diseases"

Tolerance means "inclusion," but actually that is not enough. To many people who have been made marginal in the past, inclusion sounds like, "come on in, but don't change anything." Inclusion sounds like, "you're welcome to join what we do, but we're not going to change what we do." What a different result would emerge if the meaning of tolerance for differences was widely understood to include the varieties of human beings within the norm against which equality is measured!

15

—Martha Minow, "On Neutrality, Equality, and Tolerance: New Norms for a Decade of Distinction"

5 Division and classification

Division and classification involve analyzing a subject, division by breaking a topic into its component parts, classification by grouping like items.

If one looks at the actors and activities which have dominated the news over the years, it is possible to divide much of what appears on television and in the magazines, particularly as hard news, into two types of stories. One type can be called disorder news, which reports threats to various kinds of order, as well as measures taken to restore order. The second type deals with the routine activities of leading public officials: the day-to-day decisions, policy proposals, and recurring political arguments, as well as the periodic selection of new officials, both through election and appointment. These story types in turn suggest two additional values: the desirability of social order . . . and the need for national leadership in maintaining that order.

16

—Herbert J. Gans, *Deciding What's News: A Study of* CBS Evening News, NBC Nightly News, Newsweek *and* Time

6 Comparison/contrast

In discussing similarities and differences between items, a writer can develop a paragraph by focusing on the **subject** (the items compared or contrasted) or on specific **points** of comparison or contrast. Longer comparisons are generally arranged point-by-point, shorter ones by subject.

Organizing a Paragraph of Comparison and Contrast

Comparison and contrast is a type of analysis in which parts of two (or more) *subjects* are studied and then discussed in terms of one another. Particular *points* of comparison and contrast provide the means by which to observe similarities and differences between subjects. A comparative analysis is usually arranged in one of two ways:

Arrangement by subject

Topic sentence (may be shifted to other positions in the paragraph)

Introduce Subject A
Discuss Subject A in terms of the first point to be discussed
Discuss Subject A in terms of the second point to be discussed

Introduce Subject B
Discuss Subject B in terms of the first point to be discussed
Discuss Subject B in terms of the second point to be discussed

Arrangement point-by-point

Topic sentence (may be shifted to other positions in the paragraph)

Introduce the first point to be compared and contrasted
Discuss Subject A in terms of this point
Discuss Subject B in terms of this point

Introduce the second point to be compared and contrasted
Discuss Subject A in terms of this point
Discuss Subject B in terms of this point

Conclude with a summary of similarities and differences.

Arrangement point-by-point

The twins also have their differences. One wears his hair over his forehead, the other has it slicked back with sideburns. One expresses

17

himself better orally, the other in writing. But although the emotional environments in which they were brought up were different, the profiles on their psychological inventories were much alike. 17

—Constance Holden, "Identical Twins Reared Apart"

Arrangement by subject

It took some time but finally we were able to identify most of the contrasting features of the American and British problems that were in conflict in this case. When the American wants to be alone he goes into a room and shuts the door—he depends on architectural features for screening. For an American to refuse to talk to someone else present in the same room, to give them the "silent treatment," is the ultimate form of rejection and a sure sign of great displeasure. The English, on the other hand, lacking rooms of their own since childhood, never developed the practice of using space as a refuge from others. They have in effect internalized a set of barriers, which they erect and which others are supposed to recognize. Therefore, the more the Englishman shuts himself off when he is with an American, the more likely the American is to break in to assure himself that all is well. Tension lasts until the two get to know each other. The important point is that the spatial and architectural needs of each are not the same at all. 18

—Edward Hall, *The Hidden Dimension*

7 Analogy

An analogy is a comparison of two topics that, on first appearance, seem unrelated. Analogies are often used to clarify difficult concepts.

If clothing is a language, it must have a vocabulary and a grammar like other languages. Of course, as with human speech, there is not a single language of dress, but many: some (like Dutch and German) closely related and others (like Basque) almost unique. And within every language of clothes there are many different dialects and accents, some almost unintelligible to members of the mainstream culture. Moreover, as with speech, each individual has his own stock of words and employs personal variations of tone and meaning. 19

—Alison Lurie, *The Language of Clothes*

8   Cause and effect

Development by cause and effect shows how an event or condition has come to occur.

> What happens when farm people take up "off-farm" work? The immediate result is that they must be replaced by chemicals and machines and other purchases from an economy adverse and antipathetic to farming, which means that the remaining farmers are put under yet greater pressure to abuse their land. If under the pressure of an adverse economy, the soil erodes, soil and water and air are poisoned, the woodlands are wastefully logged, and everything not producing an immediate economic return is neglected, that is apparently understood by most of the society as merely the normal cost of production.
>
> —Wendell Berry, "An Argument for Diversity"

20

Combining methods of development

Writers often combine methods of development. (See paragraphs 13 by Jessica Mitford, 18 by Edward Hall, and 19 by Alison Lurie.)

5f   Writing and revising paragraphs of introduction and conclusion

The introduction moves the reader into a paper, and the conclusion moves the reader back out, with new insights gained from reading the paper.

1   Introductions

The introduction as a frame of reference

Introductions can establish a frame of reference that alerts readers to the type of language, evidence, and logic that will be used in the subsequent paper. The following paragraph uses the language of chemistry and biology (*antidote, electrolyte, formulations*), suggests that evidence will be provided by reporting on empirical studies, and that the cause-and-effect logic will be used to support the thesis.

> When medical research yields new lifesaving therapies, too often they are complex, expensive and inaccessible to many people. Oral rehydration therapy (ORT) is a fine exception to that rule. It is an uncomplicated, low-cost and easily obtainable antidote to a major scourge: the dehydration

21

that accompanies diarrhea. A patient is simply fed an electrolyte solution to replace fluid and vital ions lost through the bowel. In an added boon, recent study has found virtue in a number of different simple formulations, many of which may offer advantages over the solution now in widest use.

21

> —Norbert Hirschhorn and William B. Greenough III,
> "Progress in Oral Rehydration Therapy"

The introduction as an invitation to continue reading

In addition to establishing a frame of reference, an introduction also catches and holds the reader's attention. Whether you prefer to write your introduction first or to wait until the paper is finished, remember to review the introduction to make sure it accurately presents to the reader a sense of what will follow.

While I was painting the downstairs hall I thought of a novel to write. Really I just thought of a character; he more or less wandered into my mind, wearing a beard and a broad-rimmed leather hat. I figured that if I sat down and organized this character on paper, a novel would grow up around him. But it was March and the children's spring vacation began the next day, so I waited.

22

> —Anne Tyler, "Still Just Writing"

Strategies for Writing Introductions

1. Announce your topic, using a vocabulary that hints at the perspective from which you will be writing. On completing your introduction, readers should be able to anticipate the type of language, evidence, and logic you will use in your paper.

2. If readers lack the background needed to understand your paper, then provide this background. In a paragraph or two, choose and develop a strategy that will both orient readers to and interest readers in your subject:
   define terms
   present a brief history
   review a controversy

3. If readers know something of your subject, then devote less (or no) time to developing background information and more time to

stimulating interest. In a paragraph or two, choose and develop a strategy that will gain the reader's attention:

raise a question

quote a source familiar to the reader

tell a story

begin directly with a statement of the thesis

4. Once you have provided background information and gained the reader's attention with an opening strategy, gradually turn that attention toward your thesis, which you will position as the last sentence of the introductory paragraph(s).

---

2 | Conclusions

While a conclusion need only summarize the essay, a good conclusion will also suggest the significance of the work or apply it to the larger world. A well written conclusion will answer the question, "So what?"

Strategies for Writing Conclusions

1. **Summary.** The simplest conclusion is a summary, a brief restatement of your paper's main points. Avoid conclusions that repeat exactly material presented elsewhere in the paper.

2. **Summary and Comment.** More emphatic solutions build on a summary in one of several ways. These conclusions will

set ideas in the paper in a larger context

call for action (or research)

speculate or warn

purposefully confuse or trouble the reader

raise a question

quote a familiar or authoritative source

tell a story

The three conclusions that follow provide examples of a summary, a call to action, and a warning.

Primarily as a result of tremendous leaps in computer power and the capabilities of graphics software, optical interferometry can now be used to perform high-resolution, two- and three-dimensional surface mapping. Adapting these techniques to surface studies has just begun. Nevertheless, we are convinced that they are destined to become important tools for both industry and academia.

> —Glen M. Robinson, David M. Perry and Richard W. Peterson, "Optical Interferometry of Surfaces"

23

It is time to experiment, time to leave the well-ordered but stuffy classroom, time to restore a vulgar vitality to poetry and unleash the energy now trapped in the subculture. There is nothing to lose. Society has already told us that poetry is dead. Let's build a funeral pyre out of the desiccated conventions piled around us and watch the ancient, spangle-feathered, unkillable phoenix rise from the ashes.

> —Dana Gioia, "Can Poetry Matter?"

24

There is greed and humility, fraud and sincerity, thugishness and wit in the animal rights movement, just as there is among Bible Belt preachers or, for that matter, environmentalists. Animal rights isn't necessarily the enemy. Let's face it, in this era of war, greed and thoughtless consumption, the earth and all her creatures need all the allies they can get. But animal rights isn't necessarily environmentalism either, no matter what its proponents say. Those who would fight the earth's battles can't help but make common cause with animal rights activists where their interests coincide—but carefully, lest the ever-elusive big picture doesn't get miniaturized into portraits of battered puppy dogs.

> —Margaret L. Knox, "The Rights Stuff"

25

3 The opening and closing frame

An introductory and concluding **frame** for a paper involves using the same story, quotation, or question to introduce the subject and to conclude the discussion.

Introduction

For a long time I have wanted to write about a vision of my father I experienced on a New York City subway train riding downtown to a literary meeting. As a historian I am skeptical of visions. I pride myself on my rationality, I rely on fact. But as a novelist I believe in visions. Now I see

26

a way to tell the story in the context of other visions of my father that have pursued me lifelong.

26

Conclusion

    I pulled a novel out of my briefcase and began to read it. The train jerked to a stop. When I looked up, the raw, dangerous man opposite me was gone. My novelist's self felt disappointed. I wished I had had the nerve to call after him, "Hey, getcha *Woild*!"

27

—Thomas Fleming, "Visions of My Father"

5g Determining paragraph length

    There is no set rule for determining paragraph length. The difficulty or complexity of content, the length of sentences, and the density of print on the page all figure in determining appropriate length. Consider paragraph length only after you have determined that your paper says what you want it to clearly and emphatically.

EXERCISE 5-1   Recognizing unity, development, and coherence in sections

On the reverse side of this page, identify the section thesis of the following passage (a section from Langston Hughes's autobiography) and then state how each paragraph expands on the thesis. Finally, using the guidelines found in the box on pages 87–88, explain how the section is unified, well developed, and coherent.

My aunt told me that when you were saved you saw a light, and something happened to you inside! And Jesus came into your life! And God was with you from then on! She said you could see and hear and feel Jesus in your soul. I believed her. I have heard a great many old people say the same thing and it seemed to me they ought to know. So I sat there calmly in the hot, crowded church, waiting for Jesus to come to me.

28

The preacher preached a wonderful rhythmical sermon, all moans and shouts and lonely cries and dire pictures of hell, and then he sang a song about the ninety and nine safe in the fold, but one little lamb was left out in the cold. Then he said: "Won't you come? Won't you come to Jesus? Young lambs, won't you come?" And he held out his arms to all us young sinners there on the mourner's bench. And the little girls cried. And some of them jumped up and went to Jesus right away. But most of us just sat there.

29

A great many old people came and knelt around us and prayed, old women with jet-black faces and braided hair, old men with work-gnarled hands. And the church sang a song about the lower lights are burning, some poor sinners to be saved. And the whole building rocked with prayer and song.

30

Still I kept waiting to *see* Jesus.

31

Finally all the young people had gone to the altar and were saved, but one boy and me. He was a rounder's son named Westley. Westley and I were surrounded by sisters and deacons praying. It was very hot in the church, and getting late now. Finally Westley said to me in a whisper: "God damn! I'm tired o' sitting here. Let's get up and be saved." So he got up and was saved.

32

Then I was left all alone on the mourner's bench. My aunt came and knelt at my knees and cried, while prayers and songs swirled all around me in the little church. The whole congregation prayed for me alone, in a mighty wail of moans and voices. And I kept waiting serenely for Jesus, waiting, waiting—but he didn't come. I wanted to see him, but nothing happened to me. Nothing! I wanted something to happen to me, but nothing happened.

33

—Langston Hughes, *The Big Sea*

SECTION THESIS:

HOW PARAGRAPHS EXPAND ON THESIS:

¶ 29

¶ 30

¶ 31

¶ 32

¶ 33

The section is unified because

The section is well developed because

The section is coherent because

EXERCISE 5-2   Recognizing unity, development, and coherence in paragraphs

In the space below, identify the main point in the following and explain how (1) the paragraph is unified, (2) the sentences in the paragraph develop the main point, and (3) the paragraph is coherent.

> In 1848 Marx and Engels wrote one of the most important political documents of modern history. This document was a short but stirring call to arms for the working class and became the creed of the Communist Party. Known as the *Communist Manifesto*, it contains the immortal words: *"Workers of the world unite! The proletarians have nothing to lose but their chains."* In consise, ringing language, the *Communist Manifesto* sets forth the basic tenets of Marxist philosophy. Telling of the bourgeoisie's (the owner's) exploitation of the proletariat (the workers), Marx predicted a proletarian uprising and an end to capitalism and exploitation.
>
> 34

> —Gary K. Bertsch, Robert P. Clark, and David M. Wood,
> *Power & Policy in Three Worlds*, Fourth Edition

MAIN POINT

The paragraph is unified because

The paragraph is well developed because

The paragraph is coherent because

EXERCISE 5-3   Recognizing unity, development, and coherence in paragraphs

Find two interesting paragraphs from textbooks, magazines, or other collections. In the space below, use your analysis of paragraph 34 by Bertsch, Clark, and Wood as a model to evaluate the unity, development, and coherence of these paragraphs. Then compare the two: Is one a better paragraph than the other? If so, why? How do the two differ in development and coherence?

EXERCISE 5-4   **Writing unified, well-developed, and coherent paragraphs**

On a separate sheet of paper, rewrite the following sentences so that they comprise a unified, well-developed, and coherent paragraph. Feel free to cut or add material as necessary. After you finish, compare your responses with classmates. How do your paragraphs differ? How are they similar? Are some paragraphs better than others? Why? (You can mark up the paragraph on this page if you wish.)

Many environmental groups decry the use of commercial household cleaners. Two women in Atlanta, Debra Kerch and Jodie Davis, began an environmentally safe cleaning service in 1990. Kerch and Davis's company, Earth Care Services, proves that you can be environmentally conscious and financially successful at the same time. Many household chemicals are toxic. Batteries are filled with acid. Bleach can do damage to groundwater. Pesticides can make people and pets ill. Animal Rights groups boycott products made by companies that conduct animal testing. The Body Shop is a chain of health-and-beauty-aids stores that produces and sells animal-safe products. Kerch and Davis use only products that are not tested on animals. They plan to market their products in addition to continuing their cleaning service. They clean homes using only products that are environmentally safe. They also dispose of recyclable items for their clients.

EXERCISE 5-5   **Recognizing topic sentences**

In the spaces provided, copy the topic sentence for each of the following paragraphs.
If the topic is implied, write "implied" and then phrase the topic in your own words.

> I went to a private school run by a French order of nuns. I was the
> poorest girl in the class, the only one who could not fork up the twenty-five
> dollars for the eighth grade trip to Washington. What story did I write in
> those days? One about a little rich boy, who lived all day behind elegant   35
> iron gates and had everything he wanted—except a friend he could confide
> in.

> —Gail Godwin, "Becoming a Writer"

¶ 9 by Stephen Jay Gould

¶ 10 by Samuel Clemens

¶ 12 by Peter Singer

EXERCISE 5-6   **Recognizing strategies to achieve coherence**

In the space below, identify the techniques that the authors use to establish coherence.

¶ 16 by Herbert Gans

¶ 18 by Edward Hall

¶ 25 by Margaret L. Knox

EXERCISE 5-7   **Using strategies to achieve coherence**

On a separate sheet of paper, rewrite the following sentences so that they comprise a coherent paragraph. After you finish, compare your response with those of your classmates. How do your paragraphs differ? How are they similar? Are some paragraphs better than others? Why? (You can mark up the paragraph on this page if you wish.)

In the 1950s prime-time television was dominated by situation comedies. Some of the programs included *The Honeymooners* and *I Love Lucy.* In the early 1960s there were situation comedies. Some of the programs included *Father Knows Best, The Dick Van Dyke Show,* and *The Donna Reed Show.* Television shows in the 1950s and '60s did not deal with controversial issues. In the early 1970s television shows began to deal with controversial issues. *All in the Family* dealt head-on with issues of race. *All in the Family* dealt with issues of gender. *All in the Family* dealt with pacifism. These were some of the issues it dealt with. *M*A*S*H* dealt with issues of pacifism. *M*A*S*H* dealt with issues of social responsibility. In the late 1970s and in the early 1980s many shows did not deal with controversial issues. Shows that were on in the late 1970s and early 1980s included *The Brady Bunch* and *Three's Company.* In the late 1980s and early 1990s some programs are beginning to deal with controversial issues. Popular shows in the late 1980s and early 1990s included *The Golden Girls* and *Roseanne. The Golden Girls* dealt with issues of aging. *The Golden Girls* dealt with issues of sexuality. *Roseanne* deals with issues of unemployment. *Roseanne* deals with issues of teenage sexuality. Television seems to be dealing with controversial issues. Television dealt with controversial issues in the early 1970s. Television did not deal with controversial issues in the 1950s. Television did not deal with controversial issues in the late 1970s and early 1980s.

EXERCISE 5-8   Developing a paragraph with specific details

Choose one set of general statements from the following list, and on a separate sheet of paper, develop a paragraph by providing specific details related to the core idea. As you develop the paragraph, keep in mind the guidelines on pages 87–88.

1. Trying to hold down a job while caring for a family (or while pursuing a college degree) can pose many problems. Frequently the individual trying to balance the two ends up shortchanging both.

2. The perfect vacation should offer equal amounts of relaxation, excitement, and enlightenment.

3. The kind of music played on radio stations in a given city can reveal a good deal about the inhabitants' ages, interests, and socioeconomic status.

EXERCISE 5-9   Developing a paragraph with specific details

Choose a different general statement from the list in Exercise 5-8, and on a separate sheet of paper, develop a paragraph using two of the patterns covered in 5e-2.

EXERCISE 5-10   Recognizing introduction strategies

Find representative introductions (of chapters, sections, essays) from the reading you're doing for courses in two different disciplines. Consider all science courses to be one discipline, all business courses to be another, all economics/sociology/ psychology/political science to be another, and all literature/language/history/ philosophy/fine arts to be another. Using what you've learned about introductions in this chapter, in the space below compose a brief comparison of the two samples, explaining how they reflect different frames of reference for readers.

EXERCISE 5-11   Recognizing conclusion strategies

Find representative conclusions (of chapters, sections, essays) from the reading you're doing for courses in two different disciplines, using the categories found in Exercise 5-10. Using what you've learned about conclusions in this chapter, in the space below compose a brief comparison of the two samples, explaining the methods they use to signal that the paper is finished, as well as the message they leave with the reader.

EXERCISE 5-12   Determining paragraph length

Mark off with a slash (/) places where the following paragraph could be divided to make it easier for the reader to follow. When you finish, compare your response with those of your classmates, explaining your decisions.

Sir Thomas More was born in 1477, the oldest son of a lawyer. He received an excellent education, studying with the Archbishop of Canterbury and attending Oxford University. While studying for the bar, More also read widely in religious and classical literature, and did a little of his own writing. Although he once believed that he had a vocation to the priesthood, he eventually settled down to married life with Jane Colt. His wife died in childbirth six years after they were married, leaving More with four children. In order to provide himself with companionship and his children with a mother, he married again shortly after his first wife died. More's literary career included a history of Richard III and his famous *Utopia*. While his Utopia was essentially a godless place, More's life remained one of Christian piety. His intense faith, in fact, prevented him from signing his name to a letter declaring Henry VIII the supreme head of the Church in England. Henry had split from the Church of Rome in a dispute over the legality of his marriage to Catherine of Aragon. Because of the respect and popular support that More enjoyed, his signature on the letter became an obsession with the King. In 1534, More was imprisoned for his refusal to sign the oath. He maintained his honor, and when he was tried he spoke eloquently of the sanctity of the human conscience and the unity of the holy Church. More was beheaded in 1535, prompting a shocked, mournful response from the European community.

CHAPTER 6

Writing and Evaluating Arguments

In everyday life as well as in the academic world, argument provides a way of knowing about and participating in the world.[1]

6a An overview of argument

An **argument** is a process of influencing others, of changing minds through reasoned discussion. Arguments consist of three parts: claim, support, and reasoning.

CLAIM   A claim is an argument's thesis, a statement about which people will disagree. There are three types of claim; whichever you use, you need to define terms with care.

- Claims about facts
- Claims about what is valuable
- Claims about policy

SUPPORT   Support consists of facts, opinions, and examples that you present to readers so that they will accept your claim. Usually, you will present several types of support for a claim. (6c)

REASONING   Reasoning is the pattern of thought that connects support to a claim. Each type of support involves a corresponding form of reasoning. Reasoning will be based on appeals to a reader's logic, respect for authority, or emotion.

- Appeals to logic (6d-1)
- Appeals to authority (6d-2)
- Appeals to emotion (6d-3)

---

[1]The approach to argument taken here is based on the work of Stephen Toulmin, as developed in *The Uses of Argument* (Cambridge: The University Press, 1958).

Sample argument

1st statement of support (appeal to logic) ⎰ If you are sitting in a crowded room in which people are smoking, you will breathe in some of that smoke. You have no choice in the matter; the smoke is in the air. **Because of the**

claim ⎰ **dangers of secondhand smoke, smoking in public places should be restricted.** According to former Secretary of Health, Education and Welfare Joseph Califano, "Study after study has associated involuntary smoking and lung cancer, pneumonia, asthma and bronchitis." The key word in this statement is *involuntary:* No one should be subjected to dangerous substances without his or

key term defined ⎰ her consent. Restricting smoking simply requires that certain areas be set aside for smokers in order protect nonsmokers.

2nd statement of support (appeal to authority)

3rd statement of support (appeal to emotion)

Analysis: The example paragraph consists of three sets of statements that support the claim. Each is based on a corresponding type of reasoning. Claim, support, and reasoning function as one persuasive whole:

(1) **Support:**	Fact (nonsmokers breathe in smoke from others)
Reasoning:	Appeal to logic (cause and effect)
Claim (about policy):	Nonsmokers should not have to worry about secondhand smoke; therefore, smoking in public places should be restricted.
(2) **Support:**	Fact (statement by Joseph Califano)
Reasoning:	Appeal to authority (Califano is considered an expert on health issues; his testimony is valuable)
(3) **Support:**	Opinion (no one should be subjected involuntarily to hazards)
Reasoning:	Appeal to emotion (sympathy will lead you to agree)
Key term defined:	Restricting means that areas will be set aside.

6b   Making a claim (an argumentative thesis)

The **claim** of a paper is a single statement that crystallizes your purpose for writing and governs the logic and development of the paper. The argumentative **claim** (or argumentative thesis) expresses your view on a subject. (See 3d for a discussion of thesis statements.)

1   Answering questions with your claim

Arguments provide answers to one of three types of questions: questions of *fact, value,* or *policy.* A *question of fact* can take the following forms: *Does X exist? Does X lead to Y? How can we define X?* A statement of fact that has been established as true can be used as evidence in other arguments. The methods of establishing the truth of a statement of fact differ both between and within disciplines.

Claims that answer questions of fact

Alcoholism is not a disease.

First-year college students are better prepared than the SAT scores suggest.

A *question of value* takes the form: *What is X worth?* In determining value, the arguer uses explicitly stated standards called *criteria.*

Claims that answer questions of value

Treating alcoholism as a disease undermines the individual's sense of control over his or her own body.

The SATs are culturally biased exams that unfairly label ethnic and racial minorities unprepared for college.

A *question of policy* takes the form: *What action should be taken?* Questions about what *ought* to be done prompt arguments based on claims of policy.

Claims that answer questions of policy

Alcoholism should be treated by restoring the individual's sense of control over his or her body.

The SATs must be completely overhauled to eliminate bias.

2 | Defining terms in the argumentative thesis

If your argument is to succeed, you must define terms carefully. Some terms (such as *humanist* or *harassment*) can be defined in different ways. In addition, sometimes it is necessary to argue for a certain definition or to explain a complicated term. If you and your audience do not agree on the definitions of your terms, then your argument is undermined.

6c | Gathering evidence

Evidence consists of the facts, opinions, and examples that support your claim. A **fact** is a statement that can be proven true or false. Facts can be verified by referring to recent, authoritative sources. An **example** is a specific instance that illustrates a point. Examples can demonstrate that a generalization is correct. An **opinion** is a statement of interpretation or judgment. Opinions are supported by referring to the opinions of experts.

CRITICAL DECISIONS

FORM, AND SUPPORT, OPINIONS: FINDING SUPPORT FOR YOUR ARGUMENTS

Once you have decided on a claim, turn your attention to gathering support. Question your claim vigorously: What will readers need to see in order to accept your view as true, probable, or desirable? Assemble support from the various categories available to you:

- **Facts:** Find sources on your topic. Take copious notes on any facts that you think are pertinent. Remember that the facts you gather should accurately represent the available data.

- **Statistics:** Again, find sources on your topic. Begin with the U.S. Government Printing Office, which publishes volumes of statistics on life in the United States. Locate other publications, with an eye particularly to statistical studies.

- **Expert opinions:** Locate experts by reviewing source materials and checking for people whose work is referred to repeatedly. Also compare bibliographies and look for names in common. Within a week or so of moderately intensive research, you will identify acknowledged experts on a topic. Quote experts when their language is particularly powerful or succinct; otherwise, summarize or paraphrase.

- **Examples:** Readers may recall a vivid example more clearly than they will your claim. Realizing this, look for multiple examples on the topic of your argument and choose examples that make your point for you—without the benefit of your comments. If examples are memorable, you will encourage readers to accept your claim.

- **Emotions:** Do not underestimate the power of emotions in swaying readers to your position. If you are arguing honestly and believe in your claim, then you can in good conscience appeal to the emotions of your readers. Discover their needs and explain, perhaps through an example, how the issues important to you affect them.

Devise an action plan: Take advantage of the various kinds of support available to you when arguing. To the extent it is appropriate for the context in which you are arguing, make appeals to logic, authority, *and* emotion. Think strategically about how best to position your facts, statistics, expert opinions, examples, and appeals to emotion.

6d Developing support for your claim

Reasoning in an argument is the pattern of thinking you use to connect statements of support to your claim. Formally, types of reasoning are referred to as **lines of argument.** Appeals to logic, authority, and emotion rest on inferences you make concerning the evidence you have assembled in support of your claim.

The following chart summarizes the main lines of argument you can use in presenting claims of fact, value, and policy. You can refer to the chart in order to determine which lines are appropriate for which types of claims.

Matching lines of argument with types of claims

	Claims of Fact	Claims of Value	Claims of Policy
Appeals to Reason			
generalization	x	x	
causation	x		x
sign	x		
analogy	x	x	x
parallel case	x	x	x
Appeals to Authority	x	x	x
Appeals to Emotion		x	x

Adapted from Wayne Brockriede and Douglas Ehninger, "Toulmin on Argument: An Interpretation and Application" *Quarterly Journal of Speech* 46 (1960): 53.

1 Appealing to logic

Argument from generalization

You can infer a **generalization** from a sufficient number of relevant examples. For instance, if you observe that seven of ten friends who crammed for a test failed, you might generalize that cramming is an unproductive way to prepare. Arguments from generalization can support claims of fact and value.

Argument of causation

In argument of **causation,** you establish a fact and claim that this fact leads to a specific effect, or result. For instance, you might establish that people who study consistently between tests receive higher scores than those who do not. You conclude, then, that consistent studying results in higher scores. Arguments of causation can support claims of fact or policy, and can be used in a problem-solution structure.

Argument from sign

In argument from **sign,** you conclude that since two things tend to occur in the presence of one another, one is a sign (not a cause) of the other. For instance, you may notice that a friend suffers from sleeplessness, loss of appetite, and moodiness before major exams. You conclude that these are signs of test anxiety. Arguments from sign can support claims of fact.

Argument from analogy

An argument from **analogy** establishes a comparison between your topic and another, apparently unrelated, topic. For instance, you might observe that preparing for exams is like keeping a car in tune—if you don't keep up with routine maintenance, then the car will eventually have major problems. Analogies are useful supplements to an argument, but at some point they break down. The car, for example, can be fixed even without regular maintenance, while failure to keep up with academic work usually results in failure. Argument from analogy can support claims of fact, value, or policy.

Argument from parallel case

An argument from **parallel case** establishes a comparison between directly related topics. The situations presented must be alike in essential ways for the argument to work. For instance, you might argue that since an instructor allowed make-up exams for last year's students, she should allow them this year as well. Argument from parallel case can support claims of fact, value, or policy.

2 Appealing to authority

You as the writer are the primary authority in your papers. You may also call upon experts on your topic.

Establishing yourself as an authority

If you are to convince your readers to abandon their views and adopt yours, you must gain their trust. Readers must be able to yield to your position and retain their self-respect. You should be honest, knowledgeable, and reasonable in tone (see 21e), and you should choose an appropriate level of language (see 3a-4).

Referring readers to experts

Although experts in every discipline disagree with one another, appealing to a recognized expert can strengthen your argument. For example, you might offer your instructor an article from *The Chronicle of Higher Education* endorsing the concept of make-up tests. You can use the following guidelines to determine whether or not an authority is reliable.

Use *Authoritative* Sources

1. Prefer acknowledged authorities to self-proclaimed ones.
2. Prefer an authority working within his or her field of expertise to one who is reporting conclusions about another subject.
3. Prefer first-hand accounts over those from sources who were separated by time or space from the events reported.
4. Prefer unbiased and disinterested sources over those who can reasonably be suspected of having a motive for influencing the way others see the subject under investigation.
5. Prefer public records to private documents in questionable cases.
6. Prefer accounts that are specific and complete to those that are vague and evasive.
7. Prefer evidence that is credible on its own terms to that which is internally inconsistent or demonstrably false to any known facts.
8. In general, prefer a recently published report to an older one.
9. In general, prefer works by standard publishers to those of unknown or "vanity" presses.
10. In general, prefer authors who themselves follow [standard] report-writing conventions.

11. When possible, prefer an authority known to your audience to one they have never heard of.

This material is quoted from Thomas E. Gaston and Bret H. Smith, *The Research Paper: A Common-Sense Approach* (Englewood Cliffs: Prentice Hall, 1988) 31-33.

Appeals to recognized authorities can be mixed with appeals to reason and emotion. (In scientific writing, authority is the primary form of appeal.) Appeals to authority can support claims of fact, value, and policy.

Appealing to emotion

While appeals to reason are logically based and appeals to authority are based on the reader's respect for expert opinion, appeals to emotion are based on the needs and values of the audience. Often an emotional appeal is necessary to get people to act. For instance, even though you have proven that make-up tests are recognized as valuable for learning, the instructor may not be prepared to take action. If she values the emotional well-being of her students, it may be effective to remind her of the mental anguish your friend faces before each test. Appeals to emotion can support claims of value and policy.

Making an Emotional Appeal

1. List the needs of your audience with respect to your subject: these needs might be physical, psychological, humanitarian, environmental, or financial.
2. Select the category of needs best suited to your audience and identify emotional appeals that you think will be persuasive.
3. In your appeal, place the issue you are arguing in your reader's lap. Get the reader to respond to the issue emotionally.
4. Call on the reader to agree with you on a course of action.

The limits of argument

Some topics—such as abortion and capital punishment—are so controversial or so tied to religious or moral beliefs that you cannot change a reader's mind. Other topics—many of them involving financial expenditures—involve vested interests, making it almost impossible to convince an unreceptive audience.

6e Making rebuttals

All arguments are subject to challenge. When you raise a challenge to your own argument, you force yourself to see the issue from a different perspective, and you heighten readers' interest. After acknowledging the opposition, you respond with a **rebuttal**, an argument of opposition. You can rebut either by challenging the logic of your opponent, or by acknowledging some merit in the opponent's argument and modifying your position accordingly. For instance, your instructor argues that make-up tests discourage students from studying for the first test. You might challenge that statement by showing reports that indicate otherwise, or you might acknowledge her position and modify your own by suggesting that each student be allowed to make up only one test.

Of course, you may decide that an opposing argument is stronger than yours. In this case, you should be willing to concede at least some of your opposition's points.

CRITICAL DECISIONS

BE ALERT TO DIFFERENCES: RESPONDING TO OPPOSING POINTS OF VIEW

Expect opposition. When you have located opposing points of view, use the occasion to extend your thinking. Let disagreement enhance the quality of your argument.

- **The facts are in dispute.** When the facts you are relying on in an argument are disputed—a potentially serious challenge—then you must investigate both the validity of your facts and the opposition's.

  Check the credibility of sources. Be sure that your sources are reliable; if you discover some dispute about reliability, you must meet this challenge head on: raise it in your argument and, if you can, establish the trustworthiness of your information. If you have trouble doing so, abandon questionable sources and be grateful to your opposition.

  If both sources (yours and the opposition's) are equally reliable, ask: Through what process of investigation were these facts established? Different methods of investigation can lead to different perceptions of the facts. Acknowledge these methods in your argument and state clearly which you (or your sources) have relied on.

- **Expert opinions are in dispute.** Experts *will* disagree, and most writers can find experts, real or so-called, to support or attack an argument.

Respond to differences of expert opinion by checking qualifications. Lacking expertise in a subject, you may have some trouble doing this. Try these strategies, both of which can help you to reaffirm, or discount, the usefulness of expert opinion:

> *Strategy 1:* To validate expertise, be sure that an author is referred to in several sources. If the author were a fringe personality, you would not find repeated, serious references to his or her work.

> *Strategy 2:* To validate expertise, locate a book written by the person in question. Locate two reviews, which will be written by someone at least familiar with the topic. From the reviews you will get a sense of a book's strengths and weaknesses, and you will learn something of the author's reputation.

If the experts holding opposing views are reliable, you will need to acknowledge the disagreement in your argument. Determine its basis. If you find a conflict of assumptions (see 1h-2), investigate and discuss these. If you find your assumptions still worth supporting, then support them—with reasons.

Devise an action plan: Use the differences you find to clarify your own thinking on a topic. When your opposition has a valid point, acknowledge it openly and adjust. Show that you expect differences and can incorporate them into your thinking.

 6f   **Preparing to write an argument**

Devising strategies for argument

Here are two time-honored strategies for arranging arguments:

Writing an Argument

The classic five-part structure

1. Introduce the topic to be argued. Establish its importance.
2. Provide background information so that readers will be able to follow your discussion.

3. State your claim (your argumentative thesis) and develop your argument by making a logical appeal based on the following factors (discussed in 6d-2 and 6d-3): generalization, causation, sign, analogy, parallel case, or authority.
4. Acknowledge counterarguments and treat them with respect. Rebut these arguments. Reject their evidence or their logic or concede some validity and modify your claim accordingly. (See 6e.)
5. A useful way to conclude is to summarize the main points of your argument. Then remind readers of what you want them to believe or do.

Note: This five-part structure for argument does not suggest, necessarily, a five-paragraph argument. Arguments can be considerably longer than five paragraphs.

Writing an argument: The problem-solution structure*

I.   There is a serious problem.
    A. The problem exists and is growing.
       (Provide support for this statement.)
    B. The problem is serious.
    C. Current methods cannot cope with the problem.
       (Provide support)
II. There is a solution to the problem. (Your claim goes here.)
    A. The solution is practical.
       (Provide support)
    B. The solution is desirable.
       (Provide support)
    C. We can implement the solution.
       (Provide support)
    D. Alternate solutions are not as strong as the proposed solution.
       (Review—and reject—competing solutions)

Note: This six-part structure for argument does not suggest, necessarily, a six-paragraph argument. A problem-solution argument can be considerably longer than six paragraphs.

*Adapted from Richard D. Rieke and Malcolm O. Sillars, Argumentation and the Decision Making Process (Glenview: Scott, Foresman, 1984) 163.

Inductive and deductive arrangements

Induction moves from support—particular facts, examples, and opinions—to a claim. Visually, the process looks like this:

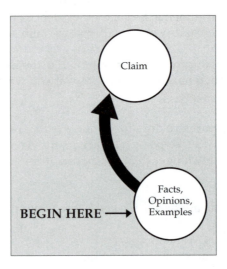

Deductive arrangement moves from a claim to support—to particular facts, opinions, and examples. Visually, the process looks like this:

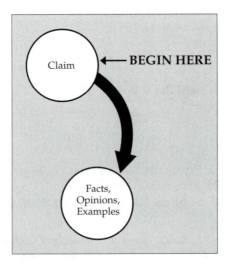

The decision to use inductive or deductive arrangement is a decision about strategy. You should consider the nature of your argument and the needs of your audience when you decide on a strategy.

Gathering materials for argument

A useful technique for preparing to write an argument is to write a *pre*-draft: a brief paper, for your eyes only, exploring your position. Before you begin a draft of an argument, you should understand the support you will present and the lines of reasoning you will use to link that support to your claim.

Gathering Materials for Your Argument

1. Gather material on your subject. Generate information on your own—see 3b; if necessary, conduct research. See Part IX of the handbook on library research.
2. Review the material you have gathered. Decide what you think about the topic, and in a single sentence answer a question of fact, value, or policy. Your one-sentence answer to the question will be the claim of your argument.
3. Understand your audience: What do they know about the topic? What do they need to know? To what sorts of appeals will they respond?
4. Plan out the lines of argument you will present in support of your claim.
5. Identify strong counterarguments and plan to rebut and neutralize them. Possibly concede some of your opposition's points.
6. Sketch your argument, deciding on placement of your claim and arrangement of your lines of argument.
7. Write a draft of your argument, realizing that you will need to backtrack on occasion to get new information or to rethink your strategy. As with the writing of any paper, writing an argument will be a messy, backward-looping activity that often requires mid-course corrections. See chapters 3 and 4 on the necessary uncertainties in preparing for and writing a first draft.
8. Revise two or three times. See chapter 4 for advice.

6g Evaluating arguments and avoiding common errors

 ### 1 Defining terms

The first part of an argument to examine is its claim. If all terms are not clearly defined (either implicitly or explicitly), then determine whether or not the failure to define terms creates problems in the argument itself. For example, an instructor who insists that each student be treated *equally* may mean that she is willing to accommodate students who are at a disadvantage because of physical handicap, emotional problems, or learning disabilities. Another instructor might interpret the term *equal* to mean that all students follow exactly the same rules, regardless of the student's particular situation.

2 Examining inferences

The following seven flaws, or logical fallacies, can undermine an argument.

1. *Faulty generalization.* A generalization is invalid if it is made without sufficient data. If you conclude that the political science department is overly conservative on the basis of your acquaintance with two of ten professors, then you have made a faulty generalization.

2. *Faulty cause and effect.* Simply because one event precedes another, it does not necessarily follow that the first event caused the second. (In Latin this fallacy is called *post hoc*, meaning "after this.") If a team's mascot is stolen, and they subsequently lose three games, it does not follow that the theft of the mascot caused the losing streak. Another related flaw is the belief that events must have *single* causes. To claim that drugs are solely responsible for city violence is to oversimplify the problem.

3. *Confusing correlation with causation.* Simply because two things are associated does not mean that one is a cause of the other. People with good study habits are often responsible on the job as well; neither, however, can be said to be a cause of the other.

4. *Faulty analogy.* If the key components of an analogy do not parallel closely the central issues of the argument, the analogy will confuse rather than clarify. To describe a child's mind as a blank slate ready to be written on is to ignore genetics and other early influences.

5. *Either/or reasoning.* When a writer tries to force a choice between only two options, then he or she is ignoring the complexity of the issue. To say, "Either

we cut programs or the state goes bankrupt" is to ignore other possible measures, such as raising taxes or streamlining government operations.

6. *Personal attacks.* Known in Latin as *ad hominem* ("to the man") arguments, personal attacks focus attention on the person him- or herself rather than on the issue. To argue that a candidate is unsuited for office because she wears flashy clothes is to shift attention from the issues to an insignificant point.

7. *The begged question.* To assume the validity of a point without proving it is to beg the question. To argue that any responsible person will accept random drug testing is to assume a definition of responsibility that not everyone will agree with.

3 Examining evidence

The following guidelines will help you examine evidence.

Facts and examples

1. *Facts and examples should fairly represent the available data.* If you cannot find sufficient evidence to support your claim, you should rethink your claim. If fifteen of twenty students report that they don't study for a test if they know there will be a make-up exam, then you cannot use the five who do study to argue for make-up exams.

2. *Facts and examples should be current.* If facts and examples are dated, they will not support your claim. You cannot use studies from fifty years ago to support your claim that students today learn better by writing papers than by taking exams.

3. *Facts and examples should be sufficient to establish validity.* Generalizations must be based on adequate and representative examples. To interview only four people about test anxiety is to base your claim on an invalid sample.

4. *Negative instances of facts and examples should be acknowledged.* It is always better to raise the evidence against your argument yourself. If, for example, several students claim that exams help them learn better than papers do, you should acknowledge this in your argument.

Statistics

5. *Use statistics from reliable and current sources.* You can determine the reliability of statistical sources by noting how often experts cite a particular source.

Government statistics are also considered reliable. The U.S. Department of Education would be a reliable source of statistics on academic life.

6. *Comparative statistics should compare items of the same logical class.* Comparisons are only valid if the items compared are related. To compare statistics from a small private junior college with those from a multi-campus state university would not produce valid results.

Expert opinions

7. *"Experts" who give opinions should be qualified to do so.* Someone who is cited as a source by many writers in a field can be considered qualified, as are those who have credentials and experience in the field in which they are writing. A business leader, for example, is not necessarily qualified to make pronouncements about how a class should be conducted.

8. *Experts should be neutral.* If an expert will profit from a particular interpretation, then that expert should be disqualified. A sales representative for a company that develops multiple-choice tests should not be consulted when determining whether objective or essay tests are preferable.

EXERCISE 6-1   Understanding the claim

For each of the following statements, (1) identify the claim as a question of fact, value, or policy, and (2) circle any terms that must be defined.

EXAMPLE   *The Adventures of Huckleberry Finn* is the
(essential) American (novel.)   ___fact___

1. If we are to maintain our civilization, alternative sources of energy must be developed.   _____

2. Despite the fall of communist governments in the 1990s, Karl Marx remains the most significant figure in modern history. _____   _____

3. Random drug testing in the workplace constitutes an infringement on individual rights.   _____

4. The film industry must rethink its "bottom-line" criteria for judging the value of a movie.   _____

5. Given the economic condition of the country at this time, it can be said that we are in a recession.   _____

6. Corporations that knowingly produce unsafe products should be held criminally liable for users' injuries.   _____

7. Monet did more to establish impressionism as a valid school of art than did any other painter.   _____

8. The government must make a legitimate commitment to funding AIDS research.   _____

9. The government has yet to make a legitimate commitment to funding AIDS research.   _____

10. Economic conditions were far more relevant to the rise of the Third Reich than was ideology.   _____

EXERCISE 6-2   **Distinguishing types of evidence**

In the following draft paragraph, the sentences that offer evidence in support of the thesis are numbered. Label each as fact, example, or opinion.

Drunk drivers should serve time in jail. (1) In the first place, although the automobile is not designed exclusively to kill, it can be considered a lethal weapon. (2) Secondly, statistics in states that jail drunk drivers show that the number of repeat offenders has dropped. (3) There is no question that an otherwise solid citizen who spends a weekend in jail will think twice about driving drunk again. (4) One business manager who "did time" announced that he never really thought about the seriousness of his offense until he shared a cell with a man awaiting trial on armed robbery charges. (5) If we consider the possible results of drunk driving—injury and death—rather than the character of the drunk driver, we should have no problem treating it as the crime it is.

1. _____

2. _____

3. _____

4. _____

5. _____

EXERCISE 6-3   **Recognizing appeals to reason and emotion**

Identify the following statements as either appeals to reason or to emotion. Then, for each appeal to reason, write an appeal to emotion, and vice-versa.

EXAMPLE   This child was made ill by eating lead paint.   <u>emotion</u>

            Studies show that lead paint causes illness in children.

1. If seatbelts were mandatory, lives and dollars would be
    saved.   _____

2. Computers can test cosmetics as precisely as animal
    experiments.   _____

3. A young mother is dead because hunting is allowed
    too close to residential areas.   _____

4. Closing an army base results in economic losses in the
    surrounding community.   _____

5. Thousands of helpless children will go hungry as a
    result of welfare cuts.   _____

EXERCISE 6-4   Preparing an argument

Using the strategies outlined in the box on page 129, prepare an argument on one of the following topics. (Or your instructor may offer a topic or allow you to choose your own.) You may use the space below for notes.

1. Papers are more useful to students' learning than are exams.

2. Living on campus prepares students for living on their own after college.

3. Colleges should include students on search committees for new faculty.

EXERCISE 6-5   Recognizing flaws in reasoning

Using the list on pages 130–132, identify and briefly explain the flaw in each of the following statements.

EXAMPLE   As soon as you've paid off your car, it will
                    break down.   <u>faulty cause/effect</u>

The financial arrangements for buying a car have no impact on the car's performance.

1. We must increase spending for education or
    we'll have a nation of illiterates.   _____

2. He can't possibly understand the problems of the
    poor; he drives a BMW.   _____

3. Having read *Beloved*, I am convinced that Toni
    Morrison is the greatest living novelist.   _____

4. An intelligent person would never vote for him.   _____

5. Of course she's emotionally unstable; her parents
    are divorced.   _____

CHAPTER 7

Constructing
Sentences

Although virtually all lifelong speakers of English have an *implicit* understanding of grammar, vocabulary, and sentence structure, writers can benefit from making that implicit knowledge *explicit*.

7a Understanding sentence parts

Meaning in language is built on the *relationship* among words. The basic unit in which words are arranged to communicate is the sentence.

1 The basics: Recognizing subjects and predicates

Every sentence has a **subject:** a noun or word group serving as a noun that engages in the main action of the sentence or is described by the sentence. Every sentence also has a **predicate:** a verb, and other words associated with it, that states the action undertaken by a subject or the condition in which the subject exists.

A **simple subject** is the single noun or pronoun that identifies what the sentence is about or produces the action of the sentence. The **simple predicate** is the main sentence verb. The simple subject is underlined once in the following sentences, the simple predicate twice.

Subject	Predicate
<u>Dogs</u> of every kind	<u>bark</u> at the worst times.
In one study, <u>researchers</u>	<u>found</u> that dogs bark for no reason.
A <u>number</u> of experts in biology,	as a result of their studies, <u>believe</u> that dogs are wolves fixated in adolescence.

2 | Nouns

A **noun** names a person, place, thing, or idea.[1] Only nouns can be introduced by articles (*a, an, the*) and accompanied by limiting words (such as *those, each, one, which*). Nouns change form to show number (*book/books*) and possession (*Rick's*). Nouns can also be classified according to use, as the accompanying box shows.

Classification of Nouns

Proper nouns, which are capitalized, name particular persons, places, or things:
> *Sandra Day O'Connor, Chevrolet, "To His Coy Mistress"*

Common nouns refer to general persons, places, or things and are not capitalized:
> *judge, automobile, poem*

Count nouns can be counted:
> *cubes, cups, forks, rocks*

Mass nouns cannot be counted:
> *sugar, water, air, dirt*

Concrete nouns name tangible objects:
> *lips, clock, dollar*

Abstract nouns name an intangible idea, emotion, or quality:
> *love, eternity, ambition*

Animate versus **inanimate nouns** differ according to whether they name something alive:
> *fox* and *weeds* versus *will* and *honesty*

Collective nouns are singular in form but plural in sense:
> *crowd, family, group, herd*

---

3 | Verbs

A **verb,** the main word in the predicate of a sentence, expresses an action, an occurrence, or a state of being.

---

[1]The discussion of parts of speech is drawn from Hulon Willis, *Modern Descriptive English Grammar* (San Francisco: Chandler, 1972).

action	The dog *barked.*
occurrence	It *happened* last night.
state of being	The dog *was* terrified.

Verbs change form on the basis of their **principal parts**, which play a major role in verb **tense** (the time of the action relative to the present).

Base Form	Past Tense	Present Participle	Past Participle
to appear	appeared	am appearing	appeared
to swim	swam	am swimming	swum

Types of verbs in English include **transitive,** which transfer action from an actor to a receiver of the action, **intransitive,** which show action with nothing acted upon, and **linking,** which allow the word or words following the verb to complete the meaning of the subject. **Auxiliary (or helping) verbs** help show tense and mood.

transitive	He <u>carried</u> the bag.
intransitive	He <u>tripped</u>.
linking	He <u>seemed</u> all right.
auxiliary	He <u>was</u> getting up. He <u>could</u> get up.

4　Verbals

A **verbal** is a verb form that functions as an adjective, an adverb, or a noun. Types of verbals are gerunds, participles, and infinitives. A **gerund** (the *-ing* form) functions as a noun; a **participle** (present or past) functions as an adjective, and an **infinitive** (or base form) can function as a noun, adjective, or adverb.

gerund	*Raking* leaves is an autumn chore.
present participle	The girl *raking* the leaves is my niece.
past participle	*Raked* leaves make great piles for jumping.
infinitive	She likes *to rake* leaves. (noun) The first one *to rake* all the leaves gets to jump into the pile. (adjective) I took the day off *to rake* leaves. (adverb)

Important Relationships between a Subject and Verb

A complete sentence must have both a subject and a verb. A word grouping that lacks a subject, a verb, or both is considered a fragment. See chapter 12 on fragments and chapter 16 for a special class of fragments—grammatically "mixed" constructions.

INCOMPLETE	At the beginning of the meeting. [There is no verb.]
REVISED	At the beginning of the meeting, the treasurer reported on recent news.
INCOMPLETE	The fact that this is an emergency meeting. [The use of *that* leaves the statement incomplete, without a verb.]
REVISED	This is an emergency meeting of the board.

A sentence must have a *logically compatible* subject and verb. A sentence in which a subject is paired with a logically incompatible verb is sure to confuse readers, as you will see in chapter 16.

INCOMPATIBLE	The meeting room is sweating. [A room does not normally sweat.]
REVISED	Those gathered in the meeting room are sweating.

A sentence must have a subject and verb that *agree in number.* A subject and verb must both be singular or plural. The conventions for ensuring consistency are found in chapter 10.

INCONSISTENT	The treasurer are a dynamic speaker. [The plural verb does not match the singular subject.]
REVISED	The treasurer is a dynamic speaker.

A sentence must have a subject close enough to the verb to ensure clarity. Meaning in a sentence can be confused if the subject/verb pairing is interrupted with a lengthy modifier. See chapter 15 for a discussion of misplaced modifiers.

INTERRUPTED	We because of our dire financial situation and our interests in maintaining employee welfare have called this meeting.
REVISED	We have called this meeting because of our dire financial situation and our interests in maintaining employee welfare.

5 Adjectives

By modifying or describing a noun or pronoun, an **adjective** provides both essential and compelling information in a sentence. Adjectives include the present and part participle forms of verbs (*rotating* shifts, *calculated* response), as well as single words (*beautiful, ordinary, quick*).

6 Adverbs

An **adverb** can modify a verb, adjective, adverb, or an entire sentence, generally answering questions such as *when, how, where,* and to *what extent.* Adverbs include single words (*already, behind, before*) and words formed by adding *-ly* to adjectives (*beautifully, ordinarily, quickly*). **Descriptive** adverbs describe individual words within a sentence (*The orchestra played* beautifully.), while **conjunctive adverbs** (such as *however, thus, furthermore*) establish relationships between entire sentences. (See chapter 19.)

7 Pronouns

Pronouns substitute for nouns. The word that a pronoun renames is called its **antecedent.** Pronouns show **number** (*I, we*) and **case** (*I, my, me*). There are eight classes of pronouns.

Personal pronouns (*I, you, us, her,* etc.) refer to people and things.

Many children want dolls to resemble *them.*

Relative pronouns (*who, which, that,* etc.) begin dependent clauses (see 7e) and refer to people and things.

It was always easy for white children to find dolls *that* were white.

Demonstrative pronouns (*this, these, that, those*) point to the nouns they replace.

Those children who were not white had to settle for white dolls.

Interrogative pronouns (*who, which, what,* etc.) form questions.

Who could find black or Asian dolls in a toy store?

Intensive pronouns (*herself, themselves,* etc.) repeat and emphasize a noun or pronoun.

A doll *itself* might be beautiful and lovable.

Reflexive pronouns (*herself, themselves,* etc.) rename—reflect back to—a preceding noun or pronoun.

> But nonwhite children could not recognize *themselves* in the doll.

Indefinite pronouns (*one, anyone, everybody,* etc.) refer to general, or nonspecific, persons or things.

> *Someone* unfamiliar with the United States might think that the population was all white.

Reciprocal pronouns (*one another, each other*) refer to the separate parts of a plural noun.

> Child care specialists believe that dolls of many colors can help children of different races appreciate *one another.*

8 Prepositions

A **preposition** links a noun (or word group substituting for a noun) to other words in a sentence. Along with the words that follow them, prepositions form **prepositional phrases**, which function as adjectives or adverbs.

Common Prepositions

Single-word prepositions

about	beyond	off
above	by	on
across	concerning	onto
after	despite	out
against	down	outside
along	during	over
among	except	through
around	for	till
as	from	to
before	in	toward
behind	into	under
below	like	up
beneath	near	with
between	of	

Multiword prepositions

according to	contrary to	on account of
along with	except for	on top of
apart from	in addition to	outside of
as for	in back of	owing to
because of	in case of	with regard to
by means of	in spite of	with respect to

 ## Conjunctions

Conjunctions join sentence elements or entire sentences in one of two ways: coordinating and correlative conjunctions, as well as conjunctive adverbs, establish an *equal* relationship among joined parts (see chapter 19); subordinating conjunctions establish an *unequal* relationship (see 7e).

Coordinating conjunctions join parallel elements from two or more sentences into a single sentence: *and, but, or, nor, for, so*

> People with sickle cell disease are prone to infection, *and* they are particularly susceptible to strokes.

Conjunctive adverbs create special logical relationships between the clauses or sentences joined: *however, therefore, thus, consequently,* etc.

> Sickle cell disease rarely affects northern European or Asian babies; *however,* in twenty-four states all babies are tested for the disease.

Correlative conjunctions are pairs of coordinating conjunctions that place extra emphasis on the relationship between the parts of the coordinated construction: *both/and, neither/nor, not only/but also,* etc.

> *Not only* does the test identify affected babies, *but* it *also* identifies carriers of the disease.

Subordinating conjunctions connect subordinate clauses to main clauses: *when, while, although, because, if, since, whereas,* etc.

> *Although* universal testing for sickle cell disease saves some lives, many in the medical profession believe that only high-risk babies should be tested.

10 | Interjections

An **interjection** is an emphatic word or phrase. When it stands alone, it is often followed by an exclamation point. As part of a sentence, it is usually set off by commas.

Oh!   Well, I guess it's over.

11 | Expletives

An **expletive** (*it, there*) is a word that fills a slot left in a sentence that has been rearranged.

basic sentence   Millions of dollars are wasted on fad diets each year.

with expletive   There are millions of dollars wasted on fad diets each year.

7b | Understanding basic sentence patterns

All of the five basic sentence patterns in English consist of a subject and a predicate. Depending on the sentence's structure, the predicate may contain a **direct object**, an **indirect object**, or a (subject or object) **complement**.

Pattern 1:

	┌─*predicate*─┐
Subject	verb
Birds	fly.

Subject: a noun or noun-like word group that produces the main action of the sentence or is described by the sentence.

Predicate: a verb and other words associated with it, that states the action undertaken by the subject or the condition in which the subject exists.

Pattern 2:

	┌──────*predicate*──────┐
Subject	verb (tr.) direct object
Birds	build nests.

Direct Object: a noun, or group of words substituting for a noun, that receives the action of a transitive verb (tr.). A direct object answers the question *What or who is acted upon?*

Pattern 3:   Subject   ┌─────────*predicate*─────────┐
                                   verb (tr.) indirect object direct object

                 Maria   gave her mother a parakeet.

        Indirect Object: a noun, or group of words substituting for a
                                noun, that is indirectly affected by the action
                                of a verb. Indirect objects typically follow
                                transitive verbs such as *buy, bring, do, give,*
                                offer, teach, tell, play, or *write.* The indirect
                                object answers the question *To whom or for*
                                whom has the main action of this sentence
                                occurred?

Pattern 4:   Subject   ┌─────────*predicate*─────────┐
                                   verb (tr.) direct object object complement

                 The parakeet   drove her mother crazy.

        Object   an adjective or noun that completes the
        Complement: meaning of a direct object by renaming or
                                describing it. Typically, object complements
                                follow verbs such as *appoint, call, choose,*
                                consider, declare, elect, find, make, select, or *show.*

Pattern 5:   Subject   ┌─────────*predicate*─────────┐
                                   verb (linking)   subject complement

                 The bird   became her nemesis.

        Subject   a noun or adjective that completes the
        Complement: meaning of a subject by renaming or by
                                describing it. Subject complements follow
                                linking verbs such as *appear, feel, seem, remain,*
                                as well as all forms of *be.*

7c   Expanding sentences with single-word modifiers

1   Modifying nouns and verbs with adjectives and adverbs

noun modified   The *noisy* parakeet drove her mother crazy.
by adjective

verb modified   The bird *quickly* became her nemesis.
by adverb

2 Positioning modifiers

An adverb can be shifted in a sentence to change rhythm or meaning. Make sure that your adverbs modify the words you intend them to modify.

shifted meaning   She was *only* cleaning the cage (that is, nothing more important than cleaning).

She was cleaning *only* the cage (that is, cleaning nothing else).

shifted rhythm   *Frequently*, Maria gave her mother gifts.
Maria *frequently* gave her mother gifts.
Maria gave her mother gifts *frequently*.

Single-word adjectives are usually positioned directly before the nouns they modify.

7d Modifying and expanding sentences with phrases

Phrases, which do not express complete thoughts, can function as modifiers and as objects, subjects, or complements. Phrases consist of nouns or verbals and the words associated with them.

1 Adding prepositional phrases

A **prepositional phrase**, consisting of a preposition and its object, can function either as an adjective or an adverb.

adjective   The bird *in the green cage* sings constantly.

adverb   Maria's mother returned the bird *after a few days*.

2 Adding verbals: Infinitive phrases

An **infinitive phrase** is a verbal consisting of the base form of a verb and its objects or modifiers. Infinitive phrases can function as adjectives, adverbs, or nouns. (See 7a-4.)

noun subject   *To hear a canary sing* is a great pleasure.

noun object   Local birds love *to build nests over my front door*.

adjective   I feel a responsibility *to keep the birds safe.*

adverb   The mother bird flies off *to get food for the chicks.*

3 | Adding verbals: Gerund and participial phrases

A **gerund phrase** is a verbal consisting of the *-ing* form of a verb and its subject (written in possessive form), objects, or modifiers. Gerund phrases function as nouns. A **participial phrase** is a past or present participle and its objects and modifiers. Participial phrases can function as adjectives.

gerund   *The bird's singing* drove Maria's mother crazy.

past participle   Maria, *frustrated with her mother*, bought another gift.

present participle   The birds *nesting over my door* greet me each morning.

4 | Adding noun phrases

A **noun phrase,** consisting of a noun accompanied by all of its modifying words, functions as the subject of a sentence, as the object of a verb or preposition, or as a complement.

subject   *A regal swan with an elegant neck* appeared in the pond.

direct object   Children fed *several brazen geese living near the pond.*

complement   Anthony is a *recognized expert on bird migration.*

5 | Adding absolute phrases

An **absolute phrase,** formed by deleting the linking verb *to be* from a sentence or by changing the main verb to its *-ing* form, modifies an entire sentence. Set off absolute phrases with commas. (See chapter 25.)

Its wings spread majestically, the eagle flew away.

Its wings spreading majestically, the eagle took flight.

6 | Adding appositive phrases

An **appositive phrase,** formed by eliminating the verb from the predicate part of Sentence Pattern 5, renames a noun. The phrase is *in apposition to*, or beside, the noun.

Seagulls, *scavengers at heart,* are often found circling over landfills.

7e Modifying and expanding sentences with dependent clauses

A **clause** is a group of words with a subject and a predicate. An **independent** (or **main**) **clause** can stand alone as a sentence; a **dependent** (or **subordinate**) **clause** cannot stand alone as a sentence. The four types of dependent clauses are adverb, adjective, noun, and elliptical.

Adding dependent adverb clauses

An **adverb clause** begins with a subordinate conjunction and functions as an adverb. When a subordinate conjunction is placed at the head of a sentence, it makes that sentence grammatically dependent, unable to stand alone.

> *When its founder died in 1989,* Judith Jamison took over as director of the Alvin Ailey American Dance Theater.

Subordinating Conjunctions and the Logical Relationships They Establish

To show condition: *if, even if, unless,* and *provided that*
To show contrast: *though, although, even though,* and *as if*
To show cause: *because* and *since*
To show time: *when, whenever, while, as, before, after, since, once,* and *until*
To show place: *where* and *wherever*
To show purpose: *so that, in order that,* and *that*

Adding dependent adjective clauses

An **adjective clause** usually begins with a relative pronoun (*which, that, who, whom,* or *whose*) and functions as an adjective. (See 8f for a discussion of when to use which relative pronoun.)

> Ailey himself chose Jamison, *who had begun her career with his troupe,* to succeed him.

Adding dependent noun clauses

A **noun clause** begins with the pronoun *which, whichever, that, who, whoever, whom, whomever, whose* or the word *how, when, why, where, whether,* or *whatever.* The noun clause functions as a subject, an object, a complement, or an appositive.

> **subject**   *Whoever took over the American Dance Theater* would find it difficult to live up to Ailey's image.

 Working with elliptical clauses

An **elliptical clause,** one in which a word or words have been omitted, functions exactly as the full clause would. In the previous sentence, *as the full clause would* is an elliptical adverb clause (the full clause would read: *as the full clause would function*).

> Jamison's artistic perspective is much the same *as Ailey's.*
> (The full clause would read: *as Ailey's artistic perspective was.*)

 Classifying sentences

 Functional definitions

The four functional types of sentences are declarative, interrogative, exclamatory, and imperative. A **declarative** sentence (the most common type) makes a statement or assertion. An **interrogative** sentence poses a question. An **exclamatory** sentence (a rare type) directly expresses emotion. An **imperative** sentence directly expresses a command.

> **declarative**   The military coup was unsuccessful.
>
> **interrogative**   Why did they go through with it? Were they prepared?
>
> **exclamatory**   What a pack of fools!
>
> **imperative**   Don't try this at home!

 Structural definitions

The four structural classes of sentences in English are simple, compound, complex, and compound-complex. A **simple sentence,** regardless of its length, has a single subject and predicate and consists of one independent clause. (The five basic sentence patterns in 7b are simple sentences.) A **compound sentence** has two subjects and two predicates and consists of two independent clauses joined by a coordinate or correlative conjunction. A **complex sentence** consists of one independent and one or more dependent clauses introduced by subordinate conjunctions or relative pronouns. A **compound-complex sentence** consists of two or more independent clauses and one or more dependent clauses.

simple Thanks to advances in computer technology, astronomers can now use telescopes from thousands of miles away.

compound Telescopes are often located in isolated places, but the new technology allows them to be operated by remote control.

complex Although other telescopes can be operated by remote control, only the new telescope in Apache Point, New Mexico is designed specifically for that purpose.

compound-complex When Apache Point is fully operational, astronomers from all over the world can use it, and students from five American universities will hook up to it with computers.

EXERCISE 7-1   **Implicit understanding of sentences**

This exercise is designed to show you just how much you really do know about sentences. In the following paragraph, mark off with a slash (/) places where you'd end a sentence. (You can also supply commas where you think they're needed, but that's not necessary for the purposes of this exercise.) Then compare your response to other students' responses. As you discuss differences, try to explain why you divided the paragraph as you did. (There are several different ways of dividing the paragraph.)

The Supreme Court hears about 125 to 130 cases during the seven months each

year that it is in session these cases are chosen from over 5,000 petitions most of

which are prepared by highly specialized law firms but every year 200 to 300

petitions are submitted by individuals on their own behalf these cases are called

pro se the Latin words for "for himself" in most years no more than one or two

pro se cases are heard and fewer result in a positive decision many of these

petitions are prepared by prisoners who have given up on lawyers one of the

most famous of these cases was that of Clarence Gideon a poor man who was

convicted without having been represented by a lawyer Gideon's petition which

he wrote out by hand was accepted by the Court and resulted in a landmark

ruling that people who can't afford lawyers must be given the opportunity to be

represented by a court-appointed lawyer.

EXERCISE 7-2   Recognizing subjects and predicates

In the following sentences, place a slash (/) between subjects and predicates. Then underline the simple subject once, and the simple predicate twice.

EXAMPLE   <u>Nations</u> embarking on military adventures / often <u><u>invoke</u></u> a deity to justify their cause.

1. The Roman emperor Titus ceremoniously called upon the god of war, Mars, when he attacked Jerusalem in A.D. 70.
2. The prophet Muhammad, founder of Islam, attributed his A.D. 630 conquest of Mecca to the power of Allah.
3. Allah, the one true god of Islam, apparently was also responsible for the victory over Jerusalem in 1187.
4. The sacking of Constantinople during the Fourth Crusade in 1204 was undertaken in the name of the Christian god.
5. The historical term "Crusades" refers to the Christian invasions of the Holy Land, which was then under the control of Muslims.
6. The Muslims themselves had a term for Holy Wars, "jihad."
7. The revolt of the Shi'ite Muslims in 685 pitted against each other two forces, both claiming the protection of Allah.
8. Union and Confederate forces in the American Civil War both claimed to be fighting for the same Christian god almost eighteen centuries later.
9. The Japanese forces that bombed Pearl Harbor in 1941 were fighting for the Emperor, who was considered the "son of heaven."
10. The Gulf War of 1990-91 between Iraq and a U.S.-led coalition again saw two armies each invoking the name of a god.

EXERCISE 7-3   Recognizing subjects, predicates, and parts of speech

Make a photocopy of a brief passage from a textbook in one of your other courses. In order to practice identifying sentence parts and parts of speech, mark off the simple subjects and simple predicates according to the instructions for Exercise 2, and then, using abbreviations ("n"-noun, "v"-verb, "adj"-adjective, "adv"-adverb, "pro"-pronoun, "prep"-preposition, "con"-conjunction, and—if there are any—"int"-interjection), try to identify as many parts of speech as you can.

EXERCISE 7-4   Understanding basic sentence patterns

For each of the following sentences, place a slash (/) between the subject and predicate, and then identify with the appropriate abbreviation each of the following: *v*—verb, *v (tr)*—transitive verb, *v (l)*—linking verb, *do*—direct object, *io*—indirect object, *oc*—object complement, and *sc*—subject complement. Finally, on the lines at the right, identify by number the basic sentence pattern.

v(tr)   do

EXAMPLE   Architects / design buildings.   __2__

1. Friedrich Kekule was an architecture student.

    _____

2. Kekule found chemistry preferable.

    _____

3. His chemistry career flourished.

    _____

4. Organic chemistry became Kekule's specialty.

    _____

5. Kekule gave organic chemistry a structural theory.

    _____

EXERCISE 7-5   Using single-word modifiers

For each of the following sentences, underline the nouns once and the verbs twice. Then rewrite the sentences, using one-word adjectives or adverbs to modify the nouns and verbs.

EXAMPLE   Rock <u>musicians</u> <u><u>make</u></u> concert <u>appearances</u>.

Dedicated rock musicians make *frequent* concert appearances.

1. Fans scream.

2. Promoters make money.

3. Musicians become exhausted.

4. An album can make a musician famous.

5. A musician needs music videos.

Name _____ Section _____ Date _____

EXERCISE 7-6   Recognizing phrases

On the lines at the right, identify the type of phrase underlined and its function in the sentence.

EXAMPLE   Nuclear energy, <u>with all its problems</u>,
           seems to be here to stay.   _____preposition/adj_____

1. People have a right <u>to know how dangerous it is.</u>   _____

2. The industry, <u>feeling besieged</u>, is engaging in a
   public relations campaign.   _____

3. Nuclear power is the cleaner <u>of the two primary
   power sources</u>, nuclear and fossil-fuel.   _____

4. <u>Until appropriate waste-removal methods are
   devised</u>, nuclear remains the most dangerous
   power source.   _____

5. <u>Generating wind and solar power</u> is a dream of
   some researchers.   _____

6. Many people would refuse <u>to pay the costs
   involved with solar power.</u>   _____

7. <u>Their lives shortened by lung disease</u>, many coal
   miners attest to the dangers of that fuel.   _____

8. Experts are abandoning research into oil,
   <u>convinced of its political dependence.</u>   _____

9. Researchers are constantly trying <u>to solve energy
   problems.</u>   _____

10. Nobody knows what will be <u>the energy source of
    the future.</u>   _____

EXERCISE 7-7   Modifying sentences with phrases

Take the following basic sentences and add modifiers and modifiers within modifiers, making sure to keep the sentence coherent. (The point at which one more modifier would make the sentence "topple" is the point at which to stop adding.) Compare your responses to those of other students: Do your responses differ primarily in style? meaning? both?

1. Arturo sang.

2. Keisha taught Mary Ellen the dance.

3. The members welcomed the non-members.

4. Ben, Alicia, and Samantha were the stars.

5. The performers made their parents proud.

EXERCISE 7-8   Modifying sentences with dependent clauses

Combine the following pairs of sentences, using subordinate conjunctions and relative pronouns to create dependent clauses.

EXAMPLE   American artist Ad Reinhardt became famous for his single-color paintings. Reinhardt was the son of immigrants.

American artist Ad Reinhardt, *who was the son of immigrants,* became famous for his single-color paintings.

1. Reinhardt was an abstract painter from the beginning of his career. Other painters embraced abstractionism at some point in their careers.

2. Picasso said, "My painting represents the victory of the forces of light and peace over the powers of darkness and evil." Reinhardt responded with, "My painting represents the victory of the forces of darkness and peace over the powers of light and evil."

3. Picasso represented reverence and ideology. Reinhardt represented irreverence and iconoclasm.

4. Reinhardt's "black" paintings seem so filled with nothingness. The viewer must stand and stare for a long time.

5. Art lovers flocked to the Los Angeles Museum of Contemporary Art in October, 1991. An Ad Reinhardt retrospective was being exhibited.

EXERCISE 7-9   Identifying sentence structures

On the lines at the right, identify the following sentences as simple, compound, complex, or compound-complex.

EXAMPLE   Legends of everyday horrors last for
            generations.   ___simple___

1. Although many people tell the tale of the
   psychopath's hook left dangling on the car
   door handle, nobody has ever produced
   any evidence that it really happened.   _____

2. Probably because of its pathos, the story of
   the dog tied to the car bumper still
   survives, and it was immortalized in the
   movie *National Lampoon's Vacation.*   _____

3. The notice of the LSD-laced children's
   stamps has made the rounds for years, but
   nobody has ever seen one.   _____

4. A famous academic story involves the
   Philosophy examination question, "Why?"
   and the student's response, "Why not?"   _____

5. This story and its variations all report that
   the professor, appreciating creativity, gives
   the student an A.   _____

EXERCISE 7-10   Review

In the space below, rewrite the following paragraph, combining sentences by converting some into single-word modifiers, phrases, and dependent clauses. You may also combine sentences by joining independent clauses with conjunctions.

Personal ownership is a concept. The concept is not innate in human nature. Native Americans did not own land. They had an idea. They belonged to the land. They could use the land. They drew their livelihood from the land. The notion of ownership was peculiar to them. The notion was from the west. The peculiarity can be seen. Consider ownership of air. Consider ownership of the seas. Ownership is personal. This is a notion. The notion seems absurd. We think about the notion of personal ownership. We begin to wonder. We wonder about its legitimacy.

CHAPTER 8

Case in Nouns
and Pronouns

If your writing is to be clear, then your choice of case for pronouns (and at times for nouns) must be appropriate. Case refers to a noun or pronoun's change in form, depending on its function in a sentence. The form of a noun remains the same regardless of the noun's function as subject or object. The form of a pronoun, however, changes when the pronoun moves from subject to object position in a sentence. Both nouns and pronouns change form to indicate possession.

8a Using pronouns as subjects

Pronouns Used as Subjects

	Singular	*Plural*
1st person	I	we
2nd person	you	you
3rd person	he, she, it	they

 Use the subjective case when a pronoun functions as a subject, as a subject complement, or as an appositive that renames a subject. (See 7d-6.)

Subject of an independent clause

Jonas Salk embarked on a crucial project in 1950; **he** began exploring ways to prevent the spread of polio.

Subject of a dependent clause

Although **he** faced numerous obstacles, Salk achieved limited success within two years.

Subject complement

It was **he** who developed the first successful polio vaccine.

Appositive that renames a subject

Two men, **he** and Albert Sabin (who later developed oral polio vaccine), are credited with saving the lives of millions of children.

2 Use the subjective case for pronouns with the linking verb *be.*

A pronoun that follows a linking verb is called the **complement** of the noun preceding the verb. (It may help to think of the pronoun as *completing* the meaning of the noun.) Since the noun is the subject of the sentence, the pronoun after the verb must be in the subjective case. Such constructions reverse the normal (subject-verb-complement) word order of a sentence. You can test to see if a pronoun is a complement by recasting the sentence in normal word order.

REVERSED	The man responsible for the first polio vaccine was he, Jonas Salk.
NORMAL	He was the man responsible for the first polio vaccine.

In nonstandard usage, the objective case is common in constructions such as: "Who's calling?" "It's **him**." However, standard academic English demands that the case of the pronoun be consistent with the case of the noun: "It's **he**." If such a construction sounds stilted, reorder the sentence: "**He's** calling."

8b Using pronouns as objects

Pronouns Used as Objects

	Singular	*Plural*
1st person	me	us
2nd person	you	you
3rd person	him, her, it	them

1 Use the objective forms for pronouns functioning as objects.

Pronouns functioning as the object of a preposition, as the object or indirect object of a verb, or as the object of a verbal take the objective form.

Object or indirect object of verb

David Souter was surprised when President George Bush appointed **him** to the Supreme Court.

His neighbors said that Souter had always given **them** reason to be proud.

Object of preposition

The Judiciary Committee asked Souter pointed questions, and he answered every one of **them** with tact and honesty.

Appositive that renames an object

With the appointment of Souter, Bush had named to key positions two New Hampshire men, John Sununu (White House Chief of Staff) and **him**.

Object of verbal

Although Souter's views were not well known, among the groups supporting **him** were conservatives and right-wing Republicans.

2 Use the objective form for pronouns functioning as the subject of an infinitive.

A pronoun that comes between a verb and an infinitive (the basic verb form preceded by *to*) takes the objective form, even though that pronoun is referred to as the subject of the infinitive.

Subject of infinitive

Liberals' concerns about Souter's record caused **them** to oppose his appointment.

8c Using nouns and pronouns in the possessive case

In addition to indicating ownership: "Billie Holiday sang with several great bands during her career," the possessive case of nouns and pronouns serves other functions as well.

Possessive Forms of Pronouns

	Singular	*Plural*
1st person	my, mine	our, ours
2nd person	your, yours	your, yours
3rd person	his, her, hers, its	their, theirs

1 **Certain possessive pronouns are used as subjects or subject complements to indicate possession.**

The possessive pronouns *mine, ours, yours, his, hers,* and *theirs* are used in place of a noun as subjects or subject complements.

Hers was one of the greatest jazz voices of the century, according to critics.

The title of First Lady of Jazz was **hers** for over a decade.

2 **Use a possessive noun or pronoun before a gerund to indicate possession.**

The possessive form is used for pronouns that come before a gerund in order to establish "ownership" of the gerund construction.

GERUND   **Her** singing revolutionized jazz vocals.

Since participles and gerunds take the same form (-*ing*), they can sometimes cause confusion. Participles require a pronoun in the objective form:

PARTICIPLE   When Lester Young's fans saw **him** performing with Holiday, they were mesmerized.

The importance of using the appropriate pronoun form is illustrated by rephrasing this sentence:

GERUND   Lester Young's fans saw **his** performing with Holiday as a turning point for modern jazz.

8d | In a compound construction, use pronouns in the objective or subjective form according to their function in the sentence.

When trying to determine the appropriate case for a pronoun in a compound subject or object, create a simplified sentence by dropping out the compound; then try choosing the pronoun:

FAULTY | Jesse and Frank James fought for the Confederacy in the Civil War; later Frank and **him** started an outlaw gang.

SIMPLIFIED | Frank started an outlaw gang; **he** did too.

REVISED | Jesse and **he** started an outlaw gang.

8e | Pronouns paired with a noun take the same case as the noun.

1 | For first-person plural pronouns (*we, us*) paired with a noun, use the same case as the noun.

Standard academic English requires that first-person plural pronouns take the same case as the nouns with which they are paired. When trying to determine the appropriate case for the personal pronouns *we* or *us* placed before a plural noun, use the following test: Drop out the paired noun from the sentence. In the simpler sentence remaining, you should be able to determine which pronoun case is required.

NONSTANDARD | Ghost stories always frightened **we** campers as we sat around the fire.

SIMPLIFIED | Ghost stories always frightened **us** . . . as we sat around the fire.

REVISED | Ghost stories always frightened **us** campers as we sat around the fire.

2 | In an appositive, a pronoun's case should match the case of the noun it renames.

Appositive refers to a word or phrase that describes, identifies, or renames a noun in a sentence. When trying to determine the appropriate case for pronouns functioning as appositives, use the following test: Drop the noun being renamed out of the sentence. The simpler sentence that remains will usually reveal what pronoun case is required.

FAULTY	Charlotte Mason was my camp counselor. It was Mason—**her** alone—who kept me from crying myself to sleep every night.
SIMPLIFIED	**She** alone kept me from crying myself to sleep every night.
REVISED	Charlotte Mason was my camp counselor. It was Mason—**she** alone—who kept me from crying myself to sleep every night.

8f   Choose the appropriate form of the pronouns *whose, who, whom, whoever,* and *whomever* depending on the pronoun's function.

The following table shows the appropriate forms of the relative pronouns *whose, who, whom, whoever,* and *whomever:*

Forms of the Relative Pronoun *Who(m)/Who(m)ever*

Subjective	Objective	Possessive
who	whom	whose
whoever	whomever	—

1   In a question, choose a subjective, objective, or possessive form of *who(m)* or *who(m)ever* according to the pronoun's function.

When trying to decide which form of these pronouns to use, answer the question, substituting the personal pronouns *I/me, we/us, he/him,* or *she/her* for the relative pronoun. The relative pronoun will take the same case as the personal pronoun.

QUESTION	(Who/Whom) did you wish to see?
ANSWER	You wished to see her.
REVISED	Whom did you wish to see?

2   In a dependent clause, choose the subjective, objective, or possessive form of *who(m)* or *who(m)ever* according to the pronoun's function within the clause.

When trying to decide which form of these pronouns to use, isolate the clause and consider the pronoun's function within the clause.

Determine whether the relative pronoun functions as the subject of a dependent clause.

A relative pronoun followed by a verb is usually subjective. In addition, if the personal pronouns *I, we, you, he* or *she* can be substituted for the relative pronoun, then use the subjective case.

EXAMPLE	A Nobel Prize means international recognition for (whoever/whomever) receives one.
ISOLATION/ SUBSTITUTION	(Whoever/Whomever) receives one. **He** receives one.
REVISED	A Nobel Prize means international recognition for **whoever** receives one.

Determine whether the relative pronoun functions as the subject of a dependent clause.

A relative pronoun followed by a noun or by the pronouns *I, we, you, he, she, few, some, many, most, it,* or *they* is usually objective. In addition, if the personal pronouns *him, her,* or *them* can be substituted for the relative pronoun when the clause is recast in normal word order, then use the objective case.

EXAMPLE	A Nobel Prize means international recognition for (whoever/whomever) it is awarded to.
ISOLATION/ RECAST/ SUBSTITUTION	It is awarded to (whoever/whomever). It is awarded to **him.**
REVISED	A Nobel Prize means international recognition for **whomever** it is awarded to.

Determine whether the relative pronoun needs to show possession.

A relative pronoun that indicates possession of the noun following it is possessive. In addition, if the personal pronouns *his, her, their,* or *its* can be substituted for the relative pronoun, then use the possessive case.

EXAMPLE	William Faulkner, _____ Nobel Prize brought him much-needed recognition, delivered a stirring address upon receiving the award.
ISOLATION/ SUBSTITUTION	**His** Nobel Prize brought him much-needed recognition.

REVISED   William Faulkner, **whose** Nobel Prize brought him
                      much-needed recognition, delivered a stirring address upon
                      receiving the award.

CRITICAL DECISIONS

CHALLENGE YOUR SENTENCES: APPLY A TEST FORM *WHO* AND *WHOM*

In a clause the relative pronouns *who* and *whom* take the place of nouns (or
pronouns) that function as subjects or objects. Choosing the correct relative
pronoun requires that you see that pronoun in relation to the words immediately
following. You cannot focus on the pronoun alone and hope to get its form right;
you must examine the broader context of the clause in which the pronoun is
located. Two questions should help you to choose between *who* and *whom*
correctly.

- Is the relative pronoun followed by a verb?

  —"Yes": choose the subjective form *who* or *whoever.*

  A relative pronoun followed by a verb indicates the pronoun occupies
  the subject position of the clause. To confirm this choice, substitute *I, we,
  you, he,* or *she* for the pronoun. If one of these and the words
  immediately following form a sentence, you have identified the need for
  the subjective case.

    Clinton, *who* won by a landslide in the electoral college, did not
    win as convincingly in the popular vote. [*Who* is followed by a
    verb and when it is converted to *he* yields a sentence: "*He* won
    by a landslide. . . ."]

  —"No": choose the objective form *whom* or *whomever.* See the next test.

- Is the relative pronoun followed by a noun or by any of these pronouns:
  I, we, you, he, she, few, some, many, most, it, or *they?*

  —"Yes": choose the objective form *whom* or *whomever.*

  A relative pronoun followed by a noun or one of the listed pronouns
  indicates that the normal order of the clause (subject-verb-object) has
  been rearranged, suggesting the need for a pronoun in its objective

form. To confirm your choice of *whom* or *whomever*, consider the pronoun and the words immediately following. Rearrange these words and substitute *him, her,* or *them* for the relative pronoun. If a sentence results, you have identified the need for the objective form.

> Clinton, *whom* most analysts counted out of the presidential race, surprised supporters and detractors alike. [*Whom* is followed by *most* and when it is converted to *him* yields a sentence: "Most analysts counted *him* out."]

| 8g | Choose the case of a pronoun in the second part of a comparison depending on the meaning intended. |

When the second part of a comparison is omitted for the sake of brevity, the case of the remaining pronoun must be chosen with care so as not to confuse the meaning of the sentence. In order to determine case, complete the construction:

EXAMPLE	Faulkner's family sometimes thought that they knew his characters better than (he, him).
COMPLETE	Faulkner's family sometimes thought that they knew his characters better than **they knew him.**
COMPLETE	Faulkner's family sometimes thought that they knew his characters better than **he knew his characters.**

Depending on the meaning intended by the writer, either of these constructions is appropriate.

If the omitted verb cannot take an object, then the remaining pronoun must be subjective. Completing the construction will also reveal the correct choice:

FAULTY	Faulkner and Andrew Lytle were contemporaries, but Lytle was not as famous as **him.**
REVISED	Faulkner and Andrew Lytle were contemporaries, but Lytle was not as famous as **he.**
COMPLETED	Faulkner and Andrew Lytle were contemporaries, but Lytle was not as famous as **he was.**

EXERCISE 8-1   **Using pronoun forms**

Fill in the blanks in the following sentences with the appropriate form of the pronoun in parentheses:

EXAMPLE   In 1966, the Surgeon General announced that cigarettes were harmful to
               health. Many smokers who heard (he) _*him*_ making the
               announcement now knew that the habit was deadly.

1. Friends and families of smokers asked (they) _____ to quit.

2. Twenty years after the first announcement, smokers were told, "(you) _____
    smoking also endangers everyone in your vicinity."

3. "It's horrible to realize that it was (I) _____ who was responsible for the health
    problems of my children," reported one smoker.

4. As pressure to ban smoking in public places grew, some smokers fought back,
    protesting, "(we) _____ smokers have rights too!"

5. In the new health-conscious climate, however, (they) _____ was a cause that was
    decidedly unpopular.

6. Children asked their parents, "How can you jeopardize the health of your
    children, (we) _____ who depend on you?"

7. Coworkers complained that it was (they) _____ , not the smokers, (who) _____
    rights were being violated.

8. Smokers countered with claims of discrimination: "Society is treating (we) _____
    smokers as second-class citizens!"

9. Gradually, over the objections of many smokers, demands to restrict (they) _____
    smoking to certain areas were met, creating what are now known as "smoke-free
    zones."

10. Nonsmokers told smokers that (they) _____ and (they) _____ habit were
    unwelcome in public places.

EXERCISE 8-2   Recognizing pronoun forms

Underline all of the pronouns in the following paragraph, and above each identify the case with the abbreviation *s*—subjective, *o*—objective, or *p*—possessive:

EXAMPLE   Although many smokers were able to kick the habit, they soon
discovered that quitting smoking had its own problems.

> Many smokers discovered that quitting made them irritable, causing problems at
> work and at home. Their job performance suffered, and spouses and children
> found that a reformed smoker isn't always a joy to her family. Said the son of one
> reformed smoker, "Sometimes I want to give her a cigarette just to have a little
> peace in the house!" Other smokers faced yet another problem in the search to
> curb their desire for nicotine. A man who quit smoking after fifteen years put it
> this way: "You think your problems are over now that you have quit, but the
> craving doesn't leave you alone. So you eat—and put on weight." Studies have
> shown that people who quit smoking do in fact gain weight, some of them as
> much as thirty pounds. Researchers warn us, however, that while smoking
> certainly plays its part in curbing our appetites, the health risks of excess weight
> cannot compare to the health risks of smoking.

EXERCISE 8-3   Using appropriate forms of *who*

Fill in the blanks in the following sentences with the appropriate forms of the pronouns *whose, who, whom, whoever,* and *whomever:*

EXAMPLE   The class was studying a poet __*whose*__ works were well known.

1. The Robert Frost poem opens with these words: "_____ woods these are I think

    I know."

2. Reading Frost's lines to the class, the professor asked if anyone could describe the

    person _____ was speaking in the poem.

3. "_____ it was, he sure loved the woods!" came one reply.

4. The professor then asked the class, "_____ is the speaker addressing in this poem?"

5. A bored student whispered, "_____ he's talking to, my only answer is '_____

    cares?' "

EXERCISE 8-4   Understanding pronoun use

Photocopy a brief passage that contains a number of pronouns from one of your textbooks. Circle all of the pronouns, and then list them. Using what you've learned about case and function so far, identify the pronouns by case and explain their function in the sentence.

CHAPTER 9

Verbs

Verb forms convey three important messages to readers: **tense** indicates when an action or state of being occurs; **mood** indicates whether a statement is a fact, a command, or an occurrence contrary to fact; and **voice** indicates whether the emphasis in on the actor or the object acted upon.

VERB FORMS

9a Using the principal parts of regular verbs consistently

All verbs other than *to be* have three **principal parts** (the base form, past tense, and the past participle), and two other basic forms (the *-s* form and the present participle).

The Forms and Principal Parts of Regular Verbs

Base Form	Present Tense (*-s form*)	Past Tense	Past Participle	Present Participle
belong	belongs	belonged	belonged	belonging
wade	wades	waded	waded	wading
kick	kicks	kicked	kicked	kicking

 1 Recognizing the forms of regular verbs

Base form + the *-s* form = present tense

The **base** (or infinitive) **form** is the form from which all changes are made. The base form takes no ending in present tense for plural nouns or for personal pronouns *I, we, you,* or *they.*

> United States businesses *function* less efficiently than their counterparts in Germany and Japan.

The **-s form** is used for third-person singular subjects.

> Overseas competition *makes* U.S. companies more innovative.

Past-tense form

The **past tense**, indicating an action that has been completed in the past, is formed by adding the suffix *-d* or *-ed* to the regular verb.

> Shortly after World War II, an influx of Japanese products entered world markets.

Two participle forms

The **past participle** of a regular verb is identical to the past tense form. Paired with *have* the past participle forms a perfect tense; paired with *be* it forms a passive construction; paired with a noun or pronoun it functions as an adjective.

> U.S. companies *have attempted* to outperform Japanese and German companies, but often they *are obstructed* by high labor costs and *depleted* resources.

The **present participle** (*-ing*) paired with *be* forms a perfect tense; paired with a noun or pronoun it functions as an adjective. When the *-ing* form functions as a noun it is called a *gerund*.

> Companies *are starting* to rely on innovative programs at an *increasing* rate in hopes of *winning*.

2 **Revising nonstandard verb forms by using standard *-s* and *-ed* forms**

Although eliminating *-s* and *-ed* endings is acceptable in nonstandard conversation, in standard English the endings must be used.

NONSTANDARD   My boss *ask* me to work overtime.

STANDARD   My boss *asked* me to work overtime.

9b Learning the forms of irregular verbs

While most English verbs follow the forms outlined above for regular verbs, irregular verbs form past tense and past participle by changing the spelling of the base verb (*draw/drew, fight/fought*).

Be

Be, the most common verb in English, is the only verb with more than five forms.

The Principal Parts of *be*

Base Form	Present Tense	Past Tense	Past Participle	Present Participle
(to) be	he, she, it *is* I *am* we, you, they *are*	he, she, it *was* I *was* we, you, they *were*	*been*	*being*

A partial list of irregular verbs follows:

Base Form	Past Tense	Past Participle
arise	arose	arisen
be (am, are, is)	was, were	been
bear	bore	borne, born
beat	beat	beaten
become	became	become
begin	began	begun
bend	bent	bent
bind	bound	bound
bite	bit	bit, bitten
bleed	bled	bled
blow	blew	blown
break	broke	broken
bring	brought	brought
build	built	built
burn	burned, burnt	burned, burnt
burst	burst	burst
buy	bought	bought
catch	caught	caught
choose	chose	chosen
cling	clung	clung

come	came	come
cost	cost	cost
cut	cut	cut
dig	dug	dug
dive	dove, dived	dived
do (does)	did	done
draw	drew	drew
drink	drank	drunk
drive	drove	driven
eat	ate	eaten
fall	fell	fallen
feel	felt	felt
fight	fought	fought
find	found	found
fling	flung	flung
flee	fled	fled
fly	flew	flown
forbid	forbade	forbidden or forbid
forget	forgot	forgotten or forgot
freeze	froze	frozen
get	got	got, gotten
give	gave	given
go	went	gone
grow	grew	grown
hang[1]	hung	hung
have (has)	had	had
hear	heard	heard
hide	hid	hidden
hit	hit	hit
keep	kept	kept
know	knew	known
lay	laid	laid
leave	left	left
lie[2]	lay	lain
lose	lost	lost
make	made	made
mean	meant	meant
pay	paid	paid
prove	proved	proved or proven
read	read	read
ride	rode	ridden

---

[1]*Hang* as an irregular verb means to *suspend*. When *hang* means to *execute*, it is regular: *hang, hanged, hanged*.

[2]*Lie* as an irregular verb means to *recline*. When *lie* means to *deceive*, it is regular: *lie, lied, lied*.

ring	rang	rung
rise	rose	risen
run	ran	run
say	said	said
seek	sought	sought
send	sent	sent
set	set	set
shake	shook	shaken
shine[3]	shone	shone
sing	sang	sung
sink	sank	sunk
sit	sat	sat
sleep	slept	slept
speak	spoke	spoken
spend	spent	spent
spring	sprang, sprung	sprung
stand	stood	stood
steal	stole	stolen
stick	stuck	stuck
strive	strove	striven
swear	swore	sworn
swim	swam	swum
swing	swung	swung
take	took	taken
teach	taught	taught
tear	tore	torn
tell	told	told
think	thought	thought
throw	threw	thrown
wake	woke, waked	waked, woken
wear	wore	worn
wind	wound	wound
wring	wrung	wrung
write	wrote	written

9c Using auxiliary verbs

The auxiliary verbs *be, have,* and *do* are used to create progressive and perfect tenses, as well as to form questions and to show emphasis or negation:

I am running.   I had run.   Did I run?   I did run.   You didn't run.

---

[3]*Shine* as an irregular verb means to *emit light.* When *shine* means to *polish,* it is regular: *shine, shined, shined.*

█ 1 **Use modal auxiliaries to refine meaning.**

Modal auxiliaries (*can, could, may, might, must, ought to, should, would*) express urgency, obligation, likelihood, possibility, and so on. They retain the same form regardless of the person or number of the subject. (The auxiliaries *will* and *shall* indicate future tense.) Meaning changes when the modal auxiliary changes:

She can forget.   She might forget.   She ought to forget.   She must forget.

█ 2 **Revise nonstandard auxiliaries by using standard forms of *be*.**

Although some dialects eliminate *be* or use its base form, standard academic English requires the appropriate form to be used.

NONSTANDARD   She be forgetting. She forgetting.

STANDARD   She is forgetting.

█ 9d Using transitive and intransitive verbs

Action verbs are classified as **transitive** and **intransitive**. A **transitive verb** transfers action from subject to object.

█ 1 **Distinguish between verbs that take direct objects and those that do not.**

While many verbs are always transitive (*hit, buy, give*) and some are always intransitive (*cling, look, sleep*), some verbs can be either transitive or intransitive, depending on their use:

He felt sick.   He felt the soft breeze.

█ 2 **Avoid confusion between the verbs *sit/set, lie/lay, rise/raise*.**

Although verbs such as *sit/set, lie/lay, rise/raise* are often interchanged in speech, the appropriate form must be used in standard academic English. The first verb in each pair is intransitive.

sit/set	I **sit** at the table.	I **set** the glass on the table.
lie/lay	You **lie** on the floor.	You **lay** the blanket on the floor.
rise/raise	I **rise** before dawn.	I **raise** the shade when the sun comes up.

The Principal Parts of *sit/set, lie/lay, rise/raise*

Base Form	Present Tense	Past Tense	Past Participle	Present Participle
sit	sits	sat	sat	sitting
set	sets	set	set	setting
lie	lies	lay	lain	lying
lay	lays	laid	laid	laying
rise	rises	rose	risen	rising
raise	raises	raised	raised	raising

TENSE

 9e Understanding the uses of verb tenses

The **tense** of a verb indicates time; simple tenses are *past, present,* and *future.* Each tense has both a **perfect** form (indicating completed action), a **progressive** form (indicating ongoing action), and a **perfect progressive** form (indicating ongoing action that will be completed at some definite time).

 1 The varied uses of the present tense

Present: I study for the exam.
    Present perfect: I have studied for the exam.
    Present progressive: I am studying for the exam.
    Present perfect progressive: I have been studying for the exam.

The simple present

For the simple present tense, use the verb's base form for first- and second-person subjects (singular or plural) and third-person plural subjects. Add *-s* to the base for the third-person singular subject. While the simple present tense indicates an action taking place in the writer's present time, simple present can also be used to indicate other time references:

I *need* a rest. When she *retires*, she will sell her house.

Tomorrow I *register* my new car.

The historical present

Because actions in any existing work (books, movies, plays, etc.) are always present to the reader, use the present tense when referring to those actions. Accepted wisdom or scientific fact is also referred to in present tense, as is repeated action:

Scarlett O'Hara *pledges* that she'll never go hungry again.

Chicken pox *strikes* thousands of children every year.

Every four years we *elect* a new President.

The present perfect tense

The present perfect tense is formed with the auxiliary *have* or *has* and the past participle, and indicates an action completed at an indefinite past time or one that continues to have an impact.

We *have traveled* forty miles. She *has donated* money to the school fund.

The present progressive tense

The present progressive tense is formed with the auxiliary *is, am,* or *are* and the present participle, and indicates an ongoing action that may continue into the future.

They *are planning* to visit Rome.

The present perfect progressive tense

The present perfect progressive tense is formed with the auxiliaries *has been* or *have been* and the present participle, and indicates an action begun in the past, continuing in the present, and possibly continuing into the future.

I *have been hoping* to see her.

 The past and future tenses

PAST TENSES

The simple past tense

The simple past tense for regular verbs is formed by adding *-d* or *-ed* to the infinitive; irregular verbs form the past tense by undergoing internal changes. The simple past tense indicates an action completed at a definite time in the past.

Many Democrats *hoped* that Mario Cuomo would run for President in 1988.

The past perfect tense

The past perfect tense is formed with the auxiliary *had* and the past participle, and indicates a past action that has occurred prior to another action.

Before the convention, several sources *had suggested* that Cuomo might reconsider.

The past progressive tense

The past progressive tense is formed with the auxiliary *was* or *were* and the present participle, and indicates an ongoing action completed in the past.

Liberal groups *were trying* to convince Cuomo to run.

The past perfect progressive tense

The past perfect progressive tense is formed with the auxiliary *had been* and the present participle, and indicates a past ongoing action completed prior to another past action.

Before the Iowa caucuses, Cuomo *had been considering* a run.

FUTURE TENSES

The future tense

The future tense is formed by the auxiliary *will* and the base verb, and indicates an action that will begin in the future. (In formal writing, the first person has traditionally taken the auxiliary *shall*.)

Atlanta *will host* the Summer Olympics in 1996.

The future perfect tense

The future perfect tense is formed by the auxiliary *will have* and the past participle, and indicates an action occurring in the future, prior to another action.

By the time the torch is lit, the city *will have spent* millions of dollars on promotion alone.

The future progressive tense

The future progressive tense is formed by the auxiliary *will be* (or *shall be*) and the present participle, and indicates an ongoing action in the future.

Atlanta residents *will be celebrating* throughout the games.

The future perfect progressive tense

The future perfect progressive tense is formed by the auxiliary *will have been* and the present participle, and indicates an ongoing action in the future that will occur before another specified, future time.

By summer of 1996, Atlanta *will have been preparing* for the games for over six years.

9f Sequencing verb tenses

In sentences that include more than one verb, be sure to indicate the proper tense for each verb. Otherwise, readers may become confused.

UNCLEAR	After Craig cleans up, he locked the store. [Present and past tense together are confusing.]
CLEAR	After Craig cleans up, he will lock the store. [Both actions in future, one earlier than the other.]
CLEAR	After Craig cleaned up, he locked the store. [Both actions in past, one earlier than the other.]

1 Sequence the events in complex sentences with care.

In complex sentences, the subordinate conjunction in the dependent clause will establish a time sequence. Be sure to make consistent the sense of time in the independent clause with the sense of time established in the dependent clause.

UNCLEAR	Before the store closed, several customers make major purchases. [A definite event in the past is established in the subordinate clause, but the action of the independent clause takes place in the present.]
CLEAR	Before the store closed, several customers made major purchases. [Both actions now take place in the past, one before the other.]

2 Choose verb tense in an infinitive phrase based on your choice of verb in the main clause.

When the infinitive phrase consists of *to* and the present tense, the action occurs at the same time or later than the action indicated by the main verb in the sentence:

When Margaret Sanger began to offer birth control information, hundreds of poor women <u>came</u> *to hear* her advice. [Both actions occurred at the same time.]

The women <u>hoped</u> *to end* their cycle of childbearing. [*To end* the cycle is a possible action that will occur later than *hoped*.]

When the infinitive phrase consists of *to* and the past participle, the action occurs before the action of the main verb:

To have offered such illegal information to poor women <u>jeopardized</u> Sanger's freedom. [Offering the information occurred in the past before the jeopardy, in fact causing the jeopardy.]

When the main clause is either past or perfect, the tense sequence is sometimes difficult.

Establishing a relationship between two events, both of which occur in the past

Use the simple past tense in the independent clause—and any of the four past tenses in the dependent clause.

The settlers <u>lived</u> where the land *supported them*. [past/past]

Frank <u>called</u> the doctor who *had operated* on him. [past/past perfect]

Shelley <u>wrote</u> her letters while she *was traveling* to Moscow. [past/past progressive]

We <u>believed</u> that she *had been working* on a solution for years. [past/past perfect progressive]

Use the past perfect tense in the independent clause and the simple past tense in the dependent clause.

Lucy <u>had</u> almost <u>decided</u> to quit smoking when she *visited* her sister. [past perfect/past]

Establishing a relationship between a past event and a future event

Use the past tense in the independent clause and the simple future, future progressive, or simple present tenses in the dependent clause.

We <u>reserved</u> tickets for the play that *will open* on Saturday night. [past/future]

We <u>reserved</u> tickets for the play that *will be opening* on Saturday night. [past/future progressive]

We <u>reserved</u> tickets for the play that *opens* on Saturday night. [past/present]

Establishing a relationship between a past event and an acknowledged fact or condition

Use the simple past tense for the main clause and the simple present tense in the dependent clause.

The study <u>concluded</u> that few people *trust* strangers. [past/present]

Helen <u>contacted</u> the lawyer who *has* the best reputation. [past/present]

We <u>found</u> evidence that the theory *is* correct. [past/present]

Use the past perfect tense for the main clause and the simple present tense in the dependent clause.

Smith <u>had argued</u> that everyone *needs* basic services. [past perfect/present]

---

3 **Choose the verb tense of a participle based on your choice of verb in the main clause.**

The present participle (*-ing*) indicates an action that occurs at the same time as the action of the main verb.

Providing birth control information to poor women, Sanger <u>incurred</u> the wrath of the religious community. [Both actions occurred at the same time in the past.]

The present perfect participle (*having*) indicates an action that occurs before the action of the main verb.

Having failed to convince authorities that her methods were compassionate, Sanger <u>left</u> for England. [The *failure* occurred before the trip to England, but both were in the past.]

The past participle (*-ed* or *-en* for regular verbs) indicates an action that occurs at the same time as or earlier than the action of the main verb.

Loved by the poor and *hated* by the authorities and religious leaders, Sanger <u>continued</u> to speak out for women's reproductive rights. [The *loving* and *hating* likely occurred before and after the *continuation* of speaking out.]

VOICE

9g Using the active and passive voices

Transitive verbs can be constructed to emphasize either the actor or the object. That emphasis is called a verb's **voice**. The **active voice** emphasizes the actor, while the **passive voice** emphasizes the object acted upon.

ACTIVE   Mozart composed *The Magic Flute.*

PASSIVE   *The Magic Flute* was composed by Mozart.

The passive voice requires a rearrangement of words, the use of *be* and the past participle, and (if the actor is to be named in the sentence) the preposition *by*.

1 Use a strong active voice for clear, direct assertions.

As the names imply, active verbs create a sense of action while passive verbs create a sense of inaction (passive constructions are also wordy). See the example above for illustration. Unless there is a specific reason for using the passive, use the active.

2 Use the passive voice to emphasize an object or to deemphasize an unknown subject.

Emphasize an object with a passive construction.

Passive voice shifts attention from the actor to the object acted upon. It is even possible to eliminate the actor from the sentence in passive voice.

ACTIVE   Researchers need adequate funding to conduct experiments.

PASSIVE   Adequate funding is needed by researchers to conduct
(subject retained)   experiments.

PASSIVE   Adequate funding is needed to conduct experiments.
(subject deleted)

Deemphasize an unknown subject with the passive voice.

The passive voice allows writers to avoid using indefinite subjects (such as *someone* or *people*).

ACTIVE	People need a substantial income in order to purchase a home.
PASSIVE (subject retained)	A substantial income is needed by people in order to purchase a home.
PASSIVE (subject deleted)	A substantial income is needed in order to purchase a home.

MOOD

9h Understanding the uses of mood

A verb's **mood** indicates the writer's judgment as to whether a statement is a fact, a command, or an occurrence contrary to fact. The most common mood, **indicative,** refers to fact, opinion, or question.

Most colleges offer courses in western civilization. [fact]

Western civilization courses are the most important in the curriculum. [opinion]

Did you take a western civilization course? [question]

Imperative mood signals a command. The subject of the command (*you*) is usually omitted, but occasionally it is expressed directly.

Don't drop that western civilization course.

Don't you drop that western civilization course!

Subjunctive mood indicates a wish, a requirement, a recommendation, or a statement contrary to fact. In the **present subjunctive** the base form of the verb is used for all subjects.

I suggest that she *drop* her western civilization course.

I suggest that they *drop* their western civilization course.

In the **past subjunctive** the past tense of the verb (or in the case of *be,* the form *were*) is used.

I wish that western civilization were an elective course.

In the **past perfect subjunctive** the past perfect form of the verb is used.

If you *had studied*, you would have passed your western civilization course.

1 **Use the subjunctive mood with certain *if* constructions.**

When an *if* clause expresses an unreal or hypothetical condition, use the subjunctive in the clause and the modal auxiliaries *would, could, might,* or *should* in the main clause.

FAULTY   If Allan *was* smart, he wouldn't have taken six courses this term. [Since he took six courses, Allan is <u>not</u> smart; the indicative is inconsistent.]

REVISED   If Allan *were* smart, he wouldn't have taken six courses this term.

Note: When the *if* clause indicates cause and effect rather than a condition contrary to fact, use the indicative mood.

If Allan *is* smart, he'll only sign up for five courses next term.

 2 **Use the subjunctive mood with *as if* and *as though* constructions.**

As if and *as though* constructions set up hypothetical comparisons that call for the subjunctive.

FAULTY   Allan talks as if he *was* a genius. [Since he's not a genius, the indicative is inconsistent.]

REVISED   Allan talks as if he *were* a genius.

3 **Revise to eliminate auxiliary *would* or *could* in subjunctive clauses with *if, as if,* or *as though*.**

The modal auxiliaries *would, could,* or *should* appear only in the main clause of a construction using *if, as if,* or *as though;* they <u>do not</u> appear in the dependent clause.

FAULTY   If Allan *would have* taken my advice, he would have passed his courses.

REVISED   If Allan *had* taken my advice, he would have passed his courses.

 4 **Use the subjunctive mood with a *that* construction.**

Use the subjunctive mood with subordinate *that* constructions expressing a requirement, request, urging, belief, wish, recommendation, or doubt. (The word *that* may be omitted.)

We suggested that Allan *take* an incomplete in one course.

He said he wished he *were* dead.

EXERCISE 9-1   Identifying main and auxiliary verbs

Underline and identify the main verb and any auxiliary verb associated with it in the following sentences. (Remember that the verbs *be* and *have* can be either main verbs or auxiliaries.)

                                          aux   *main*

EXAMPLE   Recently many companies <u>have introduced</u> "pay-for-performance" plans.

1. These plans offer financial incentives to workers based on production.

2. Some workers—but by no means all—are thrilled with the plans.

3. Many employees have been paid by the hour for years.

4. They can no longer depend on consistent paychecks.

5. However, some employees will be earning twice their regular salaries.

EXERCISE 9-2   **Using irregular verbs**

Choose five of the irregular verbs (other than *be*) from the list provided, and for each verb, construct three sentences: one using the base form, one using the past tense form, and one using the past participle form. (If you have difficulty using the past participle form, consult the sections on tense and voice.)

EXAMPLE   The bells *ring* every hour.

The bells *rang* all through the night.

The bells *have rung* at noon for fifty years.

Verb 1

Verb 2

Verb 3

Verb 4

Verb 5

EXERCISE 9-3   Distinguishing between *sit/set, lie/lay,* and *rise/raise*

Compose six sentences, one each for the verbs *sit/set, lie/lay,* and *rise/raise.*

EXAMPLE   She *set* the vase on the table carefully.

1.

2.

3.

4.

5.

6.

EXERCISE 9-4   **Understanding tense**

Using complete sentences, fill in the verb tense chart for the following verbs: *write, smile, go.*

Present:

Present perfect:

Present progressive:

Present perfect progressive:

Past:

Past perfect:

Past progressive:

Past perfect progressive:

Future:

Future perfect:

Future progressive:

Future perfect progressive:

EXERCISE 9-5   Using appropriate tenses

In the following sentences, write out the verb in parentheses in a tense appropriate to the meaning of the sentence.

EXAMPLE   Many people (study) __have studied__ the events that (make) __made__ Salem, Massachusetts infamous.

1. For years before the girls in Salem Village (begin) _____ accusing local people of witchcraft, disputes over land boundaries (plague) _____ the town.

2. In 1691 the village (be) _____ without a minister for years, but when Samuel Parris (arrive) _____ he (proclaim) _____, "Before the year (be) _____ out, I (sweep) ____ the devil from your midst!"

3. In the winter of that year, while his daughter and his niece (study) _____ Scripture, they (begin) _____ to shake and scream.

4. By the time the doctor (arrive) _____, the girls (behave) _____ strangely for days.

5. His conclusion (be) _____ chilling: "The girls (be) _____ bewitched."

6. Thus an episode (begin) _____ that (baffle) _____ us now and (baffle) _____ others in years to come.

EXERCISE 9-6   Tense and meaning

The following paragraph is written as though the main action occurred in the past. Rewrite the paragraph in the space below so that the time is the present, changing the italicized verbs as necessary (not all verbs will require changes). Remember to consider the meaning of each sentence within the passage before changing the verb tenses.

EXAMPLE   Sam *had seen* a bumper sticker in town: SPRAYED AND BETRAYED.

Sam *has seen* a bumper sticker in town: SPRAYED AND BETRAYED.

When she *told* Emmett, he *grunted* and *kept* digging. He *had* Clearasil on his face. She *realized* that not every soldier who *came* back from Vietnam *was* as weird as Emmett. She *knew* of veterans—relatives of classmates—who *had adjusted* perfectly well. They *had* nice houses and wives and kids. They *didn't* wear skirts, even for a joke, and they *didn't* refuse to get a job or buy a car. Allen Wilkins *was* one of them. He *owned* a menswear store and *coached* Little League. His daughter *was* a teen model in a Glamor Barn TV ad on Channel 6. Sam *wondered* if it *was* just her own crazy family rather than Vietnam.

Bobbie Ann Mason, *In Country*

EXERCISE 9-7   **Understanding tense sequences**

For each of the following sentences, write out the appropriate tense of the verb in parentheses. Determine tense by considering the sequence of tenses in each sentence:

EXAMPLE   Since the space program began, fourteen astronauts (die) _have died_ in the line of duty.

1. When the space program was in its infancy, nobody (believe) _____that so many astronauts would lose their lives.

2. However, if you consider the number of tests and missions in which astronauts (participate) _____ over the years, you (realize) _____ that the number (be) ___ _ actually quite small.

3. Of the fourteen, three (die) _____ in a fire on the launch pad before the capsule (launch) _____ .

4. Four others died in airplane crashes that (not relate) _____ directly to a launching.

5. And of course we all remember the Challenger disaster of 1986, when seven men and women (kill) _____ .

6. Before final plans were made to memorialize the fallen astronauts, NASA officials (consider) _____ the issue for over a year.

7. At first the idea was to build a monument to the seven who (die) _____ on the Challenger, but now officials (decide) _____ that the memorial (honor) _____ all who (die) _____ in the line of duty.

8. Conceived by a Florida architect and designed by a San Francisco firm, the memorial (be) _____ a black granite slab that (rise) _____ forty-two feet into the air.

9. In order to create a sense of light, the names of the astronauts (carve) _____ right through the granite, so that sunlight (stream) _____ through the letters.

10. Like the Vietnam memorial in Washington, D.C., the "Space Mirror," as it (call) _____ , (honor)_____ our dead for generations to come.

EXERCISE 9-8 **Recognizing active and passive verbs**

Rewrite the following paragraph in the space below, changing the italicized verbs from active to passive and vice-versa, supplying subjects where necessary.

EXAMPLE   René Jules Dubos *was well known* as a bacteriologist and an environmentalist.

People know René Jules Dubos as a bacteriologist and an environmentalist.

Although his early dreams involved athletic achievements, Dubos eventually *studied* agriculture. The young Dubos found microbiology and chemistry tedious because the subjects *were explored* by students in a laboratory setting. Later, after he *completed* doctoral studies in soil microbiology, he began working with pneumonia patients. It was through experiments based on his work that three researchers from the Rockefeller Institute for Medical Research *won* the Nobel Prize in Chemistry. Although Dubos was responsible for the first clinically useful antibiotic, known as gramicidin, he eventually concluded that ecology and not medicine *held out* the best hope for curing disease.

EXERCISE 9-9   Using the subjunctive mood

In each of the following sentences, change the mood of the underlined verb if necessary. Circle the number of any correct sentences.

EXAMPLE   The rules of slavery required that the slave woman ~~submitted~~ *submit* to her master's advances.

1. Young Harriet Jacobs often thought, "If I <u>was</u> a free woman, I'd never be abused so."

2. Her conscience dictated that she <u>resisted</u> as long as she could.

3. Her grandmother advised, "If he <u>tries</u> to get you alone, head for the door!"

4. Instead Jacobs became the lover of a sympathetic free man who treated her as though she <u>was</u> a lady of high social standing.

5. Despite the motivation behind her actions, Jacobs often lamented, "I wish I <u>was</u> a virtuous woman!"

EXERCISE 9-10   Review

Rewrite the following paragraph on a separate sheet of paper, correcting the use of
verb form, tense, and mood. If passive sentences would be more effective as active
(or vice-versa), rewrite them.

   Debate over the civil rights bill of 1991 had focused on the concept of quotas. In
the sixties they had implemented quotas in order to assure minority students rights to
higher education. But by the eighties the term "quota" became the equivalent of a
four-letter word. Gains made by civil rights groups throughout the sixties and early
seventies had been lost as the country continued its move to the right. White students
argued, "If I would have been black, I'd have no trouble getting into college!" Visions
of unqualified minority students displacing deserving white students were conjured
up by politicians eager to harness the conservative vote. But in the late eighties the
concept of quotas had been taking on a different look. Prestigious universities were
admitting that for several years they have been using quotas to limit the number of
Asian Americans on their campuses. And then someone discovered that universities
such as Harvard, Stanford, and Yale are regularly accepting athletes whose
qualifications will be lower than those of many rejected students. Furthermore, it was
discovered that the group receiving preferential treatment more often than any other
was not African Americans, Chicanos, Asian Americans, or any other minority group.
Rather, the most preferred group has consisted of children of alumni—usually very
white and very wealthy.

EXERCISE 9-11   Understanding verb use

Photocopy a brief passage from one of your textbooks, and analyze its use of verbs.
First circle all of the verbs in the passage (count verb phrases as a single verb), and
then identify the verbs by tense, voice, and mood. Finally, comment on the use of
several auxiliaries in the passage. How do the various verb forms used contribute to
the meaning of the selection?

CHAPTER 10

Agreement

The term **agreement** describes two relationships in sentences: between a **subject and verb** and between a **pronoun and antecedent.** Whenever one element in these pairs is changed, the other must be changed as well:

SINGULAR   Approximately every ten years an unwelcome *visitor* descends
                                                         subject   verb

                     upon the trees of New England.

                     The gypsy moth eats every green thing in sight as it feasts on
                           antecedent   pronoun
                     the region's foliage.

PLURAL   Approximately every ten years unwelcome *visitors* descend
                                                          subject   verb

                     upon the trees of New England.

                     Gypsy moths eat every green thing in sight as they feast on the
                           antecedent   pronoun
                     region's foliage.

SUBJECT-VERB AGREEMENT

Subjects and verbs must agree in **number** and **person.** *Number* can be singular (one) or plural (more than one); *person* can be first (the speaker), second (the person spoken to), or third (the person spoken about). Pronouns as well as nouns are classified according to person.

	First-Person Subject	*Second-Person Subject*	*Third-Person Subject*
Singular	I	you	he, she, it
Plural	we	you	they

The first and second person take verbs *without* the -s ending:

     I speak.   You speak.   We speak.

10a Make a third-person subject agree in number with its verb.

The "tradeoff" technique

Since the suffix *-s* or *-es* is added to a verb to indicate it is singular, but added to the subject to indicate it is plural, it may be helpful to visualize a tradeoff of *-s/-es* endings between most noun subjects and their verbs: if one ends with *-s/-es* then the other does not. The tradeoff technique still applies even when the plural subject does not end in *-s/es*.

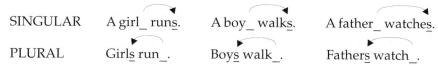

SINGULAR	A girl_ runs.	A boy_ walks.	A father_ watches.
PLURAL	Girls run_.	Boys walk_.	Fathers watch_.

Determining the Number of a Third-Person Subject

One way to establish the number of a third-person subject is to apply a simple test. Any noun in the third person can be replaced by a corresponding third-person pronoun: the singular pronouns *he, she,* or *it,* or the plural *they.* When you are uncertain about the number of a noun subject, reread the sentence and, based on its context, replace the subject with a third-person pronoun. Read the sentence once more. In most cases, you can fairly easily choose an appropriate verb that agrees with the pronoun.

UNSURE?	The experience of downwardly mobile people (*seem* or *seems?*) a strange subject for an anthropologist.
REPLACE	It *seems* a strange subject for an anthropologist. [Replacing the subject *experience* and its modifying phrase with the singular *it* clarifies the need for a singular verb.]

1 A subject agrees with its verb regardless of whether any phrase or clause separates them.

When a subject and verb are separated by a lengthy modifier, mentally eliminate the intervening phrases or clauses:

> Gypsy moths, despite their harmless appearance, **are** responsible for the defoliation of thousands of trees in the northeast.

Note: Phrases beginning with "in addition to," "along with," "as well as," "together with," or "accompanied by" do NOT create a plural subject. They should be treated as any other modifier:

FAULTY   The gypsy moth, along with other pests such as grasshoppers and beetles, **appear** in cycles.

REVISED   The gypsy moth, along with other pests such as grasshoppers and beetles, **appears** in cycles.

2 A compound subject linked by the conjunction *and* is in most cases plural.

Unless it refers to a single person, place, or thing, a compound subject is considered plural:

PLURAL   Spraying and taping **are** two techniques used to control gypsy moths, according to Catherine Mahoney.

SINGULAR   However, this farmer and town planner **insists** that she simply lets nature take its course.

3 When parts of a compound subject are linked by the conjunction *or* or *nor*, the verb should agree in number with the nearer part of the subject.

When both parts of a compound subject are the same number, agreement poses no problem. When part is singular and part plural, the verb agrees with the nearer subject:

SINGULAR   Either Jessica or Cassandra **is** scheduled to work today.

                Neither the Martins nor Hal Simonson **cleans** windows.

PLURAL   Either the windows or the carpets **have** to be cleaned.

                Neither salary nor related factors **influence** his decisions.

Note: If the singular part of the compound subject is nearest the verb, the sentence will sound awkward. Revise to place the plural nearest the verb.

4 Most indefinite pronouns have a singular sense and take a singular verb.

The following indefinite pronouns always have a singular sense:

another	more
any	much
anybody	neither
anyone	nobody
anything	none, no one
each one	other
either	one
every	somebody
everybody	someone
everyone	something
everything	

Everyone **sings** beautifully in the shower.

Nothing **is** worse than having to listen to a "shower soprano."

The indefinite pronouns *both, ones,* and *others* have a plural sense and take a plural verb.

My mother and my sister are shower sopranos; both **are** impatiently waiting to be "discovered."

The indefinite pronouns *all, any, more, many, enough, none, some, few,* and *most* have a singular or plural sense, depending on the meaning of a sentence.

Substituting a personal pronoun or looking at the context of a sentence can provide clues about the number of its subject:

SINGULAR   I too am impatient; most of this singing **drives** me crazy.

PLURAL   Among shower sopranos, some **are** more accomplished than others.

5 **Collective nouns have a plural or a singular sense, depending on the meaning of a sentence.**

The context of the sentence will help you determine whether a collective noun refers to a single unit or individual parts of that unit:

SINGULAR   A team of researchers **has been studying** Lyme disease.

PLURAL   The team **disagree** among themselves on how to deal with the ticks that cause the disease.

6 Nouns plural in form but singular in sense take singular verbs.

Although nouns such as *athletics, economics, mathematics, news, physics,* and *politics* are plural in form, they are singular in meaning.

> News of Lyme disease **is spreading** almost as fast as the disease itself.

7 A linking verb agrees in number with its subject, not with the subject complement.

When the complement of a linking verb is different in number from the subject, the verb agrees with the subject.

SINGULAR   The cause of Lyme disease **is** tiny insects called ticks.

PLURAL   Tiny insects called ticks **are** the cause of Lyme disease.

8 In sentences with inverted word order, a verb should agree in number with its subject.

Typical subject-verb word order is reversed when expletives *it* and *there* are used, as well as in questions. Find the subject in order to determine the number of the verb.

SINGULAR   There **is** a cure for Lyme disease.

What **is** the cure for Lyme disease?

PLURAL   There **are** antibiotics available to treat people bitten by Lyme ticks.

Are antibiotics effective against Lyme disease?

9 The verb of a dependent clause introduced by the pronoun *which, that, who,* or *whom* should agree in number with the pronoun's antecedent.

The number of both the pronoun subject and the verb in a dependent clause is determined by the antecedent in the main clause.

SINGULAR   The offending tick can be found on an animal that **wanders** through infested areas.

PLURAL   The offending tick can be found on animals that **wander** through infested areas.

10 **Phrases and clauses that function as subjects are treated as singular and take singular verbs.**

No matter how long the phrase or clause, nor its content, a noun clause or a gerund (or infinitive) phrase always takes a singular verb.

> <u>Wearing long sleeves and pants tucked into socks</u> **protects** people against tick bites.

> <u>That they must wrap themselves up like mummies even on hot days</u> **annoys** people who live in tick-infested areas.

11 **Titled works, key words used as terms, and companies are treated as singular in number and take singular verbs.**

When the group of words has a singular sense, the verb is singular.

> <u>"Protecting Yourself Against Lyme Disease"</u> **is** a pamphlet put out by one Connecticut town.

> <u>Preventive medicine</u> **is** the best protection, the pamphlet states.

PRONOUN-ANTECEDENT AGREEMENT

An **antecedent** is a word—usually a noun, sometimes a pronoun—that is renamed by a pronoun. An antecedent must be clearly identified, and the pronoun and antecedent must agree in *number, person,* and *gender. Gender* can be masculine (*he*), feminine (*she*), or neuter (*it*). In the following sentence the pronoun agrees with its antecedent in number (singular), person (third), and gender (feminine).

> <u>Alice Walker</u> says that **she** was influenced by Zora Neale Hurston's *Their Eyes Were Watching God.*

10b Pronouns and their antecedents should agree in number.

Since the number of a noun is not always clear, number agreement between pronoun and antecedent can pose problems. Use the following conventions to determine the number of an antecedent.

 1 **A compound antecedent linked by the conjunction *and* is usually plural.**

PLURAL   <u>Hurston *and* Walker are both novelists</u>. **They** tell tales of African American women.

SINGULAR   Walker is well known. <u>The novelist, essayist, and poet</u> **has become** one of the most respected writers in the United States.

The exception is the compound antecedent that has a singular sense.

2 **When parts of a compound antecedent are linked by the conjunction *or* or *nor*, a pronoun should agree in number with the nearer part of the antecedent.**

SINGULAR   Neither the other African American writers nor <u>Hurston</u> was read widely in <u>her</u> day.

PLURAL   Neither Hurston nor other African American <u>writers</u> were read widely in **their** day.

Note: If the singular part of the compound antecedent is nearest the verb, the sentence will sound awkward. Revise to place the plural nearest the pronoun, as in the second example.

3 **Make pronouns agree in number with indefinite pronoun antecedents.**

Indefinite pronouns such as *each, anyone,* and *everyone* usually have a singular sense.

<u>Each</u> of Walker's books tells a story in **its** own way.

Indefinite pronouns such as *both* or *others* have a plural sense.

<u>Both</u> of the novelists use colloquial language in **their** work.

Indefinite pronouns such as *some, more,* or *most* can have a singular or plural sense, depending on the context of the sentence.

SINGULAR   <u>Some</u> of Walker's novels are difficult because of **their** language.

PLURAL   <u>Some</u> of Walker's work is difficult because of **its** language.

4 **Make pronouns agree in number with collective noun antecedents.**

Collective nouns such as *audience, band, group,* or *team* will be singular or plural depending on the meaning of the sentence.

SINGULAR   Hurston's <u>audience</u> recognizes **its** social responsibility.

PLURAL   Walker's <u>audience</u> disagree on **their** reactions to the movie version of *The Color Purple.*

10c | Rename indefinite antecedents with gender-appropriate pronouns.

In the past it was acceptable to use the **generic *he* or *his*** to rename an indefinite antecedent that signified both males and females.

A novelist learns **his** craft by writing novels.

Many people would be offended by this sentence's implicit exclusion of female novelists. To avoid giving such offense, apply the guidelines shown in the Critical Decision Units that follow.

CRITICAL DECISIONS

SET ISSUES IN A BROADER CONTEXT: UNDERSTAND THE GENDER MESSAGES IMPLIED BY YOUR PRONOUNS

Gender-specific pronoun use can be inaccurate and offensive. Be aware, when choosing a pronoun, of the larger social setting in which you work. To avoid unintentional sexism, use five techniques, either alone or in combination. For more discussion on gender reference, see 21g.

1. **Use the constructions *he or she, his or her,* and *him or her* in referring to an indefinite pronoun or noun.** Choose this option when the antecedent of a pronoun must have a singular sense. Realize, however, that some readers object to the *he or she* device as cumbersome. The variants *(s)he* and *he/she* are considered equally cumbersome. The *he or she* device can work, provided it is not overused in any one sentence or paragraph.

AWKWARD	To some extent, *a biologist* must decide for <u>him or herself</u> which system of classification <u>he or she</u> will use.
REVISED	To some extent, *a biologist* must decide which system of classification *he or she* will use.
REVISED	To some extent, *a biologist* must decide on which system of classification to use. [The infinitive *to use* avoids the *he or she* difficulty.]

2. **Make a pronoun's antecedent plural.** If the accuracy of a sentence will permit a plural antecedent, use this device to avoid unintentional sexism in pronoun selection.

PLURAL To some extent, *biologists* must decide for <u>themselves</u> which system of classification *they* will use. [Note the possible shift in meaning: *biologists* may imply a group discussion.]

3. **Use the passive voice to avoid gender-specific pronouns—but only if it is appropriate to de-emphasize a subject.** Note, however, that using the passive voice creates its own problems of vague reference. (See 9g-2 and 17b-1.)

NEUTRAL It is every biologist's responsibility to specify which system of classification *is being used.*

4. **Reconstruct the entire statement so as to avoid the problem.** Often it is easier to rewrite sentences to avoid pronouns altogether.

NEUTRAL When choosing among competing systems of classification, the biologist makes a choice that greatly affects later work both in the field and in the lab. [*Later work* is left without a limiting, gender-specific modifier.]

BE ALERT TO DIFFERENCES: APPLY A TEST FOR CHOOSING COMPARATIVE FORMS—FEW/FEWER/FEWEST, LITTLE/LESS/LEAST, MANY, MUCH

When making comparisons, note the differences between elements that can be counted and those that cannot. (See 7a-2 and 42a-1.) Then choose the appropriate form for your comparison.

- For nouns that can be counted, downward comparisons must be made with *few, fewer,* or *fewest:*

FAULTY Frozen yogurt has *less* calories than ice cream. [Since *calories* can be counted, *less* is the wrong comparative term.]

REVISED Frozen yogurt has *fewer* calories than ice cream.

- For mass nouns, which cannot be counted (see 7a-2), downward comparisons must be made with *little, less,* or *least:*

FAULTY "Drinker's Delight" coffee has *fewer* caffeine than regular coffee. [Since caffeine is a mass noun and cannot be counted, *fewer* is the wrong comparative term.]

REVISED "Drinker's Delight" coffee has *less* caffeine than regular coffee.

- For nouns that can be counted, use the adjective *many,* not *much:*

FAULTY   Ice cream has *much* calories. [Since *calories* can be counted, *much* is the incorrect adjective form.]

REVISED   Ice cream has *many* calories.

Name _____ Section _____ Date _____

EXERCISE 10-1   Subject-verb agreement

In the following sentences, determine whether the subject is singular or plural, and circle the appropriate verb.

EXAMPLE   Heroes (embody/embodies) qualities valued in a given culture.

1. Everybody (has/have) a hero.
2. In some cultures, courage and bravery in battle (constitute/constitutes) heroic qualities.
3. Young people, whether they live in the United States or Europe, often (glorify/glorifies) rock performers.
4. The singer and performer (act/acts) as a role model for youth.
5. In religious communities, the person who is able to overcome persecution at the hands of nonbelievers (is/are) often considered heroes.
6. The saint, along with other types of heroes, (become/becomes) the subject of legends.
7. Heroes are not always remembered throughout the ages; some (is/are) forgotten all too soon.
8. Every generation (has/have) heroes to admire.
9. Often members of the same generation (disagree/disagrees) about who is a hero.
10. The person who values action and adventure (admire/admires) one hero, while people who value contemplation and serenity (admire/admires) another.
11. Athletics (is/are) an area that (produce/produces) many heroes.
12. There (is/are) many reasons to admire a great athlete.
13. Training the body to perform strenuous feats (is/are) considered admirable.
14. *The Hero With a Thousand Faces* (is/are) Joseph Campbell's analysis of heroes in mythology.
15. No single hero or god (satisfy/satisfies) everyone's requirements.
16. Some, however (has/have) come close.
17. Their ability to help humans feel the presence of the divine (make/makes) Buddha, Jesus, and Mohammed heroes that have endured through the ages.
18. The cause of hero worship (is/are) people themselves.
19. Yes, people (is/are) the cause of hero worship.
20. To worship heroes (is/are) to be human.

EXERCISE 10-2   Pronoun-antecedent agreement: collective nouns

In the following sentences, determine whether the collective noun has a singular or a plural meaning, and circle the appropriate verb.

EXAMPLE   The team was about to lose (its, their) fourth game in a row.

1. After the loss, the team bickered among (itself, themselves).
2. The crowd booed heartily, expressing (its, their) disapproval.
3. A Brownie troop could have forged (its, their) way around the field more effectively than this team.
4. The press corps shook (its, their) heads in disbelief.
5. A couple who had both bet against the team happily collected (its, their) winnings.

EXERCISE 10-3   Using gender-appropriate pronouns

In the following sentences, replace gender-specific pronouns by using any of the five conventions listed in the chapter. Remember to change other elements in the sentence as needed.

> *he or she*
> EXAMPLE   When ~~he~~ enters an urban office building, the average person is drawn into a bustling world of activity. (Or: "When *entering. . . .*")

1. A receptionist is busy tending to her telephone while a security guard walks his lobby beat.

2. Once in the heart of the building, the visitor sees a businessman making his deals and a secretary typing her letters.

3. The world of business keeps a person constantly on his guard.

4. Often an attorney is involved with business deals, offering his best legal advice.

5. When the papers are signed, it's time for the file clerk to do her job and file the documents.

EXERCISE 10-4   Review

On a separate sheet of paper, revise the following paragraph by correcting errors in subject-verb and pronoun-antecedent agreement. Eliminate any inappropriate gender references as well.

In the past twenty years, consumers have become more and more aware of the environment. After World War II this society became not only a consumer society but they became a disposable society as well. A person used paper plates and plastic flatware when eating his dinner, and cleaned up afterward with paper towels. Consumers bought health and beauty aids packaged in layers of plastic and cardboard. Babies wore disposable diapers, and parents wiped his or her bottom with disposable cloths. If an alien had landed anywhere in the United States during the middle part of this century, they would have considered us the most wasteful people on earth. And we probably were. The earth was being polluted. And the cause of the pollution were people. After Earth Day in 1970, however, we began to change all that. Now bottles, cans, and paper is recycled. We check the ingredients on a can to see if it's dangerous to the earth. We fertilize our lawns with organic material rather than chemicals. And we forswear use of disposable items. What is the consequences of our environmental awareness? Many results are heartening, but some results of this new environmentalism is bad. Each of the environmental groups have their own goals, some of them conflicting. In addition, the ordinary citizen, as well as the educated environmentalist, sometimes think that the problem is solved. There is many dangers here, primary among them a tendency toward complacency. This planet, with her magnificent oceans, majestic forests, and solemn deserts, need our full attention now.

CHAPTER 11

Adjectives and Adverbs

Adjectives and adverbs provide clarity and vitality in a sentence. Consider the following sentences:

John Brown addressed the crowd.

With the hangman's rope hovering over his grizzled head, a still passionate John Brown addressed the volatile crowd that had gathered to witness his execution.

In the second sentence, the layers of descriptive words, phrases, and clauses make the sentence come alive. This chapter will cover single-word adjectives and adverbs.

11a Distinguishing between adjectives and adverbs

Adjectives and adverbs differ because of the words they modify and the questions they answer.

Distinguishing Adjectives from Adverbs

An **adjective** modifies a noun and pronoun and answers these questions:
Which: The **latest** news arrived.
What kind: An **insignificant** difference remained.
How many: The **two** sides would resolve their differences.

An **adverb** modifies a verb and answers these questions:
When: **Tomorrow,** the temperature will drop.
How: The temperature will drop **sharply.**
How often: Weather patterns change **frequently.**
Where: The weather patterns **here** change frequently.

An **adverb** also modifies adjectives, adverbs, and entire clauses:
Modifying an adjective: An **especially** large group enrolled.
Modifying an adverb: Courses at this school **almost** never get closed.
Modifying a clause: **Consequently,** the registrar closed the course.

You can determine whether to use an adjective or an adverb by first determining what is to be modified and then using the conventions in this chapter.

1 | Identifying and using adjectives

An **adjective** modifies a noun or pronoun by answering any of several questions: *Which*—the *old* book; *what kind*—the *battered* book; *how many*—*five* books. Single-word adjectives normally appear before the word they modify; compound adjectives or phrase/clause adjectives sometimes follow the word. "Pure" adjectives are not derived from other words: *tall, blue, heavy, great*. Many adjectives, however, are formed by adding suffixes to nouns and verbs.

Basic Word	Suffix	Adjective
energy	-ic	energetic
season	-al	seasonal
respect	-ful	respectful
provoke	-ive	provocative

2 | Identifying and using adverbs

An **adverb** modifies a verb by answering any of several questions: *When*—I read the book *earlier*; *how*—I read the book *quickly*; *where*—I read the book *here*; *how often*—I read the book *once*. Adverbs can modify adjectives: It was an *extremely* long book; they can modify other adverbs: I read the book *only* once; some can also modify entire sentences: *Consequently,* I didn't understand the book. Adverbs can be placed at the beginning, the middle, or the end of a sentence.

"Pure" adverbs are not derived from other words: *always, here, well, now*. Many adverbs, however, are formed by adding the suffix *-ly* to adjectives. (Be careful not to mistake adjectives such as *friendly* for adverbs, however.)

Adjective	Add *-ly*	Adverb
bright		brightly
seasonal		seasonally
large		largely
respectful		respectfully

11b | Use an adverb (not an adjective) to modify verbs as well as verbals.

Since adverbs can appear in various places in a sentence, it's important to determine which word is being modified.

FAULTY	Fifteen years ago people talked of sharks **fearful.**
REVISED	Fifteen years ago people <u>talked</u> of sharks **fearfully.**

| FAULTY | People tended to approach sharks **cautious,** even in aquariums. |
| REVISED | People tended <u>to approach</u> sharks **cautiously,** even in aquariums. |

11c Use an adverb (not an adjective) to modify another adverb or an adjective.

While adjectives such as *real* are used as adverbs in conversation ("real exciting"), standard academic usage calls for adverbs to modify other adverbs and adjectives.

| NONSTANDARD | The movie *Jaws* portrayed shark hysteria **perfect.** |
| REVISED | The movie *Jaws* portrayed shark hysteria **perfectly.** |

11d Use an adjective (not an adverb) after a linking verb to describe a subject.

Linking verbs include *be* in all its forms, as well as the following verbs: *appear, become, feel, grow, look, remain, seem, smell, sound, stay,* and *taste*. The word that completes the subject-linking verb construction, since it refers to a noun or pronoun, must be a noun, a pronoun, or an adjective. However, linking verbs that can also express action (*feel, grow, look, smell, taste*) are modified by adverbs.

LINKING	The shark looked **menacing.**
	The sea felt **calm.**
ACTION	The shark looked **menacingly** at the swimmers.
	The swimmer felt **cautiously** for fins in the water.

Good, well, bad, badly

Because they are used interchangeably in conversation, the words *good/well* and *bad/badly* cause problems for writers. Here are the appropriate uses of these words.

1 Good and well

Good is an **adjective.**

> The swimmer looked **good** to the hungry shark.
>
> She was a **good** swimmer and got away.

Well can be either an **adverb** or, when referring to health, an **adjective.**

> The shark swims **well.**
>
> She didn't feel **well** after she escaped the shark.

2   Bad and badly

Bad is an **adjective.**

Did the shark feel **bad** about missing dinner?

Badly is an **adverb.**

The coast guard handled the situation **badly.**

11e   Using comparative and superlative forms of adjectives and adverbs

The basic form for adjectives and adverbs is called the **positive** form. When using adjectives and adverbs to compare things, the **comparative** form is used for two elements and the **superlative** for three or more. Short adjectives and adverbs show comparison by adding the suffixes *-er* and *-est*; longer words use *more* and *most*. Negative comparisons are shown with the words *less* and *least*.

	Positive	*Comparative*	*Superlative*
Adjectives	clear	clearer/less clear	clearest/least clear
	happy	happier/less happy	happiest/least happy
	wonderful	more/less wonderful	most/least wonderful
Adverbs	soon	sooner	soonest
	quickly	more/less quickly	most/least quickly
	courteously	more/less courteously	most/least courteously

1   Use irregular adjectives and adverbs with care.

It's best to memorize adjectives and adverbs that form comparatives and superlatives with internal changes.

Irregular Forms of Comparison

	Positive	*Comparative*	*Superlative*
Adjective	good	better	best
	bad	worse	worst
	little	less	least
	many	more	most
	much	more	most
	some	more	most

Adverb	well (also adj.)	better	best
	badly	worse	worst

Note: Comparisons among nouns that can be **counted** are made with the adjectives *many/more/most* and *few/fewer/fewest*; nouns that cannot be counted (**mass**) use *much* (or *some*) *more/most* and *little/less/least*.

COUNT NOUN	Coves have **fewer** shark <u>attacks</u> than open seas.
	Many <u>articles</u> have been written about sharks.

MASS NOUN	Coves have **less** shark <u>activity</u> than open seas.
	Much <u>attention</u> has been paid to sharks.

2 **Express comparative and superlative relationships accurately, completely, and logically.**

Accuracy

Comparative form is for two items, superlative for three or more.

TWO ITEMS	People are **more** dangerous than sharks.
MULTIPLES	Of all creatures on earth, people are the **most** dangerous.

Completeness

Each element in a comparison must be mentioned, either explicitly or implicitly.

INCOMPLETE	People are more dangerous. [than what?]
REVISED	People are more dangerous <u>than sharks</u>.
	People are the most dangerous <u>creatures</u>.

Logic

Adjectives that have an absolute meaning (*absolute, dead, final, first, infinite, last, perfect, unique*) cannot logically be compared. Comparisons must be made with qualifying words such as *almost* or *nearly*.

ILLOGICAL   Sharks are **more perfect** feeders than any other animal.

REVISED   Sharks are **more nearly perfect** feeders than any other animal.

11f Avoid double comparisons, double superlatives, and double negatives.

Double comparisons/superlatives

With comparatives and superlatives that are formed by adding *-er* or *-est*, do not use the words *more, most, less,* or *least*.

FAULTY   Researchers at several universities are working on the **most tiniest** machines ever built.

REVISED   Researchers at several universities are working on the **tiniest** machines ever built.

Double negatives

Although fairly common in nonstandard usage, double negatives are unacceptable in standard academic English. Combine the negatives *not, never, neither/nor, hardly,* or *scarcely* with *any, anything,* or *anyone*. Do not combine them with *no, none, nothing,* or *no one*.

FAULTY   Twenty years ago researchers had hardly **none** of the technology necessary to develop these micromachines.

REVISED   Twenty years ago researchers had hardly **any** of the technology necessary to develop these micromachines.

11g Avoid overusing nouns as modifiers.

Many nouns can function as adjectives modifying other nouns (*birthday* party, *school* book, *tree* house, *copy* machine). Using too many noun modifiers for the same noun can result in a confusing sentence. Noun modifiers should be varied with other forms of modifiers, such as possessives or phrases.

UNCLEAR   **University research laboratory micromachine** technology is relatively new.

REVISED   Micromachine technology conducted in research laboratories of universities is relatively new.

EXERCISE 11-1   Recognizing adjectives and adverbs

Make a photocopy of a brief passage from one of your textbooks. Circle the adjectives and adverbs and draw arrows to the words they modify. Explain how the adjectives enhance meaning.

EXERCISE 11-2   Using adjectives and adverbs

Add adjectives and adverbs to the sentences below to make them clearer and more lively. (Remember that adjectives and adverbs can be phrases and clauses as well as single words.)

EXAMPLE   Martin needed a change.

Weary Martin *desperately* needed a *significant* change.

1. Martin planted a garden.

2. The plants grew.

3. Martin took a vacation.

4. Sherry looked after the garden.

5. Everything in the garden died.

EXERCISE 11-3   Distinguishing between adjectives and adverbs

In the following sentences, determine whether the modifier should be an adjective or an adverb. Then choose the appropriate modifier from the pairs of words in parentheses. (The first word in each pair is an adjective, the second an adverb.)

EXAMPLE   Micromachine technology is progressing quite (quick, (quickly)).

1. This kind of research had been conducted (previous, previously) in electronics laboratories.

2. The speed of developments from electronics to mechanics has been (startling, startlingly).

3. Micromachines will (sure, surely) be useful in medicine.

4. Researchers in the field are looking (excited, excitedly) to the future.

5. Researchers in the field are looking (excited, excitedly) about the future.

EXERCISE 11-4   Using *good/well* and *bad/badly*

In the following sentences, fill in the blank with *good* or *well*, *bad* or *badly*. Then draw an arrow from the word chosen to the word modified.

EXAMPLE   After the accident, Eleanor looked __bad__ .

1. The fact that she drives _____ kept the accident from being more serious.

2. She certainly is a _____ driver.

3. Also, if she didn't smell so _____ , she'd never have noticed the leaking gasoline.

4. She said that in the hospital everything tasted _____ .

5. Regardless, after a few days she'll feel _____ again.

EXERCISE 11-5   **Comparative and superlative forms**

In the following sentences, correct any errors in comparative and superlative forms.

EXAMPLE   Of the New York City Ballet and the Bolshoi, some consider the
                        better
            Bolshoi to be the ~~best~~.

1. The New York company was directed for years by George Balanchine, believed to be the better choreographer.
2. When Balanchine died in 1983, he was succeeded by one of the most youngest directors ever to head a famous company.
3. Peter Martins scarcely had no trouble filling Balanchine's shoes.
4. Under his direction, the New York City Ballet has become the most fine company in the world.
5. Martins is now in the most perfect position: talented, respected, and young.

EXERCISE 11-6   Review

In the following paragraph, correct any errors in the use of adjectives and adverbs.

The term "third world" refers to those countries which don't belong neither to

the first, or western capitalist world nor the second, or eastern communist world. In

terms of standard of living, the first world is considered the better. Both the first and

the second worlds, however, haven't had no trouble maintaining the most minimum

standard of living for their populations. In the third world such is not the case. The

citizens of third world countries are the most poorly on earth, even if some of them are

governed by the most wealthiest individuals. Some theories blame third-world

poverty on the industrial nations, while others cite factors within the third-world

countries themselves. It is true that industrial nations don't seem to feel too badly

when faced with the real deplorable conditions of life in much of the world's most

poor countries. However, the multitude of internal problems—from overpopulation to

underdevelopment—within third-world countries themselves also plays a role in their

poverty. Washington think tank third-world research economists tend to favor the

latter theories. Regardless of which is the valider theory, the difficultest economic

problems facing the world today have their roots in the divisions between the third

world and the rest of the world.

CHAPTER 12

Sentence Fragments

A **sentence fragment** is a partial sentence punctuated as if it were a complete sentence. Sentence fragments are grammatically incorrect because they lack either a subject or a predicate, both of which are necessary for a complete sentence. But even more important for your writing, sentence fragments relate incomplete ideas, causing confusion for your readers.

 12a Check for completeness of sentences.

The following three tests will help you determine that your sentences are grammatically complete:

1. Locate a verb.

2. Locate the verb's subject.

3. Be certain that a subject and verb are not preceded by a subordinating conjunction.

First test: Locate a verb.

Neither participles (verb forms with *-ing* or *-ed*, *-en* endings) nor infinitives (basic verb forms with *to*) alone can function as the main verb in a sentence. The underlined words in the following sentences are fragments.

FRAGMENT   The camera focused on the star. <u>Singing the national anthem</u>.

<u>A seasoned veteran of the Metropolitan Opera</u>. She moved the crowd to tears.

It was a thrill. <u>To be in the presence of such greatness</u>.

REVISED   The camera focused on the star singing the national anthem.

A seasoned veteran of the Metropolitan Opera, she moved the crowd to tears.

It was a thrill to be in the presence of such greatness.

Second test: Locate the verb's subject.

Once you have located a verb, ask *who* or *what* makes its assertion or action and you will find the subject.

FRAGMENT   Everyone reacted as I did. <u>Cheered until our voices were hoarse.</u>

REVISED   Everyone reacted as I did. We cheered until our voices were hoarse.

Note that imperative sentences such as "Sing another song!" are complete because the implied subject is *you*.

Third test: Check for subordinating conjunctions or relative pronouns.

Subordinate clauses beginning with subordinating conjunctions or relative pronouns are not complete sentences.

FRAGMENT   Nobody paid any attention to the game. <u>Because we were so impressed with the singer.</u>

    The fans were a real disappointment to the team. <u>Who went on to a 16-0 defeat.</u>

REVISED   Nobody paid any attention to the game because we were so impressed with the singer.

    The fans were a real disappointment to the team, who went on to a 16-0 defeat.

Subordinating conjunctions are *after, although, as if, because, before, if, once, since, until, while,* and *how.* Relative pronouns are *that, which, whichever, who, whoever, whom,* and *whomever.*

Note that a relative pronoun can introduce a complete sentence if that sentence is a question, such as "Who can remember anything about the game?"

12b Eliminate fragments: Revise dependent clauses set off as sentences.

Subordinate clauses set off as sentences can be revised by converting the clause to an independent clause or by joining the clause to a new sentence.

1 **Convert the dependent clause to an independent clause.**

Deleting the subordinating conjunction, or substituting a noun or pronoun for a relative pronoun, results in a complete sentence.

FRAGMENT   After Vladimir Ilyich Lenin's brother was executed for an attempt on the life of the czar.

Lenin, who was arrested himself in 1897.

REVISED   ~~After~~ Vladimir Ilyich Lenin's brother was executed for an attempt on the life of the czar.

Lenin, ~~who~~ was arrested himself in 1897.

~~Lenin, who~~ He was arrested himself in 1897.

2 **Join the dependent clause to a new sentence.**

A fragment resulting from setting off a relative clause as a sentence can be revised by attaching the relative clause to an independent clause.

FRAGMENT   The city of St. Petersburg was renamed to honor Lenin. Who was a hero of the Bolshevik revolution.

REVISED   The city of St. Petersburg was renamed to honor Lenin, who was a hero of the Bolshevik revolution.

Eliminating Fragments from Your Writing

1. **Revise subordinate clauses set off as sentences.**

Convert a subordinate clause to an independent clause.

FRAGMENT   Because animal rights activists launched a campaign.

REVISED   ~~Because~~ Animal rights activists launched a campaign.

Join a dependent clause to a new sentence.

FRAGMENT   Because animal rights activists launched a campaign. Many major cosmetics manufacturers have abandoned animal testing.

REVISED   Because animal rights activists launched a campaign,
               many major cosmetics manufacturers have abandoned
               animal testing.

2. Revise phrases set off as sentences.

No phrase—verbal, prepositional, absolute, or appositive—can
stand alone as a sentence.

FRAGMENT   After the campaigns against cosmetics companies.
            Activists turned their attention elsewhere.

REVISED   After the campaigns against cosmetics companies,
            activists turned their attention elsewhere.

3. Revise repeating structures or compound predicates set off as sentences.

Incorporate repeating elements and compound structures into
existing sentences.

FRAGMENT   Animal rights has become a political cause. A popular
            cause.

REVISED   Animal rights has become a political cause—a popular
            cause.

FRAGMENT   Campaigns are attracting more supporters. And funds.

REVISED   Campaigns are attracting more supporters and funds.

12c   Eliminate fragments: Revise phrases set off as sentences.

Phrases set off as sentences can be revised by adding words to convert the
phrase into a complete sentence or by joining the phrase to a new sentence.

1   Revising verbal phrases

Participial and gerund phrases (functioning as modifiers or nouns)

FRAGMENT   Making 160 times what the average blue-collar worker makes.

REVISED   Chief Executive Officers of large corporations ~~making~~ make 160 times what the average blue-collar worker makes.

REVISED   Chief Executive Officers of large corporations are well compensated, making 160 times what the average blue-collar worker makes.

REVISED   Making 160 times what the average blue-collar worker makes is one of the perks of being a Chief Executive Officer of a large corporation.

Infinitive phrases (functioning as nouns)

FRAGMENT   To justify their raises while workers are being laid off.

REVISED   CEOs are finding it difficult to justify their raises while workers are being laid off.

2 Revising prepositional phrases (functioning as modifiers)

FRAGMENT   In a recession period.

REVISED   In a recession period, more and more shareholders are demanding that CEOs take pay cuts.

3 Revising absolute phrases (modifying an entire sentence)

FRAGMENT   Their salaries subjected to intense scrutiny.

REVISED   Their salaries subjected to intense scrutiny, CEOs are becoming nervous.

REVISED   Their salaries have been subjected to intense scrutiny.

4 Revising appositive phrases (renaming or describing other nouns)

FRAGMENT   A tactic that may not work in hard economic times.

REVISED   CEOs have resorted to "stonewalling," a tactic that may not work in hard economic times.

REVISED   "Stonewalling" is a tactic that may not work in hard economic times.

12d Eliminate fragments: Revise repeating structures or compound predicates set off as sentences.

Join repeating elements and compound predicates to existing sentences.

Repeating elements

FRAGMENT	College presidents find themselves in a different situation. An unpleasant one.
REVISED	College presidents find themselves in a different situation, an unpleasant one.
FRAGMENT	Their salaries are less than those of corporate CEOs. About 75% less.
REVISED	Their salaries are less than those of corporate CEOs—about 75% less.

Compound predicates

FRAGMENT	Shrinking budgets mean that college presidents must often cut salaries. Or eliminate programs.
REVISED	Shrinking budgets mean that college presidents must often cut salaries or eliminate programs.
REVISED	Shrinking budgets mean that college presidents must often cut salaries. Or they must eliminate programs.

12e Use fragments intentionally on rare occasions.

Occasionally fragments are used for effect in fiction and expressive writing; in academic prose intentional fragments are even more rare. Writers should understand that unless the intentional fragment is effective, it will be considered an error by most readers.

EFFECTIVE FRAGMENT	As Althea walked slowly toward the door, she realized that she was in for the fight of her life. As the moment approached she became more and more frightened. Terrified, in fact.
INEFFECTIVE FRAGMENT	It is common for people facing unpleasant confrontations to experience anxiety. And sometimes real fear.

EXERCISE 12-1   Identifying fragments

Using the three-part test, identify and explain the fragments in the sentences below. Circle the number of any complete sentences.

EXAMPLE   Beginning in Anaheim, California in 1955.   <u>frag—no verb</u>

1. Hailed as the prototype amusement park of the twentieth century.   _____

2. Because Disneyland California had been so wildly successful.   _____

3. With the 1971 opening of Walt Disney World in Orlando, Florida.   _____

4. And soon became one of the most popular tourist attractions in the country.   _____

5. But Disney Enterprises wasn't content with the success of Disneyland and Disney World.   _____

6. A new park that provided a glimpse of the future.   _____

7. A place called Experimental Prototype Community of Tomorrow, or EPCOT.   _____

8. Followed by the 1983 opening of Tokyo Disneyland.   _____

9. Despite protests by French citizens concerned about the effect of the new Euro Disneyland outside Paris.   _____

10. However, Euro Disneyland has been tremendously successful.   _____

EXERCISE 12-2   **Correcting fragments**

The paragraph below contains five fragments formed by setting off subordinate clauses as complete sentences. Correct each of the fragments by joining the subordinate clauses to independent clauses.

EXAMPLE   Sociologists study how humans behave. When they are in groups.

Sociologists study how humans behave when they are in groups.

Social communities have been recognized among humans for thousands of years. But it is only within the last century. That humans have become aware of social communities among other animals. After studying primates, and monkeys in particular. Researchers have concluded that these creatures have relatively sophisticated methods of communication, employing different sounds to signal different meanings. Because calls warning of danger are recognizably different from calls indicating the approach of another monkey. Researchers believe that their "language" is based on survival skills. There is also a hierarchy among members of monkey groups, especially among vervet monkeys. Vervets identify themselves according to family, community, and social rank, and their behavior is governed by some concept of social relationships. In this way vervets are very much like humans. Who also define themselves in terms of their relationships to others. Although vervets do not have the intellectual capacity of humans. Their communities often run far more smoothly than do their human counterparts.

EXERCISE 12-3   Identifying and correcting fragments

In the pairs of sentences below, identify each fragment by naming the type of phrase it represents and correct the fragments by joining phrases to independent clauses. Circle the number of any sentence that is correct.

EXAMPLE   <u>To collect great art.</u> One must have a good

deal of money.   ___infinitive___

<u>To collect great art,</u> one must have a good deal of money.

1. Walter H. Annenberg is a great art collector. Having
   spent a considerable fortune on works by the world's
   most renowned painters.   _____
2. The son of an immigrant who ended up in jail for tax
   evasion. Annenberg overcame many obstacles in his
   own rise to success.   _____
3. Throughout his life Annenberg has been known for his
   philanthropy. Particularly making substantial
   donations to many art museums.   _____
4. One of Annenberg's prize possessions is his impressionist
   collection. One of the finest collections in the world.   _____
5. This collection, as well as Annenberg's
   post-impressionist collection, will go to New York's
   Metropolitan Museum of Art. After his death.   _____
6. In 1991. The Annenberg collection toured the country.   _____
7. Among the collection's stops were museums in New
   York, Philadelphia, Los Angeles, and Washington, D.C.   _____
8. Museums hosting the tour have been rewarded with
   increased attendance. Providing them with
   much-needed additional funds.   _____
9. The collection includes paintings by Renoir, Gauguin,
   and Monet. Three of the most highly respected
   impressionists of their day.   _____
10. The Metropolitan Museum is fortunate indeed. To
    know that the collection will one day hang on its walls.   _____

EXERCISE 12-4   Identifying and correcting fragments

In the pairs of sentences below, identify the fragments formed by repeating elements and compound predicates and join them to the independent clauses. Circle the number of any sentence that is correct.

EXAMPLE   The international community is becoming more aware of how nations deal with crime and punishment. Especially punishment.

The international community is becoming more aware of how nations deal with crime and punishment—especially punishment.

1. The United States is one of a decreasing number of prominent nations to use capital punishment. Otherwise known as the death penalty.
2. In extradition cases, the United States currently faces a problem. A serious problem.
3. Countries that have outlawed capital punishment question the U.S. policy. And sometimes refuse to extradite suspects facing the death penalty here.
4. Countries that still use capital punishment include China, South Africa, and Cuba. And, of course, the United States.
5. The extradition problem is extremely sensitive. So sensitive that leaders are often reluctant to discuss it.

EXERCISE 12-5   Review

In the following paragraph, correct fragments either by creating independent clauses or by joining the fragments to independent clauses. Underline any fragment that seems particularly effective.

Martha Graham was one of the most prominent names in dance in the twentieth century. Rejecting traditional ballet. Graham brought dancers to the floor first. There they contracted their bodies. And felt the pull of gravity. In her early Vaudeville days she played more than one fighting woman. This image recurred throughout her career. Which spanned six decades. Graham's style was known for its intensity and fierceness as well as for its beauty. Although she rejected tradition. She eventually began a tradition of her own. It is a considerable understatement. To say that Graham influenced virtually every choreographer in modern dance. However, her influence extended beyond dance itself to theater and film. Among her students were many well known figures. Great actresses such as Bette Davis. Davis considered Graham a genius. Who had revolutionized the world of dance and movement. Graham was ninety-six years old when she died, but her legacy will live on. Forever.

EXERCISE 12-6   Revising

Look through your graded papers to find instructor's comments regarding fragments. Reread the papers, identifying the fragments as you read by using the three-part test. Then identify the cause of the fragment and correct it. (If you don't have any graded papers handy, look through any body of writing you've done recently.)

CHAPTER 13

Comma Splices and Fused Sentences

If readers are to understand your prose, they must be able to recognize appropriate boundaries between your sentences. Independent clauses, or sentences, must be separated by a period, a semicolon, a colon, or a conjunction with appropriate punctuation.

Five Ways to Mark the Boundary between Sentences

Mark a sentence boundary with punctuation.

1. Use a period: He laughed. He danced. He sang.

2. Use a semicolon: He laughed; he danced; he sang.

Mark a sentence boundary with a conjunction and punctuation.

3. Use a coordinating conjunction: He laughed, and he danced.

4. Use a subordinating conjunction: While he laughed, he danced.

5. Use a conjunctive adverb: He laughed; moreover, he danced.

Sentence boundaries can become blurred in two ways:

In the **fused** (or **run-on**) **sentence,** the writer fails to recognize the end of one independent clause and the beginning of the next. In a **comma splice,** the writer recognizes the boundary between the end of one independent clause and the beginning of the next but marks the boundary between the two incorrectly—with a comma.

FUSED SENTENCE The blurring of sentence boundaries can create a comprehension problem readers must often stop to decipher which combinations of words form meaningful units.

COMMA SPLICE   The blurring of sentence boundaries can create a comprehension problem, readers must often stop to decipher which combinations of words form meaningful units.

13a   Identify fused sentences and comma splices.

Before submitting a draft of your work for a fellow student's or a professor's review, read your sentences aloud. Sometimes the ear can pick up errors that the eyes can't. Be aware of sentences with more than one thought, or sentences that can't be read without taking a breath in the middle. Fused sentences and comma splices tend to occur in three circumstances:

1. **A sentence of explanation, expansion, or example** is frequently spliced together with another sentence that is being explained, expanded upon, or illustrated. Regardless of how close the topics are, the two sentences must remain distinct.

FUSED SENTENCE   In 1988 a presidential election took place in the United States France also elected a president that year.

COMMA SPLICE   In 1988 a presidential election took place in the United States, France also elected a president that year.

REVISED   In 1988 a presidential election took place in the <u>United States. France</u> also elected a president that year.

2. **The pronouns** *he, she, they, it, this,* and *that,* when renaming the subject of a sentence, can signal a comma splice or a fused sentence. Regardless of whether or not the subjects are identical, the two sentences must remain distinct.

FUSED SENTENCE   In the United States, President Ronald Reagan was not running he had already served two terms.

COMMA SPLICE   In the United States, President Ronald Reagan was not running, he had already served two terms.

REVISED   In the United States, President Ronald Reagan was not <u>running, because</u> he had already served two terms.

3. **Conjunctive adverbs** (such as *therefore* and *consequently*) **and transitional expressions** (such as *for example* and *on the other hand*) are commonly found in fused or spliced clauses. Because conjunctive adverbs and transitions always link complete sentences, they must be paired with a period or a semicolon (not a comma).

FUSED SENTENCE   In France, President François Mitterand had only been in office for one term therefore he was eligible to run.

COMMA SPLICE   In France, President François Mitterand had only been in office for one term, therefore he was eligible to run.

REVISED   In France, President François Mitterand had only been in office for one <u>term; therefore</u> he was eligible to run.

13b Correct fused sentences and comma splices in one of five ways.

1 Separate independent clauses with a period (and sometimes a colon).

A period is the most obvious way to separate sentences, especially if they're not closely related. When the first sentence emphatically introduces an explanation, example, or appositive in the second sentence, use a colon to separate the two.

FUSED SENTENCE   The choice in France was clear either endorse the Socialists or make a move to the right.

COMMA SPLICE   The choice in France was clear, either endorse the Socialists or make a move to the right.

REVISED   The choice in France was <u>clear. Either</u> endorse the Socialists or make a move to the right.

REVISED   The choice in France was <u>clear: Either</u> endorse the Socialists or make a move to the right.

2 Link clauses with a comma and a coordinating conjunction.

Use a comma placed *before* a coordinating conjunction (*and, but, or, nor, for, so,* and *yet*) to link closely related sentences of equal importance. Be careful to choose a coordinating conjunction that indicates clearly the relationship between the two sentences.

FUSED SENTENCE   The right-wing Jacques Chirac was Socialist Mitterand's Prime Minister now the two were running against each other.

COMMA SPLICE   The right-wing Jacques Chirac was Socialist Mitterand's Prime Minister, now the two were running against each other.

REVISED	The right-wing Jacques Chirac was Socialist Mitterand's Prime <u>Minister, but</u> now the two were running against each other.

 3 **Link clauses with a semicolon.**

Use a semicolon instead of a comma and a coordinating conjunction to link closely related sentences of equal importance. A semicolon is appropriate when the relationship between the sentences is clear, or when you want to leave the relationship up to the reader.

FUSED SENTENCE	The choice in the U.S. was between George Bush and Michael Dukakis the Republicans endorsed Bush and the Democrats Dukakis.
COMMA SPLICE	The choice in the U.S. was between George Bush and Michael Dukakis, the Republicans endorsed Bush and the Democrats Dukakis.
REVISED	The choice in the U.S. was between George Bush and Michael <u>Dukakis; the</u> Republicans endorsed Bush and the Democrats Dukakis.

4 **Link clauses with a semicolon (or period) and a conjunctive adverb.**

Use conjunctive adverbs (such as *however, consequently, therefore,* and *moreover*) to link closely related sentences of equal importance. Conjunctive adverbs are similar to coordinating conjunctions, but they're more formal and forceful; moreover they establish different rhythms in the sentences they join.

A period between sentences joined by a conjunctive adverb indicates a full separation of ideas, while a semicolon emphasizes a link between the two sentences. If a conjunctive adverb is placed at the beginning of a sentence, it is usually followed by a comma. If placed in the middle, it is usually set off by a pair of commas. And if placed at the end, it is preceded by a comma. The period or semicolon always precedes the conjunctive adverb.

FUSED SENTENCE	After August Dukakis's popularity steadily dwindled ultimately, he lost by a landslide.
COMMA SPLICE	After August Dukakis's popularity steadily dwindled, ultimately, he lost by a landslide.
REVISED	After August Dukakis's popularity steadily dwindled. Ultimately, he lost by a landslide.

REVISED	After August Dukakis's popularity steadily dwindled; ultimately, he lost by a landslide.
REVISED	After August Dukakis's popularity steadily dwindled. He lost, ultimately, by a landslide.
REVISED	After August Dukakis's popularity steadily dwindled. He lost by a landslide, ultimately.

 5 Link clauses with a subordinating conjunction or construction.

Use a subordinating conjunction or construction to link sentences when one is less important than the other. The subordinating conjunction or relative pronoun makes the clause in which it is used dependent, functioning as a modifier of the main clause. If the dependent clause comes first, follow it with a comma. A comma is not always necessary when the main clause comes first.

FUSED SENTENCE	The left wing remained strong in France Mitterand was re-elected by a landslide.
COMMA SPLICE	The left wing remained strong in France, Mitterand was re-elected by a landslide.
REVISED	<u>Because</u> the left wing remained strong in <u>France, Mitterand</u> was re-elected by a landslide.
REVISED	Mitterand was re-elected by a <u>landslide because</u> the left wing remained strong in France.
REVISED	Mitterand was re-elected by a <u>landslide that</u> indicated the strength of the left wing in France.

Critical Decisions

Challenge and be challenged: Choosing a method to link independent clauses

Sentence boundaries clearly marked with a period help readers to focus on, and understand, one thought at a time. When you want to show the relationship *between* sentences and get readers to consider one thought in light of another, then you should link clauses. You have various options for doing so; which option you choose depends on the relationship you want to establish between independent clauses.

- Do you want one independent clause to announce another? If so, use a colon to make the announcement (see 13b-1).

    SEPARATED   The race was postponed for one reason. The sponsors withdrew their support.

    LINKED   The race was postponed for one reason: the sponsors withdrew their support.

- Do you want to relate but maintain equal emphasis between two independent clauses? If so, use a coordinating conjunction with a comma, a conjunctive adverb with a semicolon or period, or a semicolon to link the clauses (see 13b-2–4 and 19a).

Coordinating conjunction with a comma

    SEPARATED   Runners had already arrived. They were angry with the postponement.

    LINKED   Runners had already arrived, and they were angry with the postponement.

Conjunctive adverb with a semicolon or a period

    SEPARATED   The sponsors cited financial worries. They had political concerns as well.

    LINKED   The sponsors cited financial worries; however, they had political concerns as well.

Semicolon

    SEPARATED   One faction of runners wanted to boycott all future races in that city. Another faction wanted to stage a protest march.

    LINKED   One faction of runners wanted to boycott all future races in that city; another faction wanted to stage a protest march.

- Do you want to link two independent clauses but emphasize one more than the other? If so, use a subordinating conjunction to link the clauses (see 13b-5 and 19b).

SEPARATED   The press was embarrassing. The sponsors canceled the race permanently.

LINKED   Because the press was embarrassing, the sponsors canceled the race permanently.

Conjunctions and Punctuation

Coordinating Conjunctions

and but so or for nor yet

Use coordinating conjunctions with punctuation in this pattern:

Independent clause , CONJUNCTION independent clause

FUSED SENTENCE   Newton developed calculus he discovered laws of gravity.

COMMA SPLICE   Newton developed calculus, he discovered laws of gravity.

REVISED   Newton developed calculus, and he discovered laws of gravity.

Conjunctive Adverbs

moreover however furthermore thus therefore consequently

Use conjunctive adverbs with punctuation in these patterns:

Independent clause ; CONJUNCTION , independent clause
Independent clause . CONJUNCTION , independent clause

REVISED   Newton developed calculus; moreover, he discovered laws of gravity.

REVISED   Newton developed calculus. Moreover, he discovered laws of gravity.

Subordinating Conjunctions

after   although   because   once   since   though   while

Use subordinating conjunctions with punctuation in these patterns:

CONJUNCTION   clause   ,   independent clause
Independent clause   CONJUNCTION   clause

REVISED   After Newton developed calculus, he discovered laws of gravity.

REVISED   Newton discovered laws of gravity after he developed calculus.

EXERCISE 13-1   Identifying comma splices and fused sentences

Identify each of the following sentences as a comma splice (*cs*) or a fused sentence (*f*). Then use a slash (/) to indicate the point at which the sentence should be separated.

EXAMPLE   The medicine chest is an important part of any home, you
don't need to spend a lot of money to keep it well stocked.

The medicine chest is an important part of any home,/ you
don't need to spend a lot of money to keep it well stocked.   *cs*

1. One of the most basic items in the medicine chest isn't
   normally considered a medicine at all it's usually found in the
   kitchen cabinets.   _____

2. Baking soda can be used a number of ways, it can be a
   deodorant, a salve for mosquito bites or poison ivy, a
   toothpaste or mouthwash, or an antacid.   _____

3. Tea can also be used to soothe bites or sunburn it should not
   be used on a serious burn.   _____

4. Another kitchen staple that can do double duty is vinegar,
   mixed with water it can be used to relieve "swimmer's ear."   _____

5. Many of today's adults recall drinking ginger ale to soothe an
   upset stomach, carbonated drinks of any kind still do the
   trick.   _____

6. Among first-aid items that should be in a medicine chest are
   band aids, cotton balls, and tweezers, rubbing alcohol is
   important, too.   _____

7. The well-stocked medicine chest should also have medicines
   aspirin or non-aspirin pain reliever, decongestant, and cough
   syrup are medicine chest staples.   _____

8. The medicine chest is no place for children, precautions
   should be taken in homes with small children.   _____

9. Some people have overstocked medicine chests others don't
   have even the bare necessities.   _____

10. Every home should have basic supplies what's in the
    medicine chest depends on the needs of the family.   _____

EXERCISE 13-2   **Revising comma splices and fused sentences**

Rewrite each of the following sentences from Exercise 13-1 as specified in parentheses.

EXAMPLE   The medicine chest is an important part of any home, you don't need to spend a lot of money to keep it well stocked. (coordinate conjunction)

The medicine chest is an important part of any home, *and* you don't need to spend a lot of money to keep it well stocked.

1. One of the most basic items in the medicine chest isn't normally considered a medicine at all it's usually found in the kitchen cabinets. (semicolon & transitional expression)

2. Baking soda can be used a number of ways, it can be a deodorant, a salve for mosquito bites or poison ivy, a toothpaste or mouthwash, or an antacid. (colon)

3. Tea can also be used to soothe bites or sunburn it should not be used on a serious burn. (period & conjunctive adverb)

4. Another kitchen staple that can do double duty is vinegar, mixed with water it can be used to relieve "swimmer's ear." (colon)

5. Many of today's adults recall drinking ginger ale to soothe an upset stomach, carbonated drinks of any kind still do the trick. (semicolon)

6. Among first-aid items that should be in a medicine chest are band aids, cotton balls, and tweezers, rubbing alcohol is important, too. (period & transitional expression)

7. The well-stocked medicine chest should also have medicines aspirin or non-aspirin pain reliever, decongestant, and cough syrup are medicine chest staples. (semicolon & transitional expression)

8. The medicine chest is no place for children, precautions should be taken in homes with small children. (semicolon & conjunctive adverb)

9. Some people have overstocked medicine chests others don't have even the bare necessities. (comma & subordinate conjunction)

10. Every home should have basic supplies what's in the medicine chest depends on the needs of the family. (comma & subordinate conjunction)

EXERCISE 13-3   **Revising comma splices and fused sentences**

Correct each of the following comma splices and fused sentences in two different ways. Be prepared to discuss the effect of punctuating the sentences differently.

EXAMPLE   Humans have been fascinated by time travel at least since the days of H. G. Wells, Einstein's theories took the notion out of the realm of science fiction.

Humans have been fascinated by time travel at least since the days of H. G. Wells; however, Einstein's theories took the notion out of the realm of science fiction.

Although humans have been fascinated by time travel at least since the days of H. G. Wells, Einstein's theories took the notion out of the realm of science fiction.

1. One of Wells's most famous novels was *The Time Machine* it introduced Victorian society to the fascination of time travel.

2. Einstein declared time to be the fourth dimension, suddenly physicists began to think of traveling in time as they thought of traveling through space.

3. The laws of physics don't include anything to indicate that time travel is impossible the possibility calls into question the foundations of physics.

4. On the one hand, time travel should be theoretically possible, on the other, the implications of time travel upset the laws of physics.

5. In general terms, the implications involve laws of cause and effect how can the effect come before the cause, which is what time travel would allow?

6. More specific questions abound, what would happen if a person traveled back in time and somehow killed her grandmother?

7. A physicist from Princeton University, J. Richard Gott, has constructed a theoretical time machine its journey would involve movement around a pair of "cosmic strings."

8. At the California Institute of Technology a similar machine was designed it would speed through a "wormhole."

9. Laypersons have difficulty understanding the complex theories behind these models they do have access to more fanciful time machines.

10. When they think about traveling through time most people would prefer a more glamorous machine Doc's Delorean in *Back to the Future* fits the bill perfectly.

EXERCISE 13-4   Review

Rewrite the following paragraph on a separate sheet of paper, correcting the comma splices and fused sentences by using different strategies. As you determine which strategies to use, keep in mind the smooth flow of sentences as well as the correctness of the structures.

In some totalitarian countries citizens worry about the governments listening in on their private conversations, monitoring their movements, and generally invading their privacy. Most United States citizens rarely worry about such government intrusion, a very real threat to privacy does exist. That threat comes from business. Certainly the FBI and state or local police organizations collect information on certain citizens the DMI has information on thousands. The DMI, or Direct Marketing Information, sells mailing lists to businesses that use the mails to contact potential customers, many of these businesses can also get information on individuals' buying habits, their family size, their income and savings records, and many other areas that most of us consider quite private. This invasion of privacy is a result primarily of the technology boom the existence of cordless phones, the sophistication of computers, and the emergence of "voice-mail" systems on telephone networks all contribute to the problem. The invasion-of-privacy business is also aided by the government. It's not that the government regularly sells information on private citizens, it's that the government does little to prevent others from doing so. Regulations on business steadily declined throughout the nineteen eighties now it seems to be open season on citizens' private lives.

EXERCISE 13-5   Revising

Look through your graded papers to find instructor's comments regarding fused sentences and/or comma splices. Reread the papers, identifying the errors as you read by using the three guidelines presented earlier. Then revise the errors. (If you don't have any graded papers handy, look through any body of writing you've done recently.)

CHAPTER 14

Pronoun Reference

If a **pronoun** does not refer clearly to the noun it replaces, confusion can result. Sentences with unclear pronoun reference need to be revised to keep readers from having to pause to determine which pronoun goes with which noun.

UNCLEAR   Although Bob Woodward and Carl Bernstein achieved fame as a team, they didn't work together much after the Watergate stories. **He** continued on **his** own to write books about the Supreme Court and the CIA under William Casey. **His** latest work is about the planning and implementation of the Gulf War of 1991.

REVISED   Although Bob Woodward and Carl Bernstein achieved fame as a team, they didn't work together much after the Watergate stories. **Woodward** continued on **his** own to write books about the Supreme Court and the CIA under William Casey. **His** latest work is about the planning and implementation of the Gulf War of 1991.

14a   Make pronouns refer clearly to their antecedents.

Revise a sentence whenever a pronoun can refer to more than one antecedent. Be particularly careful about reporting someone's words indirectly.

CONFUSING   The city editor of the *Post* assigned both Woodward and Bernstein to work on the same story. **He** was very apprehensive about the assignment.

REVISED   **Bernstein** was very apprehensive about the assignment.

CONFUSING   When Bernstein and Woodward first worked together, Bernstein said **he** didn't like **him.**

REVISED   When Bernstein and Woodward first worked together, Bernstein said, "**I** don't like **him.**"

REVISED   When Bernstein and Woodward first worked together, Bernstein said **he** didn't like **Woodward.**

14b Keep pronouns close to their antecedents.

When several nouns appear in a sentence between the pronoun and its antecedent, revise by moving the pronoun closer to the antecedent or by restating the noun.

CONFUSING   <u>Woodward and Bernstein</u> eventually shed their animosity, and went on to expose government corruption. Various government officials, including some of the President's own staff members, were involved in illegal dealings. **They** couldn't believe what was happening.

REVISED   <u>Woodward and Bernstein</u> eventually shed their animosity, and went on to expose government corruption. **They** couldn't believe what was happening. Various government officials, including some of the President's own staff members, were involved in illegal dealings.

REVISED   Woodward and Bernstein eventually shed their animosity, and went on to expose government corruption. Various government officials, including some of the President's own staff members, were involved in illegal dealings. **Woodward and Bernstein** couldn't believe what was happening.

When the relative pronouns *who*, *which*, and *that* are used to introduce a modifying adjective clause, they should be placed close to the noun they modify.

CONFUSING   The <u>two reporters</u> interviewed scores of government officials and employees, **who** weren't always sure of what they were looking for.

REVISED   The <u>two reporters</u>, **who** weren't always sure of what they were looking for, interviewed scores of government officials and employees.

14c State a pronoun's antecedent clearly.

If a pronoun's antecedent—which can only be a noun—is not stated directly, vagueness or confusion can result.

 1 **Make a pronoun refer to a specific noun antecedent, not to a modifier that may imply the antecedent.**

Sentences in which an adjective serves as an antecedent should be revised to include a noun antecedent.

CONFUSING   Woodward and Bernstein remained <u>persistent</u> throughout their investigations, and eventually **it** paid off.

REVISED   Woodward and Bernstein remained persistent throughout their investigations, and eventually **their persistence** paid off.

REVISED   Woodward and Bernstein practiced <u>persistence</u> throughout their investigations, and eventually **it** paid off.

2   **Make a pronoun refer to a noun, not the possessive form of a noun.**

Sentences in which a noun's possessive form serves as an antecedent should be revised to include a noun antecedent.

CONFUSING   The <u>reporters'</u> final story made history. **They** exposed a constitutional crisis that resulted in President Nixon's resignation.

REVISED   The <u>reporters</u> put together a final story that made history. **They** exposed a constitutional crisis that resulted in President Nixon's resignation.

3   **Give the pronouns *that, this, which,* and *it* precise reference.**

Sentences in which the pronouns *that, this, which,* and *it* refer to the overall sense of a preceding sentence (as opposed to a specific word) should be revised to include a specific antecedent.

CONFUSING   Catacombs housing hundreds of tombs have been found on a site in Arizona. **This** has caused archaeologists to rethink their attitudes toward some ancient tribes.

REVISED   Catacombs housing hundreds of tombs have been found on a site in Arizona. **This find** has caused archaeologists to rethink their attitudes toward some ancient tribes.

4   **Avoid indefinite antecedents for the pronouns *it, they,* and *you.***

Although indefinite pronouns without a clear reference are common in nonstandard usage and conversation ("you know," "they say," "it figures"), in standard academic writing *you* must refer to the reader (unless it is part of a direct quotation); *it* and *they* must refer to particular things, ideas, or people.

NONSTANDARD	**They** used to think that these tribes had no regard for their dead. **You** can understand why, given the brutish nature of the tribes' existence.
STANDARD	**Archaeologists** used to think that these tribes had no regard for their dead. **Anyone** can understand why, given the brutish nature of the tribes' existence.

How to Revise Unclear Pronoun Reference

1. Provide a clear, nearby antecedent.

2. Replace the pronoun with a noun and thereby eliminate the problem of ambiguous reference.

3. Totally recast the sentence to avoid the problem of ambiguous reference.

5 | **Avoid using a pronoun to refer to the title of a paper in the paper's first sentence.**

Since the title is not an actual part of the paper itself, a noun in the title cannot serve as the antecedent for a pronoun in the paper.

UNCLEAR	The <u>Catacombs</u> of Casa Malpais
	Archaeologists found **them** deep in the ground under a large room used for special ceremonies.
REVISED	The Catacombs of Casa Malpais
	Archaeologists found **the catacombs of Casa Malpais** under a large room used for special ceremonies.

Avoid mixing uses of the pronoun *it*.

Do not use *it* as both a pronoun (referring to a noun) and an expletive (a filler in a rearranged sentence) in the same sentence.

UNCLEAR	**It** is evident that the archaeological expedition met **its** goals.
REVISED	Evidently, the archaeological expedition met **its** goals.

14e Use the relative pronouns *who*, *which*, and *that* appropriately.

1 Selecting relative pronouns

Relative pronouns introduce dependent clauses that usually function as adjectives. While all relative pronouns refer to the nouns they follow, your choice of pronoun depends on the nature of the noun. *Who* refers to people (and sometimes animals or deities); *which* refers to animals and things; and *that* refers to people, animals, or things.

Isadora Duncan, **who** scandalized much of Europe with her exotic behavior, performed dances **that** expressed her vitality. The dances, **which** were like nothing the theater world had seen before, shocked her audiences.

2 Using relative pronouns in essential and nonessential clauses

Use *that* or *which* (with no commas around the dependent clause) to denote an essential (or restrictive) modifier—one that provides information crucial for identifying a noun. Use *which* (with commas around the dependent clause) to denote a nonessential (or nonrestrictive) modifier—one that simply provides additional information about the noun. *Who* can be used for either essential or nonessential modifiers.

ESSENTIAL	A dancer **who** scandalized much of Europe with her exotic behavior performed dances **that** expressed her vitality.
NONESSENTIAL	Isadora Duncan, **who** scandalized much of Europe with her exotic behavior, performed expressive dances. The dances, **which** were like nothing the theater world had seen before, shocked her audiences.

CRITICAL DECISIONS

BE ALERT TO DIFFERENCES: APPLY A TEST FOR CHOOSING *WHO, WHICH* OR *THAT*—WITH OR WITHOUT COMMAS.

Writers can be unsure of themselves when choosing relative pronouns (*who, which,* and *that*) and when using commas with relative clauses. Relative pronouns begin relative clauses, and these function in a sentence as if they were adjectives: they modify nouns. You can apply three tests for deciding which pronoun to use and whether or not to use commas.

Identify the noun being modified.

- Is this a proper noun—the name of a *specific* person (Larry), place (Baltimore), or thing (Levis)? If yes, then use the pronoun *who, whom,* or *whose* (for a person) or *which* (for a place or thing)—*with* commas. The noun does not need the modifying clause to specify its meaning. This clause is *nonessential* (see 25d).

  My friend George, *who* is constantly angry, has developed a stress disorder.

  The harbor area in Baltimore, *which* is the largest city in Maryland but not the capital, has changed significantly in the last twenty years.

  The Levis, *which* fit me well, were on sale.

- Is the noun being modified a common noun—an unspecified person (man), place (city), or thing (pants)? If yes, then it is quite likely that the modifying information of the clause is essential for specifying the noun's identity. Use *who, whom,* or *whose* (for a person) and *which* or *that* (for a place or thing) *without commas*. The modifying clause is *essential* (see 25d).

  People *who* are constantly angry often develop stress disorders.

  The cities *that* are of greatest interest to me are all accessible by train.
  The cities *which* are of greatest interest to me are all accessible by train.

  The pants *that* fit me best were on sale.

- If, in the context of a paragraph, the identity of the common noun being modified is made clear and specific to the reader, then treat the common noun in the same way that you would a proper noun: use a relative clause, with commas.

  Over a year ago, I met the woman *who* is seated at that table in the corner. The woman, *whose* name I can't remember, is a friend of Joan's.

  [In the first sentence, the relative clause *who is seated . . .* is needed to identify which woman, presumably in a roomful of people. In the second sentence, the reader knows who is being referred to, so the relative clause in that sentence (*whose name . . .*) is nonessential and takes commas.]

EXERCISE 14-1   **Correcting faulty pronoun reference**

Check the following sentences for clear pronoun reference. If pronoun reference is
unclear, then replace pronouns with nouns or move pronouns closer to their
antecedents. Circle the number of any correct sentences.

EXAMPLE   Upton Sinclair's novel *The Jungle* was published in 1906, the same year
            that Samuel Hopkins Adams's *Great American Fraud* was
                    Sinclair
            published. ~~He~~ also published several other books, among them *Oil!* and
            Boston.

1. Sinclair wrote *The Jungle* to expose corruption in Chicago's meat packing industry,

    especially mistreatment of workers and unsanitary conditions. It became very well

    known.

2. Sinclair was one of a group of writers active primarily in the cities of pre-World

    War I United States who questioned the morality of the capitalist system.

3. The term "muckraker" was coined by Theodore Roosevelt and applied to writers

    like Sinclair because of the nature of their writing, which refers to a line from John

    Bunyan's *Pilgrim's Progress*.

4. The muckrakers were at odds with the industrialists and many politicians. They

    didn't approve of their methods for making money.

5. In part as a result of the muckrakers' work, the Beef Inspection Act was passed. It

    curbed abuses in the industry.

EXERCISE 14-2   Correcting faulty pronoun reference

Check the following sentences for problems with stating pronoun reference directly. Revise by providing direct antecedents for pronouns; making sure that pronouns don't refer to possessive nouns; and making sure that relative pronouns and the pronouns *it, they,* and *you* are used appropriately. Circle the number of any correct sentences.

EXAMPLE   Organizations ranging from the National Institute of Child Health to
the American Cancer Society have warned about the dangers of
These warnings have
excessive alcohol consumption. ~~This has~~ resulted in a heightened
awareness of alcohol abuse.

1. People's attitudes toward alcohol are ambivalent. They understand the dangers,
    but they live in a society that glorifies drinking.

2. You can drink moderately with no risk to your health, but you should avoid heavy
    drinking.

3. Health officials are determined to educate people, and it seems to be having some
    effect.

4. Even liquor companies, that depend on the use of alcohol for their profits, are
    beginning to preach moderation.

5. It was not too long ago that some people praised alcohol because it was a remedy
    for many ills.

6. The Surgeon General's Office, who are the watchdogs of the nation's health, has
    issued warnings about alcohol use during pregnancy.

7. Since a pregnant woman's fetus can be irreparably harmed by alcohol, she is
    better off abstaining for the duration of the pregnancy.

8. Alcohol is not harmful if used moderately; thus it is not considered dangerous to
    the entire population.

9. They conclude that one drink per day is not dangerous for the average person.

10. Drunk driving is responsible for half of the fatal automobile accidents in this
    country, more than half of fire deaths, and a significant proportion of drownings,
    home accidents, and violent crimes as well, which means that alcohol is surely a
    dangerous drug.

EXERCISE 14-3   **Recognizing clear pronoun reference**

Photocopy several paragraphs from one of your textbooks. Try to find a passage that narrates an event: a scientist's discovery, an historical figure's accomplishments, or a section of a short story or novel. Circle all of the pronouns in the selection, and draw arrows to their antecedents. Then, in the space below, answer the following questions: How frequently does the writer keep pronouns close to their antecedents? If there are cases in which the two are separated by long phrases or clauses, is the pronoun reference still clear? If your answer is "no" for any parts of the passage, rewrite those parts to make the reference clearer.

EXERCISE 14-4   **Revising**

Look through your graded papers to find instructor's comments regarding unclear pronoun reference. Reread the papers, identifying the errors as you read by using the strategies outlined in this chapter. Then revise the errors. (If you don't have any graded papers handy, look through any body of writing you've done recently.)

CHAPTER 15

Misplaced and Dangling Modifiers

The function of a modifier is to describe a noun, verb, or other modifiers (see 7c). In order to function most effectively, a modifier should be placed as close as possible to the word it modifies.

MISPLACED MODIFIERS

 15a **Position modifiers so that they refer clearly to the words they should modify.**

When a modifier is not closely linked with the word it modifies, readers can become confused.

CONFUSING   The city of Leningrad received its name from the Bolsheviks, which sits on the shores of the Gulf of Finland.

Sitting on the shores of the Gulf of Finland, the Bolsheviks gave the city of Leningrad its name.

REVISED   The city of Leningrad, which sits on the shores of the Gulf of Finland, received its name from the Bolsheviks.

Sitting on the shores of the Gulf of Finland, the city of Leningrad got its name from the Bolsheviks.

15b **Position limiting modifiers with care.**

Depending on their position in a sentence, **limiting modifiers** (such as *only*, *almost*, *just*, *nearly*, *even*, and *simply*) can change meaning significantly. They should be positioned in a sentence with care. Notice the different meanings in these two sentences:

The city had been called Petrograd for **nearly** ten years when the name was changed after Lenin died.

The city had been called Petrograd for ten years when the name was changed after Lenin **nearly** died.

15c   Reposition modifiers that describe two elements simultaneously.

Squinting modifiers—words that can modify either the preceding or the following words—should be repositioned so that they modify only one word.

CONFUSING	People who objected to the change **quietly** talked of their dismay.
REVISED	People who **quietly** objected to the change talked of their dismay.
REVISED	People who objected to the change talked of their dismay **quietly**.

CRITICAL DECISIONS

CHALLENGE YOUR PLACEMENT OF MODIFIERS

Modifiers provide much of the interest in a sentence; but when misused, they undermine communication by forcing readers to stop and figure out your meaning. In every case, you should know precisely *which* word in a sentence you are modifying. Posing three questions should help you to be clear.

- What modifiers am I using in this sentence? To use modifiers effectively and correctly, you should be able to recognize modifiers when you write them. Single words, phrases, and clauses can function as modifiers.

Modifying word (see 7c)

ADJECTIVE	The artist made a *deliberate* effort.
ADVERB	The artist succeeded *brilliantly.*

Modifying phrase (see 7d)

ADJECTIVE	The painting, *displayed on a dark wall*, glowed.
ADVERB	Patrons responded *with an unusual mix of excitement and nervousness.*

Modifying clause (see 7e)

ADJECTIVE	Many attended the opening, *which had become a much-anticipated event.*
ADVERB	*After the gallery closed that evening,* the staff celebrated.

- What word is being modified? (See 15a–c.)

The artist made a *deliberate* effort. [The noun *effort* is being modified.]

The artist succeeded *brilliantly.* [The verb *succeeded* is being modified.]

Several patrons who returned repeatedly called the young artist "a wonder." [Confusing: The single-word modifier *repeatedly* seems to modify two words, *returned* and *called.*]

Having made a commitment of time and money, it was gratifying to see a successful show. [Confusing: The phrase *having made a commitment of time and money* does not modify any specific word.]

- Does the modifying word, phrase, or clause clearly refer to this word? (See 15a–c, 15h.)

On returning, several patrons repeatedly *called* the young artist "a wonder." [The modifier *repeatedly* now clearly modifies the verb *called.*]

Having made a commitment of time and money, *the manager* was gratified to see a successful show. [The modifying phrase now clearly modifies the noun *manager.*]

15d Reposition a lengthy modifier that splits a subject and its verb.

It is acceptable to place a modifier between a subject and its verb. However, if a modifier is so long that it breaks the link between subject and verb, it should be repositioned.

CONFUSING Another name change, **approved by those who want Lenin's name purged from Soviet life but opposed by those who decry the cost,** has been proposed.

REVISED **Approved by those who want Lenin's name purged from Soviet life but opposed by those who decry the cost,** another name change has been proposed.

REVISED Another proposed name change has been **approved by those who want Lenin's name purged from Soviet life, but those who decry the cost** oppose the change.

Avoid Splitting Paired Sentence Elements with Lengthy Modifiers

Each of the five basic sentence patterns (see 7b) presents paired parts of speech that function together to create meaning. Avoid splitting the following paired elements with lengthy modifiers that disrupt meaning: subject and verb, verb and object, verb and indirect object, indirect object and object, object and complement, linking verb and subject complement.

Pattern 1:

┌─Predicate─┐
Subject   verb
Sarah   arrived.

Pattern 2:

┌──────Predicate──────┐
Subject   verb (tr.)   direct object
Sarah   embraced   her family.

Pattern 3:

┌────────────Predicate────────────┐
Subject   verb (tr.)   indirect object   direct object
Sarah   brought   them   presents.

Pattern 4:

┌────────────Predicate────────────┐
Subject   verb (tr.)   direct object   object complement
Sarah   considered   her family   a blessed sight.

Pattern 5:

┌──────────Predicate──────────┐
Subject   verb (linking)   subject complement
Sarah   was relieved   to be home.

15e Reposition a modifier that splits a verb and its object or a verb and its complement.

While one- or two-word modifiers can come between a verb and its object or complement, a lengthy adverb phrase or clause should be moved to the beginning or the end of the sentence.

CLEAR   Scientists are **always** excited about new discoveries.

AWKWARD   Scientists are, **because of their naturally skeptical natures,** hesitant to declare a discovery.

REVISED   **Because of their naturally skeptical natures**, scientists are hesitant to declare a discovery.

15f Reposition a modifier that splits the parts of an infinitive.

Although it is acceptable to split an infinitive (*to* + the base form of the verb) in conversation, the standards of written English are more rigid. In general, lengthy modifiers that split infinitives should be repositioned. Some readers, however, do not accept any modifiers between the two parts of the infinitive. If a modifier cannot be repositioned clearly, then the sentence should be revised to eliminate the infinitive form.

SPLIT   Only the most massive stars are believed to **on their deaths** become black holes.

       The apparent discovery of a new black hole causes astronomers to **quickly** abandon whatever they are working on.

REVISED   Only the most massive stars are believed to become black holes **on their deaths.**

       The apparent discovery of a new black hole finds astronomers **quickly abandoning** whatever they are working on.

15g Reposition a lengthy modifier that splits a verb phrase.

While a verb phrase (a verb and its auxiliaries) can be split with brief modifiers, a lengthy modifier in the middle of a verb phrase can cause confusion. Such modifiers should be relocated.

CLEAR   The gravity of a black hole is so intense that not even light can **ever** escape.

CONFUSING Astronomers can **because of the sensitivity of their measurements** detect a black hole by its pull on nearby matter.

REVISED   **Because of the sensitivity of their instruments,** scientists can detect a black hole by its pull on nearby matter.

DANGLING MODIFIERS

15h Identify and revise dangling modifiers.

A modifier is said to "dangle" when the word it modifies is not clearly visible in the same sentence. Correct the error by rewriting the sentence, making sure to include the word modified.

1   **Give introductory clauses or phrases a specific word to modify.**

Because the writer knows what a long introductory clause or phrase modifies, sometimes he or she neglects to include that word in the main clause of the sentence. Revision involves asking what the opening clause of the phrase modifies and rewriting the sentence to provide an answer.

DANGLING   **Offering astronomers a forum for sharing their discoveries,** scientists engage in vigorous discussion.

REVISED   **Offering astronomers a forum for sharing their discoveries,** scientific journal articles are the subject of vigorous discussion.

2   **Rewrite passive constructions to provide active subjects.**

Because the passive voice deletes the subject (see 9g), an introductory phrase or clause modifying a passive construction will dangle. Rewriting the sentence in the active voice will provide the word to be modified.

DANGLING   **Examining distant galaxies,** a black hole is discovered.

REVISED   **Examining distant galaxies,** astronomers discover a black hole.

EXERCISE 15-1   **Misplaced and squinting modifiers**

Rewrite the following sentences by repositioning misplaced and squinting modifiers or by recasting the sentence so that it reads clearly. (You can choose which word you want a squinting modifier to describe.) Circle the number of correct sentences.

EXAMPLE   Budgets for major motion pictures include provisions for advertising, which seem to be growing steadily.

Budgets for major motion pictures, *which seem to be growing steadily,* include provisions for advertising.

1. Concentrating on producing the movie itself, considerations such as an advertising budget rarely concerned producers of the past.

2. Within the last two decades, producers who understood the business thoroughly approved budgets for marketing purposes.

3. Television seems to be the reason for the increasing importance of marketing campaigns, which dominates the leisure lives of many Americans.

4. An audiovisual medium itself, television provides the perfect advertising ground for movies.

5. Early movie advertising on TV consisted of a voiceover and a shot of the movie's title, usually a deep male voice.

6. Marketing executives who recognized the value of TV ads for movies clearly began to take advantage of the medium.

7. Consisting of a quick, exciting scene from an upcoming movie, producers make millions on movie "teasers."

8. Also called "trailers," people seem taken in by these vignettes.

9. Too many trailers can ruin business for a movie with exciting features.

10. Trailers themselves seem to have become entertainment for some people, taking on a life of their own.

EXERCISE 15-2   Limiting modifiers

Rewrite the following sentences, repositioning the limiting modifier to give the sentence a different meaning.

EXAMPLE   Birth order seems to be an important factor only in the development of some children.

Birth order *only* seems to be an important factor in the development of some children.

1. Just where you are in relation to your siblings can have an effect on your personality.

2. Psychologists say that birth order is almost as important as parent-child bonding to all children.

3. Even amateurs can trace some of their personality characteristics to birth order.

4. The eldest, for example, is always a person who takes responsibility seriously.

5. Simply being the youngest can make a person dependent on everyone.

EXERCISE 15-3   Repositioning modifiers

Rewrite the following sentences, repositioning modifiers so that there are clear links between subjects, verbs, and objects or complements. Circle the number of any correct sentences.

EXAMPLE   When Graham Greene died in 1991, he over the course of his life had written more than fifty books.

When Graham Greene died in 1991, he had written more than fifty books *over the course of his life.*

1. Greene's writing was to the public that bought over twenty million copies of his books the work of a master storyteller.

2. Most novelists write, according to literary and popular culture critics, either "serious" literature or "escape" literature.

3. Greene's writing included, much to the chagrin of narrow-minded literary scholars, both types of literature.

4. The writer, Greene remarked on a number of occasions, should not be ashamed of being popular among non-academics.

5. Greene was, as a young child and even as a young man, occasionally suicidal.

6. He, in 1920, at the age of 16, underwent psychoanalysis.

7. In 1925, because he was engaged to marry a Catholic, Greene converted to Catholicism.

8. Catholic theology provided because of its concepts of sin and salvation Greene with the central theme for most of his work.

9. Greene won with this adventure story that also explored the notion of redemption both critical and popular acclaim.

10. He was, in the eyes of most literary critics, one of the great voices of the twentieth century.

EXERCISE 15-4   Repositioning modifiers

Rewrite the following sentences, repositioning modifiers in order to repair split
infinitives and to restore clear links between main verbs and their auxiliaries. Circle
the number of any correct sentences.

EXAMPLE   A number of men at a 1976 American Legion convention in
                     Philadelphia began to gradually show signs of pneumonia.

                     A number of men at a 1976 American Legion convention in
                     Philadelphia *gradually* began to show signs of pneumonia.

1. Similar outbreaks had, according to medical statistics, occurred in several other
    places.

2. In order to fully understand the disease, local physicians called in the U.S. Centers
    for Disease Control.

3. All of the men were clearly suffering from the same disease.

4. Researchers had by the end of their investigation discovered a new bacillus, which
    they named *Legionella pneumophilia.*

5. The disease came to eventually be known as "Legionnaire's Disease."

EXERCISE 15-5   **Repairing dangling modifiers**

Rewrite the following sentences, repairing the dangling modifiers by revising the sentence to restore the word modified. Circle the number of any sentences that are correct.

EXAMPLE   Responding to medical advice about healthy diets, fish is being eaten more and more these days.

Responding to medical advice about healthy diets, people are eating fish more and more these days.

1. Searching for the perfect seafood dinner, haddock is a good choice.

2. With its mild flavor and smooth texture, there is good reason for the demand.

3. Discouraged by high costs and poor catches, commercial fishing has been abandoned in many coastal areas.

4. More efficient and more profitable, "fish farming" is slowly replacing commercial fishing.

5. Like animals raised on farms, a number of chemicals are injected.

269

EXERCISE 15-6   Misplaced and dangling modifiers

Rewrite the following paragraph on a separate sheet of paper, revising sentences to eliminate misplaced and dangling modifiers.

EXAMPLE   Soaring effortlessly through the air, people have always envied birds.

People have always envied birds, soaring effortlessly through the air.

Inventors were, centuries before Wilbur and Orville Wright first left the ground in Kitty Hawk, imagining ways in which people could fly. But the fascination didn't end with the advent of commercial air flight. Hang gliders became in the seventies the rage, and now the latest fad for would-be fliers is bungee jumping. Bungee jumping, apparently originating in Europe and Australia, combines the thrill of flight with the adventure of parachuting. Jumpers attach themselves to a strong cord, usually made of rubber, and then freefall. Reaching speeds of up to 60 m.p.h. and falling sometimes 100 feet, a "high" that not many people can tolerate is experienced. Bungee jumpers had to at first avoid police, because their favorite jumping spot, bridges, were off limits according to the law. Now more legal spots for jumping are appearing, among them a 140-foot tower in Colorado. And one of the most popular spots from which to jump is itself airborne—a hot air balloon. People who jump often describe the experience as exhilarating.

EXERCISE 15-7   Revising

Look through your graded papers to find instructor's comments regarding misplaced or dangling modifiers. Reread the papers, identifying the errors as you read by using the strategies outlined in this chapter. Then revise the errors. (If you don't have any graded papers handy, look through any body of writing you've done recently.)

CHAPTER 16

Shifts and Mixed Constructions

SHIFTS

Sentences must be consistent in a number of areas: person, number, tense, mood, voice, tone, and discourse.

16a Revise shifts in person and number.

Person and **number** help to identify the subject of a sentence.

Pronoun Forms (Subjective Case)

	Singular	*Plural*
First Person	I	we
Second Person	you	you
Third Person	he, she, it	they, people
	one, a person	

---

1 **Revise shifts in person by keeping all references to a subject consistent.**

Maintaining consistency in person keeps the subject's identity clear.

INCONSISTENT   Anyone with fair skin should avoid sunlight; otherwise you might get a serious sunburn.

REVISED   Anyone with fair skin should avoid sunlight; otherwise he or she might get a serious sunburn.

2 **Revise shifts in number by maintaining consistent singular or plural forms.**

Maintaining consistency in number also keeps the subject's identity clear.

271

INCONSISTENT	If a fair-skinned person spends too much time in the sun, they risk developing cancer.
REVISED	If fair-skinned people spend too much time in the sun, they risk developing cancer.

16b Revise shifts in tense, mood, and voice.

When tense, mood, and voice are not consistent within a sentence, readers can become confused.

Sequencing Verb Tenses in a Sentence

To establish a relationship between two events, both of which occur in the past:

- Use the simple past tense for one past event—and any of the four past tenses for the other event (see 9f-1).

To establish a relationship between a past event and a future event:

- Use the past tense in the independent clause and the simple future, future progressive, or simple present tenses in the dependent clause.

To establish a relationship between a past event and an acknowledged fact or condition:

- Use the simple past tense for the main clause and the simple present tense in the dependent clause.
- Use the past perfect tense for the main clause and the simple present tense in the dependent clause.

---

1 Revise shifts in tense by observing the appropriate sequence of verb tenses.

If the pattern of verb tenses in a sentence is not consistent, readers will have difficulty following a paragraph. (See 9e, f.)

INCONSISTENT	When my father had been young, people thought a tan was a sign of health.
REVISED	When my father was young, people thought a tan was a sign of health.

The historical present refers to material read in books or articles or to action in a film. (See 9e-1.)

HISTORICAL PRESENT	In Fitzgerald's novel *Tender is the Night*, the main characters spend much of their time lying in the sun.

 2 Revise for shifts in mood.

When a writer shifts mood (indicative, subjunctive, and imperative) in a sentence, readers cannot be sure of the intended judgment about the information presented. Avoid confusion by choosing a mood (most often the indicative) and using it consistently. (See 9h.)

INCONSISTENT	If everyone was conscious of the dangers of too much sun, the beaches would all be empty.
REVISED	If everyone were conscious of the dangers of too much sun, the beaches would all be empty.

 3 Revise for shifts in voice.

If a writer shifts between active and passive voice in the same sentence, readers will be confused about whether or not the subject is emphasized. Avoid this difficulty by choosing either active or passive voice in any one sentence.

INCONSISTENT	When the Nazis marched through Europe, many great works of art were taken.
REVISED	When the Nazis marched through Europe, they took many great works of art.

16c Revise for shifts in tone.

Shifts in tone—from formal to casual, from light to serious—are disconcerting to readers.

DISCONCERTING	During their relentless onslaught the Nazis ripped off countless museums, galleries, and libraries.
REVISED	During their relentless onslaught the Nazis pillaged countless museums, galleries, and libraries.

16d Maintain consistent use of direct or indirect discourse.

Shifting between direct (quoting exactly) and indirect (reproducing the sense of a quotation) discourse can disorient readers. Within a given sentence, choose between the two forms of discourse.

INCONSISTENT	According to art expert Klaus Goldmaan, Nazis wished to destroy other cultures, and they believed that "if you destroy a people's art, then you destroy their historical identity and confidence."
REVISED	According to art expert Klaus Goldmaan, Nazis wished to destroy other cultures, and they believed that if they could destroy a people's art, then they could destroy their historical identity and confidence.

MIXED CONSTRUCTIONS

A **mixed construction** occurs when a sentence begins with one grammatical pattern and then shifts abruptly to another pattern.

16e Establish clear, grammatical relations between sentence parts.

Although mixed constructions are rarely confusing in casual conversation, the absence of gestures and intonation in writing make it necessary to maintain consistent patterns in written work. Mixed constructions are likely to occur with certain introductory patterns: the expression "The fact that," adverb clauses, and prepositional phrases.

MIXED	The fact that in wartime pillaging is rampant.
	When pillaging is rampant can be demoralizing for people under siege.
	By pillaging treasures can demoralize a people under siege.
REVISED	The fact that in wartime pillaging is rampant cannot excuse the destruction of a culture's treasured art.
	When pillaging is rampant, it can be demoralizing for people under siege.
	By pillaging treasures, invaders can demoralize a people under siege.
REVISED	In wartime pillaging is rampant.
	Rampant pillaging can be demoralizing for people under siege.
	Pillaging treasures can demoralize a people under siege.

16f   Establish consistent relations between subjects and predicates.

Faulty predication occurs when the predicate part of a sentence does not logically complete its subject. Faulty predication is likely to occur in sentences with linking verbs that follow the pattern A = B (or A *is* B). When the subject complement begins with the word *when, where,* or *because,* beware of faulty predication. Revise so that the subject complement is an adjective or a noun, or change the linking verb to another verb.

FAULTY	Inflation is when prices steadily increase and the value of money decreases.
	Insolvency is where a person doesn't have enough money to pay off debts.
	The reason for this recession is because the country has been living on borrowed money.
REVISED	Inflation is an economic condition in which prices steadily increase and the value of money decreases.
	Insolvency is a situation in which a person doesn't have enough money to pay off debts.
	The reason for this recession is that the country has been living on borrowed money.
REVISED	Inflation occurs when prices steadily increase and the value of money decreases.
	Insolvency occurs when a person doesn't have enough money to pay off debts.
	This recession occurred because the country has been living on borrowed money.

INCOMPLETE SENTENCES

16g   Edit elliptical constructions to avoid confusion.

In **elliptical constructions** a writer eliminates certain words in a sentence to streamline communication. However, essential words should not be eliminated.

1   Use *that* when necessary to signal sentence relationships.

Omit *that* from a sentence only if it will not confuse readers.

CLEAR	Shakespeare and his contemporaries believed ~~that~~ drama should tell the stories of important people.
UNCLEAR	Audiences appreciated Shakespeare wrote about noble men and women.
REVISED	Audiences appreciated that Shakespeare wrote about noble men and women.

2   Provide all the words needed for parallel constructions.

Words can be omitted from parallel constructions only if the omitted words match exactly the words in the other part of the construction.

CLEAR	Shakespeare wrote about noble men and women, Ibsen ~~wrote~~ about ordinary people.
UNCLEAR	Shakespeare's Hamlet and Lear are royalty, Ibsen's Nora ~~is~~ a housewife.
REVISED	Shakespeare's Hamlet and Lear are royalty; Ibsen's Nora is a housewife.

3   Use the necessary prepositions with verbs in parallel constructions.

In parallel constructions, prepositions that are part of verb phrases can only be omitted if they are identical to the preposition remaining.

CLEAR	Nora had trust ~~in~~ and faith in her husband.
UNCLEAR	She believed ~~in~~ and relied on him for support.
REVISED	She believed in and relied on him for support.

16h   Make comparisons consistent, complete, and clear.

In order to be effective, the elements in a comparison should be logically consistent, and they should be stated completely and clearly.

1   **Keep the elements of a comparison logically related.**

ILLOGICAL   The traditional role of housewife in the 1890s differed from Nora, who took on financial responsibility.

REVISED   The traditional housewife in the 1890s differed from Nora, who took on financial responsibility.

2   **Complete all elements of a comparison.**

Revise incomplete comparisons so that readers can understand which elements in a sentence are being compared.

INCOMPLETE   In the end, Nora displayed greater moral courage.

REVISED   In the end, Nora displayed greater moral courage than her husband.

3   **Make sure comparisons are clear and unambiguous.**

Revise comparisons that can be interpreted in more than one way.

UNCLEAR   Nora believed that honor was more important than her children.

REVISED   Nora believed that honor was more important than her children were.

EXERCISE 16-1   **Correcting shifts**

Rewrite each of the following sentences to correct shifts in person, number, tense, mood, or voice. (There is more than one way to correct some of the sentences.) Circle the number of any correct sentences.

EXAMPLE   Universities in the United States receive government funding, for which you provide information on research costs and "indirect costs."

Universities in the United States receive government funding, for which <u>they</u> provide information on research costs and "indirect costs."

1. If a university received funds, it must provide a clear accounting of how it spent those funds.

2. Universities are granted funds by government agencies for scientific research and development; when you apply, you estimate what your "indirect costs" will be.

3. What are indirect costs? They are any costs not directly related to the research itself; it includes administration, maintenance, and libraries.

4. For example, if a university were to apply for a grant from the Defense Department, it estimates not only the costs incurred by conducting the research, but general costs involved in operating the university as well.

5. Some people prefer to call indirect costs "overhead," while they are called "padding" by skeptical observers.

6. The government agency granting the funds is supposed to oversee the disbursement; you do this by auditing the university's overhead charges.

7. If any discrepancies emerge during the audit, they are to be reconciled before additional funds are dispersed.

8. During the 1980s Stanford University received major funding from the Office of Naval Research; not only did it fail to report overhead costs adequately, but they apparently used some of the funds on things like yachts and flowers.

9. When the Stanford story broke, many observers had blamed the hopelessly confusing regulations involved in university research.

10. Not only will Stanford have to return millions to the federal government, but their books will have to be kept carefully in future years.

EXERCISE 16-2   Correcting shifts

Rewrite the following sentences, correcting shifts in tone and in the use of direct or indirect discourse. Circle the number of any correct sentences.

EXAMPLE   Scientists have always had a heck of a time studying gamma rays because the earth's atmosphere shields it from most of the rays.

Scientists have always had <u>difficulty</u> studying gamma rays because the earth's atmosphere shields it from most of the rays.

1. Scientists believe that gamma rays were created during the "big bang" that began the universe and are "the strongest kind of radiation we know."

2. In the past, gamma rays have been studied through the use of totally humongous balloons.

3. Early in 1990, NASA launched the Gamma Ray Observatory, which will circle the earth at a height of almost 300 miles catching up on what's happening in the universe.

4. Researchers involved in the development of the GRO have said "It's a major breakthrough in the study of gamma rays," and that it will provide scientists with information for up to eight more years.

5. One scientist said that he'd been studying gamma rays for twenty years and "this is the most exciting thing I've ever seen."

6. Scientists from all over the world have been involved both in the design of GRO and in its operation—the launching has people psyched up in many countries.

7. One researcher called the project a "fishing expedition," referring to the fact that scientists don't know exactly what they're looking for with the GRO.

8. It should, however, provide additional information on the origins of the universe, and "we expect to have to rethink our theories of its size as well."

9. If the GRO doesn't screw up, the next few years should see profound changes in the way we envision the universe.

10. One NASA official put it this way: "GRO promises to open up the whole universe to us" and that it will surely keep scientists busy for decades.

EXERCISE 16-3   **Correcting mixed constructions**

Rewrite each of the following sentences in two ways to eliminate mixed
constructions and faulty predication. Circle the number of any correct sentences.

EXAMPLE   Psychotherapy is where an analyst and a patient delve into the patient's
           past to help explain and control behavior.

           Psychotherapy is a clinical situation in which an analyst and a patient
           delve into the patient's past to help explain and control behavior.

           In psychotherapy an analyst and a patient delve into the patient's past
           to help explain and control behavior.

1. When psychotherapy is a success means that the patient trusts the analyst.

2. By undergoing analysis can help many troubled individuals overcome anxiety.

3. Because of the success of psychoanalytic theory is responsible for the popularity of
    psychotherapy in past years.

4. One reason for the recent decline in the popularity of psychotherapy is because of
    the rigidity of its rules.

5. The fact that few patients can benefit from psychotherapy, and the process is a long one.

6. Although psychotherapy is no longer as popular as in the past, but some people still swear by its benefits.

7. Group therapy is when a single analyst works with several patients at once.

8. The evolution of psychotherapy is interested in serving a complex society.

9. Rather than abandon psychotherapy completely, many analysts have adapted it.

10. In discussing psychotherapy is recognized as a significant but limited success.

EXERCISE 16-4

Rewrite the following sentences to correct problems with elliptical constructions and comparisons. Circle the number of any correct sentences.

EXAMPLE   Audiences always had great respect and faith in Leonard Bernstein.

Audiences always had great respect <u>for</u> and faith in Leonard Bernstein.

1. Audiences in the United States loved Bernstein better than other composers.

2. Many consider Bernstein is the greatest American composer to date.

3. Bernstein's conducting style was flamboyant, and his scores lively.

4. Traditional conducting was far more formal than Bernstein.

5. His devotion and belief in children led him to conduct many "Young People's Concerts."

6. Bernstein began playing piano at age ten, and orchestras at twenty-three.

7. Critics have said his genius was legendary.

8. His compositions were often more daring than those of his contemporaries.

9. Some of his later works were not as popular.

10. Bernstein will be remembered more for his popular work, especially *West Side Story*.

EXERCISE 16-5   Review

Rewrite the following paragraph in the space below, revising sentences to eliminate shifts, mixed constructions, and incomplete sentences.

The cost of medical care in the United States has become the subject of more intense debate. A system that in the past was capable of providing the best care in the world will now be in danger of collapse. Among the issues involved in this debate are Medicaid and Medicare costs, the financial situation of hospitals, and escalating health insurance premiums. Since both state and federal governments are not in good financial shape is the reason why Medicaid and Medicare payments to care providers are shrinking. And those payments are only trickling in. Someone who has been dropped from the Medicaid rolls still needs medical care, and some of them very expensive care. These people all end up as nonpaying patients in county or city hospitals; it's foolish to consider such patients aren't a burden on the community. In addition, the cost of doing business, along with increased malpractice insurance rates, have sent hospital finances into a tailspin. (But increases in malpractice premiums are a problem for doctors too.) Add to this group insurance premiums that strain the budgets of management and employees alike, and what you have is a health care crisis of major proportions.

EXERCISE 16-6   **Recognizing consistency**

Photocopy a brief passage from one of your textbooks, and pay close attention to the sequencing of tenses, consistency of mood, the use of voice, and the consistency and completeness of sentences. Answer the following questions in the space below: How does the writer's use of verbs help the reader understand the passage? How effectively are comparisons presented? How does the author handle elliptical constructions? Are there any apparent inconsistencies (in voice, for example)? If so, can you explain why the writer may have chosen this shift?

EXERCISE 16-7   **Review**

Look through your graded papers to find instructor's comments regarding shifts and/or mixed constructions. Reread the papers, identifying the specific types of problems and revising accordingly. (If you don't have any graded papers handy, look through any body of writing you've done recently.)

CHAPTER 17

Being Clear, Concise, and Direct

17a Revise to eliminate wordiness.

1 Combine sentences that repeat material.

If two sentences provide the same information, combine them.

WORDY   Many famous people **were left handed.** Alexander the Great, Leonardo da Vinci, Michelangelo, and Napoleon **were left handed.**

REVISED   Many famous people, including Alexander the Great, Leonardo da Vinci, Michelangelo, and Napoleon, **were left handed.**

2 Eliminate wordiness from clauses and phrases.

Reduce clauses and phrases to single words, and eliminate relative pronouns.

WORDY   **In addition to these people,** Paul Klee, **who was** a great artist, was left handed.

REVISED   Paul Klee, a great artist, was **also** left handed.

3 Revise sentences that begin with expletives.

Unless an expletive (*it is, there are, there were*) is necessary, eliminate it.

WORDY   **There are many difficulties** that left-handed people encounter.

WORDY   Left-handed people encounter many difficulties.

4 Eliminate buzzwords.

Nouns such as *area, aspect, case, character, element, factor, field, kind, sort, type, thing, nature, scope, situation,* and *quality* can be buzzwords, unnecessary "fillers" in a sentence. Buzzwords can also be adjectives such as *nice, good, interesting, bad, important, fine, weird, significant, central,* and *major,* or adverbs such as *basically, really, quite, very, definitely, actually, completely, literally,* and *absolutely.* Unless a buzzword is necessary, eliminate it.

WORDY	**Basically,** left-handedness is **really** a **very weird sort of thing.**
REVISED	Left-handedness is unusual.

5 | Eliminate redundant writing.

Unless repetition is being used for effect, eliminate redundant material.

WORDY	Left-handedness is only found in about ten percent of the population, **a very small percentage.**
	Left-handers in the population are very few **in number.**
REVISED	Left-handedness is only found in about ten percent of the population.
	Left-handers in the population are very few.

Expressions to Avoid

Wordy	*Direct*
at this moment (point) in time	now, today
at the present time	now, today
due to the fact that	because
in order to utilize	to use
in view of the fact that	because
for the purpose of	for
in the event that	if
until such time as	until
is an example of	is
would seem to be	is
the point I am trying to make*	—

in a very real sense*   —

in fact, as a matter of fact*   —

*These final expressions are fillers and should be eliminated.

---

6 Eliminate long-winded phrases.

Substitute simple words for phrases that do nothing but pad writing.

WORDY   **At the present time, it would seem** that left-handers have
              something more to worry about, **due to the fact that** two
              researchers have linked left-handedness with shorter life spans.

REVISED   **Now** left-handers have something more to worry about,
              because two researchers have linked left-handedness with
              shorter life spans.

17b Use strong verbs.

When revising, circle all verbs and replace weak verbs with forceful ones.

1 Give preference to verbs in the active voice.

Passive verbs not only de-emphasize the actor, but they also require more
words in the sentence (see 9g). Unless you intend to focus on the object of the action,
use active verbs.

PASSIVE/   Spike Lee's film *Do the Right Thing* **is believed by** critics **to have**
WORDY   ushered in a new genre, the ghetto film.

REVISED   Critics **believe** that Spike Lee's film *Do the Right Thing* **has**
              ushered in a new genre, the ghetto film.

2 Use forms of *be* and *have* as main verbs only when no alternatives exist.

Unless the verbs *be* and *have* are being used as auxiliaries, or unless *be* is being
used to define something, these verbs are weak and should be replaced.

WEAK/   Critics **are of the opinion** that *Do the Right Thing* makes a
WORDY   tough, honest statement about race relations.

              The film **had the impact** of shocking audiences.

REVISED   Critics **believe** that *Do the Right Thing* makes a tough, honest statement about race relations.

The film **shocked** audiences.

 3   **Revise nouns derived from verbs.**

Using nouns derived from verbs (*enchantment, location, deliverance*) often results in indirect, wordy sentences. When possible, restore the original verb form of nouns derived from verbs.

INDIRECT/   *Do the Right Thing* **gave emphasis** to the need for action on
WORDY   racial issues.

REVISED   *Do the Right Thing* **emphasized** the need for action on racial issues.

Write Clearly, Concisely, Directly

When revising a draft for clarity, conciseness, and directness, be critical of every sentence.

1. Combine repetitive sentences.
2. Reduce an adjective clause to a phrase or to one word.
3. Eliminate relative pronouns whenever possible.
4. Reduce adverbial and prepositional phrases to one word.
5. Eliminate expletives.
6. Eliminate buzzwords.
7. Eliminate redundant writing.
8. Eliminate long-winded phrases.
9. Use verbs in the active voice, not the passive.
10. Substitute strong verbs for *be* and *have*.
11. Convert nouns made from verbs back to verbs.

EXERCISE 17-1   Eliminating wordiness

Rewrite the following sentences, eliminating wordiness by combining sentences, reducing clauses and phrases to single words, and deleting unnecessary expletives. Circle the number of any correct sentences.

EXAMPLE   At the present time many babies who are born prematurely can be saved.

Today many premature babies can be saved.

1. There are many babies who would have died within hours of birth ten years ago who live healthy lives today.

2. Babies do not have to wait until birth to be treated for some conditions. Even before birth, babies can be treated for some conditions.

3. Doctors can perform surgery on fetuses who are as young as 24 weeks.

4. Premature babies have many problems. Premature babies frequently suffer from developmental problems.

5. An unspecified number of babies need therapy to overcome disabilities.

6. Hydrotherapy involves working with children in water to improve motor skills.

7. Speech/communication therapy involves working with children's abilities to verbalize and use words.

8. There are entire families of disabled children that can sometimes benefit from therapy.

9. It is often the demands of a disabled child that can disrupt normal family life.

10. When the entire family is involved with the therapy for the disabled child, the life of the family runs more smoothly.

EXERCISE 17-2   **Eliminating wordiness**

Eliminate wordiness in the following sentences by deleting buzzwords, redundant writing, and long-winded phrases. Circle the number of any correct sentences.

EXAMPLE   In the early 1960s, International Business Machines (IBM) established itself in a very real sense as an absolute giant.

In the early days of the electric typewriter, International Business Machines (IBM) established itself as a giant corporation.

1. When computers basically came into use in businesses, IBM was literally there to fill the needs.
2. In point of fact, IBM became known for its large "mainframe" computers.
3. In 1977, IBM saw what was to become its primary and most significant competition, when the Apple II was produced.
4. Since 1977, IBM has been identified as the computer-of-choice for business use, while Apple has taken over the personal computer (PC) market.
5. IBM came out with a PC in 1981, but the aspects of its cost and difficulty prevented it from really edging out the Apple.
6. In 1984, as a matter of fact, Apple introduced the Macintosh, a small in size and powerful PC that was "user friendly."
7. As more businesses moved quite definitely away from mainframes, IBM started to begin to rethink its position.
8. In 1991, due to the fact that IBM was struggling to maintain its position, rumors began to surface about the nature of the future of the computer industry.
9. As a matter of fact, some analysts foresaw increased competition, including many small companies.
10. In the final end, many were definitely surprised when IBM and Apple announced that they would join their forces together.

EXERCISE 17-3 **Eliminating wordiness**

Rewrite the following sentences, eliminate wordiness by changing passive verbs to active, replacing *be* and *have,* and revising nouns derived from verbs. Circle the number of any correct sentences.

EXAMPLE   In May of 1935, two recovering alcoholics had a meeting to try to help one another overcome their dependence on alcohol.

In May of 1935, two recovering alcoholics <u>met</u> to try to help one another overcome their dependence on alcohol.

1. William Griffith Wilson and Robert Holbrook Smith gave support to one another as the two made attempts to lead sober lives.

2. Their experience was so successful that *Alcoholics Anonymous* was written by them in 1939, marking the beginning of the organization.

3. Alcoholics Anonymous is an organization that provides recovering alcoholics with the kind of support Wilson and Smith provided each other.

4. Current AA membership is about a million.

5. Spiritual values are stressed by AA, often mentioning God by name.

6. Recently other groups have sprung up in the belief that religion need not be a part of the recovery process.

7. The new groups, such as the Secular Organization for Sobriety (SOS), give emphasis to the alcoholic's own willpower rather than the intervention of a higher power.

8. A group created especially for women alcoholics, Women for Sobriety (WFS) is an organization that has a focus on women alcoholics.

9. Another group, Rational Recovery (RR), emphasizes the power that the individual has to overcome alcoholism.

10. People are helped to maintain sobriety by all of these groups.

EXERCISE 17-4   Review

Rewrite the following paragraph, eliminating wordiness with the techniques discussed in this chapter.

In 1954 a decision that would shake the nation was handed down by the Supreme Court in the case of *Brown* v. *Board of Education of Topeka*. There are many people who have some familiarity with the case that declared segregation in public schools unconstitutional. Not many, however, are knowledgeable about the fact that Thurgood Marshall was in point of fact the attorney who argued the case before the Supreme Court. In part as a result of this victory, and because he had succeeded in winning the case, President Lyndon Johnson appointed Marshall to the Supreme Court thirteen years later. The first black African American to sit on the high court, Marshall was born in Baltimore and received his education at Howard University Law School. As the legal director of the NAACP, Marshall was the one who brought to the Supreme Court many cases in addition to *Brown*. From 1938 to 1958 he argued more than thirty cases before the high court, winning all but three. Many of the cases he argued basically set in motion the machinery that continues to eliminate segregation at the present time. When he was appointed to the Supreme Court Marshall vowed to give interpretations of the Constitution in terms of the promises it makes to protect the weakest, least powerful members of society. Marshall voted with the liberal majority of the court during the last final years of Chief Justice Earl Warren's tenure. As the court took on a tone that was more conservative, Marshall wrote many opinions that were dissenting in civil liberties cases. When William Brennan retired from the Supreme Court in 1990, Marshall was in a position that found himself isolated. A year after that point in time, as his health deteriorated and got worse, Marshall made the announcement of his resignation from the Court, ending an era of activism on behalf of civil rights that changed the country and made it a different place.

EXERCISE 17-5   **Recognizing concise, clear, and direct prose**

Photocopy an essay from a popular magazine such as *Time* or *Newsweek* (essays are usually on the last page of those two magazines). First, circle all of the verbs. How many are passive? Why do you suppose the writer made those verbs passive? Would any have been more effective in the active voice? How many instances can you find of *be* or *have* used as main verbs? Are those verbs necessary, or could any of them have been replaced by more active verbs? Then underline all of the nouns derived from verbs. Could any of these have been recast as verbs? Why do you suppose the writer chose to keep them as nouns? Finally, how do strong verbs contribute to the effect of the passage? Write your responses below.

EXERCISE 17-6

As you revise drafts of papers you're working on at present, concentrate on conciseness, clarity, and directness. Try to identify the specific kinds of problems you have in this area so that you can look out for them in future drafts. Now compare your revisions to the originals: How much shorter are the revisions? How much clearer?

CHAPTER 18

Maintaining Sentence Parallelism

Parallelism in writing involves repeating grammatical structures to achieve logical, easy-to-read sentences.

18a Use parallel words, phrases, and clauses with coordinating conjunctions.

Words, phrases, or clauses joined by coordinating conjunctions (*and, but, for, or, nor, so, yet*) must share an equivalent grammatical form. If compound elements do not share equivalent grammatical forms, revise the sentence by determining the parallel elements and making sure that they are grammatically equivalent.

FAULTY PARALLELISM	For over a generation bootleggers have been **taping** radio concerts, **copying** the tapes, and **will sell** them to fans.
REVISED	For over a generation bootleggers have been **taping** radio concerts, **copying** the tapes, and **selling** them to fans.

CRITICAL DECISIONS

BE ALERT TO DIFFERENCES *AND* SIMILARITIES: MATCH PARALLEL CONTENT WITH PARALLEL PHRASING

Words and word groups that refer to comparable content should show comparisons with parallel phrasing. The only indication of *faulty parallelism* may be that a sentence sounds "off" or illogical. Learn to recognize situations that call for parallel structures and to correct sentences with faulty parallelism.

Recognize situations that call for parallel structures.

Any time you use a coordinating conjunction (*and, but, or,* or *nor*), you are combining elements from two or more sentences into a single sentence.

The children are fond of ice cream. The children are fond of salty pretzels.

Combined elements are logically comparable, and they should share a single grammatical form, otherwise they are not parallel.

PARALLEL	The children are fond of ice cream and salty pretzels. The children are fond of eating ice cream and salty pretzels.
NOT PARALLEL	The children are fond of ice cream and eating salty pretzels.

Correct faulty parallelism.

> 1. *Recognize a sentence that is not parallel.*

NOT PARALLEL	Before they had horses, Indians hunted buffalo by chasing them over blind cliffs, up box canyons, or *when they went* into steep-sided sand dunes.

To revise a sentence with faulty parallelism, *determine which elements should be parallel* (that is, logically comparable), and then *revise the sentence so that these elements share an equivalent grammatical form.* Think of parallel elements as word groupings that complete slots in a sentence. The same grammatical form that you use to complete any one slot in a parallel structure must be used to complete all remaining slots.

> 2. *Determine the parallel elements.*

> by chasing them <u>Slot 1</u>, <u>Slot 2</u>, and <u>Slot 3</u>.
> by chasing them <u>*over blind cliffs,*</u> <u>Slot 2,</u> and <u>Slot 3.</u>

Because Slot 1 is completed with a prepositional phrase (*over blind cliffs*), Slots 2 and 3 should be filled with prepositional phrases. The series *over blind cliffs, up box canyons, or <u>when they went</u> into steep-sided sand dunes* lacks parallel structure because the third element in the series introduces a *when* clause, which is not consistent with the grammatical form of Slot 1.

> 3. *Revise so that parallel elements have equivalent grammatical form.*

PARALLEL	Before they had horses, Indians hunted buffalo by chasing them *over blind cliffs, up box canyons,* or *into steep-sided sand dunes.*

1 Using parallel words

Words that appear in a pair or a series are related in content and should be parallel in form.

FAULTY PARALLELISM	Bootlegging is **excitement** and **lucrative.**
	Authorities are **surprised** and **discouraged by** the extent of bootlegging.
REVISED	Bootlegging is **exciting** and **lucrative.**
	Authorities are **surprised at** and **discouraged by** the extent of bootlegging.

2 Using parallel phrases

Parallel phrases should have the same grammatical structure.

FAULTY PARALLELISM	Recording artists have been **fighting back, taking charge, and to beat the bootleggers** at their own game.
REVISED	Recording artists have been **fighting back, taking charge, and beating the bootleggers** at their own game.

3 Using parallel clauses

Parallel clauses should have the same grammatical structure.

FAULTY PARALLELISM	Artists such as Frank Zappa and Bob Dylan hope that releasing their own bootleg discs will **discourage** bootleggers **and to stop** the drain on legitimate profits.
REVISED	Artists such as Frank Zappa and Bob Dylan hope that releasing their own bootleg discs will **discourage** bootleggers **and stop** the drain on legitimate profits.

18b Use parallelism with correlative conjunctions.

Parts of sentences joined by correlative conjunctions (*either/or, neither/nor, both/and, not only/but also*) must share an equivalent grammatical form. If elements do not share equivalent grammatical forms, revise the sentence by determining the parallel elements and making sure that they are grammatically equivalent.

FAULTY PARALLELISM	The conquest of Mexico resulted both **from the technological superiority** of the Spanish and **the political structure** of the Aztec civilization.
REVISED	The conquest of Mexico resulted both **from the technological superiority** of the Spanish and **from the political structure** of the Aztec civilization.
	The conquest of Mexico resulted **from** both **the technological superiority** of the Spanish and **the political structure** of the Aztec civilization.

18c Use parallelism in sentences with compared and contrasted elements.

Elements that are compared or contrasted in a sentence (using expressions such as *rather than, as opposed to, on the other hand, not, like, unlike,* and *just as/so too*) must share an equivalent grammatical form. If elements do not share equivalent grammatical forms, revise the sentence by determining the parallel elements and making sure that they are grammatically equivalent.

FAULTY PARALLELISM	Recently historians have characterized the conquest as **a destructive force** rather than **civilizing** the native people.
REVISED	Recently historians have characterized the conquest as **a destructive force** rather than **a civilizing influence on** the native people.
	Recently historians have characterized the conquest as **destroying** rather than **civilizing** the native people.

18d Use parallelism among sentences to enhance paragraph coherence.

Using parallel sentences highlights the logic of a paragraph and binds it into a coherent unit.

Spanish soldiers claimed that they were saving souls. The Aztecs, however, saw the Spaniards slaughtering bodies. When European civilization arrived, native civilization was crushed. The influence of Europe in the New World expanded, as the dominance of the Aztecs in the New World contracted.

18e Use parallel entries when writing lists or outlines.

To emphasize the logical connections in outlines and lists, make sure that the elements are of equivalent grammatical form.

 Making lists

A list that is not parallel can be confusing, while one that is parallel highlights the logical connections between items on the list.

FAULTY PARALLELISM	Areas that need attention include: • repairing windows • what to do about missing shingles? • to trim hedges • paint doors
REVISED	Areas that need attention include: • repairing windows • replacing missing shingles • trimming hedges • painting doors
REVISED	Areas that need attention include: • repair windows • replace missing shingles • trim hedges • paint doors

2 Making outlines

An outline in which elements from the same level of generality are not parallel can be confusing; an outline that uses parallel structures will highlight logical connections within the outline.

FAULTY PARALLELISM	The Age of Realism and Naturalism A. The influence of Darwin B. How capitalism affected writers C. Reacting against romanticism D. Differer regions are celebrated
REVISED	The Age of Realism and Naturalism A. The influence of Darwin B. The effects of capitalism C. The reaction against romanticism D. The celebration of regionalism

EXERCISE 18-1   Eliminating faulty parallelism

Rewrite the following sentences, eliminating faulty parallelism. (While some
sentences may be correct, they can be improved with parallel structure.) Circle the
number of any correct sentences.

EXAMPLE   In mid-nineteenth-century New England the Transcendentalists
                   flourished, publishing a magazine, teaching schoolchildren, and they
                   tried to set up an ideal community.

                   In mid-nineteenth-century New England the Transcendentalists
                   flourished, publishing a magazine, teaching schoolchildren, and trying
                   to set up an ideal community.

1. The Transcendentalists supported both abolition and for women to have equal
   rights.

2. Among the most famous Transcendentalists were Bronson Alcott, whose daughter
   Louisa May became a famous novelist, and Ralph Waldo Emerson, writing great
   essays and delivering powerful lectures.

3. Transcendentalism did not offer any clear set of beliefs; rather, it was suggesting a
   way to view the world.

4. While traditional Christianity believed that divine intervention was necessary to
   improve human nature, for the Transcendentalists humanity could be improved
   by relying on its own strength.

5. Transcendentalism was an offshoot of Unitarianism, which had rejected Calvinism and liberal beliefs were embraced by them.

6. Those who joined the Transcendentalists were often ministers and people who wrote for a living.

7. Margaret Fuller's contribution to Transcendentalism included editing the magazine *The Dial* and she also conducted discussions for women.

8. Brook Farm, an experiment in communal living, was established both to help support the group and educate children.

9. The more literary members of the group included poets, novelists, and lecturers.

10. Perhaps the greatest legacy of Transcendentalism is not its religious or philosophical belief but how it influenced great literature.

EXERCISE 18-2   **Creating parallel structures**

Combine the following sentences, using parallel words, phrases, and clauses.

EXAMPLE   On October 3, 1990, Germans raised one flag. They shed the names
           "East" and "West." They were a unified country again.

           On October 3, 1990, Germans raised one flag, shed the names "East"
           and "West," and became a unified country again.

1. For several months there was rejoicing. People danced in the streets.

2. After the celebration, Germans realized that they had economic problems to face.
   They also had social problems. There were problems in politics as well.

3. East German politicians were accustomed to governing by decree. West Germans
   relied on vigorous debate in order to govern.

4. In the East, factories used outmoded machinery. They also had no restraints on
   pollution. The products they produced were inferior to Western products.

5. West Germans welcomed their fellow citizens. They gave assistance in finding lost
   relatives. Promises were made to improve the lives of Easterners.

6. Within months, Westerners recognized that they would have to make sacrifices. They were beginning to realize that unification would be costly.

7. Factories need to be retooled. There are many unemployed people who have to find jobs. The political structure will have to accommodate Easterners.

8. At first, Western leaders thought that reunification would be completed in two or three years. But now ten years is what most experts think it will take.

9. There is friction between Easterners and Westerners. The Easterners think Westerners are greedy. The Westerners think Easterners are pathetic.

10. Most Germans still believe that reunification will create harmony. They think it will make the country stronger. Their dreams will be fulfilled.

EXERCISE 18-3   Creating parallel structures

Study the paragraph by Abraham Lincoln below, reproduced from Chapter 18 of the handbook. Write an imitation of Lincoln's paragraph, beginning with one of the following sentences (or choose your own):

> A teenage marriage cannot last.
> A great concert can revitalize the soul.
> A child born in the ghetto will never be free.

A house divided against itself cannot stand. I believe this government cannot endure, permanently half slave and half free. I do not expect the Union to be dissolved. I do not expect the house to fall. But I do expect it will cease to be divided. It will become all one thing, or all the other.

EXERCISE 18-4

Rewrite the following outline, keeping elements at the same level of generality in parallel form.

Section Title: Preparing for surgery

      A. Doctor takes a medical history
      B. Blood tests by lab technician
      C. Anesthesiologist—explaining procedure, asking questions
      D. "Prep" undertaken by nursing staff
          1. Any hair in immediate area shaved off
          2. They thoroughly clean area
          3. Isolation of area

EXERCISE 18-5   Recognizing parallel structures

Photocopy a page or two from one of your textbooks, and underline all parallel words, phrases, and clauses. Rewrite a couple of the sentences, eliminating the parallel structure. Compare the two: How does the use of parallelism contribute to the meaning of the passage? How does it affect the style of the piece? Write your responses below.

EXERCISE 18-6   Revising

As you revise drafts of any papers you're working on at present, look for places where parallel structure would make the paper more effective. It may be a series of words, or two phrases or clauses, or even a pair of sentences. Occasionally a paragraph can be arranged around parallel structures (as in Exercise 18-3).

CHAPTER 19

Building Emphasis with Coordination and Subordination

Once your main points are presented clearly in a draft, you can concentrate on employing specific, concrete images (chapter 21 c, d), concise and direct language (chapter 17), parallel structures (chapter 18), and sentence variety (chapter 20). All of these techniques help give your writing emphasis.

COORDINATION

19a Use coordinate structures to emphasize equal ideas.

When you use coordination in your writing, you give equal emphasis to each element in the coordinate structure.

CRITICAL DECISIONS

CHALLENGE SENTENCES: KNOW WHEN TO COORDINATE OR SUBORDINATE SENTENCE ELEMENTS

Coordination and subordination are methods of linking sentences and sentence parts. The following sentences can be joined in various ways to establish coordinate or subordinate relationships. Presently, each sentence—*because* it is a sentence—receives equal emphasis.

> (1) A complete suit of armor consisted of some 200 metal plates. (2) The armor of the fifteenth century offered protection from crossbows. (3) Armor offered protection from swords. (4) Armor offered protection from early muskets. (5) A suit of armor weighed 60 pounds. (6) A suit of armor would quickly exhaust the soldier it was meant to protect.

Choosing when to link sentences with coordination or subordination requires that you be clear about (1) the level of emphasis you want to give particular information and (2) the specific logical relationships you want to establish.

WHY CHOOSE COORDINATE RELATIONSHIPS?

Coordinating Conjunctions and the Relationships They Establish

To show addition: *and*   **To show contrast:** *but, yet*
To show choice: *or, nor*   **To show cause:** *for*
To show consequences: *so*

Use coordinating conjunctions to link sentences by giving equal emphasis to specific words (in this case, words from sentences 2, 3, and 4).

The armor of the fifteenth century offered protection from crossbows, swords, and early muskets.

Use coordinating conjunctions to link sentences by giving equal emphasis to specific phrases (in this case, verb phrases from sentences 1 and 5).

A complete suit of armor consisted of some 200 metal plates **and** weighed 60 pounds.

Use coordinating conjunctions to link and give equal emphasis to whole sentences, in this case sentence 6 and the combination of sentences 2, 3, and 4.

The armor of the fifteenth century offered protection from crossbows, swords, and early muskets; **but** the armor would quickly exhaust the soldier it was meant to protect.

Conjunctive Adverbs and the Relationships They Establish

To show contrast: *however, nevertheless, nonetheless,* and *still*
To show cause and effect: *accordingly, consequently, thus,* and *therefore*
To show addition: *also, besides, furthermore,* and *moreover*
To show time: *afterward, subsequently,* and *then*
To show emphasis: *indeed*
To show condition: *otherwise*

Use conjunctive adverbs to link and give equal emphasis to two sentences. Conjunctive adverbs can be shifted from the beginning, to the middle, to the end of the second sentence (which is not possible with coordinating conjunctions—see 19a-3):

The armor of the fifteenth century offered protection from crossbows, swords, **and** early muskets; **however,** the armor would quickly exhaust the soldier it was meant to protect.

Conjunctive adverbs vs. coordinating conjuctions: Both conjunctive adverbs and coordinating conjunctions give equal emphasis to and establish similar logical relations between the sentences they join. Why choose one over the other? Differences are subtle and, if the sentences are punctuated correctly, both choices are correct. Because a conjunctive adverb's *only* function is to join whole sentences, it is the more emphatic choice. Use a conjunctive adverb when the sentences being joined are long or complicated (when the content requires a strong logical connection) or when you otherwise want to emphasize the relationship between sentences.

WHY CHOOSE SUBORDINATE RELATIONSHIPS?

Subordinating Conjunctions and the Relationships They Establish

> **To show condition:** *if, even if, unless,* and *provided that*
> **To show contrast:** *though, although, even though,* and *as if*
> **To show cause:** *because* and *since*
> **To show time:** *when, whenever, while, as, before, after, since, once,* and *until*
> **To show place:** *where* and *wherever*
> **To show purpose:** *so that, in order that,* and *that*

Subordinating conjunctions link whole clauses but, in the process, give one clause greater emphasis. Use a subordinating conjunction when you want one of the two sentences you are linking to modify (that is, to describe or to comment on) the other.

> Because it weighed 60 pounds, a suit of armor would quickly exhaust the soldier it was meant to protect.

Designate one sentence as subordinate by placing a conjunction at its head; thereafter, the sentence is referred to as a *dependent clause* (in this example, *Because it weighed 60 pounds*). Emphasis in a sentence linked with subordination is given to the *independent clause:* in this example, to *a suit of armor . . . protect*. See the discussion on relative pronouns (14e, 19b-2, 25d-1&2), which also begin dependent clauses.

---

1 Give equal emphasis to elements with coordinating conjunctions.

Coordinating conjunctions (*and, but, or, nor, so, for, yet*) allow writers to combine parallel elements from two or more sentences into a single sentence.

To establish equality between words

Howard Cosell is a noted sports announcer **and** journalist.

To establish equality between phrases

Cosell believes that the importance of sports lies not in the games themselves **but** in the causes that arise within sports.

To establish equality between phrases

Cosell states that Muhammad Ali is remembered for his boxing career, **yet** he should be remembered for his fight against the draft.

2 **Give equal emphasis to elements by using correlative conjunctions.**

Correlative conjunctions (*either/or, both/and, not only/but also, neither/nor, whether/or*) function in the same way as coordinating conjunctions, but provide greater emphasis.

Cosell asserts that boxing is both a brutal sport and a corrupting influence.

3 **Use conjunctive adverbs to give balanced emphasis to sentence elements.**

Conjunctive adverbs (e.g., *however, otherwise, indeed, nevertheless, afterward, still*) are used to join two independent clauses sharing balanced emphasis. Conjunctive adverbs can be moved around in a sentence.

Cosell was known as one of the best boxing announcers in the business. **However,** he now refuses to be associated with the sport.

Cosell was known as one of the best boxing announcers in the business. Now, **however,** he refuses to be associated with the sport.

4 **Revise sentences that use illogical or excessive coordination.**

Faulty coordination

Revise sentences in which coordinated elements are not logically related.

FAULTY   Calls to 900 numbers are expensive, and they offer callers horoscopes, travel information, celebrity trivia, and many other bits of information.

REVISED   Calls to 900 numbers are expensive. They offer callers horoscopes, travel information, celebrity trivia, and many other bits of information.

Excessive coordination

Revise sentences in which coordination is used excessively and without attention to logical connections.

FAULTY   The increasing popularity of 900 lines can be attributed to people's insatiable desire for information, and many entrepreneurs have discovered that the profits from 900 lines can be great, but those profits must be shared with telephone companies, and the entire business is complicated, and that is because of the lack of regulations.

REVISED   The increasing popularity of 900 lines can be attributed to people's insatiable desire for information. Many entrepreneurs have discovered that the profits from 900 lines can be great, but those profits must be shared with telephone companies. The entire business is complicated by the lack of regulations.

SUBORDINATION

19b Use subordinate structures to emphasize a main idea.

In **subordination,** a **dependent clause** is joined to an **independent clause,** emphasizing the idea in the independent clause (see chapter 7e).

 Use subordinating conjunctions to form dependent adverb clauses.

Two sentences can be joined to create a **complex sentence** in which the independent clause will receive the greater emphasis.

The residents of Walpole, Massachusetts no longer wanted their town's name to be associated with a prison. The prison's name was changed from Walpole to Cedar Junction.

Because the residents of Walpole, Massachusetts no longer wanted their town's name to be associated with a prison, the prison's name was changed from Walpole to Cedar Junction.

Emphasis and logical sequence determine whether a dependent adverbial clause will appear at the beginning of a sentence, in the middle, or at the end.

When it was a colony of Great Britain, Rhodesia was its name.

The name was changed, **because of its colonial implications,** to Zimbabwe.

The country has been known as Zimbabwe **since Ian Smith's white government was ousted.**

2 Use *that*, *which*, and *who* to form dependent adjective clauses.

Two sentences can be combined so that one becomes an **adjective clause** that modifies a noun in the independent clause. The adjective clause begins with a **relative pronoun** (*who* for people; *that* for people, animals, or things; *which* for animals or things).

The early British settlers in this country called their community "New England." The settlers still felt close ties with their homeland.

The early British settlers called their community "New England." The settlers still felt close ties with their homeland.

The early British settlers, who still felt close ties with their homeland, called their community "New England."

3 Use subordination accurately to avoid confusion.

Three errors are commonly associated with subordination: inappropriate and ambiguous use of subordinating conjunctions, illogical subordination, and excessive subordination.

Inappropriate and ambiguous use of subordinating conjunctions

Revise sentences in which the subordinating conjunction *as* is used to indicate cause.

CONFUSING	**As** they wished to remind themselves of home, the settlers named their new towns after British towns.
REVISED	**Because** they wished to remind themselves of home, the settlers named their new towns after British towns.

Revise sentences in which the preposition *like* is used as a subordinating conjunction. While *like* is appropriate in informal conversation, *as* belongs in formal, standard English.

NONSTANDARD	New Englanders cherished their heritage **like** their counterparts in England did.
REVISED	New Englanders cherished their heritage **as** their counterparts in England did.

Illogical subordination

Revise sentences in which the subordinating conjunction does not reflect a logical relationship between the dependent and the independent clauses.

FAULTY	**Where** the settlers named their communities after their home towns, the natives named places for natural phenomena.
REVISED	**While** the settlers named their communities after their home towns, the natives named places for natural phenomena.

Excessive subordination

Revise sentences in which excessive subordination obscures relationships between clauses and threatens to confuse readers.

FAULTY	Because the settlers believed that human nature is basically evil, they established a strong government, which oversaw the everyday lives of each resident, even though some of the settlers, who did not hold the same religious beliefs, felt that they were being persecuted.
REVISED	Because the settlers believed that human nature is basically evil, they established a strong government. The government oversaw the everyday lives of each resident, even though some of the settlers, who did not hold the same religious beliefs, felt that they were being persecuted.

OTHER DEVICES FOR ACHIEVING EMPHASIS

19c Use special techniques to achieve emphasis.

Other techniques, such as repetition, contrast, and punctuation, can be combined with coordination and subordination to achieve emphasis.

1 Punctuate, capitalize, and highlight to emphasize words.

Capitalization, boldface, exclamation points, and **italics** should be used sparingly, and only when wording alone will not achieve the appropriate emphasis.

Horace Rumpole calls his wife She Who Must Be Obeyed.

In the British legal system, there is a difference between a **barrister** and a **solicitor.**

You may not believe this, but judges, barristers, and solicitors in a British courtroom still wear *wigs!*

Words following a **colon** are emphasized.

Horace Rumpole has a special place in his creator's heart: John Mortimer based the Rumpole character on barristers he encountered in his career.

Dashes and **parentheses** are also effective tools for achieving emphasis. The dash creates a pause and the expectation that a significant comment will follow, while parentheses set off material that is interesting but not essential.

Rumpole's trademarks—his crumpled raincoat and his fat cigar—have endeared him to millions of viewers.

Mortimer created an entire cast of characters (Guthrie Featherstone, Phyllida Erskine-Brown, Uncle Tom, and Henry the clerk) based on his experiences.

 2   **Repeat words, phrases, and clauses to emphasize ideas.**

Repeating a structure two or three times in a sentence can create emphasis. Used sparingly within a paragraph, repetition can help readers understand material and appreciate key points.

Given **time**—**time** not in years but in millennia—life adjusts, and a balance has been reached. For **time** is the essential ingredient; but in the modern world there is no **time.**

—Rachel Carson, *Silent Spring*

A nation is **as great,** and only **as great**, as her rank and file.

—Woodrow Wilson

She was intensely sympathetic. She was immensely charming. She was utterly unselfish.

—Virginia Woolf, "Professions for Women"

3   **Use contrasts to emphasize ideas.**

When placing elements in **contrast** to one another, be sure that they have parallel structures.

We know through painful experience that freedom is never voluntarily given by the oppressor; it must be demanded by the oppressed.

—Martin Luther King, "Letter from Birmingham Jail"

Use specialized sentences to create emphasis.

You can achieve emphasis by using an occasional sentence that does not conform to readers' expectations.

The brief sentence

An especially brief sentence located anywhere in a paragraph will call attention to itself.

> . . . In December 1988, the supreme court of Canada ruled that parts of Bill 101 [which banned any language but French on commercial signs] were illegal. According to the court, Quebec could order that French be the primary language of commerce, but not the only one. As an immediate response, 15,000 francophones marched in protest through the streets of Montreal and many stores that had bilingual signs were vandalized, often by having the letters FLQ (for Front de Libération de Québec) spray-painted across their windows. One was firebombed.
>
> —Bill Bryson, *The Mother Tongue*

The one-sentence paragraph

While the one-sentence paragraph often either opens or closes an essay, it can be effectively placed between two longer paragraphs as well.

> . . . Sometimes, walking in the star-sprinkled evenings, I think of that almost forgotten theory of Arrhenius that the spores of life came originally from outer space.
>
> **Perhaps that explains it, I think wistfully—life reaching out, groping for a billion years, life desperate to go home.**
>
> The nineteenth-century mechanists, at least, did not find our origins in the abyss. . . .
>
> —Loren Eiseley, *The Immense Journey*

The periodic sentence

Because most sentences are **cumulative** (that is, they begin with the subject and add detail as the sentence progresses), using the occasional **periodic sentence** (that is, one in which the subject and verb are delayed until the end) can create emphasis.

> By the last day of the tour, when a limousine picked me up at my Beverly Hills hotel for my last round of satellite TV interviews, I knew I had to stop.
>
> —Randy Shilts, "Talking AIDS to Death"

EXERCISE 19-1   Creating emphasis

Using coordinating conjunctions, correlative conjunctions, and conjunctive adverbs, combine the following sentences to achieve equal emphasis.

EXAMPLE   Weather forecasting is a fascinating science. Weather forecasting is also a complex science.

Weather forecasting is a fascinating and complex science.

1. In the past, the National Weather Service sent balloons into the atmosphere. If they did not launch balloons, they looked to radar systems for weather readings.

2. The service uses computers as well. Most of them are hopelessly outdated.

3. A good deal of information reaches the service from satellites. The satellites are also showing signs of wear.

4. Much of the Weather Service's equipment is outdated. Its forecasts are more accurate than they were a generation ago.

5. Accurate weather forecasts allow people to plan their activities. Accurate forecasts can save lives.

6. Officials who know a tornado is headed their way can warn citizens to take cover. Officials who know it is headed elsewhere don't have to warn citizens.

7. In 1986 the Weather Service established a modernization plan. The plan is both overbudget. The plan is behind schedule.

8. The new satellites must be launched soon. If they are not launched soon, the Weather Service will receive no information from space.

9. The new computers and radar systems must be put into operation soon. They are needed now.

10. With up-to-date equipment, the Weather Service can make accurate short-range forecasts. With up-to-date equipment, the Weather Service can make accurate long-range forecasts.

EXERCISE 19-2   Achieving emphasis with dependent clauses

Combine the following pairs of sentences by converting one in each pair into a dependent clause.

EXAMPLE   The Industrial Revolution brought people into factories. At an earlier time, people's work and home lives were intertwined.

Before the Industrial Revolution brought people into factories, their work and home lives were intertwined.

1. Work began to be concentrated in factories. At this point the time people spent on the job became time spent away from the family.

2. Time spent on the job began to take precedence. The reason for this was that the worker's wages kept the family fed and clothed.

3. A worker spent more time at the factory. This worker was viewed as a dedicated family man.

4. Women did not work in the factories. They only worked if they were unmarried, or at least childless.

5. Managers measured a worker's worth by time spent on the job. The reason managers did this was that they were responsible for production.

6. A worker took time off to tend to a sick family member. That worker was considered undependable.

7. Managers still measure worth in terms of hours. This happens despite the fact that the assembly line is no longer the model of American industry.

8. More women with children enter the workforce. This phenomenon has caused managers to reluctantly rethink their ideas about time and worth.

9. Human services professionals have studied work/family problems. These same human services professionals encourage corporations to become more flexible about time spent on the job.

10. At some point corporations will become more sensitive to the time constraints faced by workers. Meanwhile, both family and business will suffer.

EXERCISE 19-3   Revising for emphasis

Revise the following sentences by eliminating illogical or excessive coordination; inappropriate or ambiguous use of subordinating conjunctions; and illogical or excessive subordination.

EXAMPLE   By the age of four, Wolfgang Amadeus Mozart's musical ability was well known in Salzburg, and he became the court organist for the Archbishop.

By the age of four, Wolfgang Amadeus Mozart's musical ability was well known in Salzburg, where he became the court organist for the Archbishop.

1. As his fame had spread before he was seven, he was invited to tour Europe in 1763.

2. Throughout his life, he composed in his head, where other composers agonized over the clavier.

3. By the time Mozart was fourteen, he had played for the crowned heads of Europe, and he played for the Pope also, and he had been writing sonatas for seven years at this time, and the Pope conferred on him the order of the Golden Spur, but Mozart did not think much of the award.

4. During his early years, Mozart performed in Germany, Austria, and Italy, and several heads of state commissioned sonatas and operas from him.

5. Mozart, like many composers before him, wrote music for religious occasions.

6. In 1777 the Archbishop, who knew that Mozart wished to move on, allowed the young man to take on other work, after which Mozart traveled to Paris and Munich, which were then centers of great music, because he wanted to expand his experience.

7. He spent a good deal of time in Vienna, as he wanted desperately to secure an appointment at the imperial court.

8. In late 1787 the Emperor finally hired Mozart and paid the young man less than half what his predecessor had been paid.

9. While employed by the Emperor, Mozart wrote operas and concertos, and he often performed himself, and some of his performances included improvisations, and the audience went wild over them.

10. Where he wrote in many forms, Mozart is most highly regarded for his operas.

EXERCISE 19-4   **Recognizing emphasis**

Make three photocopies of several consecutive paragraphs from one of your textbooks. On the first copy, underline all coordinate structures, and identify the words indicating equal ideas as coordinating conjunctions, correlative conjunctions, or conjunctive adverbs. How many times does the writer use coordination? How often are words joined? Phrases? Clauses? How does the use of coordination help the writer achieve emphasis in the passage? Write your responses below.

Using the second photocopy, underline all subordinate structures and circle each subordinating conjunction. What kind of relationship does each subordinating conjunction establish? (Refer to the list in this chapter.) How many times does the writer use subordination? How often are subordinate clauses placed at the beginning of the sentence? In the middle? At the end? How does the use of subordination help the writer achieve emphasis in the passage?

Using the third photocopy, underline and identify all special techniques for achieving emphasis. How many times does the writer use special techniques? How many different techniques does the author use? How does the use of special techniques help the writer achieve emphasis in the passage?

EXERCISE 19-5   Review

Rewrite the following paragraph in the space below, combining sentences with the techniques for achieving emphasis covered in this chapter.

In the past ten years there has been a boom in medicine in this country. That boom has not been in human medicine. Dogs and cats who suffered illnesses were once "put to sleep." Now they are treated in much the same way as humans are. Some people consider pet health care a frivolous notion. Thousands of owners spend millions of dollars annually on treatment for their pets. Many owners consider their pets part of the family. These owners see nothing wrong with spending money for veterinary care. More people wish to treat rather than euthanize their sick pets. Pet health insurance programs are available around the country. Pet health care may be an indication of compassion. It may be an indication of misplaced priorities. It looks like many people will continue to pay the veterinarian to cure the family dog.

EXERCISE 19-6   Revising

As you revise drafts of any papers you're working on at present, use the techniques covered in this chapter to achieve emphasis. Remember that the ideas you want to communicate will determine the specific technique you use. Compare the revision to the original. How has adding emphasis improved the effectiveness of your paper?

CHAPTER 20

Controlling Length and Rhythm

20a Monitoring sentence length

1 Track the length of your sentences.

Until you develop intuition about sentence length, it is wise to find out what your average sentence length is, and vary the number of words from sentence to sentence.

Tracking Sentence Length

Any given sentence in a paragraph is long or short in relation to the *average* number of words per sentence in that paragraph. A simple process of counting and dividing will reveal to you your average sentence length.

1. Number the sentences in a paragraph and on a scrap of paper write those numbers in a column.

2. Count and record the number of words in each sentence.

3. Count the total number of words in the paragraph. (Add together the word counts for step 2.)

4. Divide the number of words in the paragraph (step 3) by the number of sentences in the paragraph (step 1): this number is your average sentence length for the paragraph.

Consider a sentence to be **average** in length if it has **5 words more or less** than your average. Consider a sentence **long** if it is **6 or more** words longer than your average and **short** if it is **6 or fewer words shorter.**

5. Return to the listing you made in step 2, and designate each sentence of your paragraph as being of **average** length, **short,** or **long**. These designations apply to your writing only. They are relative terms, representing different sentence lengths for different writers.

2   **Vary sentence length and alternate the length of consecutive sentences.**

Once you have tracked the length of your sentences, you can vary sentence length.

Varying Sentence Length and Alternating the Length of Consecutive Sentences

While no precise formula exists for determining how many long or short sentences should be used in a paragraph, you may find these general principles helpful:

- Determine the average length of sentences in a paragraph.
- Plan to vary from that average by using short and long sentences.
- Use short sentences to break up strings of longer ones.
- Avoid placing short sentences consecutively unless you are doing so for specific stylistic effect.
- Avoid placing more than two or three long sentences consecutively.
- Avoid placing more than three or four sentences of average length consecutively.

20b   Strategies for varying sentence length

1   **Control the use of coordination.**

While coordination eliminates redundancy and reduces the overall length of a paragraph, it also results in longer sentences. Learn to use coordination to vary sentence length, being careful not to make sentences too long.

REDUNDANT	Sculptor Lynda Benglis is known as a minimalist. Benglis is also a feminist. Benglis uses metal tubing. She also uses plastic sheeting. She also uses chicken wire to construct her sculptures.
REVISED	Sculptor Lynda Benglis is known as both a minimalist and a feminist, and she uses metal tubing, plastic sheeting, and chicken wire to construct her sculptures.

REVISED   Sculptor Lynda Benglis is known as both a minimalist and
                   a feminist. She uses metal tubing, plastic sheeting, and
                   chicken wire to construct her sculptures.

2 **Control the use of modifying phrases and clauses.**

Controlling the extent to which you use modifying phrases and clauses (see
chapter 7, d and e) can help you control sentence length. Modifying phrases and
clauses can function as adjectives or adverbs, and they include the following:

Type	**Example**
Infinitive Phrase	Benglis left college **to become an artist.** (adv)
Prepositional Phrase	She had a great deal of talent **to exploit.** (adj) The power **of Benglis's work** is striking. (adj)
Participle Phrase	Her work is displayed **in several cities.** (adv) **Returning to her roots,** Benglis uses bright colors. (adj)
Appositive Phrase	New York, **an artist's haven,** welcomed her. (adj)
Subordinate Clause	**Before Benglis arrived on the scene,** minimalist sculpture was considered impersonal. (adv)
Relative Clause	Benglis, **who is only forty-nine,** has a bright future ahead of her. (adj)

Convert modifying clauses to phrases.

If a sentence is too long in relation to surrounding sentences, reduce its length
by converting a modifying clause to a phrase.

CLAUSE   **Unless they take medication constantly,** some allergy sufferers
                  are miserable for months on end.

PHRASE   **Without constant medication,** some allergy sufferers are
                  miserable for months on end.

Move modifying phrases from one sentence to another.

If a sentence is too long, try moving a modifier from it to an adjacent sentence.

LONG   The allergy sufferer's immune system, **which is responsible for the allergic reaction,** is sensitive to many substances, such as pollen and mold, that are harmless to the body.

REVISED   The allergy sufferer's immune system **is responsible for the allergic reaction.** It is sensitive to many substances, such as pollen and mold, that are harmless to the body.

Substitute a single-word modifier for a phrase- or clause-length modifier.

Sentences can be shortened by converting phrases or clauses to single-word adjectives or adverbs.

CLAUSE   An allergy attack **that comes on suddenly** can be serious.

SINGLE
WORD   A **sudden** allergy attack can be serious.

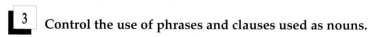 **Control the use of phrases and clauses used as nouns.**

Sentences can be combined by converting the key words of one sentence into a phrase or clause that then functions as a noun in the second sentence. **Infinitive phrases, gerund phrases, and noun phrases and clauses** can function as nouns.

Type	**Example**
Infinitive Phrase	**To protect the body from harmful substances** is the job of the immune system. (subject)
Gerund Phrase	It works by **attacking foreign bodies.** (object)
Noun Phrase	Allergic reactions result from **a case of mistaken identity.** (object)
Noun Clause	**The fact that pollen is not harmful** means nothing to the oversensitive immune system. (subject)

If a sentence containing a noun phrase or clause is too long, move the noun phrase to another sentence.

LONG   Because of **the fact that medical researchers do not know what causes the immune system to react to allergens,** it is difficult for doctors to treat allergies effectively.

REVISED   **Medical researchers do not know what causes the immune system to react to allergens. Thus** it is difficult for doctors to treat allergies effectively.

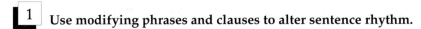

20c | Strategies for controlling sentence rhythm

1 | Use modifying phrases and clauses to alter sentence rhythm.

Moving modifiers to different places within a sentence can change the rhythm of the sentence. Sentences with only a few brief modifiers have their own rhythm.

Vary the position of phrases.

While phrases that function as adverbs can be moved within a sentence, sometimes such movement changes the meaning of the sentence. Phrases that function as adjectives should always remain close to the nouns they modify.

Adverb phrases:

ORIGINAL   The Prime Minister resigned **on Tuesday,** hoping that Parliament would respond quickly.

SHIFTED   **On Tuesday,** the Prime Minister resigned, hoping that
RHYTHM   Parliament would respond quickly.

SHIFTED   The Prime Minister resigned, hoping that Parliament would
MEANING   respond quickly **on Tuesday.**

Adjective phrases:

ORIGINAL   Parliament, **voting no confidence in the Prime Minister,** had forced his resignation.

SHIFTED   **Voting no confidence in the Prime Minister,** Parliament had
RHYTHM   forced his resignation.

FAULTY   Parliament had forced his resignation, **voting no confidence in the Prime Minister.**

Vary the position of clauses.

Shifting the position of adverb clauses in a sentence can alter its rhythm. An adjective clause must remain close to the noun it modifies.

Adverb clauses:

ORIGINAL **Because she is chosen by members of the parliament,** the Prime Minister usually represents the majority party.

REVISED The Prime Minister, **because she is chosen by members of the parliament,** usually represents the majority party.

REVISED The Prime Minister usually represents the majority party, **because she is chosen by members of the parliament**.

Adjective clauses:

ORIGINAL Margaret Thatcher, **who had been a dominant figure in world politics,** resigned in 1990.

SHIFTED RHYTHM A dominant figure in world politics, Margaret Thatcher resigned in 1990.

FAULTY Margaret Thatcher resigned in 1990, **who had been a dominant figure in world politics.**

Vary the position of transitions.

Moving transitions within a sentence can change its rhythm.

ORIGINAL Many countries are governed by a parliamentary system. **However,** not all parliamentary systems are the same.

REVISED Many countries are governed by a parliamentary system. Not all parliamentary systems, however, are the same.

REVISED Many countries are governed by a parliamentary system. Not all parliamentary systems are the same, however.

2 Revise individual sentences with a disruptive rhythm.

Sentences with repeated stops and starts should be revised, sometimes resulting in two sentences.

DISRUPTIVE The English language, because of its diversity, is spoken differently in different places, and has changed over time.

REVISED Because of its diversity, the English language is spoken differently in different places. It has also changed over time.

3 | Revise groups of sentences to avoid a repetitive rhythm.

When sentences in the same paragraph repeat the same rhythm, restructure one or more of them.

REPEATING   In France, the Académie Française oversees the language, regulating usage and passing judgment on grammar and spelling. In the United States, there is no official body charged with governing our speech and writing. Because of its frequent shifts and evolutions, many linguists express fondness for English.

REVISED   In France, the Académie Française oversees the language, regulating usage and passing judgment on grammar and spelling. There is no official body charged with governing our speech and writing in the United States. Because of its frequent shifts and evolutions, many linguists express fondness for English.

4 | Vary sentence types.

In English there are four types of sentences based on function (see 7f-1). The direct statement is a **declarative sentence:** *English is spoken almost everywhere.* The question is an **interrogative sentence:** *How many people speak English?* The exclamation, or **exclamatory sentence,** expresses emotion: *I hate English class!* The command, or **imperative sentence,** expresses an order or strong desire: *Do your English homework.*

Use occasional questions for variety and focus.

In addition to focusing content, a question placed in the midst of declarative sentences creates a unique rhythm.

American English contains words from many different languages. Why is this so? In part, it's because we have been "borrowing" expressions from immigrants for two centuries.

Vary the structure of sentences.

In English there are four types of sentences based on function (see chapters 7 and 19). A **simple sentence** has a single subject and a single verb or predicate. A **compound sentence** has two subjects and two predicates. A **complex sentence** has one independent clause and one or more dependent clauses. A **compound-complex** sentence has at least two independent clauses and one dependent clause. (In the following examples, simple subjects are underlined once, simple predicates twice, and dependent clauses are set in italics.)

SIMPLE	Upon arrival in this country, many <u>immigrants</u> <u><u>knew</u></u> little English.
COMPOUND	Either <u>they</u> <u><u>relied</u></u> on relatives to translate, or <u>they</u> <u><u>learned</u></u> English as best they could.
COMPLEX	*Because immigrants had little political power*, <u>official agencies</u> rarely <u><u>provided</u></u> translations for them.
COMPOUND-COMPLEX	*When immigrants arrive today*, <u>they</u> often <u><u>find</u></u> a more welcoming bureaucracy, and <u>they</u> seldom <u><u>need</u></u> to rely on their own translators.

Varying Sentence Rhythm

Variety in sentence structures and rhythms is the mark of stylistically strong writing. While no rules govern just how a writer should vary rhythm from sentence to sentence, you may find these general principles helpful.

- Use phrases, clauses, and transitional expressions to vary sentence beginnings.

- Consciously shift the location of phrase- and clause-length modifiers in a paragraph: locate modifiers at the beginning of some sentences, in the middle of others, and at the end of others.

- Use short sentences to break up strings of long, heavily modified sentences.

- Limit your concentration of phrase- and clause-length modifiers to one and possibly two locations in a sentence. Heavily modifying a sentence at the beginning, middle, *and* end will create a burden stylistically.

- Vary sentence types.

EXERCISE 20-1   **Tracking sentence length**

Using the guidelines provided at the beginning of the chapter, track the sentence length in the following paragraph. Compare your analysis with those of your classmates to make sure that you know the procedure. Then choose three paragraphs you have written recently and analyze them. What conclusions can you draw about your own style? (For example, do you need to use more long sentences? Do you need to vary length more?)

(1) On every frontier, pioneers brought old habits to new lands. (2) Wheat, bluegrass, and white clover accompanied settlers over the Appalachians. (3) The Portuguese harvested sugar cane, and grapes thrive on the Madeira islands. (4) But most frontiers have been in the temperate regions, where soils and climate were not unlike the home country's. (5) The Amazon, by contrast, is a tropical frontier, a "torrid zone," that part of the planet for which countless conquistadors "have had the teeth but not the stomach," wrote historian Alfred W. Crosby. (6) Back in 1903, Euclydes da Cunha, the Brazilian explorer and journalist, described the challenge of the Amazon as "The Thousand Years' War against the unknown." (7) Nearly a century later, an assorted few have taken up the challenge.

—Mac Margolis, "Heroes of the Amazon"

EXERCISE 20-2   **Varying sentence length**

Using the strategies covered in 20b, vary sentence lengths in the following paragraph. Among the conjunctions you may use are: **Coordinating conjunctions:** *and, but, or, nor, for, so, yet.* **Correlative conjunctions:** *not only / but also, either / or, both / and.* **Conjunctive adverbs:** *however, moreover, furthermore, therefore, consequently.* **Subordinating conjunctions:** *when, although, while, since, because, before.* **Relative pronouns:** *who, which, that.*

In Newport, Rhode Island, a stone tower sits atop a hill. Colonial Governor Benedict Arnold used the tower to house a windmill. There is speculation about whether or not Arnold built the mill. Some say he adapted a structure. The structure had existed on the site since the twelfth century. These observers claim that the tower was built by Vikings. The Vikings landed at Narragansett Bay. Their landing preceded Columbus' first sighting of the New World. Others contend that the structure is no more than three hundred years old. There is some evidence of Viking artifacts in the general area. Most experts agree. They think that if the edifice were indeed constructed by Leif Ericsson's men, then archaeologists would have unearthed many more artifacts. These artifacts would have been unearthed by now. Some they believe that the tower is a Viking construction. Some do not believe this. Most people agree that it has created in Newport an intriguing mystery. The mystery is better left unsolved.

EXERCISE 20-3   Controlling length and rhythm

Rewrite each of the following sentences by moving the modifiers and transitions to as many different positions as possible in each sentence. Then read all of the sentences aloud to get a sense of the different rhythms.

EXAMPLE   Although it seems to be a simple word, "territory" can mean many different things.

Territory, **although it seems to be a simple word,** can mean many different things.

Territory can mean many different things, **although it seems to be a simple word.**

1. For example, one's personal territory is the immediate area surrounding one's body.

2. In geographical terms, territory refers to a specified area of land.

3. Among nations, territory means the land governed by a particular state.

4. In cities, certain territories belong to different gangs.

5. For people living in the suburbs, territory might be the neighborhood.

6. Animals, however, also have territories.

7. A fox, for example, spreads its scent to mark the perimeter of its territory.

8. When animals are in unfamiliar territory, they are constantly on guard.

9. Similarly, humans are on guard in unfamiliar territory.

10. People will build fences to guard their territory.

EXERCISE 20-4   Review

Using the techniques found in this chapter, rewrite the paragraph below, varying sentence length and rhythm.

The advent of television was in 1927. The basic technology of transmitting images has remained the same since then. The image we see on the screen is transmitted in waves. This is how the sounds we hear from the radio are transmitted. This is the same way Philo T. Farnsworth produced television images in San Francisco over sixty years ago. Technology became advanced enough to produce color images in 1954. Stereo sound was introduced thirty years later. But these advances were still based on the same transmission standard. Now all of that is about to change. Scientists are working on technologies that will alter television. The introduction of the compact disk altered audio recording technology almost the same way. Television images will soon be transmitted digitally. This will allow for much clearer pictures, among other things. The sets designed to receive the new images will at first be prohibitively expensive. But eventually high-definition television, or HDTV, will find its way into every home. Television is finally stepping into the computer age.

EXERCISE 20-5   Identifying strategies for achieving length and rhythm

Photocopy a brief passage from one of your textbooks, and identify some of the techniques the author uses to achieve variety in sentence length and rhythm. How does the author's style contribute to the content of the passage? How does it contribute to your reading pleasure? Write your responses below.

EXERCISE 20-6   Revising

As you revise drafts of papers you're working on at present, concentrate on controlling sentence length and rhythm. First analyze the paragraphs for sentence length, then for position of modifiers and types of sentences. After you have finished, compare the revision to the originals. How have you improved your presentation?

CHAPTER 21

Choosing the Right Word

21a Learning denotation and connotation

Denotation refers to the dictionary definition of a word. Occasionally, words that look similar are mistaken for one another: *flaunt* (to display ostentatiously) and *flout* (to scorn), for example. **Connotation** refers to a word's implications, associations, and nuances of meaning. For example, while *gathering, crowd,* and *mob* all refer to groups of people, *gathering* implies friendship, *crowd* implies anonymity, and *mob* implies angry intentions. When you choose words in your own writing, pay careful attention to both denotation and connotation.

21b Revising awkward diction

Four common errors lead to awkward diction: inappropriate connotation, inappropriate idiom, straining to sound learned, and unintentional euphony (rhyming, etc.).

1 Choosing words with an appropriate connotation

Inappropriate connotation can confuse readers and disrupt your prose.

INAPPROPRIATE   The mob at the class reunion shared old memories.

REVISED   The gathering at the class reunion shared old memories.

2 Following standard English idioms

Idiom refers to phrases that native speakers understand intuitively, but that do not conform to any general rules. Only use idiomatic expressions if you are certain of their form.

NOT IDIOMATIC   The class clown **turned out** at the reunion.

IDIOMATIC   The class clown **turned up** at the reunion.

Some Common Idioms in American English

He will *admit **to*** nothing.
We *arrived **at*** a conclusion.

We *arrived **in*** time.
We *arrived **on*** time.
We *brought **in*** the cake.
We *brought **up*** the rear of the parade.
*Except **for*** my close friends, no one knows of my plan.
Don't call, *except **in*** emergencies.
I often *get **into*** jams.
*Get **up*** the courage to raise your hand.
I *got **in*** just under the deadline.
Good friends will *make **up*** after they argue.
How did you *make **out*** in your interview?
We'll *take **out*** the trash later.
Next week, the Red Sox *take **on*** the Orioles.
The senate will *take **up*** the issue tomorrow.
A large crowd *turned **out.***
At midnight, we'll *turn **in.***
The request was *turned **down.***

---

3 Writing directly rather than straining to sound learned

It is far better to write simply and directly than to falter while trying to sound scholarly. Sometimes such attempts result in the creation of words that do not exist in English, and sometimes they result in unnecessarily long, complicated phrases.

AWKWARD Attempts to sound learned will **undoubtfully** fail.

      Some usage of an inappropriate nature is considered humorous by this reader.

REVISED Attempts to sound learned will **surely** fail. [The correct word is *undoubtedly*, but if you can't use it properly, use a simpler word.]

      I am amused by some inappropriate usage.

4 Listening for unintentional euphony

While **euphony**—the pleasing sound produced by certain word combinations—is desirable in poetry, it is inappropriate in most essays and reports. Reading your work aloud will alert you to any unintentional euphony.

AWKWARD Euphony **sounds sweet** and **soothing** in **some** writing.

REVISED Euphony **creates a sweet, calming effect** in **some** writing.

21c Using general and specific language

A proper mix of **general** and **specific** language is necessary to help readers understand an essay. Language that is too general often fails to convince readers, while language that is too specific fails to lead readers to the "big picture."

GENERAL   Moreover, a disturbing political phenomenon is afoot: the disillusionment of Latin American voters with traditional democratic politics.

SPECIFIC   In all recent presidential elections except two, the incumbent party has been rejected at the polls. In many cases, voters have chosen newcomers with no strong allegiances or organizations, such as Collor and Peru's President Fujimori, a self-effacing engineer whose low-budget campaign promised nothing more than honesty and hard work.
            —Pamela Constable

The preceding general statement offers no support to convince readers of its truth, while the specific statement offers no unifying point to make it meaningful. Taken together, however, they constitute an effective paragraph that balances general claims with specific evidence.

21d Using abstract and concrete language

Abstract language is used to name categories or ideas, and appeals to the intellect. **Specific** or **concrete** language, on the other hand, is used to provide details, and appeals to the senses. A proper balance of abstract and concrete language helps readers understand the ideas in an essay from both an intellectual and a sensory perspective.

ABSTRACT   The Old West here comes into direct conflict with the New.

CONCRETE   The leathery rancher in Wyoming with his herd to water vs. the condo-dwelling Sybarite in Laguna Beach with a Porsche to wash and two hot tubs to keep filled.
            —Jeanne McDowell and Richard Woodbury

The first sentence above provides abstract terms to convey the idea of the Old and the New West; the second provides concrete images such as rancher, cattle herd, urbanite, and hot tubs. (In fact, the two sentences are joined in the original with a colon.)

21e Using formal English as an academic standard

Although descriptive linguists agree that no dialect of English is more "correct" than any other, there is good reason to adopt a standard dialect. Communication is enhanced when all parties adhere to the same guidelines. In academic writing, that standard is **formal English.** To inject regional or ethnic dialects, slang, or colloquial language into communication for a general audience is to confuse a segment of that audience.

CRITICAL DECISIONS

SET ISSUES IN A BROADER CONTEXT: CHOOSING THE RIGHT TONE AND REGISTER FOR YOUR PAPERS

Every sentence of every paper you write has a characteristic tone which, intended or not, communicates information about you: about your assumptions concerning the reader and about your knowledge of and attitude toward your topic. Choose a tone that helps you to meet the expectations of readers while satisfying your purpose as a writer. You will choose a formal, informal, or popular tone and register (3a-4).

Choosing an appropriate tone requires that you carefully analyze the writing occasion (see 3a-4)—the topic, your purpose, and your audience—and that you then make decisions about your document's level of content, language, and style.

- Match the tone and register of your writing to the writing occasion—to your topic, your purpose, and the needs of your audience:

    FORMAL. *Likely audience*—specialists or knowledgeable nonspecialists. *Content*—choose content that goes beyond introductory material. *Language*—to the extent that you understand and are comfortable with technical language, use it whenever needed for precision. *Style*—adhere to all the rules and conventions expected of writing in the subject area. Complicated and, if necessary, long sentences are acceptable if needed for precision. For guidance on format, see pieces similar to the one you are writing or consult a discipline-appropriate style guide.

    POPULAR. *Likely audience*—nonspecialists willing to follow a detailed presentation. *Content*—choose content similar to that of a formal presentation, but avoid any examples or explanations

that require specialized understanding. Emphasize (but do not necessarily limit yourself to) content that intersects with the readers' experiences and will keep them engaged.
Language—avoid specialized terms whenever possible, though if you must use them for precision, carefully prepare for and define them. *Style*—adhere to all conventions of grammar, usage, spelling, etc. Some slang or colloquial language is acceptable, but keep it to a minimum. Avoid specialized formats, but organize content in a sensible, orderly way. Closely monitor your sentences, alternating length and rhythm for best effect (see chapter 20).

INFORMAL. *Likely audience*—nonspecialists looking for general information. *Content*—choose content that closely intersects your readers' experiences; otherwise, readers will lose interest. Coverage of topic should be introductory. Draw only on the most accessible examples and cases. *Language*—do not use specialized terms. Generally, keep sentences brief. *Style*—adhere to conventions of grammar, usage, spelling, etc. Slang or colloquial language is accepted, especially when you are familiar with the local or in-group speech of your readers. A narrative, first-person format may be useful.

---

1   Revise most slang expressions into standard English.

For members of the in-group, **slang** is easy to understand. However, for people outside the group, it can be confusing. The word *wicked* means something totally different to an adolescent and an older adult; *bad* has opposite meanings for inner-city youth and suburban adults. When writing for a general audience, replace slang with standard English.

2   Replace regionalisms and dialect expressions with standard academic English.

If you ask for *tonic* in New England, you'll be given a soft drink; in any other part of the country you'll be given tonic water. Such **regional** expressions can interfere with communication for a general audience. Similarly, **dialect** expressions are meaningful only to a narrow audience. The omission of the verb *be* is perfectly logical within some dialects, for example, while it only serves to confuse those who do not understand the dialect.

3 Reduce colloquial language to maintain clarity and a consistent level of academic discourse.

Colloquial language is informal, conversational language. While most speakers of English understand colloquialisms, their presence in academic prose creates inconsistencies in tone. Expressions such as the following should be translated into formal English.

Colloquial	**Formal**
flunked	failed
jerk	foolish person
tough break	unfortunate
rub the wrong way	irritate
hang in there	persevere

4 Revise to restrict the use of jargon.

Among certain groups of professionals, **jargon** provides linguistic short cuts. A sportscaster uses the acronym *ERA* to refer to a pitcher's earned-run average, while a feminist uses the same acronym to refer to the Equal Rights Amendment. Doctors speak of *contraindications*, politicians of *damage control*, and artists of *minimalism*. Outside the professional group, these terms can only confuse an audience. If jargon must be used for a general audience, it is necessary to define terms. However, jargon should be avoided in standard academic prose.

21f Using figures of speech with care

Similes, analogies, and **metaphors** are **figures of speech,** carefully controlled comparisons that clarify or intensify meaning. In academic writing, figurative language is used across disciplines, though in some disciplines more freely than in others.

1 Using similes, analogies, and metaphors

In a **simile,** two different things—one usually familiar, the other not—are compared, using *like* or *as.*

> . . . before it is done this field trip to a slaughterhouse will have become for me a descent into Hades, a vision of life that perhaps it would have been better never to know.
>
> —Richard Selzer

Like a simile, an **analogy** compares an unknown concept in terms of something known. It is often more direct than a simile; its intended purpose is to clarify an idea. Analogies can be as brief as a sentence or as long as an essay.

It is a serious matter to shoot a working elephant—it is comparable to destroying a huge and costly piece of machinery—and obviously one ought not to do it if it can possibly be avoided.

—George Orwell

Longer analogies often begin with cue words such as *consider, by analogy,* and *just as;* transitions include *similarly, just so, so too,* and *in the same way.* (See chapter 6 for use of analogies in building an argument.)

Metaphors differ from similes and analogies in that the comparison is implicit; neither *like* or *as* nor other cue words are used.

Every word that falls from the mouth is a coin lost.

—Maxine Hong Kingston

2 Revise mixed metaphors.

In order to be effective, metaphors must be consistent. A **mixed metaphor** involves combinations that defy logic.

MIXED
METAPHOR   The President charted a course for the ship of state that had all citizens playing for the same team.

REVISED   The President laid out a game plan that had all citizens playing for the same team.

3 Replace worn-out metaphors (clichés) with fresh figures.

Metaphors that have become so worn that they no longer command attention indicate an unwillingness on the writer's part to seek out vivid expressions. Such clichés include *piece of cake, tough as nails, nose to the grindstone,* and *over the hill.*

21g Eliminating biased, dehumanizing language

The old children's rhyme "Sticks and stones may break my bones, but names can never hurt me" is a lie. Language can be used to hurt, to offend, and to exclude.

Sexism in diction

The so-called "generic" masculine pronoun, used to designate both men and women, prevailed in a time when women played a less visible role in public life. Many people take offense at the generic masculine, along with such gender-specific titles as *businessman, woman lawyer,* and *male nurse.*

Some Potentially Offensive Gender-Specific Nouns

Avoid	*Use*
stewardess (and similar nouns)	flight attendant
chairman	chair, chairperson
woman driver, male nurse	woman who was driving, man at the nursing station
mankind	people, humanity, humankind
workmen, manpower	workers, work force, personnel
the girls in the office	the women, the manager, the typist
mothering	parenting, nurturing

1   **Rewrite gender-stereotyping nouns as neutral nouns.**

SEXIST   All **salesmen** are covered by **workman's** compensation.
A **man's** worth cannot be counted in dollars.

NEUTRAL   All **salespeople** are covered by **worker's** compensation.
A **person's** worth cannot be counted in dollars.

2   **Balance reference to the sexes.**

SEXIST   The softball league is open to **men** and **girls.**

NEUTRAL   The softball league is open to **men** and **women.**

3   **Make balanced use of plural and gender-specific pronouns.**

See the Critical Decisions Box in 10c for four strategies that will help you to correct gender problems with pronoun use.

SEXIST   A good manager consults **his** employees on major decisions.

NEUTRAL   Good managers consult **their** employees on major decisions.

21h Avoiding euphemistic and pretentious language

1 Restrict the use of euphemisms.

Euphemisms are designed to soften the effect of words that may offend some readers. They are usually longer than the original word, however, and they sometimes convey a lack of sincerity. It is usually better to be direct rather than to rely on euphemism; phrasing can be used to soften effect.

EUPHEMISM   They are contemplating a **reduction in the work force.**

REVISED   A **layoff** is being contemplated.

2 Eliminate pretentious language.

Pretentious language indicates that a writer is more concerned with sounding lofty than with communicating. Avoid pretentious expressions such as the following:

Pretentious	**Direct**
In the opinion of this writer	I believe
utilize	use
In the event that	If
edifice	building

In specialized areas of study, technical terms are necessary. You should distinguish between legitimately complex terminology and pretentious writing.

Distinguishing Pretentious Language from Legitimate Technical Language

Bear in mind two principles when attempting to eliminate pretentious language:

- **Be concise:** Use as few words as possible to communicate clearly. Delete whole sentences or reduce them to phrases that you incorporate into other sentences; reduce phrases to single words; choose briefer words over longer ones. (See 17a for a full discussion of conciseness.)

- **Be precise:** Make sure your sentences communicate your *exact* meaning. If you need to add clarifying words, add as few words as possible. Use technical language for precision only when no other language will do.

These principles can help you eliminate pretentious language from your writing.

PRETENTIOUS	Individuals involved in thespian pursuits oftentimes partake of comestibles and potables in the culinary establishment referred to as Sardi's.
REVISED	Actors often eat and drink at Sardi's restaurant.
TECHNICAL (needs no revision)	. . . the concept of physical dependence on alcohol is a useful criterion for alcoholism, and the occurrence of withdrawal symptoms is a serviceable indicator in empirical studies.

—J. Michael Polich and Bruce R. Orvis

EXERCISE 21-1   **Eliminating inappropriate language**

Revise the following sentences, eliminating inappropriate connotation, non-idiomatic English, "learned" language, and unintentional euphony.

EXAMPLE   Alzheimer's disease affects the older people, causing them to
have trouble remembering
~~disremember~~ simple things.

1. In the past, Alzheimer's was referred by as *senile dementia*, and was not distinguished from other forms of craziness.

2. Doctors guess that about fifteen percent of the population over sixty-five suffer from the disease, ten percent of whom are capable to carry on normal lives.

3. In persons past their prime, difficulty remembering is a common occurrence, irregardless of the cause.

4. Most researchers agree to the idea that Alzheimer's results from the rotting of brain cells.

5. Absent-minded people need not trepidate that they have Alzheimer's, according with researchers, because absent-mindedness is a clearly common condition.

EXERCISE 21-2

Label each of the following sentences as *general* or *specific*. For each general sentence, provide an additional sentence with specific detail. For each detailed sentence, provide an additional sentence that makes a general statement.

EXAMPLE   There is a great variety of programs on television.   _general_

Television programs include dramas, news programs, and situation comedies.

1. Toddlers love *Sesame Street*.   _____

2. Tom Brokaw of *The NBC Nightly News* is as famous as any movie star.   _____

3. Situation comedies are very popular.   _____

4. *Baby Talk* and *M*A*S*H* were both adapted from popular movies.   _____

5. Some television shows have led to movies as well.   _____

6. People rely on television to provide news in times of crisis.

    ————————

    ————————

7. Lucille Ball, Mary Tyler Moore, and Roseanne Barr all starred in their own television shows.

    ————————

8. *Masterpiece Theatre* and *Mystery!* are both imported from Britain.

    ————————

9. Some actors have starred in more than one series.

    ————————

10. *All in the Family* focused on controversial issues of the seventies.

    ————————

EXERCISE 21-3   **Recognizing abstract and concrete language**

Photocopy a brief passage from one of your textbooks. Underline all of the general and abstract words, and circle all of the specific and concrete words. What is the proportion of general to specific words? of abstract to concrete? How do the words relate to one another? How does the combination contribute to the effectiveness of the passage? Write your response below.

EXERCISE 21-4   **Distinguishing between abstract and concrete language**

Label each of the following items *abstract* or *concrete*. For each abstract item, provide a concrete expression or sentence. For each concrete item, provide an abstract concept.

EXAMPLE   integrity   <u>abstract</u>

           Ralph Nader is incorruptible.

1. pain   _____

2. a cool spring rain   _____

3. activism   _____

4. a baby's first cry   _____

5. sweating palms and beating heart   _____

EXERCISE 21-5   Eliminating slang, jargon, and other inappropriate language

Revise the following paragraph to eliminate slang, regionalisms and dialect expressions, colloquial language, jargon, sexist language, and euphemistic or pretentious language.

he or she

EXAMPLE   A serious student of literature must be sure that ~~he~~ understands the Romantic movement. (Or *students . . . they. . . .*)

The Romantic Movement in England got going as a reaction to the

rationalism of the Enlightenment. In the final years of the eighteenth century, the

silver-tongued bards, the lilting creators of harmonies, and the bold masters of

the canvas began to get turned off by the materialism of the previous century

and got off on nature, imagination, and emotion. While the Enlightenment had

celebrated the mind, the Romantic Movement celebrated the heart. Writers such

as Wordsworth, Keats, and the woman novelist Mary Shelley interfaced with

nature and got in touch with human experience through the senses rather than

the intellect. The Romantics deemed it plausible that the heavy truths of the

natural and the spiritual worlds were best understood through the individual

man's imagination. As a result, explorations of life and passing on, of the

supernatural, and of the exotic characterized Romantic literature. The bottom

line is that the literature of the Romantic period would influence writers for

generations to come.

EXERCISE 21-6   **Recognizing figurative language**

Locate a selection in a literature anthology—it can be a poem, a story, a play, or an essay—and read through several pages looking for similes, analogies, and metaphors. Write down several that you find powerful, and explain why they impress you.

TITLE:

AUTHOR:

SIMILES/ANALOGIES/METAPHORS:

EXERCISE 21-7   **Revising**

As you revise drafts of papers you're working on at present, concentrate on controlling diction. Pay attention to the connotations of words, to standard English forms, and to the balance between general/abstract and specific/concrete language. Identify any instances of biased, euphemistic, or pretentious language. Finally, determine whether or not figures of speech would make your writing more vivid.

CHAPTER 22

Dictionaries and Vocabulary

USING DICTIONARIES

22a Exploring dictionaries of the English language

1 Understanding standard entry information in dictionaries

A dictionary provides a great deal of information about a word, including the following:

- spelling (including variations, especially British vs. American spellings—see chapter 23)
- word division (indicating syllabication and where a word should be divided, if necessary)
- pronunciation (including variations)
- grammatical functions (parts of speech)
- grammatical forms (plurals, principal parts of verbs, including irregular forms)
- etymology (a given word's history/derivation)
- meanings (arranged either according to currency or frequency of use, or earliest to most recent use)
- examples in context
- related words (including synonyms and antonyms)
- usage labels
- field labels (for specific disciplines)
- idioms that include the word

2 Usage labels

Usage refers to how, where, and when a word has been used in speech and in writing. Some common usage labels found in dictionaries include the following:

- colloquial: used conversationally and in informal writing
- slang: in-group, informal language; not standard
- obsolete: not currently used (but may be found in earlier writing)
- archaic: not commonly used; more common to earlier writing
- dialect: restricted geographically or to social or ethnic groups; used only in certain places with certain groups
- poetic, literary: used in literature rather than everyday speech

22b │ Choosing a dictionary

1 │ Comparing abridged dictionaries

An **abridged,** or shortened dictionary tries to give as much information as possible in one portable volume. Some of the more widely used abridged dictionaries include the following:

The American Heritage Dictionary, 2nd college ed.
The Concise Oxford Dictionary of Current English
Webster's Ninth New Collegiate Dictionary
Webster's New World Dictionary of the American Language

2 │ Comparing unabridged dictionaries

An **unabridged** dictionary attempts to be exhaustive both in recounting the history of a word and in describing its various usages. Some of the more widely used unabridged dictionaries include the following:

The Oxford English Dictionary, 2nd ed (commonly known as *OED*)
The Random House Dictionary of the English Language
Webster's Third New International Dictionary of the English Language

22c │ Using specialized dictionaries of English

1 │ Dictionaries of usage

The following dictionaries provide extensive information on usage:

A Dictionary of Contemporary American Usage
Dictionary of Modern English Usage
Dictionary of American-English Usage
Modern American Usage

2 │ Dictionaries of synonyms

The following dictionaries focus on synonyms:

Webster's Dictionary of Synonyms
The New Roget's Thesaurus of the English Language in Dictionary Form

3 Other specialized dictionaries

Dictionaries of origins/etymologies

The following dictionaries provide extensive information on word origins:

Dictionary of Word and Phrase Origins
The Oxford Dictionary of English Etymology
Origins: A Short Etymological Dictionary of Modern English

Dictionaries of slang and idioms

The following dictionaries describe terms rarely found in standard dictionaries:

The New Dictionary of American Slang
Dictionary of Slang and Unconventional English
Dictionary of American Slang

Dictionaries of regionalism or foreign terms

The following dictionaries describe regional expressions and foreign terms:

Dictionary of American Regional English
Dictionary of Foreign Phrases and Abbreviations, 3rd ed.
Dictionary of Foreign Terms

BUILDING VOCABULARY

22d Learn root words, prefixes, and suffixes.

English vocabulary is derived from over 100 different languages. Words have entered the language as a result of many things, including invasions, wars, religious movements, and industrial progress. An unabridged dictionary will include the etymology of each word listed. Often the **root** word becomes the core of other words that are formed with **prefixes** and **suffixes**—letters coming before or after the root.

1 Becoming familiar with root words

If you can identify the root of an unfamiliar word, you can often infer—with help from the context in which the word appears—an appropriate definition. Many of the root words in English come from Latin and Greek. A brief sampling follows.

Common Root Words

ROOT	DEFINITION	EXAMPLE
acus [Latin]	needle	acute, acumen
basis [Greek]	step, base	base, basis
bene- [Latin]	good	beneficiary, benevolent
bio- [Greek]	life	biography, biology, bionic
cognoscere [Latin]	to know	recognize, cognizant, cognition
dormier [Latin]	to sleep	dormant, dormitory
ego [Latin]	I	ego, egocentric, egotistical
fleure [Latin]	flow	flow, fluid, effluence
gravis [Latin]	heavy	grave, gravity, aggravate
grandis [Latin]	large	grandiose, aggrandize
graphein [Greek]	to write	graph, graphic
gratus [Latin]	pleasing	gratis, gracious, graceful
hupnos [Greek]	sleep	hypnosis, hypnotic
hydro [Greek]	water	hydraulic, dehydrate
jur, jus [Latin]	law	jury, justice
lumen [Latin]	light	illuminate, luminary
manu- [Latin]	hand	manage, management, manual, manipulate
mare [Latin]	sea	marine, marinate, marina, marinara
matr- [Latin]	mother	maternal, matrilineal
pathos [Greek]	suffering	empathy, sympathy
patr- [Latin]	father	paternal, patriarch
polis [Greek]	city	metropolis, police
primus [Latin]	first	primitive, prime, primary
psych [Greek]	soul	psychological, psyche
sentire [Latin]	to feel	sentiment, sentimental, sentient, sense, sensitive
scrib, script [Latin]	to write	describe, manuscript
sol [Latin]	sun	solstice, solar, solarium
solvere [Latin]	to release	solve, resolve, solution, dissolver, solvent
tele [Greek]	distant	telegraph, telemetry
therm [Greek]	heat	thermal, thermos
truncus [Latin]	trunk	trunk, trench, trenchant
veritas [Latin]	truth	verity, verify, veritable
vocare [Latin]	to call	vocal, vocation, avocation

2 Recognizing prefixes

A prefix—letters coming before the root—can indicate number, size, status, negation, and relations in time and space.

Prefixes indicating number

PREFIX	MEANING	EXAMPLE
uni-	one	unison, unicellular
mono-	alone, single	monogamy, monolithic, monotone
bi-	two	bimonthly, bicentennial, bifocal
duo-	two	duplex, duplicate
tri-	three	triangle, triumvirate
quadr-	four	quadrant, quaduple
quint-	five	quintet
pent-	five	Pentecost, pentatonic (scale)
multi-	many, multiple	multiply, multifaceted
omni-	all, universally	omnivorous, omniscient
poly-	many, several	polytechnic, polygon

Prefixes indicating size

PREFIX	MEANING	EXAMPLE
micro-	very small	microscopic, microcosm
macro-	very large	macroeconomics
mega-	great	megalomania, megalith

Prefixes indicating status or condition

PREFIX	MEANING	EXAMPLE
ad-, ac-, af-	to, toward	address, accompany, affect
al-, ap-, as-, at-	to, toward	allege, appoint, assign, attend
hyper-	beyond, super	hyperactive, hypercritical
necro-	dead	necromancy, necropolis
neo-	new	neonate, neophyte
para-	akin to	parachute, paramilitary
pseudo-	false	pseudoscience, pseudosophisticate, pseudonym
quasi-	in some sense	quasi-official, quasi-public

Prefixes indicating negation

PREFIX	MEANING	EXAMPLE
a-, an-	not, without	amoral, asexual, anomalous
anti-	against	antibiotic, antidote, anticlimax
counter-	contrary	counterintuitive, counterfeit
de-	to reverse, remove, reduce	deactivate, detoxify, dethrone, decapitate, detract
dis-	to do the opposite	disable, dislodge, disagree
il-, in-, im-, ir-	not	illegitimate, inactive, immovable, irresolution
mal-	bad, abnormal, inadequate	maladjusted, malformed, malcontent, malapropism
mis-	bad, wrong	misinform, mislead, misnomer
non-	not, reverse of	noncompliance, nonalcoholic, nonconformist, nonessential
un-	not	unhappy, unproductive

Prefixes indicating spatial relations

PREFIX	MEANING	EXAMPLE
inter-	around	circumspect, circumscribe
intra-	between	intercede, intercept
intro-	within	intravenous, intramural
sub-	inside	introvert, intrude
super-	beneath	submarine, subterranean
trans-	above, over	superintend, supervise
	across	transfer, translate

Prefixes indicating relations of time

PREFIX	MEANING	EXAMPLE
ante-	before	antecedent, anterior
paleo-	ancient	Paleolithic, paleography
pre-	prior to	prehistory, precook, predecessor
post-	after	postdate, postwar, posterior
proto-	first	protohuman, prototype

3 Analyzing suffixes

A suffix—letters coming after the root—changes a word's grammatical function, making it a different part of speech.

Noun-forming suffixes

VERB	+	SUFFIX	(MEANING)	=	NOUN
betray		-al	(process of)		betrayal
participate		-ant	(one who)		participant
play		-er	(one who)		player
construct		-ion	(process of)		construction
conduct		-or	(one who)		conductor

NOUN	+	SUFFIX	(MEANING)	=	NOUN
parson		-age	(house of)		parsonage
king		-dom	(office, realm)		kingdom
sister		-hood	(state, condition of)		sisterhood
strategy		-ist	(one who)		strategist
Armenia		-n	(belonging to)		Armenian
master		-y	(quality)		mastery

ADJECTIVE	+	SUFFIX	(MEANING)	=	NOUN
pure		-ity	(state, quality of)		purity
gentle		-ness	(quality of, degree)		gentleness
active		-ism	(act, practice of)		activism

Verb-forming suffixes

NOUN	+	SUFFIX	(MEANING)	=	VERB
substance		-ate	(cause to become)		substantiate
code		-ify	(cause to become)		codify
serial		-ize	(cause to become)		serialize

ADJECTIVE	+	SUFFIX	(MEANING)	=	VERB
sharp		-en	(cause to become)		sharpen

Adjective-forming suffixes

NOUN	+	SUFFIX	(MEANING)	=	ADJECTIVE
region		-al	(of relating to)		regional
claim		-ant	(performing, being)		claimant
substance		-ial	(of relating to)		substantial
response		-ible	(capable of, fit for)		responsible
history		-ic	(form of, being)		historic
Kurd		-ish	(of, relating to)		Kurdish
response		-ive	(tends toward)		responsive

VERB	+	SUFFIX	(MEANING)	=	ADJECTIVE
credit		-able	(capable of)		creditable
abort		-ive	(tends toward)		abortive

22e Strategies for building a vocabulary

1 Use contextual clues and dictionaries.

If the root and affix (prefix or suffix) do not indicate for you the meaning of an unfamiliar word, consider the context in which the word appears. Often the ideas in a passage and the sentence surrounding the word will help you to determine its meaning. If all else fails, consult a dictionary.

2 Collect words—and use them.

Words that you encounter more than twice in any context are words that you should learn. In order to make such words a part of your own vocabulary, you may want to create a file of new words.

A Personal Vocabulary File

- Make a list of flash cards with a new word and the sentence in which it appears on one side of the card; place the definition on the other side.

- Review the cards regularly. Categorize them by discipline or by parts of speech. Practice changing the vocabulary word's part of speech with suffixes.

- Expand entries in your file when you find a previously filed word used in a new context.

- Consciously work one or two new words into each paper that you write, especially when the new words allow you to be precise in ways you could not otherwise be.

---

3   Use the thesaurus with care.

While a **thesaurus,** which lists the synonyms (and often the antonyms) of words, is a useful reference tool, you must be careful not to choose synonyms with which you are not familiar. Before using a word found in a thesaurus, make sure that you understand fully both the word's denotation and connotation (see chapter 21a).

4   Build discipline-appropriate vocabularies.

Discipline-specific vocabularies consist of two types of words: those that are unique to the discipline—molecule, for example—and those that are found elsewhere, though with different meanings. Take the word depression, for example. In general terms it indicates an area that has been pressed down; in psychology it indicates an emotional disorder, and in economics it indicates a period of low economic activity.

EXERCISE 22-1   Using an abridged dictionary

Identify the abridged dictionary that you use for this exercise. (If your instructor has assigned a particular dictionary, use that one.)

A. For each of the following words, first divide the word into syllables, then indicate its part of speech, and finally write out the current meaning listed in the dictionary. (Remember that the current meaning is not listed first in every dictionary.)

EXAMPLE	**Syllabication**	**Part of Speech**
magnanimous	<u>mag nan i mous</u>	<u>adjective</u>
noble, generous		

1. dispassionate _____ _____

2. solecism _____ _____

3. peripatetic _____ _____

4. tremulous _____ _____

5. hortatory _____ _____

6. vague _____ _____

7. evanescent   _____   _____

8. quintessence   _____   _____

9. zoomorphism   _____   _____

10. bathos   _____   _____

B. List all of the parts of speech that each of the following words can serve as.

EXAMPLE   market   <u>noun   verb   adjective</u>_____

1. contract   _____

2. practice   _____

3. degenerate   _____

4. reserve   _____

5. mirror   _____

C. Write out all possible plural forms for the following nouns.

EXAMPLE   bench   ___<u>benches</u>_____

1. wharf   _____

2. moose   _____

3. attorney   _____

4. radius   _____

5. synthesis   _____

D. Fill in the past, past participle, and present participle forms of the following verbs.

EXAMPLE

	Past	**Past Participle**	**Present Participle**
think	thought	thought	thinking

1. swim _____ _____ _____

2. dream _____ _____ _____

3. cling _____ _____ _____

4. forget _____ _____ _____

5. hide _____ _____ _____

E. Fill in the comparative and superlative forms of the following adjectives and adverbs.

EXAMPLE

	Comparative	**Superlative**
wonderful	more wonderful	most wonderful

1. possible _____ _____

2. quickly _____ _____

3. steep _____ _____

4. rapid _____ _____

5. final _____ _____

F. Fill in the usage label assigned to each of the following words.

EXAMPLE   rumble (a fight)   slang

1. wicked (really) _____

2. grinder (sandwich) _____

3. thine _____

4. post (courier) _____

5. post (to mail) _____

EXERCISE 22-2   Using an unabridged dictionary

Identify the unabridged dictionary that you use for this exercise.

A. In order to get a rudimentary sense of the history of modern English, find an
   English "family tree" in an unabridged dictionary, and trace modern English back
   to its origins. In reverse order, list all of the other languages that evolved into
   modern English. List also the other modern languages that are "cousins" of English.

B. Briefly describe the origins, history, and various uses of one of the following words:

   1. clerk

   2. riot

   3. mystery

EXERCISE 22-3   Building vocabulary

Locate in one of your textbooks a passage that includes several words that are new to
you. Before looking them up in the dictionary, try to determine their meaning based
on the context. Write out your tentative definition in the space below, and then check
it with the dictionary definition. If the meanings are close, you've done a good job of
making an educated guess.

EXERCISE 22-4   **Using specialized and discipline-specific dictionaries**

Identify the dictionaries you use for this exercise.

Choose a specialized dictionary and look up a sample entry. (Your instructor may assign specific dictionaries to individual students.) Then find the same entry in a standard college dictionary. In the space below, briefly describe the kinds of information each dictionary provides.

ENTRY

SPECIALIZED DICTIONARY

STANDARD DICTIONARY

EXERCISE 22-5   **Using prefixes and suffixes**

Add a prefix and/or a suffix to each of the following words, and then write each new word in a sentence:

EXAMPLE   complicate   **complication**

The surgery took longer than expected because of a complication.

1. comfort

2. attend

3. impose

4. direct

5. lone

CHAPTER 23

Spelling

You can master spelling by learning a few rules and their exceptions, and by recognizing the words you commonly misspell and remembering devices for committing their correct spelling to memory.

Overcoming spelling/pronunciation misconnections

Recognizing homonyms and commonly confused words

Words that sound similar or exactly alike (*accept/except, whole/hole, rain/reign/rein*) are called **homonyms.** Use this list of homonyms to check your own spelling. When in doubt, consult a dictionary.

Commonly Confused Homonyms and Near Homonyms

accept [to receive]
except [to leave out]

advice [recommendation]
advise [to recommend]

affect [to have an influence on]
effect [result; to make happen]

all ready [prepared]
already [by this time]

bare [naked]
bear [to carry, endure; an animal]

board [piece of wood]
bored [uninterested]

brake [stop, device for stopping]
break [to smash, destroy]

buy [purchase]
by [next to, through]

capital [city seat of government]
capitol [legislative or government building]

cite [quote, refer to]
sight [vision, something seen]
site [place, locale]

complement [something that completes]
compliment [praise]

conscience [moral sense, sense of right/wrong]
conscious [aware]

discreet [respectfully reserved]
discrete [distinct, separate]

dominant [controlling, powerful]
dominate [to control]

elicit [to draw out]
illicit [illegal]

eminent [distinguished]
immanent [inborn, inherent]
imminent [expected momentarily]

fair [just; light-complexioned; lovely]
fare [fee for transportation; meal]

gorilla [ape]
guerilla [unconventional soldier]

heard [past tense of *to hear*]
herd [group of animals]

hole [opening]
whole [entire, complete]

its [possessive form of *it*]
it's [contraction of *it is*]

lead [heavy metal]
led [past tense of *to lead*]

lessen [decrease]
lesson [something learned]

loose [not tight, unfastened]
lose [misplace, fail to win]

moral [object-lesson, knowing right from wrong]
morale [outlook, attitude]

passed [past tense of *to pass*]
past [after; beyond; a time gone by]

patience [forbearance]
patients [those under medical care]

peace [absence of war]
piece [part or portion of something]

personal [private, pertaining to an individual]
personnel [employees]

plain [simple, clear, unadorned; flat land]
plane [carpenter's tool, flat surface, airplane]

presence [attendance, being at hand]
presents [gifts; gives]

principal [most important; school administrator]
principle [fundamental truth, law, conviction]

scene [setting, play segment]
seen [past participle of *see*]

stationary [standing still]
stationery [writing paper]

straight [unbending]
strait [narrow waterway]

than [besides; as compared with]
then [at that time; therefore]

their [possessive form of *they*]
there [opposite of *here*]
they're [contraction of *they are*]

threw [past tense of *throw*]
through [by means of, finished]
thorough [complete]

to [toward]
too [also, in addition to]
two [number following *one*]

weak [feeble]
week [seven days]

weather [climatic conditions]
whether [which of two]

whose [possessive form of *who*]
who's [contraction of *who is*]

your [possessive form of *you*]
you're [contraction of *you are*]
yore [the far past]

---

2 | Recognizing words with more than one form

Some words sound alike but appear in different forms (*always/all ways, already/all ready, maybe/may be, everyday/every day, into/in to, altogether/all together*). *All right* and *a lot* are always written as two words. When in doubt, consult a dictionary.

3 | Memorizing words with silent letters or syllables

The easiest way to remember the spelling of words with silent letters or letters that are rarely pronounced (e.g., *kneel, library*) is to memorize them. The following list includes some frequently used words that contain silent letters.

aisle	foreign	pneumonia
candidate	government	privilege
climb	interest	probably
condemn	knight	quantity
depot	marriage	solemn
environment	mischievous	Wednesday
February	paradigm	

4 Distinguishing between noun and verb forms of the same word

When the noun form is spelled differently from the verb form of a word (*advise/advice, enter/entrance, renounce/renunciation*), misspellings often occur.

5 Distinguishing American from British and Canadian spellings

Although both spellings (e.g., *color/colour, center/centre, criticize/criticise*) are correct, when writing for an American audience, you should use American spelling.

23b Learn basic spelling rules for *ie/ei*.

The elementary school rhyme, *i* before *e* except after *c*, or when sounded like *ay*, as in *neighbor* or *weigh*, still holds true, as indicated in these words: *brief, relief; ceiling, perceive; beige, vein.* Exceptions to this rule include the words *ancient, height,* and *weird.* Also, words in which the *ie* constitutes two syllables (*science, atheist*).

23c Learn rules for using prefixes.

The addition of a prefix never alters the spelling of the base word: *un/common, dis/oriented, pre/school.*

23d Learn rules for using suffixes.

Spelling difficulties often arise when the root word must be changed before the suffix is added.

1 Learn rules for keeping or dropping a final *e*.

Rule: If the suffix begins with a vowel, drop the final silent *e*: *relate + ion = relation.* **Exceptions:** To distinguish homonyms (*dyeing/dying*), to prevent mispronunciation (*mileage*), and to keep the sound of *c* or *g* soft (*courageous, noticeable*).

Rule: If the suffix begins with a consonant, keep the final silent *e: care + less =* *careless.*

Exceptions: When the final silent *e* is preceded by another vowel, the *e* is dropped (*argument*). Other exceptions include *judgment, acknowledgment, awful,* and *wholly.*

2 **Learn rules for keeping or dropping a final *y*.**

Rule: When the letter immediately before the *y* is a consonant, change the *y* to *i* and then add the suffix: *supply + er = supplier.* **Exceptions:** With the suffix *-ing* (*worrying*); for some one-syllable roots (*crying*); for proper names (*Kennedys*); and when the final *y* is preceded by a vowel (*playing*).

3 **Learn rules for adding *-ally*.**

Rule: Add *-ally* to make an adverb out of an adjective that ends with *ic: emphatic + ally = emphatically.*

4 **Learn the rule for adding *-ly*.**

Rule: Add *-ly* to make an adverb out of adjectives that don't end with *ic: vigorous + ly = vigorously.* **Exception:** *publicly.*

5 **Learn the rule for adding *-cede*, *-ceed*, and *-sede*.**

Rule: Words that sound like *seed* are almost always spelled *-cede: secede.* **Exceptions:** *supersede, exceed, proceed, succeed.*

6 **Learn rules for adding *-able* or *-ible*.**

Rule: If the root word is an independent word, use the suffix *-able: treat + able = treatable.* If the root word is not an independent word, use the suffix *-ible: plausible.* **Exceptions:** *culpable, probable, resistible.*

7 **Learn rules for doubling the final consonant.**

Rule: Double the final consonant when a one-syllable word ends in a consonant preceded by a single vowel: *swim + ing = swimming.* Double the final consonant when adding a suffix to a two-syllable word if a single vowel precedes the final consonant and if the final syllable is accented once the suffix is added: *submit + ing = submitting.*

Rule: Don't double the final consonant when it is preceded by two or more vowels, or by another consonant: *gleam + ing = gleaming, resist + ing = resisting.* Don't double the final consonant if the suffix begins with a consonant: *commit + ment = commitment.* Don't double the final consonant if the word is *not* accented on the last syllable, or if the accent shifts from the last to the first syllable when the suffix is added: *season + al = seasonal, refer + ence = reference.*

23e   Learn rules for forming plurals.

1   Learn the basic rule for adding -s/-es.

Adding -s: For most words: *plant/plants, department/departments.*

Adding -es: For words ending in -s, -sh, -ss, -ch, -x, or -z: *focus/focuses, mash/mashes, pass/passes, patch/patches, ax/axes, fizz/fizzes.* For words ending in -o, if the o is preceded by a consonant: *veto/vetoes.* **Exceptions:** If the final o is preceded by a vowel: *patios;* also *pros, pianos, solos, sopranos.*

2   Learn the rule for plurals of words ending in -f or -fe.

Rule: To form the plural of some nouns ending in -f or -fe, change the ending to -ve before adding the -s: *leaf/leaves.* **Exceptions:** *beliefs, proofs, motifs, scarfs* (or *scarves*), *hoofs* (or *hooves*).

3   Learn the rule for plurals of words ending in -y.

Rules: For words that end in a consonant followed by *y*, change the *y* to *i* before adding -es to form the plural: *vanity/vanities.* For words ending in a vowel followed by *y*, add -s: *toy/toys.* **Exception:** proper names (*Kennedys*).

4   Learn the rule for plurals of compound words.

Rules: When compound nouns are written as one word, make the last part of the compound plural: *shoelace/shoelaces.* When compound nouns are hyphenated or written as two words, make plural the most important part of the compound word: *district attorney/district attorneys, commander in chief/commanders in chief, mother-in-law/mothers-in-law.*

5 Learn the irregular plurals.

Some words change internally to form plurals: *man/men, mouse/mice*. Some Latin and Greek words change final *-um, -on,* or *-us* to *-a* or *-i: datum/data, criterion/criteria, stimulus/stimuli*. For some words, the singular and the plural forms are the same: *elk/elk, rice/rice*.

23f Developing spelling skills

In addition to learning the preceding spelling rules, use the following devices:

- Memorize commonly misspelled words.

- Keep track of the words that give you trouble. See if you can discern a pattern, and memorize the relevant rule.

- Use the dictionary. Check words whose spelling you're not sure of, and add them to your personal list of difficult-to-spell words. If you are not sure of the first few letters of a word, look up a synonym of that word to see if the word you need is listed as part of the definition.

- Pay attention when you read: your mind will retain a visual impression of a word that will help you remember how it's spelled.

- You may also develop mnemonic devices—techniques to improve memory—for particularly troublesome words. For instance, you might use the *-er* at the end of *paper* and *letter* as a reminder that *station<u>er</u>y* means writing paper, while *station<u>ar</u>y* means standing still.

- Edit and proofread carefully, paying particular attention to how the words look on the page. You will find as you train yourself that you will begin to recognize spelling errors, and that you actually know the correct spelling but have made an old mistake in haste or carelessness.

- On word processors, use a spell checker, but realize that this computer aid will only identify misspelled words: if you have used an incorrect homonym, but have spelled it correctly, the spell checker will not highlight the word.

EXERCISE 23-1   Distinguishing homonyms and words with more than one form

Within each set of parentheses are sets of homonyms or words with more than one form. Circle the correct word in each set.

EXAMPLE   We were (already/all ready) for (are/our) trip to the (capitol/capital) city.

We were (already/(all ready)) for (are/(our)) trip to the (capitol/(capital)) city.

1. Our nosy neighbor was just (dieing/dying) to find out if we left on time, so we slipped out of the house (discretely/discreetly).

2. We let the car coast (passed/past) the neighbor's house before turning on the engine, and (then/than) made a (rite/right) turn onto the main street.

3. We drove (strait/straight) (threw/through) to the city, (where/were) we finally stopped for directions to our hotel.

4. It seems we had remembered everything (accept/except) the directions, which didn't cause (to, too, two) much trouble.

5. We drove (in to, into) the city in bumper-to-bumper traffic; all we could (here/hear) were horns and squealing (breaks/brakes).

6. We stopped to ask a woman (who's/whose) hair was bright purple (weather/whether) we were headed in the (rite/right/write) direction.

7. I'd never (scene/seen) such a (cite/site/sight) before, and I could hardly keep my eyes (of/off) her.

8. "(Its/It's) just down (to/too/two) blocks, and (bare/bear) left at the (forth/fourth) donut shop."

9. The (affect/effect) that hair had on us was magical: we were (no/know) longer edgy or (board/bored).

10. We wondered (allowed/aloud) if we'd (meat/mete/meet) (anymore/any more) characters like this before our trip was over.

EXERCISE 23-2   **Distinguishing between homonyms**

Choose five sets of words from the list of homonyms and near homonyms. If possible, choose sets that you have difficulty with. For each set, write one sentence incorporating all words in the set.

1.

2.

3.

4.

5.

EXERCISE 23-3   Adding suffixes

Using the rules from this chapter, combine the following words and suffixes. Use a dictionary if necessary to check your choices.

EXAMPLE   grieve + ance   _grievance_

1. place + ment   _____

2. mince + ing   _____

3. vacate + ion   _____

4. revile + ing   _____

5. fancy + ful   _____

6. city + fy   _____

7. dry + ing   _____

8. enjoy + ment   _____

9. artistic + (ly/ally)   _____

10. excited + (ly/ally)   _____

11. slavish + (ly/ally)   _____

12. pro + (cede/ceed/sede)   _____

13. inter + (cede/ceed/sede)   _____

14. irresist + (able/ible)   _____

15. commend + (able/ible)   _____

16. restrain + ing   _____

17. quit + er   _____

18. occur + ence   _____

19. confer + ence   _____

20. adroit + ness   _____

EXERCISE 23-4   **Forming plurals**

Form the plurals of the following words, using the dictionary if necessary to check your choices.

EXAMPLE   wish   _wishes_

1. sewing machine   _____

2. calf   _____

3. church   _____

4. carload   _____

5. incubus   _____

6. editor in chief   _____

7. thesis   _____

8. analogy   _____

9. moose   _____

10. brief   _____

EXERCISE 23-5   **Applying the *ie* and *ei* rule**

Using a dictionary if necessary to check your choices, fill in the blanks with *ie* or *ei*.

EXAMPLE   counterf_ei_t

1. sc____ntist   6. w____gh
2. n____ce   7. exped____nt
3. sl____gh   8. d____ty
4. l____sure   9. suffic____nt
5. b____r   10. inv____gh

EXERCISE 23-6   Review

There are ten misspelled words in the following paragraph. Cross out the words and
write them correctly.

One of the most important words to understand when talking about
exercise is "moderation." The person who lifts wieghts seven days a week is not
any healthyer than one who takes a half-hour brisk walk three times a week.
What doctors have discovered in the passed decade is that moderate exercise can
actually slow the ageing process. Exercise is advisible because it reduces the risk
of heart disease, cancer, high blood pressure, and many other aillments. It may
seem unbelieveable, but one affect of exercise is that an active eighty-year-old
can be functionly the same age as a sedentary sixty-five-year-old. This is good
news for men and woman who feel guilty about not working out seven days a
week. Now they can take their exercise in moderation and still reap the benefits.

EXERCISE 23-7   Revising

Begin your personal spelling list now. Go over papers that have been handed back to
you recently and list all the words that were misspelled. Make two columns next to
that list. In the first, write the words correctly, and in the second, write the reason for
the misspelling. When you scan the reasons, you'll probably find out that your
problem lies with one or two rules. Keep up the list, and you'll soon know which
rules to memorize.

EXAMPLE: acceptible   acceptable   ible/able endings

MISSPELLING   CORRECT SPELLING   REASON

CHAPTER 24

End Punctuation

The end of an English sentence is signaled by a period, a question mark, or an exclamation point.

THE PERIOD

24a Using the period

1 Placing a period to mark the end of a statement or a mild command

A period is placed after a statement, a mild command, and a restatement of a question.

Philip Sokolof had a heart attack on October 27, 1966.

Listen to his story.

He wondered how this could happen to him.

2 Placing periods in relation to end quotation marks and parentheses

A period is always placed inside a quotation that ends a sentence. When a parenthesis ends a sentence, a period is placed inside the end parenthesis only if the parenthetical remark is a complete sentence.

Sokolof says, "I worked out and ran a mile once or twice a week."

He was in very good shape (at 5 feet 10 inches, 145 pounds).

But his diet was unhealthy. (He loved all sorts of fatty, greasy foods.)

3 Using a period with abbreviations

Abbreviations that are punctuated with a period include *Mr., Ms., Ave., Dr.,* and *R.N.* When an abbreviation ends a sentence, use a single period, but when an abbreviation falls in the middle of a sentence, punctuate it as if the abbreviated word were spelled out (as illustrated in the previous sentence). Acronyms (*NATO*), names of large organizations (*TWA*), and government agencies (*FBI*) are not punctuated with periods.

THE QUESTION MARK

24b Using the question mark

1 Using a question mark after a direct question

Why do fatty foods contribute to heart disease?

What's wrong with eating ice cream? drinking whole milk? frying foods?

2 Using a question mark after a quoted question within a statement

Place the question mark *inside* the quotation marks when it applies directly to the quoted material. Place the question mark *outside* the quotation marks when the sentence as a whole, but not the quoted material itself, forms a question.

In 1984 Sokolof asked himself, "How can I awaken people to the dangers of a fatty diet?"

Did you know that he formed the National Heart Savers Association "to save peoples lives"?

Do not combine a question mark with any other punctuation mark.

FAULTY "Do you know your cholesterol level?," asked the doctor.

REVISED "Do you know your cholesterol level?" asked the doctor.

3 Using a question mark within parentheses to indicate that the accuracy of information is in doubt even after extensive research

Alphabetic writing was invented in Syria in 1500 B.C. (?).

Do not use the question mark in parentheses to make snide comments.

FAULTY Ancient history class is stimulating (?).

REVISED Ancient history class is far from stimulating.

THE EXCLAMATION POINT

24c | Using the exclamation point

1 | Using the exclamation point—sparingly—to mark an emphatic statement or command

While it is preferable to let your words convey emphasis, exclamation points can be used occasionally in academic writing to highlight a memorable sentence, or to duplicate spoken dialogue.

> Rameses II was apparently a vital man. He fathered one hundred sixty-two children!

> You can't be serious!

2 | Making mild exclamations with periods or commas

You must be joking.

Do not combine an exclamation point with a period, comma, or question mark.

FAULTY   "That's an incredible story!," she exclaimed.

REVISED   "That's an incredible story!" she exclaimed.

EXERCISE 24-1   Using the period

Add, delete, or move periods as needed in the following sentences, paying particular attention to quotation marks and parentheses.

EXAMPLE   The United Nations was born in San Francisco in 1945

        The United Nations was born in San Francisco in 1945.

1. The end of World War II. brought many changes to the balance of power in the world

2. Much of Eastern Europe came under Soviet control (Tito, however, successfully retained Yugoslavia's sovereignty).

3. The allies formed the North Atlantic Treaty Organization to protect western Europe from aggression

4. N.A.T.O. became known as "the protector of European democracy".

5. France and England eventually gave up many of their colonies The battle over Algerian independence from France was finally settled by Gen Charles De Gaulle.

6. The U.N. intervened in the civil war in Korea in 1950 (between the Soviet-supported North and the U. S.-supported South.).

7. The superpowers which emerged at the end of W. W. II. were the United States and the Union of Soviet Socialist Republics, or U. S. S. R..

8. The Soviet Union's Nikita Khrushchev threatened the US, "We will bury you.".

9. Mr Khrushchev did more to instill fear of communism in American schoolchildren than did Stalin, according to Catherine Mahoney, PhD..

10. President Eisenhower swore that "Communism will never prevail.", comforting children across the country.

EXERCISE 24-2   Using the question mark

Add, delete, or move question marks as needed in the following sentences, paying particular attention to quotation marks.

EXAMPLE   The question to be considered is, do children lie in court testimony.

The question to be considered is, do children lie in court testimony**?**

1. Did you hear the judge ask, "Are you sure this is what happened?"?
2. The defense attorney asked why the child had changed his testimony?
3. Were the prosecutors and the child's father "playing games?"
4. The defense called in an expert (?) to support the mother's testimony.
5. Could the child have been prompted, convinced that his story was true, perhaps even provided with the story.
6. Experts disagree on whether or not children lie in court?
7. A figure of 2% (?) is usually cited as the percentage of children who lie in court.
8. Some researchers are asking if that percentage is valid?
9. Which studies should we believe.
10. "How can we ever know?", asked one psychologist.

EXERCISE 24-3   Using exclamation points

Add, delete, or move exclamation points as needed in the following sentences.

EXAMPLE   Some people believe that the end of the world is at hand!

Some people believe that the end of the world is at hand.

1. "The Gulf War signaled the beginning of Armageddon!", cried one believer.
2. Actually, the events of 1990-91 do parallel some biblical prophecies. It's incredible.
3. The repeated cry is, "Are you ready for the rapture?!"
4. This isn't the first time people have claimed that the end is at hand!
5. If it's true, then there's only one thing to do: Prepare.

EXERCISE 24-4   **Review**

Provide periods, question marks, and exclamation points as needed in the following paragraph.

David Attenborough has spent his life asking questions And what a life He is a noted scientist, a respected author, and a successful producer for television Mr Attenborough criticizes theories that explain the purpose of human life in purely biological terms If human beings exist solely to carry on the species, he asks, then how do you explain the arts philanthropy educational reform Attenborough explains these phenomena as "externalized inheritance" It doesn't take a Ph D, he says, to see that society contributes as much to an individual's development as does genetics An individual's development is shaped not only by personal heredity, but by the Rockefeller Foundation, humanist philosophy, and UNICEF, among other things According to one student of Attenborough's, "This man believes in limitless possibilities for the human race"

CHAPTER 25

Commas

25a Using commas with introductory and concluding expressions

1 Place a comma after a modifying phrase or clause that begins a sentence.

A comma after an introductory word or brief phrase is optional. After a longer introductory phrase, use a comma.

> **Before medical technology took over the process,** women giving birth were assisted by midwives. **At present (,)** few women give birth without the assistance of a physician.

There are several basic patterns of comma placement:

Basic Patterns of Comma Placement

Place a comma after a modifying element that introduces a sentence (see 25a-1, 2).

MODIFYING ELEMENT, SENTENCE.

> Obviously, only a small sample of a large archaeological site can be dug and analyzed.

> In these days of high digging costs, archaeologists rely heavily on sampling techniques.

Set off contrasting elements with one or two commas (see 25a-3).

SENTENCE, CONTRASTING ELEMENT.

> President Wilson spoke of making the world "safe for democracy," not of protecting American commercial interests.

SENTENCE BEGINS, CONTRASTING ELEMENT, SENTENCE CONTINUES

> Wilson, not Roosevelt, said this.

Place a comma *before* a coordinate conjunction that joins independent clauses (see 25b).

COORDINATE CONJUNCTION

```
                          and  but
INDEPENDENT CLAUSE,  nor  for   INDEPENDENT CLAUSE.
                          or   so
```

Marsupial infants are born at an immature stage, **AND** they continue their development attached to a nipple in a special protective pouch of the mother.

Use a comma to set off elements in a series (see 25c-1).

. . . ELEMENT 1, ELEMENT 2, AND/OR ELEMENT 3. . . .

The development of hard disks, floppy disks, and laser disks makes storage of vast amounts of information readily available to anyone who uses personal computers.

Place a comma between coordinate adjectives (see 25c-2).

. . . ADJECTIVE 1, ADJECTIVE 2 MODIFIED NOUN. . . .

The left hemisphere of the brain thinks sequential, analytical thoughts.

Set off nonessential elements with one or two commas (see 25d-1, 2).

SENTENCE, NONESSENTIAL ELEMENT.

The number of overweight Americans has reached 60 million, about one quarter of the population.

SENTENCE BEGINS, NONESSENTIAL ELEMENT, SENTENCE CONTINUES.

Obese Americans, overweight by 20 per cent or more, number 43 million.

---

2 **Place a comma after a transitional word, phrase, or clause that begins a sentence.**

A transition at the beginning or end of a sentence is set off by one comma; a transition that comes in the middle of a sentence is set off by two commas.

However, more women are opting for home birth.

Obstetricians, **of course,** are skeptical of the trend.

The trend will continue, **regardless of the skepticism.**

3 **Use a comma (or commas) to set off a modifying element that ends or interrupts a sentence** *if* **the modifier establishes a qualification, contrast, or exception.**

Home childbirth seems to be relatively safe, **provided there are no complications.**

Childbirth assisted by a midwife, **as opposed to a physician,** is sometimes less stressful for the mother.

> Today's women, **except those whose pregnancies are risky,** may opt for a home birth.

25b   Using a comma before a coordinating conjunction to join two independent clauses

Unless the independent clauses have internal punctuation (in which case a semicolon is used), use a comma before the coordinating conjunction.

> Midwives may be acceptable to many women, **but** some doctors are still reluctant to encourage the practice.

> A doula, a trained, experienced mother, sometimes assists in childbirth**; and** recent studies of such births are very encouraging.

25c   Using commas between items in a series

1   Place a comma between items in a series.

Unless the items have internal punctuation or consist of long, independent clauses (in which case semicolons are used), use commas between items in a series. The final comma in the series can be omitted or not.

> Art museums are being assaulted by **skyrocketing costs, reduced funding (,) and prohibitive insurance premiums.**

> The art world has seen **masterpieces auctioned off, often at astronomical figures; spectacular heists in which entire collections are stolen; and a sagging economy resulting in a financial drought.**

2   Place a comma between two or more coordinate adjectives in a series, if no coordinating conjunction joins them.

Adjectives are considered coordinate if they can be reversed, or if they can be joined by a coordinating conjunction. Only coordinate adjectives are separated by a comma.

> Vincent van Gogh was a **tormented young** man who created **brilliant, passionate** paintings.

25d   Using commas to set off nonessential elements

1   Identify essential (restrictive) elements that need no commas.

A modifier that provides information necessary for defining a word is called **essential** or **restrictive,** and is not set off by commas.

An exhibition **that toured the United States and England in 1990** was called "Monet in the '90s."

2 | **Use a pair of commas to set off nonessential (nonrestrictive) elements.**

When a modifier is not essential for defining a word, set it off with commas.

Van Gogh's "Portrait of Dr. Gachet," **which sold for $82.5 million in 1990,** broke the record for paintings sold at auction.

Punctuating Modifying Clauses with *Which*, *Who*, and *That*

The relative pronouns *who*, *which*, and *that* begin modifying clauses that can interrupt or end sentences.

WHO

Who can begin a clause that is essential to defining the word modified.

Formal organizations designate managers *who help administrative units meet their specific goals.* [essential]

Who can also begin a nonessential clause. Note the presence of commas in this sentence.

Frank Smith, *who is an administrative manager,* helps his administrative unit meet its goals. [nonessential]

WHICH

Similarly, *which* can begin an essential or a nonessential modifying clause.

Two archaeological sites *which flourished in the dim yet documented past* are Saxon London and medieval Winchester. [essential]

Some historical archaeologists excavate sites like Saxon London or medieval Winchester, *which flourished in the dim yet documented past.* [nonessential]

THAT

That always denotes an essential clause. Do not use commas to set off a modifying clause beginning with *that*.

Two archaeological sites *that flourished in the dim yet documented past* are Saxon London and medieval Winchester. [essential]

---

3 **Use commas to set off parenthetical or repeating elements.**

Parenthetical remarks and repeating elements are not essential to the meaning of a sentence, and thus are set off by a comma or commas.

> The ceiling of the Sistine Chapel, **completed in 1512,** was restored in the late twentieth century.

> The ceiling took **four years to paint, almost five hundred to deteriorate, and ten to restore.**

An **appositive** phrase, which renames a noun, is set off by commas unless it consists of a series of items separated by commas (in which case it is set off by dashes).

> Julius II, **Pontiff of Rome,** commissioned the work in 1508.

> Michelangelo—**sculptor, architect, poet, and painter**—created the masterpiece almost single-handedly.

CRITICAL DECISIONS

FORM, AND SUPPORT, OPINIONS: WITHIN A SENTENCE, DISTINGUISH ESSENTIAL FROM NONESSENTIAL INFORMATION

Comma placement regularly depends on a decision you make about whether certain qualifying (or additional) information in a sentence is or is not essential to the meaning of a particular word. Your decision about this content determines how you punctuate your sentence.

A Test to Determine if Qualifying Information Is Essential or Nonessential

1. Identify the single word in the sentence being qualified by a word group.
2. Identify the qualifying word group.
3. Drop the qualifying word group from the sentence.
4. Ask of the single word from #1, above: Do I understand which one or who?
   a. If you can give a specific answer to this question, the qualifying information is nonessential: Set the information off from the sentence with a *pair* of commas.
   b. If you cannot give a specific answer to the question, the qualifying information *is* essential: Include the information in the main sentence with *no* commas.

Example Sentences

Example 1: The bill which placed a fifty cent tax on every pack of cigarettes was defeated.

1. Word being qualified: *bill*
2. Qualifying word group: *which placed a fifty cent tax on every pack of cigarettes*
3. New sentence: *The bill was defeated.*
4. Do I understand which one? *No.*

Therefore, the qualifying information is essential; include it in the sentence *without* commas.

The bill which placed a fifty cent tax on every pack of cigarettes was defeated.

Example 2: Bill 307 which placed a fifty centy tax on every pack of cigarettes was defeated.

1. Word being qualified: *Bill 307*
2. Qualifying word group: *which placed a fifty cent tax on every pack of cigarettes*
3. New sentence: *Bill 307 was defeated.*
4. Do I understand which one? *Yes.*

Therefore, the qualifying information is nonessential; set it off from the sentence with a *pair* of commas.

Bill 307, which placed a fifty cent tax on every pack of cigarettes, was defeated.

25e Using commas to acknowledge conventions of quoting, naming, and various forms of separation

1 Use a comma to introduce or to complete a quotation.

W. C. Fields is supposed to have said, "Anyone who hates children and dogs can't be all bad."

"On the whole," he wrote as his epitaph, "I'd rather be in Philadelphia."

2 Use a comma to set off expressions of direct address. If the expression interrupts a sentence, set the word off with a *pair* of commas.

Ladies and gentlemen, enjoy the show.

The show, ladies and gentlemen, is about to begin.

3 Use a comma to mark the omission of words in a balanced sentence.

Some critics consider Fields' greatest talent to have been his comic timing; **others, his creativity; still others, his improvisational capability.**

4 Place a comma between paired "more/less" constructions.

The more I read, **the less** I understand.

5 Use a comma to set off tag questions that conclude a sentence.

You've read that book, **haven't you?**

6 Use a comma to set off yes/no remarks and mild exclamations.

Yes, I read it last year.

Thank goodness, I'll never have to read it again.

7 Use commas according to convention in names, titles, dates, numbers, and addresses.

Commas with names and titles

Place a comma between a name and a title. Set off a title in commas when writing a sentence.

Melinda Shute, M.D.

Christine Krupa, Ph.D., addressed the convention.

Commas with dates

Follow conventions for using commas with dates.

December 19, 1980   December 1980   19 December 1980

Friday, December 19, 1980   the nineteenth of December, 1980

Commas with numbers

Place a comma to denote thousands, millions, and so forth. A comma is optional in four-digit numbers divisible by fifty.

>   132   1,320   13,200   132,000   1350 (or 1,300)

Commas are not used in phone numbers, addresses, page numbers, or years.

Commas with addresses

In addresses, commas are placed only between city (or county) and state, unless the address is written into a sentence.

> Ms. Tiffany Morin   Douglas County, Kansas
> 1440 Jayhawk Drive
> Lawrence, Kansas 66044

> Shannon's new pen pal was Tiffany Morin, 1440 Jayhawk Drive, Lawrence, Kansas 66044.

8 Use commas to prevent misreading.

In certain situations a comma helps prevent misreading of a sentence. Use your judgment to determine when commas are necessary.

> By ten, three of the guests still hadn't arrived.

> Those who had, complained about the latecomers.

> Moments after, the stragglers finally showed up.

> When you leave, leave through the front door.

25f Editing to avoid misuse or overuse of commas

1 Eliminate the comma splice.

> FAULTY   In 1991 The United States began to eliminate barriers to free trade with Mexico, environmentalists were vocal opponents of the arrangement.

> REVISED   In 1991 The United States began to eliminate barriers to free trade with Mexico; environmentalists were vocal opponents of the arrangement.

For ways to revise comma splices, see chapter 13.

2   **Eliminate commas misused to set off essential (restrictive) elements.**

FAULTY   One group, which threatened to oppose the agreement, was the AFL-CIO.

REVISED   One group which threatened to oppose the agreement was the AFL-CIO.

3   **Eliminate commas that are misused in a series.**

Do not use commas in a series of two, or after the second of two coordinate adjectives. Do not place a comma before the first or after the last item in a series.

FAULTY   Others opposed to the trade agreement included Greenpeace, and Ralph Nader.

Greenpeace felt that the agreement would herald devastating, irreversible, damage to the environment.

Unions and environmental groups feared that, loss of jobs, industrial sprawl, and air pollution, would result from the agreement.

REVISED   Others opposed to the trade agreement included Greenpeace and Ralph Nader.

Greenpeace felt that the agreement would herald devastating, irreversible damage to the environment.

Unions and environmental groups feared that loss of jobs, industrial sprawl, and air pollution would result from the agreement.

4   **Eliminate commas that split paired sentence elements.**

Do not place commas between subjects and verbs, between verbs and objects/complements, or between prepositions and objects.

FAULTY   Many of those who opposed the agreement for environmental reasons, recognized its political value.

The agreement promised to strengthen considerably, relations between Mexico and the United States.

Politicians had expected resistance, but had not anticipated so many groups entering into, the discussions.

REVISED   Many of those who opposed the agreement for environmental reasons recognized its political value.

The agreement promised to strengthen considerably relations between Mexico and the United States.

Politicians had expected resistance, but had not anticipated so many groups entering into the discussions.

5 Eliminate misuse of commas with quotations.

A comma is not used after a quotation that ends with a question mark or an exclamation point; nor is it used to introduce words quoted (or italicized) for emphasis.

FAULTY   "Are you ready to take a vote?," the chairperson asked.

George Bush wanted to be known as, "the education President."

REVISED   "Are you ready to take a vote?" the chairperson asked.

George Bush wanted to be known as "the education President."

EXERCISE 25-1   **Using commas with introductory and concluding expressions**

In the following sentences, insert commas to set off introductory elements and interrupting elements. Circle the number of any sentences in which no comma is needed.

EXAMPLE   The medical technology boom that began in the late nineteenth century according to scientific historians resulted in the abandonment of many home remedies.

The medical technology boom that began in the late nineteenth century, **according to scientific historians,** resulted in the abandonment of many home remedies.

1. Before the boom people used herbs and natural concoctions to treat injuries and illness.
2. For example camphor was often used to ease headache pain.
3. Honey not cough medicine was used to relieve nagging coughs.
4. People have been returning to natural remedies in the past few years.
5. In addition they have been taking advantage of unfamiliar medical treatment especially acupuncture.
6. In acupuncture thin needles are placed just under the skin.
7. Alternative medical treatment regardless of its growing popularity is viewed with skepticism by traditionally educated doctors.
8. That skepticism is understandable of course.
9. In the first place natural remedies and alternative medicines do not operate on the same principles as traditional medicine.
10. Perhaps even more important such remedies compete with traditional medicine for business and respect.

EXERCISE 25-2   **Using a comma and a coordinating conjunction between independent clauses**

Combine the following sentences to form sentences in which two independent clauses are joined by a coordinating conjunction. Add commas or semicolons as needed.

EXAMPLE   Some developers are beginning to rethink the American suburb. They are looking to old-fashioned small towns for their inspiration.

Some developers are beginning to rethink the American suburb, **and** they are looking to old-fashioned small towns for their inspiration.

1. One of the characteristics of the contemporary suburb is that residents have to drive everywhere. A new generation of planners is changing all that.

2. Because most housing developments have been built to accommodate vehicular traffic, pedestrian needs are often unmet. That emphasis on traffic has contributed to the isolation of the suburbs.

3. Planners Andres Duany and Elizabeth Plater-Zyberk design towns with old-fashioned town centers. The towns are completely up-to-date.

4. The emphasis in the towns designed by Duany and Plater-Zyberk is on community rather than on accessibility to highways. They don't worry about laying out streets that all feed into the nearest freeway entrance.

5. People living in such communities do not have to drive to a convenience store. They do not feel that the streets belong to cars rather than people.

EXERCISE 25-3   Using commas between items in a series

Add commas as necessary to the following sentences, placing optional commas in parentheses. If no commas are necessary, be prepared to explain why.

EXAMPLE   Among the many social problems in the United States are inadequate health care malnutrition and illiteracy among the poor.

Among the many social problems in the United States are inadequate **health care, malnutrition(,) and illiteracy** among the poor.

1. One of the problems most difficult to solve is chronic widespread homelessness.
2. Homelessness grew in the early eighties as a result of high housing costs severe drug problems and release of patients from state institutions.
3. Homelessness has emerged as a severe complex problem in American cities.
4. Many of the homeless simply need jobs medical care and housing.
5. Others need treatment for drug and alcohol addiction.
6. Still others cannot survive outside a protective controlled institution.
7. Many of the old reliable solutions don't seem to work.
8. Homeless people include families addicts and emotionally disturbed people.
9. The complexity of the problem makes it difficult to define analyze and solve.
10. A nation with such wealth education and technological skill should be able to solve the problem.

EXERCISE 25-4   **Comma use with essential and nonessential elements**

In the following sentences, determine whether or not the underlined phrases and clauses are essential or nonessential. Use commas accordingly.

EXAMPLE   Many writers <u>who chronicle the African American experience</u> have been recognized in the United States for decades.   essential—no commas

1. Langston Hughes <u>whose poetry expresses the frustrations of racial injustice</u> is studied in literature programs across the country.   _____

2. Zora Neale Hurston <u>a contemporary of Hughes's</u> provided inspiration for Alice Walker.   _____

3. Within the past few years, African American art <u>which had not received much attention previously</u> has been discovered by critics.   _____

4. One of the more respected artists is Romare Bearden <u>a collagist</u>.   _____

5. The work <u>that Bearden has produced in the last thirty years</u> has revolutionized the art of collage.   _____

6. Bearden founded Spiral <u>a black artists' group</u> in the 1960s.   _____

7. Much of the work <u>produced by members of the group</u> was motivated by the civil rights movement.   _____

8. Bearden <u>whose own work has moved from abstract painting to collage</u> is finally getting the recognition he deserves.   _____

9. Museum curator <u>Sharon Patton</u> expresses excitement at Bearden's well-deserved recognition.   _____

10. Bearden's work <u>which has toured the country</u> includes both urban and rural images.   _____

EXERCISE 25-5   **Using commas according to convention and to clarify meaning**

Insert commas as needed in the following sentences.

EXAMPLE   The lecturer asked the audience "Who was the most influential person
of all time?"

The lecturer asked the audience, "Who was the most influential person
of all time?"

A. Quotations, direct address, and tag questions

1. "I'd say it was either Mohammed, Jesus, or Confucius wouldn't you?"
2. "Couldn't it be" suggested the lecturer "someone more contemporary?"
3. "I think it was Karl Marx" offered one member of the audience.
4. "But his influence is already waning isn't it?"
5. "Members of the audience please make up your minds."

B. Balanced sentences, "more/less" constructions, and yes/no remarks

1. Half the audience believed that Marx was overrated; the other half that he
   deserved his position in history.
2. "No I wouldn't consider Marx one of the most influential people in history."
3. One person considered Plato the most influential person; another Aristotle.
4. The more the audience discussed the matter the less they agreed with each other.
5. "Oh well it isn't essential that we all agree."

C. Names, titles, dates, numbers, addresses; clarifying meaning

1. The lecturer was Kristin M. McArthur Ph.D.
2. She spoke before an audience of 1340 people.
3. By eight five hundred people were waiting at the doors.
4. The lecture was telecast on Friday August 23 1991.
5. Requests for transcripts should be addressed to Tara Fitzgerald Vice President for
   Operations Northeast Speakers' Bureau 147 Atlantic Avenue Salem New
   Hampshire 03079.

EXERCISE 25-6   **Eliminating misuse of commas**

In the following sentences, remove inappropriate commas. Circle the number of any sentences in which commas are used appropriately.

EXAMPLE   The Sandinista revolution, overthrew the Somoza government in Nicaragua in 1979.

                  The Sandinista revolution overthrew the Somoza government in Nicaragua in 1979.

1. The international community first became aware of the corruption in the Somoza regime after the 1972 earthquake, relief funds were diverted to the private use of Somoza and his cronies.
2. The assassination of newspaper editor, Pedro Chamorro, in 1978 provided added impetus to revolutionary forces.
3. The Somoza government left Nicaragua in economic, and social ruin.
4. Initially the revolutionary government, led by the Sandinistas, was immensely popular.
5. Dissatisfaction began as the government had trouble keeping, the promises it had made.
6. Resistance to Daniel Ortega's government was organized by the CIA, and right-wing forces in Nicaragua.
7. Elections were held in Nicaragua a little over a decade after the Sandinistas took power, the world was startled when Ortega lost.
8. The new President was Violeta Chamorro, widow of Pedro Chamorro.
9. Chamorro's coalition government, faced severe economic and political problems.
10. The inflation, that had plagued the Sandinistas, continued after Chamorro took office.

EXERCISE 25-7   Review

In the following paragraph, insert commas where appropriate, using the guidelines provided in the chapter.

Ever since the first astronomer looked through a telescope astronomers have relied on these devices to help them understand the heavens. Early telescopes were useful only to receive visible light, but in the past thirty years scientists have developed more sophisticated telescopes some of which can receive radio waves gamma rays and ultraviolet light. At the present time scientists are working on a telescope that can receive infrared light a development that will prove invaluable to space exploration. The infrared telescope will allow astronomers to see configurations invisible to ordinary telescopes. The telescope will be able to explore among other phenomena the development of planets from clouds of gas and dust. The telescopes will also be able to help astronomers to better understand black holes. The cost of an earth-mounted telescope is estimated to be $80000000; the cost of an airborne telescope $230000000. According to John Bahcall Ph.D. of the Institute for Advanced Studies in Princeton New Jersey the cost will be well worth it. The study of infrared light will allow astronomers physicists and other scientists to tell us a great deal about how our universe was formed and it will help them determine what will happen to our universe in the future. As one researcher explained "The more we know about what's out there the better we understand what's down here." The infrared telescope sounds like an exciting development don't you think?

CHAPTER 26

Semicolons

26a **Use a semicolon, not a comma, to join independent clauses that are intended to be closely related.**

FAULTY   Agriculture is one part of the biological revolution, the domestication and harnessing of village animals is the other.

REVISED   Agriculture is one part of the biological revolution; the domestication and harnessing of village animals is the other.

The following Critical Decisions box outlines the four basic ways of establishing a relationship between clauses.

CRITICAL DECISIONS

CHALLENGE SENTENCES: USING A PERIOD TO SEPARATE SENTENCES VERSUS A SEMICOLON OR COMMA (WITH A CONJUNCTION) TO LINK SENTENCES

As a writer, you have options for separating or linking sentences by using coordination or subordination. (See chapter 19.) This discussion focuses on using punctuation to communicate degrees of linkage between sentences and suggests varieties of coordinate, or equal, relationships.

WHY SEPARATE SENTENCES WITH A PERIOD?

Use a period to show a full separation between sentences.

   Dante Alighieri was banished from Florence in 1302. He wrote the *Divine Comedy* in exile.

WHY LINK SENTENCES WITH A SEMICOLON?

Use a semicolon, alone, to join sentences balanced in content and structure. Also use a semicolon to suggest that the second sentence completes the content of the first. The semicolon suggests a link but leaves it to the reader to infer how sentences are related.

BALANCED SENTENCE   Agriculture is one part of the biological revolution;
                     the domestication of animals is the other.

SUGGESTED LINK   Five major books and many articles have been
                     written on the Bayeux tapestry; each shows just
                     how much the trained observer can draw from
                     pictorial evidence.

WHY LINK SENTENCES WITH A CONJUNCTIVE ADVERB AND A SEMICOLON OR PERIOD?

Use a semicolon with a conjunctive adverb (*however, therefore,* etc.) to emphasize
one of the following relationships: addition, consequence, contrast, cause and
effect, time, emphasis, or condition (see 19a-3). With the semicolon and
conjunctive adverb, linkage between sentences is closer than with a semicolon
alone. The relationship between sentences is made clear by the conjunctive
adverb.

> Patients in need of organs have begun advertising for them; **however,** the
> American Medical Association discourages the practice.

Use a period between sentences to force a pause and then to stress the
conjunctive adverb.

> Patients in need of organs have begun advertising for them. **However,** the
> American Medical Association discourages the practice.

WHY LINK SENTENCES WITH A COMMA AND A COORDINATING CONJUNCTION?

Use a comma and a coordinating conjunction to join sentences in a coordinate
relationship that shows addition, choice, consequence, contrast, or cause (see
19a-1). Since two sentences are fully merged into one following this strategy,
linkage is complete. At the same time, this method offers the *least* emphasis in
showing a coordinate relationship.

> Robotics has increaseed efficiency in the automobile industry, **but** it has put
> thousands of assembly-line employees out of work.

Use semicolons to join closely related independent clauses, not to string
unconnected statements together.

OVERUSED   Agriculture was the first part of the biological revolution; the
            development of crop rotation and irrigation contributed to it;
            another important part was the harnessing of village animals.

REVISED   Agriculture, the first part of the biological revolution, was aided by the development of crop rotation and irrigation. There was also another part of the revolution; this was the harnessing of village animals.

26b Use a semicolon, not a comma, to join two independent clauses that are closely linked by a conjunctive adverb.

A semicolon (or a period) is used to join two independent clauses linked by a conjunctive adverb, regardless of where in the sentence the conjunctive adverb is located. (See chapters 13, 19.)

FAULTY   When Benjamin Bradlee became editor of the *Washington Post*, it was a nondescript newspaper, however, within ten years it had become a Pulitzer Prize-winning organization.

REVISED   When Benjamin Bradlee became editor of the *Washington Post*, it was a nondescript newspaper; however, within ten years it had become a Pulitzer Prize-winning organization.

When Benjamin Bradlee became editor of the *Washington Post*, it was a nondescript newspaper; within ten years, however, it had become a Pulitzer Prize-winning organization.

When Benjamin Bradlee became editor of the *Washington Post*, it was a nondescript newspaper. However, within ten years it had become a Pulitzer Prize-winning organization.

26c Join independent clauses with a semicolon before a coordinating conjunction when one or both clauses contain a comma or other internal punctuation.

Katherine Graham, who had taken over the *Post* after the death of her husband, began as a cautious publisher; but after she settled into the job, she became known for taking worthwhile risks.

26d Use a semicolon to separate items in a series when each item is long or when one or more items contain a comma.

Some of the more famous episodes in Ben Bradlee's career were the publication, against the advice of the newspaper's lawyers, of the Pentagon Papers; the investigation by Bob Woodward and Carl Bernstein of the Watergate scandal; and the paper's own scandal when Janet Cooke falsified information in a drug addiction story.

26e Place semicolons *outside* of end quotation marks.

One colleague commented, "Bradlee is the best in the business"; almost everyone else in the business would heartily agree.

26f Edit to avoid common errors.

1 Use a comma, not a semicolon, after an introductory subordinate clause.

FAULTY When it was discovered that Janet Cooke had invented the child drug addict in her story; Bradlee returned the Pulitzer prize the paper had won.

REVISED When it was discovered that Janet Cooke had invented the child drug addict in her story, Bradlee returned the Pulitzer prize the paper had won.

2 Use a colon, not a semicolon, to introduce a list.

FAULTY Being a good editor requires three things; a readiness to take risks, the determination to get the story, and a willingness to admit error.

REVISED Being a good editor requires three things: a readiness to take risks, the determination to get the story, and a willingness to admit error.

EXERCISE 26-1   Using a semicolon to join independent clauses

Combine the following sentences, using semicolons (with or without conjunctive adverbs) to join independent clauses.

EXAMPLE   In 1972, Dartmouth College hired an anthropology instructor to head a new program in Native American Studies. The man's name was Michael Dorris.

In 1972, Dartmouth College hired an anthropology instructor to head a new program in Native American Studies; the man's name was Michael Dorris.

1. Dorris had lived for a time on an Indian reservation. Most of his early years were spent in Louisville, Kentucky.

2. As a single man, Dorris adopted three children. He provided them with a family atmosphere.

3. One of his children had trouble learning. Dorris took him to many doctors.

4. The doctors in New Hampshire could not diagnose his son's problem. The director of an Indian program on a South Dakota reservation recognized fetal alcohol syndrome.

5. Dorris's book about his son, *The Broken Cord*, sold over 75,000 copies. The story has touched people across the country.

6. When Louise Erdrich married Dorris, she had no children of her own. She adapted well to her instant family.

7. Erdrich was also a writer. Her first novel, *Love Medicine,* won the National Book Critics Circle Award for 1984.

8. Dorris and Erdrich regularly edit and criticize each other's work. In 1988, they actually began writing a novel together.

9. *The Crown of Columbus* is a reflection on the 500th anniversary of Columbus's discovery of America. It explores the discovery from the perspective of the native people.

10. Individually, Dorris and Erdrich have written a total of nine books. *Crown* is the first book they have written together.

EXERCISE 26-2   **Using a semicolon to prevent misreading**

Insert semicolons as needed in the following sentences to prevent misreading.

EXAMPLE   The Parker River National Wildlife Refuge, which provides nesting areas for the endangered piping plover, is sometimes closed to human traffic, but many people who use the area for recreation feel that the service is not responsive to their concerns.

The Parker River National Wildlife Refuge, which provides nesting areas for the endangered piping plover, is sometimes closed to human traffic; but many people who use the area for recreation feel that the service is not responsive to their concerns.

1. The refuge is used by hikers, who find the beach trails peaceful, by sports enthusiasts, who consider the ocean and river fishing incomparable, and by sunbathers, who recognize the beach at the refuge as one of the finest in New England.

2. Closing the beach is clearly an unpopular decision, according to Jack Fillio, the manager of the refuge, and area residents who depend on the beach for recreational activities have reason to be angry.

3. Fillio emphasizes that the business of the Fish and Wildlife Service is to protect animals, not to provide recreation for humans, but privately he acknowledges that decisions to close popular areas are difficult not only for vacationers, but for the local economy as well.

4. Among the threats to piping plovers are beachgoers, who often trample newborn chicks, animal predators, which are attracted by human garbage, and pollution, which destroys the plovers' food.

5. Soon after they hatch, plover chicks can walk on their own, but they cannot fly for at least a month, making it difficult for them to evade the human onslaught on sunny summer days.

EXERCISE 26-3   Review

In the following paragraph, insert, move, or replace semicolons as needed, according to the guidelines provided in the chapter.

On a ranch outside Dillon, Montana; big business has met big sky. The ranch, which looks like a traditional western locale from old movies, is in fact a highly successful business that could stand up to any Wall Street operation, but it also represents an unusual venture in international relations. When the ranch was sold in 1989 to a Japanese company, a few changes were in order; first, Japanese management principles were introduced, second, Japanese sales managers were sent to the ranch to learn about cattle raising, and third, the American ranchers were educated about the tastes of Japanese beef consumers. Said one rancher, "We were very skeptical of the whole operation at first;" since that time, most of the locals have embraced the new owners. Among the goodwill gestures of the Japanese company were sponsoring a bowling team, a popular pastime in the area, supporting the local hospital, sorely in need of funds, buying machinery from local dealers rather than importing it, and distributing jackets and hats sporting the company logo to all employees of the ranch. The gestures were well received by the community, however, the attempt to use Japanese management techniques was a failure. In all, the Montana community and the Japanese company seem to have become good neighbors; not all such ventures will be productive; but international business is here to stay.

EXERCISE 26-4   Revising

Now that you have a good understanding of the various uses of the semicolon, apply that knowledge when revising your papers. Reread the drafts of any papers you're working on at present, and decide where semicolons might be appropriate—perhaps you've written two sentences that are very closely linked, or you have a list including lengthy items. Check also for instances where you may have misused or overused semicolons.

CHAPTER 27

Apostrophes

The **apostrophe (')** is used to show possession, mark the omission of letters or numbers, and mark plural forms.

27a Using apostrophes to show possession with single nouns

1 **For most nouns and for indefinite pronouns, add an apostrophe and the letter *s* to indicate possession.**

If the singular noun ends with the letter *s*, add an apostrophe and *s* unless the new word is difficult to pronounce or read.

Jonathan's calculator		Chris's roommate
Francis's sandwich	or	Francis' sandwich

2 **Eliminate apostrophes that are misused or confused with possessive pronouns.**

Personal pronouns *never* use apostrophes to show possession. (See chapters 7 and 8.) It is important to distinguish between personal pronouns in their possessive form and personal pronouns that are contractions. (See 27c for contractions.)

Possession with Personal Pronouns

its	the book's binding	*its* binding
whose	Who owns the book?	*Whose* book is this?
your	the book owned by you	*your* book
yours	the book owned by you	The book is *yours.*
their	a book owned by Bob and Sue	*their* book
theirs	a book owned by Bob and Sue	The book is *theirs.*
her	a book owned by Sue	*her* book
hers	a book owned by Sue	The book is *hers.*
our	a book owned by us	*our* book
ours	a book owned by us	The book is *ours.*
his	a book owned by Bob	*his* book
his	a book owned by Bob	The book is *his.*

Personal Pronouns: Contractions Formed with *be*

it's	*It is* doubtful he'll arrive.	*It's* doubtful he'll arrive.
who's	*Who is* planning to attend?	*Who's* planning to attend?
you're	*You are* mistaken.	*You're* mistaken.
there's	*There is* little to do.	*There's* little to do.
they're	*They are* home.	*They're* home.

FAULTY   The sign read, "Dining at it's best."

REVISED   The sign read, "Dining at its best."

---

3 **For a plural noun ending with *s*, add only an apostrophe to indicate possession. For a plural noun not ending with *s*, add an apostrophe and the letter *s*.**

children's hospital   the Swensons' house

CRITICAL DECISIONS

BE ALERT TO DIFFERENCES: TEST YOUR PLACEMENT OF APOSTROPHES WITH NOUNS AND WITH INDEFINITE PRONOUNS

The personal pronouns *his, hers, ours, its, yours,* and *theirs* **never** use apostrophes. By contrast, nouns and indefinite pronouns (such as *somebody, other,* and *no one*) do use apostrophes to show possession. Nouns and indefinite pronouns also form plurals with the suffix *-s*. Apply the following tests to determine whether or not you should be using an apostrophe and *s* (*'s*) or the suffix *-s*, with no apostrophe.

Is the noun or indefinite pronoun followed by a noun? If so, then you probably intend to show possession. Use the possessive form *'s*.

government's <u>policy</u>   hospital's <u>program</u>
                noun   **noun**

family's <u>holiday</u>   other's <u>comment</u>
          noun   **noun**

Is a noun or indefinite pronoun followed by a verb or a modifying phrase? If so, then you probably intend to make the noun or indefinite pronoun plural. Use the suffix *-s*, with *no* apostrophe.

governments <u>in that part of the world</u>
                modifying phrase

famil*ies* <u>having two or more children</u>
modifying phrase

hospital*s* <u>that have large staffs</u>
modifying clause

other*s* <u>believe</u>
verb

But if an omitted word is involved, you may need a possessive form.

Eric's friends attend Central High. Frank*'s* attend Northern.

[In the second sentence, the omitted noun *friends* is clearly intended as the subject of the sentence. The *'s* is needed to show whose friends—*Frank's.*]

27b Using apostrophes to show possession with multiple nouns

1 **To indicate possession when a cluster of words functions as a single noun, add an apostrophe and the letter *s* to the last word.**

editor in chief's office   maid of honor's dress

2 **To indicate possession of an object owned jointly, add an apostrophe and the letter *s* to the last noun (or pronoun) named.**

Matthew is Dan and Rosanne's son.

3 **To indicate individual possession by two or more people, add an apostrophe and the letter *s* to each person named.**

Mary's and Bill's accounts of the accident were entirely different.

27c Using apostrophes in contractions to mark the omission of letters and numbers

1 **Use an apostrophe to indicate the omission of letters in a contraction.**

I'll = I will   don't = do not

2 Use an apostrophe to indicate the omission of numbers in a date.

the '20s   the '50s

3 Eliminate apostrophes from verbs in their -*s* form.

FAULTY   Catherine run's the accounting office.

REVISED   Catherine runs the accounting office.

27d   Using apostrophes to mark plural forms

1 Use an apostrophe and the letter *s* to indicate the plural of a letter, number, or word referred to as a word.

Underline (on a typewriter) or italicize (in typeset) letters, number , and words referred to as words, and then add apostrophe *s*. (Exception: add *s* only to proper names.)

Typewriter   Typeset

There are two <u>s</u>'s in <u>dessert</u>.   There are two *s*'s in *dessert*.

Our group has three <u>Claires</u>.   Our group has three *Claires*.

2 Use an apostrophe and the letter *s* to indicate the plural of a symbol, an abbreviation with periods, and years expressed in decades.

Symbols, abbreviations, or decades are not italicized when made plural. With decades, abbreviations without periods, and symbols, the apostrophe is optional.

There were four Ph.D.'s in the room.

1980's	or	1980s
CPA's	or	CPAs
&'s	or	&s

3 Eliminate any apostrophes misused to form regular plurals of nouns.

FAULTY   Ballplayer's are grossly overpaid.

REVISED   Ballplayers are grossly overpaid.

EXERCISE 27-1   Possessive forms

Fill in the appropriate possessive form for each of the following nouns, using apostrophes when necessary.

EXAMPLE   women   ___women's___

1. prioress   _____
2. it   _____
3. master of ceremonies   _____
4. Melissa and Jason (jointly)   _____
5. The Blakes   _____
6. her   _____
7. Shannon and Jim (individually) _____
8. sergeant-at-arms   _____
9. oxen   _____
10. movie   _____

EXERCISE 27-2   **Distinguishing between possessives and contractions, plural nouns, and singular verbs**

In the following sentences, circle the appropriate form of each word in parentheses.

EXAMPLE   If (your/(you're)) trying to lose weight, beware of the quick and painless programs.

1. (Doctors/Doctor's) agree that the only way to lose weight and keep it off is to change (your/you're) eating habits.
2. Most people who use a commercial diet program regain (their/they're) weight within two years.
3. You should understand that a commercial (programs/program's) interests sometimes lie more in the profits (their/they're) going to make than in (your/you're) well-being.
4. If the program (guarantees/guarantee's) that you will lose weight, (your/you're) probably going to be disappointed.
5. A program that places good nutrition at (its/it's) center is the best choice.

EXERCISE 27-3   **Using apostrophes in contractions and plural forms**

A. Combine the following words to form contractions.

EXAMPLE   would + not   _____wouldn't_____

1. could + have   _____

2. they + will   _____

3. we + are   _____

4. you + had   _____

5. have + not   _____

6. she + is   _____

7. she + has   _____

8. will + not   _____

9. we + will   _____

10. they + are   _____

B. Form the plurals of the following letters, words, and numbers.

1. 7   _____

2. r   _____

3. #   _____

4. trust (referred to as a word)   _____

5. D   _____

EXERCISE 27-4   Review

Insert or delete apostrophes as needed in the following paragraph.

PBS's series *I, Claudius* is based on Robert Graves book. Various historians accounts of this period are used by Graves, who begins his tale with reference to Antony's and Cleopatra's defeat. Chronicling the Roman emperors from Augustus to Claudius, the series focus's on the corruption and treachery that eventually led to the fall of Rome. Of all the villains in the series, Claudius grandmother Livia is perhaps the worst. In order to insure that her son Tiberius will become emperor, Livia either poisons or otherwise arranges the death's of various members of her family, including her husband. (Its even suggested that she poisons her own son.) The emperor of Romes position at the time was all powerful; Rome ruled much of the world, and the emperor almost single-handedly ruled Rome. Livias activities are designed to help history on it's way. Claudius comes to suspect her treachery, but few people take him seriously because hes a cripple and he stutter's. His stammering buh-buh-buhs annoy the family, but they also protect him—nobody believes that Claudius is smart enough to be dangerous. The result is that Claudius outlives his ill-fated family. The history that he writes at the end of his life is their's.

CHAPTER 28

Quotation Marks

28a Quoting prose

1 **Use double quotation marks (" ") to set off a short direct quotation from the rest of a sentence.**

When you reproduce exactly the words of another, enclose the material in double quotation marks if it takes up four or fewer lines of your manuscript. (Longer quotations are set off by indentation.) When you reproduce someone's words inexactly, do not use quotation marks.

DIRECT	"My grandmother had a reverence for the sun," writes N. Scott Momaday.
INDIRECT	N. Scott Momaday writes that his grandmother had a reverence for the sun.

2 **Use single quotation marks (' ') to set off quoted material or the titles of short works within a quotation enclosed by double (" ") marks.**

The instructor said, "Momaday refers to his tribe's houses as 'sentinels in the plain.' "

3 **Use commas to enclose explanatory remarks that lie outside the quotation.**

Commas set off explanatory remarks (except those ending in *that*) that introduce, interrupt, or follow a quotation.

Momaday writes, "Houses are like sentinels in the plain."

"Houses," Momaday writes, "are like sentinels in the plain."

"Houses are like sentinels in the plain," Momaday writes.

Momaday writes that "houses are like sentinels in the plain."

4 **Display—that is, set off from text—lengthy quotations. Quotation marks are *not* used to enclose a displayed quotation.**

Quotations that run more than four lines of your manuscript are indented, and presented without quotation marks.

In his memoir *The Way to Rainy Mountain*, N. Scott Momaday writes lovingly of his grandmother:

> My grandmother had a reverence for the sun, a holy regard that now is all but gone out of mankind. There was a wariness in her, and an ancient awe. She was a Christian in her later years, but she had come a long way about, and she never forgot her birthright. As a child she had been to the sun dances; she had taken part in that annual rite, and by it she had learned the restoration of her people in the presence of Tai-me.

5 **Place periods and commas inside the end quotation mark.**

Unless a quotation ending with a period is followed by a page reference in parentheses, always place periods and commas inside quotation marks.

Allan Bloom asserts, "Classical music is dead among the young."

"Classical music is dead among the young," asserts Allan Bloom.

Allan Bloom asserts, "Classical music is dead among the young" (71).

6 **Place colons, semicolons, and footnotes outside end quotation marks.**

Bloom contends that his students' ignorance of classical music is "a constant surprise": previously, his students knew more about that music than he did.

Bloom believes that "rock has the beat of sexual intercourse"; indeed, he states that young rock fans are aware of rock's sexual overtones.

According to Bloom, "Never was there an art form directed so exclusively to children."

7 **Place question marks and exclamation points inside or outside end quotation marks, depending on meaning.**

Question marks and exclamation points that apply directly to the quotation or to the entire sentence are placed within the quotation marks; otherwise, they are placed outside the quotation marks.

After reading Bloom, the instructor asked, "Is he right?"

Who responded, "Does he really believe all this?"

Bloom expects us to believe that the rock business "has all the moral dignity of drug trafficking"!

8 **Place dashes inside quotations only when they are part of the quoted material.**

Bloom's students "who have had a serious fling with drugs—and gotten over it—" are often apathetic.

Bloom argues that rock music—"like the drugs with which it is allied"—provides artificial rapture.

CRITICAL DECISIONS

SET ISSUES IN A BROADER CONTEXT: INCORPORATING QUOTATIONS INTO YOUR WRITING

Knowing when to quote is something of an art, and you should see 34g of the *Allyn & Bacon Handbook* for guidance on this matter. This discussion assumes you have decided to quote. The focus here is on determining *how much* to quote and on how to *incorporate* quoted materials into the logic and rhythm of your sentences.

The following examples draw on the following passage about shopping malls by the noted anthropologist Richard Marks (*The New American Bazaar*).

> When they are successful, shopping malls in American cities fulfill the same function as *bazaars* did in the cities of antiquity. The bazaars of the ancient and medieval worlds were social organisms—if we mean by this term self-contained, self-regulating systems in which individual human lives are less important (and less interesting) than the interaction of hundreds, and sometimes thousands, of lives.

HOW MUCH TO QUOTE

Quote other writers when you find their discussions to be particularly lively, dramatic, or incisive or especially helpful in bolstering your credibility. In general, quote as little as possible so that you keep readers focused on *your* discussion.

- Quote a word or a phrase, if this will do.

  Anthropologist Richard Marks refers to the American shopping mall as a "social organism."

- Quote a sentence, if needed.

  Marks sees in shopping malls a modern spin on an ancient institution: "When they are successful, shopping malls in American cities fulfill the same function as *bazaars* did in the cities of antiquity."

- Infrequently quote a long passage as a "block."

Long quotations of five or more lines are set off as a block (see 28a-4). Limit your use of block quotations, which tempt writers to avoid the hard work of selecting for quotation *only* the words or sentences especially pertinent to the discussion at hand. If you decide that a long quotation is needed, introduce the quotation with a full sentence and a colon. The following might introduce the passage previously quoted from *The New American Bazaar.*

> Various commentators have claimed that shopping malls serve a social function. Anthropologist Richard Marks compares the mall to the bazaar in cities of old:
>
> > When they are successful, shopping malls . . .

- Use attributive phrases

By using attributive phrases like *Jones argues, Smith says,* or *According to Marks,* you alert readers to the fact that you are about to present someone else's words. Tie these attributive phrases into the logic of your own sentences, linking the quotation with the content of your paper.

> Every American city now has its shopping malls. According to anthropologist Richard Marks, successful malls "fulfill the same function as *bazaars* did in the cities of antiquity."

- Interrupt a quotation with an attributive phrase

Place your attributive comment between a quotation's subject and verb or after an introductory phrase or clause in order to emphasize a key word. The word emphasized will come just before or after the interruption.

> "When they are successful," says Richard Marks, "shopping malls in American cities fulfill the same function as *bazaars* did in the cities of antiquity." [The interruption focuses attention on *shopping malls.*]

Split a quotation with an attributive remark to maintain the rhythm or continuity of your own paragraph. Compare these two versions of a quoted sentence.

ACCEPTABLE   Every American city has its shopping malls, its equivalents of the ancient bazaar. As anthropoligist Richard Marks points out, "The bazaars of the ancient and medieval worlds were social organisms . . ."

PREFERRED   Every American city has its shopping malls, its equivalents of the ancient bazaar. "The bazaars of the ancient and medieval worlds," says anthropologist Richard Marks, "were social organisms . . ." [This version maintains paragraph coherence by keeping the reader's focus on the word *bazaar.*]

28b Quoting poetry, dialogue, and other material

1 **Run-in brief quotations of poetry with your sentences. Indicate line breaks in the poem with a slash (/). Quote longer passages in displayed form.**

Shakespeare writes:

> Yet in these thoughts myself almost despising,
> Haply I think on thee, and then my state,
> Like to the lark at break of day arising
> From sullen earth, sings hymns at heaven's gate;
>   For thy sweet love rememb'red such wealth brings,
>   That then I scorn to change my state with kings.

The last lines of Shakespeare's sonnet, "For thy sweet love rememb'red such wealth brings, / That then I scorn to change my state with kings," speak eloquently of the depth of his love.

2 **Use quotation marks to quote or write dialogue.**

Start a new paragraph whenever the speaker changes.

"I've always had difficulty understanding Shakespeare," Ellen admitted after the discussion of his sonnets.

"I know what you mean," agreed Kelly. "But I love his poetry all the same."

3 **Indicate the titles of brief works with quotation marks: chapters of books, short stories, poems, songs, sections from newspapers, essays, etc.**[1]

"Lying Doggo" is one of my favorite Bobbie Ann Mason stories.

Sarah always thinks of her old roommate when she hears Warren Zevon singing "Werewolves of London."

---

[1]**Note**: When you prepare the final drafts of your own essays, do not put the title in quotation marks.

4   Use quotation marks occasionally to emphasize words or to note invented words.

Once a word has been placed in quotation marks for emphasis, subsequent uses of the word do not call for quotation marks. Words being referred to as words, or being defined in a sentence, can either be italicized (underlined on a typewriter) or placed in quotation marks.

"Idiot" was a term used frequently in the past. An idiot in today's language usually is one who behaves foolishly.

Surgical strike is a euphemism for a bombing raid.

28c   Eliminating misused or overused quotation marks

1   Eliminate phrases using quotation marks to note slang or colloquial expressions.

MISUSED   In spite of many setbacks, George "hung in there."

REVISED   In spite of many setbacks, George persevered.

2   Eliminate phrases using quotation marks to make ironic comments.

MISUSED   Alicia's sour expression revealed that she was just "thrilled" with the performance.

REVISED   Alicia's sour expression revealed that she was disgusted with the performance.

3   Eliminate quotation marks used to emphasize technical terms.

MISUSED   We have become fascinated with "deconstruction" theory.

REVISED   We have become fascinated with deconstruction theory.

4   Eliminate quotation marks that are overused to note commonly accepted nicknames.

Use quotation marks with nicknames only if the names are unusual.

MISUSED   "Jimmy" Carter was an underrated President.

REVISED   Jimmy Carter was an underrated President.

APPROPRIATE   John "Hondo" Havlicek is a legend in Boston Celtics history.

EXERCISE 28-1   Quoting prose

Rewrite the following sentences, using the appropriate marks to indicate quotations, and making sure that quotation marks and other marks are placed appropriately. Words to be quoted are underlined; double underlining indicates quoted material within quotations.

EXAMPLE   In *Children of War*, Roger Rosenblatt describes Cambodian refugee children as <u>astonishingly beautiful</u>.

In *Children of War*, Roger Rosenblatt describes Cambodian refugee children as astonishingly beautiful.

1. Ty Kim Seng is a boy who was <u>forced to join one of the mobile work teams instituted by Pol Pot for the Khmer children's education and well being</u>, according to Rosenblatt.

2. In talking to children of war-torn countries, Rosenblatt discovers that he has been <u>defining vengeance conventionally</u>; one child he speaks to says, <u>To me revenge means that I must make the most of my life</u> (471).

3. Rosenblatt asks himself, <u>Could their idea of revenge thus be a way of dealing with the fear of evil in themselves?</u>

4. Rosenblatt keeps hearing the same refrain—<u>revenge is to make a bad man better than before</u>—in his talks with the children.

5. Is it any wonder that these children believe that <u>peace is worth more than gold</u>?

EXERCISE 28-2   Quoting dialogue

Rewrite the following dialogue, supplying the appropriate paragraphing, quotation marks, and other punctuation.

EXAMPLE   Have you ever heard, asked Joanne, of Max Ernst?

"Have you ever heard," asked Joanne, "of Max Ernst?"

I replied, no, tell me about him. Joanne thought for a moment: well, she said, he created bizarre images—collages, really—that juxtaposed beasts, plants, and humans. When did he do his work, I asked. Joanne replied, He painted from 1920 until well into the '50s, but his best work was done before 1940. I asked where I could see his work displayed. Most of it is in European galleries, Joanne reluctantly admitted.

EXERCISE 28-3   Review

Insert, move, or delete quotation marks as needed in the following paragraph.

I was reminded the other day of a statement from Margaret Mead's book *Male and Female:* "Every home is different from every other home. (76)" As I think back over my childhood, I realize how right she was. In our home, we answered not only to my mother and father, but to my grandmother and Pop-Pop as well. My best friend "Cindy," however, found our large family strange: Why are there so many people in your house—and so many bosses? she would ask. I, on the other hand, could not understand the rigid "sex roles" in her family. I could never visit her house without thinking of the children's story Dick and Jane Play Grownup. The story had always seemed so strange to me, with its clear distinctions between men's work and women's work. And again, as I think back on that time, I remember Margaret Mead's words. I once heard her tell a story about what she called the greatest threat to sex roles in the American family: taking out the garbage. Mead was talking about the fact that traditional sex roles call for males to be responsible only for outside work and females for inside work. Since garbage originates inside the home, she explained, smiling benignly, but ends up outside, whose job is it to take out the garbage? I appreciate that story now as my husband and I take turns with the garbage and I think of how different the family we have built is from either his family or mine. I find it "totally awesome" that what Mead wrote and talked about years ago remains true today.

CHAPTER 29

Other Marks

In this chapter you will read about the colon, dashes, parentheses, brackets, ellipses, and slashes—marks of punctuation that have important, if specialized, uses.

THE COLON

29a Using the colon

The colon follows a complete independent clause to signal an announcement.

1 **Edit to eliminate colons misused within independent clauses.**

FAULTY   A new field called geoengineering is: using technology to solve ecological problems.

REVISED   A new field called geoengineering is using technology to solve ecological problems.

              We have a new field called geoengineering: using technology to solve ecological problems.

2 **Use a colon to announce an important statement or question.**

Environmental groups think geoengineering ignores the real cause of our ecological problems: we refuse to consider the impact of our habits and lifestyle on the natural world.

3 **Use a colon to introduce a list or a quotation.**

A list

The ways in which we contribute to the destruction of the planet are many: burning fossil fuels, packaging products in non-recyclable plastics, eating and drinking from styrofoam containers, and pouring chemicals into the water.

A quotation

At least one geophysicist worries that relying on geoengineering rather than on changing our habits could be dangerous: "Technological fixes can turn around and bite you."

4 **Use a colon to set off an appositive phrase, summary, or explanation.**

Appositive

We are now facing the most serious environmental problem in history: the ozone layer is vanishing.

Summary

Shooting dust particles into the air to deflect dangerous ultraviolet rays could cost up to $30 million; mirrors and reflecting balloons could run over $200 million; installing lasers on high mountains could have a price tag of $2 billion: geoengineering is an expensive solution.

Explanation

Even with new guidelines for reducing the use of chlorofluorocarbons, the ozone layer is in danger: it will take three-quarters of a century for existing CFCs to dissipate.

  Use a colon to distinguish chapter from verse in Biblical citations, hours from minutes, and titles from subtitles or subsidiary material.

Biblical citation

"*One* generation passeth away, and *another* generation cometh: but the earth abideth for ever" (Ecclesiastes 1: 4).

Hours from minutes

5:33 A.M.

Title from subtitle

"Grant and Lee: A Study in Contrasts"

6 **Use a colon after the salutation in a formal letter, and in bibliographic citations.**

Dear Ms. Grassis:

Angelou, Maya. *I Know Why the Caged Bird Sings*. New York: Random House, 1969.

THE DASH

 29b Using dashes for emphasis

1 **Use dashes to set off nonessential elements.**

Nonessential elements are sharply emphasized when dashes (two hyphens on the typewriter) are used to set them off.

When Do Writers Need Dashes?

Sentence constructions rarely *require* the use of dashes. The dash is a stylist's tool, an elective mark. It halts the reader within a sentence by creating a cha-cha, dance-like syncopation. On seeing the dash, readers pause; then they speed up to read the words you've emphasized. Then they pause once more—reflectively, before returning to the main part of your sentence.

EFFECTIVE   Zoologist Uwe Schmidt discovered that shortly after birth, vampire bat pups are given regurgitated blood—in addition to milk—by their mothers.

Use the single dash to set off elements at the beginning or end of a sentence and a pair to set off elements in the middle. With elements set off at the end of a sentence or in the middle, you have the choice of using commas or parentheses instead of dashes. Whatever punctuation you use, take care to word the element you set off so that it fits smoothly into the structure of your sentence. For instance, the following sentence with its nonessential element would be awkward.

AWKWARD   Zoologist Uwe Schmidt discovered that shortly after birth, vampire bat pups are given regurgitated blood—they drink milk too—by their mothers.

BETTER   Zoologist Uwe Schmidt discovered that shortly after birth, vampire bat pups are given regurgitated blood—in addition to milk—by their mothers.

Brief modifiers in mid-sentence

Bei Dao's poetry—translated into over twenty languages—reflects his ambivalent feelings about today's China.

Lengthy modifiers

Exile has been difficult for Bei Dao—at one time a proud young soldier in Mao Zedong's Red Guard.

Appositives

Bei Dao began to question his revolutionary beliefs during the Cultural Revolution—Chairman Mao's campaign to rid China of Western influences.

2 | Use dashes to set off a significant repeating structure or an emphatic concluding element.

Repeating structure

Bei Dao's words inspired—and continue to nurture—Chinese dissidents.

Emphatic concluding remark

Poetry will continue to be Bei Dao's spiritual link to his homeland—until he can return again in person.

3 | Use a dash to set off an introductory series from a summary or explanatory remark.

Images, sounds, rhythms—poetry continues to sustain troubled souls.

4 | Use a dash to express an interruption in dialogue.

"Will you ever—"

"Write again? Only if the spirit moves me."

5 | Use a dash to set off an attribution (by name), following an epigram.

All's fair in love and war.
　　　　　　　　—Anonymous

PARENTHESES

29c Using parentheses to set off nonessential information

Parentheses ( ) are used to indicate information that is interesting but unnecessary to an understanding of the entire sentence.

1 Use parentheses to set off nonessential information: examples, comments, appositives.

Examples

In the nineteenth century, the British Empire encompassed much of what is now called the third world (for example, India and Burma).

Comments—explanatory or editorial

Indian politicians often refer to their country as the world's largest democracy (although representatives of western democracies shake their heads at the characterization).

Appositives

The Nehru family (Jawaharlal Nehru, Indira Gandhi, and Rajiv Gandhi) headed India's government almost without interruption for over forty years.

 2 Use parentheses to set off dates, translations of non-English words, and acronyms.

Dates

When India gained independence from Great Britain (1947), there was hope that a great social-democratic state would emerge.

Translations

The Nehru family belong to the Brahman caste (the highest caste, consisting of priests and scholars).

Acronyms

India's poor have received a great deal of assistance from WHO (the World Health Organization).

3 Use parentheses to set off numbers or letters that mark items in a series, when the series is run-in with a sentence.

Parentheses are only used to mark items in a series if the series is written into the sentence itself.

Several factors have contributed to the instability of Indian society: (1) religious antipathy, especially between Muslims and Hindus, (2) regional rivalry, and (3) corruption within the government itself.

Several factors have contributed to the instability of Indian society:
1. religious antipathy, especially between Muslims and Hindus,
2. regional rivalry, and
3. corruption within the government itself.

4 Punctuate parentheses according to convention.

Complete sentences within parentheses are punctuated according to convention; if the parenthetical remark is not a complete sentence, end punctuation appears outside the parentheses.

Indian politics has been riddled with violence. (Mahatma Gandhi, Indira Gandhi, and Rajiv Gandhi were all assassinated.)

Three of India's leaders have been assassinated (Mahatma Gandhi, Indira Gandhi, and Rajiv Gandhi).

BRACKETS

29d Using brackets for editorial clarification

1 Use brackets to insert your own words into quoted material.

Brackets to clarify a reference

In the latest volume of her autobiography, Maya Angelou writes, "In the United States, during segregation [before the Civil Rights movement of the 1960s], Black American travelers, unable to stay in hotels restricted to White patrons, stopped at churches and told the black ministers or deacons of their predicaments."

Brackets to weave quoted language in with your sentences

When church leaders brought unexpected guests to a home, the family relied on "surreptitious knocks [that] would sound on the back door," indicating that neighbors were bringing food to help feed the guests.

Brackets to show your awareness of an error in the quoted passage

"Maya Angelo [sic] has written poetry as well as prose."

Brackets to note emphasis

"My skin color, features and the Ghana cloth I wore made me look like any young Ghanian woman. I could pass *if I didn't talk too much* [italics mine]."

2   Use brackets to distinguish parentheses inserted within parentheses.

Angelou writes lyrically of her visit to Africa (where she tried to avoid visiting Cape Coast Castle [site of the dungeons holding newly captured slaves] for over a year).

ELLIPSES

29e   Using an ellipsis to indicate a break in continuity

Ellipses (. . .) show that you have deleted either words or entire sentences from a passage you are quoting. The following quotations come from William Least Heat Moon's *Blue Highways*. The original passage reads as follows:

> I was the only non-Catholic at the table of four other guests and three monks. While the conversation rambled over papal encyclicals and the chances of the Atlanta Braves, I watched the monks closely, knowing they might talk a good ballgame, but, sooner or later, they would betray their medievalism by lapsing into Latin or intoning prayer. All I had to do was watch. They would try to root the heresy out of me or sell an indulgence. But they ate their hotdogs with ketchup or mustard and their lips turned Kool-Aid blue just like mine. Then, as if to a tolling only they heard, they rose and disappeared, the other guests with them. Alone again.

1   Know when *not* to use an ellipsis.

Do *not* use ellipses to note words omitted from the beginning of a sentence. Do *not* use ellipses if the passage you quote ends with a period and ends your sentence as well.

> As they talked at the dinner table, recalls Moon, "I watched the monks closely, knowing they might talk a good ballgame, but, sooner or later, they would betray their medievalism by lapsing into Latin or intoning prayer."

Moon is certain that the monks will attempt to "root the heresy out of me or sell an indulgence."

2 Use an ellipsis to indicate words deleted from the middle of a sentence.

If the words omitted directly follow an internal mark of punctuation, retain that mark and then add the ellipses.

"Then, . . . they rose and disappeared, the other guests with them."

3 Use an ellipsis to indicate words deleted from the end of a sentence.

Moon says that the monks "ate their hotdogs with ketchup or mustard and their lips turned Kool-Aid blue. . . ."

4 Use an ellipsis to show a pause or interruption.

He wondered about being different from the others . . . but put the thought out of his mind and went off to bed.

THE SLASH

29f Using the slash

1 Use slashes to separate the lines of poetry run in with the text of a sentence.

Robert Frost contemplates the importance of a seemingly innocent choice when he writes, "Two roads diverged in a wood, and I— / I took the one less travelled by, / And that has made all the difference."

2 Use slashes to show choice.

You may read the book and/or watch the movie.

3 Use a slash in writing fractions or formulas to note division.

7/12   5 3/4

EXERCISE 29-1   Using the colon

In the following sentences, insert and delete colons where necessary. Circle the number of any correct sentences.

EXAMPLE   In the 1950s, some liberal-leaning parents feared three things, Senator Joseph McCarthy, the crusading newspapers, and their children.

In the 1950s, some liberal-leaning parents feared three things: Senator Joseph McCarthy, the crusading newspapers, and their children.

1. Many refused to take seriously the specter of child-informants: in fact, they scoffed at the idea.

2. Some, however, related stories of: radio commentators urging children to inform on parents and teachers quizzing students about their parents' politics.

3. Regardless of the legitimacy of these fears, one thing was abundantly clear: McCarthy's campaign was tearing some families apart.

4. Some observers see a similar situation with today's children: except that today, children are criticizing their parents for ecological reasons.

5. One eight-year old wrote a formal letter to her mother. "Dear Mom, Stop running the water when you brush your teeth. Love, Leanne."

6. Kids by the thousands are buying an ecology handbook by The EarthWorks Group, *Fifty Things Kids Can Do to Save the Earth* (Kansas City, Andrews and McMeel, 1990).

7. Today's children express concern about pollution, depletion of the ozone layer, animal rights, and human health; they're a generation of eco-activists.

8. Many parents who came of age in the sixties see their children as: crusaders for a better world.

9. They like what they see, a generation committed to a better world.

10. One parent put it this way, "If my kids pester me about saving energy, then I know I've done a good job bringing them up."

EXERCISE 29-2   **Using the dash**

In the following sentences, insert dashes where appropriate for emphasis.

EXAMPLE   Recently a forgotten group of holocaust survivors hidden children
began to speak up.

Recently a forgotten group of holocaust survivors—hidden
children—began to speak up.

1. These children spent the World War II years in hiding, an experience that was
sometimes as frightening as being in the concentration camps.
2. One survivor describes her situation huddled in a basement with a dozen other
frightened children as one in which the fear of being caught plagued everyone
constantly.
3. These hidden children have often been told that they were lucky, they survived.
4. Explaining why she has finally begun to speak of her experience, Nicole David
says, "If we don't tell our story it will be forgotten, or falsified or denied."
5. Separation from parents, denial of heritage, fear of discovery, these were the daily
concerns of hidden children.

EXERCISE 29-3   Using parentheses

Add parentheses where appropriate in the following sentences, altering placement of punctuation as necessary.

EXAMPLE   The Food and Drug Administration FDA has begun to investigate misleading labels on prepared foods.

The Food and Drug Administration (FDA) has begun to investigate misleading labels on prepared foods.

1. As consumers become more health conscious they find themselves mystified by the various claims found on labels such as "low cholesterol," "all natural," and "fresh."

2. David Kessler the tough new commissioner of the FDA wants consumers to have the information they need to make informed choices.

3. Kessler is meeting resistance from many large food companies worried, of course, about what the new labeling requirements will cost them.

4. The laissez faire "hands off" attitude of the FDA in the eighties has definitely changed.

5. Kessler's proposed changes will help consumers by 1, requiring complete nutritional information on labels, 2, eliminating meaningless claims, and 3, requiring honesty in labeling.

EXERCISE 29-4   Using brackets, ellipses, and the slash

Follow the instructions for each item, using brackets, ellipses, and the slash as appropriate.

EXAMPLE   <u>Delete the second verb</u>: "Most people do not remember or appreciate Zachary Taylor's contributions to the American presidency."

"Most people do not remember . . . Zachary Taylor's contributions to the American presidency."

1. <u>Add the clarification "Old Rough and Ready" to indicate the nickname</u>: "Those who gave Taylor his nickname would be amazed at his obscurity."

2. <u>Rewrite the fraction in digits</u>: Taylor died after serving only a little more than one quarter of his term.

3. <u>Delete the final phrase</u>: "Historians had agreed that Taylor died from food poisoning, until novelist Clara Rising suggested that he may have been poisoned by political enemies."

4. <u>Acknowledge the misspelling</u>: "Tailor is now more famous than he had ever been in the past."

5. <u>Indicate a pause at the end of the first sentence</u>: Suppose we discover that Taylor really was poisoned. What do we do then?

EXERCISE 29-5   Review

Add colons, dashes, parentheses, brackets, ellipses, and slashes as needed in the following paragraph.

Red Adair The Forgotten John Wayne Hero

War heroes, renegades from the Old West, sturdy pioneers, these are the characters portrayed on the big screen by John Wayne. Not many ordinary citizens have been immortalized by the Duke. One relatively obscure person who can make such a claim is Red Adair his adventures were the subject of a 1969 movie called *The Hellfighters*. Adair was not a war hero or pioneer, and he wasn't a notorious renegade from the Old West. So why does he have the honor of having been played by The Duke? Its Adair's business that made him so appealing to Hollywood. *Hellfighters* refers to those men and women in Adair's prime, mostly men who fight fires in oil wells. Unlike ordinary fires, oil fires are fed constantly by the fuel in the wells. And they're powerful so powerful that only a select few companies can take on the task of extinguishing an oil-well fire. Adair is a combination cowboy daredevil technician whose successes in putting out fires in Texas and Oklahoma inspired the Wayne movie. One of the hellfighters who works for Adair describes his boss in these terms "Red is Red is Well, Red is like no other man I've ever met. He looks just like a regular guy. But he can take on a well that's pumping flames 5,000 pounds of pressure." Such testimony is one of the reasons why Adair's company was called in to douse the oil fires left in Kuwait after the Gulf War "We wanted the best, and *Adair is better than the best* italics mine," said one Kuwaiti official. Red Adair may not have been a war hero when John Wayne portrayed him, but if he's successful in Kuwait, he'll finally be one.

CHAPTER 30

Capitals and Italics

CAPITALS

30a Capitalize the first letter of the first word in every sentence.

Fly-fishing is a demanding sport. Few people ever truly master it.

1 Reproduce capitalization in a quoted passage.

Unless the quotation is being run into the structure of your sentence, capitalize the first word. (Use brackets to indicate a change in capitalization.)

Says one fly-fishing enthusiast, "It's not a sport for amateurs."

One fly-fishing enthusiast says that "[i]t's not a sport for amateurs."

2 Capitalize the first word in a parenthetical statement if the remark is a sentence.

Unless you have placed the parentheses within a sentence of your own, capitalize the first word in parentheses.

Lee Wulff was a legend in fly-fishing. (He made a living from the sport for over sixty years.)

Wulff, who loved risks (he once jumped into a raging river to prove that his waders would hold him up), died at age 86 while piloting his piper cub.

3 In a series of complete statements or questions, capitalize the first word of each item.

Capitalization in a series of incomplete questions and in a displayed series is optional. If the series is run in with the sentence, no capitalization is required.

What made Wulff so legendary—His (his) stamina? His (his) love of risk? His (his) skill?

Several things made Wulff so legendary:
1. his (His) stamina,
2. his (His) love of risk, and
3. his (His) skill.

Several things made Wulff so legendary: (1) his stamina, (2) his love of risk, and (3) his skill.

4 **Capitalizing the first word of a sentence following a colon is optional.**

Wulff took on many roles: He (he) was a fisherman, a pilot, and an environmentalist.

30b Capitalize words of significance in a title.

Capitalize all significant words in a title. Unless a conjunction, article, or preposition of fewer than five letters comes at the beginning of the sentence or follows a colon, do not capitalize these words.

American Fly Fishing: A History

"Fishing the Waters of the Northwest"

Do not capitalize the word *the* unless it is part of a title or proper name. With hyphenated words, capitalize both words unless the second is very short.

"the Anglers Club of New York" "The Life of Lee Wulff"

"Fly-Fishing for Amateurs" "Bottoms-up on the River"

30c Capitalize the first word in every line of poetry.

Because I could not stop for death—
He kindly stopped for me—
—Emily Dickinson

30d Capitalize proper nouns—people, places, objects; proper adjectives; and ranks of distinction.

1 **Capitalize names of people or groups of people.**

People's names (Brian, Sheila) are capitalized, as are titles showing family relationships if the title is part of the person's name (Aunt Eileen *but* my aunt). Also capitalized are names of political groups and formal organizations (Republicans, the New Left).

2 **Capitalize religions, religious titles and names, and nationalities.**

Unitarianism	Buddhist	the Koran
Allah	Kenyan	Filipino

3 **Capitalize places, regions designated by points on the compass, and languages.**

Atlanta	Center Street	the Southwest	Spanish

Designations that are not part of a title are not capitalized (the street, turn west).

4 **Capitalize adjectives formed from proper nouns, and titles of distinction that are part of proper names.**

Belgian chocolate	Governor Wilder (*but* the governor)
Brendan Kearney, M.D.	the President (*but* a president)

5 **Capitalize the names of days, months, holidays, and historical events or periods.**

Wednesday	December	Labor Day	Civil War

Decades and centuries are not capitalized (the fifties, the tenth century), nor are seasons unless being personified (winter, Winter's rages).

6 **Capitalize particular objects and name-brand products.**

World Trade Center	Great Wall of China	Mazda Miata

7 **Use capitals with certain abbreviations, prefixes, or compound nouns.**

Capitalize abbreviations only when the words abbreviated are themselves capitalized (Elm Street/Elm St.).

Capitalize acronyms (WHO—World Health Organization).

Capitalize the prefixes *ex*, *un*, and *post* only when they begin a sentence or are part of a proper name or title (a post-Civil War event, the Post-Civil War South).

Capitalize the first word in a compound number that is part of a name or title (the Twenty-fifth Olympiad).

ITALICS

30e Underline or italicize words if they need a specific emphasis.

If used rarely, italics (or underlining on a typewriter) can emphasize words or change meaning in sentences.

By November of 1990, President Bush had become convinced that the economic blockade of Iraq was clearly *not* going to do the job.

Do *you* believe that?   Do you *believe* that?   Do you believe *that?*

Overuse of italics can make your writing unconvincing.

OVERUSED   The Joint Chiefs of Staff didn't *want* to resort to armed response, but the President *insisted* that the sanctions couldn't go on *forever.*

REVISED   The Joint Chiefs of Staff were extremely reluctant to resort to armed response, but the President was adamant in his conviction that the sanctions would lose effectiveness over time.

30f Underline or italicize words, letters, and numbers to be defined or identified.

1 Use italics for words to be defined.

In fiction, *setting* refers to the time, place, and locale of the story.

It is also acceptable to use quotation marks for a word to be defined ("setting").

2 Use italics for expressions recognized as foreign.

Use italics only for words that have not been assimilated into English (*joie de vivre, hombre*). If a word has been assimilated, no italics are necessary (de facto, hors-d'oeuvres).

3 Use italics to designate words, numerals, or letters referred to as such.

The word *bad* means different things to different groups.

The rule is: *i* before *e* except after *c*.

There are four *s*'s in *Mississippi*.

30g Use underlining or italics for titles of book-length works separately published or broadcast, as well as for individually named transport craft.

1 Use italics for books, long poems, and plays.

The Great Gatsby   *The Iliad*   *Romeo and Juliet*

Do not use italics for titles of sacred documents (the Koran) and legal or public documents (the Declaration of Independence).

2 Use italics for newspapers, magazines, and periodicals.

With newspapers, do not capitalize, underline, or set in italics the word *the*, even if it is part of the newspaper's title (the *New York Times*). Do not italicize the name of a city or town if it is not part of the newspaper's title (Salem *Observer*). The full title of a magazine is set in italics (*American Heritage*).

3 Use italics for works of visual art, long musical works, movies, and broadcast shows.

the *Mona Lisa*   *The Barber of Seville*

Citizen Kane   *L.A. Law*

4 Use italics for individually named transport craft: ships, trains, aircraft, and spacecraft.

H.M.S. *Queen Elizabeth*   the *Orient Express*

the *Enola Gay*   the *Challenger*

EXERCISE 30-1   Using capitals

In the following sentences, add or delete capitals as necessary. Circle the number of any correct sentences.

EXAMPLE   On november 22, 1963, John F. Kennedy was assassinated.

On November 22, 1963, John F. Kennedy was assassinated.

1. Kennedy was the fourth president to be assassinated. (the other three were Lincoln, Garfield, and McKinley.)
2. When Kennedy announced plans to go to dallas, democrats were concerned about his reception in the south.
3. Governor Connally of Texas met the president's plane, and the Governor assured Kennedy that texans would welcome him.
4. The general population was indeed receptive, except for a man perched in a window of the texas school book depository.
5. A former marine with a russian wife was arrested, spawning rumors of a communist conspiracy.
6. Before Lee Harvey Oswald could be tried, Businessman Jack Ruby shot him.
7. Since then, questions about conspiracy have continued to haunt the country: did Oswald act alone? was he part of a conspiracy? if so, who was behind the assassination? was cuba involved? did the mafia have Kennedy killed?
8. From north to south, east to west, the rumors flew.
9. The warren commission report concluded that Oswald acted alone, but new orleans district attorney Jim Garrison investigated and found conspiracy.
10. Since the Sixties, various theories about the Kennedy Assassination have been suggested, but to this day nobody can be sure of what really happened that day at dealey plaza.

EXERCISE 30-2   Using Italics

In the following sentences, underline words that should be italicized, and circle words that should not. Circle the number of any correct sentences.

EXAMPLE   In the months following the assassination, the country became (*obsessed*) with it.

1. *Idlewild Airport* in New York was renamed *Kennedy Airport;* schools were named for the dead President; even *children* were named after him.

2. Marguerite Oswald, mother of the alleged assassin, was interviewed on The CBS Evening News.

3. Jim Bishop's book, The Day Kennedy was Shot, became a national best-seller.

4. Stories with titles like *"Did Oswald Act Alone?"* appeared in newspapers.

5. Even in foreign newspapers like Paris's *Le Monde,* articles appeared for months after the assassination.

6. When writing about Oswald, reporters had to remember the meaning of the word alleged.

7. The CBS program 60 Minutes conducted its own critique of the *Warren Commission Report.*

8. As late as 1978, the *U.S. Congress* commissioned an investigation of the assassination.

9. Five years after the assassination, the country was abuzz with talk about the President's widow *marrying* Greek tycoon Aristotle Onassis.

10. In 1991, Oliver Stone completed a film called JFK, based on the conspiracy theories.

EXERCISE 30-3   **Review**

Correct the use of capitals and italics in the paragraph below.

Anyone who has wondered at the power it takes to sing the leads in operas such as Otello or Madama Butterfly will appreciate the fragility of the operatic voice. An article in the may 6, 1991 issue of Time magazine, *"Why golden voices fade,"* explores the choices opera Stars have to make in order to preserve their voices. A singer simply *cannot* sing demanding parts and expect his or her voice to remain pure. In fact, what is true of Opera Singers is also true of others who use their voices professionally. Lecturers and actors must also worry about what Doctors refer to as voice abuse, or the *excessive* and *improper* use of the vocal chords. A Senator who spends a great deal of time addressing large groups will fight laryngitis far more often than someone who doesn't speak publicly. According to italian operatic legend Luciano Pavarotti, people who use their voices for a living—especially opera singers—must treat their Vocal Chords like precious jewels. One who does not care for his or her voice will have a short career.

CHAPTER 31

Abbreviations and Numbers

ABBREVIATIONS

31a Abbreviating titles of rank both before and after proper names

Abbreviations such as *Mr., Mrs., Ms.,* and *Dr.* come before proper names. For titles such as *General, Senator,* and *Honorable,* abbreviate only when using full names (Senator Rudman/Sen. Warren Rudman).

Titles that come after a name are separated by commas (Kevin Fitzgerald, M.D., Ph.D). Do not mix titles that precede names with titles that come after names.

Except when referring to academic titles, do not use abbreviations in sentences without attaching them to a name.

FAULTY	Laurel Markey is the M.D. across the hall.
REVISED	Laurel Markey is the physician across the hall.
ACCEPTABLE	Laurel Markey received her M.D. degree in 1980.

31b Abbreviating specific dates and numbers

When necessary, use abbreviations to indicate dates.

B.C.E. (before the common era)   C.E. (of the common era)

B.C. (before Christ)   A.D. (*Anno Domini,* "in the year of the Lord"—abbreviation precedes date)

Abbreviations for clock time can be upper or lower case (7:15 A.M., 7:30 p.m.)

Numbers are used with standard abbreviations (No. 40, 35 mph, 3 ft. 7 in.)

453

Abbreviations for time, numbers, units, or money should be used only with reference to specific dates or amounts.

FAULTY   The furniture is scheduled to arrive on Tuesday P.M.

REVISED   The furniture is scheduled to arrive on Tuesday afternoon.

REVISED   The furniture is scheduled to arrive on Tuesday at 3:00 P.M.

 31c Using acronyms, uppercase abbreviations, and corporate abbreviations

Acronyms (uppercase pronounceable abbreviations) should be spelled out first if there is an chance that readers may be unfamiliar with them.

We buy Christmas cards from the United Nations' Children's Fund (UNICEF).

Like acronyms, other uppercase abbreviations do not use periods (NAACP, FBI, ACLU).

Helping Readers to Understand Acronyms

Unless an acronym or uppercase abbreviation is common knowledge, courtesy obligates you to write out the full word, term, or organizational name at its first mention. Then you follow with the abbreviation in parentheses. In subsequent references to the person, word, or organization, use the abbreviation:

> The World Health Organization (WHO) studies infant mortality around the globe. The WHO lists the infant mortality rate in the United States as alarmingly high for a first-world nation.

In lengthy documents where you will be using many uppercase abbreviations and acronyms, consider creating a glossary in addition to defining abbreviations the first time you use them. Creating a glossary, which you would locate at the end of the paper as an appendix, will give readers one convenient place to make identifications, sparing them the trouble of flipping through pages and hunting for an abbreviation's first defined use.

Abbreviations used by companies and organizations vary according to the usage of the organization. When referring directly to a specific organization, use its own preferred abbreviations. In a sentence that does not refer directly to a specific corporation, do not abbreviate.

FAULTY   The corp. uses a P.O. box as its mailing address.

REVISED   The corporation uses a post office box as its mailing address.

REVISED   The Mitre Corp. uses P.O. Box 2117 as its mailing address.

31d Using abbreviations for parenthetical references

In main sentences, replace Latin abbreviations (such as *e.g., i.e., etc.*) with their English equivalents (such as *for example, that is, and so on*).

Bibliographical abbreviations (such as *p., ed., vol.*) should not be used in main sentences.

31e Revise to eliminate all but conventional abbreviations from sentences.

Except for common, standard abbreviations such as *mph* and *rpm*, abbreviations should not appear in main sentences.

FAULTY   The dr.'s office is on the third flr. of the Bixby Bldg.

REVISED   The doctor's office is on the third floor of the Bixby Building.

Writing in the Disciplines

Conventions differ in the disciplines about when and how much writers should use abbreviations—and about which abbreviations are common knowledge and therefore need not be defined. Across disciplines, abbreviations are avoided in titles. For specific abbreviations lying beyond common knowledge, writers in all disciplines follow the convention of defining the abbreviation on first use. As a demonstration, a sketch of conventions for abbreviating in some of the science disciplines is provided here.

- In scientific writing, courtesy dictates that writers define words that are later abbreviated.

  Before they determined that virtually all persons with early symptoms develop full-blown acquired immune deficiency syndrome (AIDS), researchers labeled a less serious form of the disease AIDS-related complex (ARC).

- Units of measure are generally abbreviated when they are paired with specific numbers. When not thus paired, the units are written out.

  In the next stage, 14 g were added.

  Several grams of the material were sent away for testing.

- Abbreviations of measurements in scientific writing need not be defined on first use.

- Symbol abbreviations are standardized, and you will find lists of accepted abbreviations in the *CBE Style Manual*. Generally, the use of abbreviations in titles is not accepted in science writing. Limited abbreviations—without definition—in tables are accepted.

NUMBERS

31f	**Write out numbers that begin sentences and numbers that can be expressed in one or two words.**

four	thirty-nine	five-sixths
two and one-eighth	four million	the forties (*or* the 40's)

Numbers that begin sentences should be written out.

Either write out the number beginning a sentence, or rearrange the sentence so that the number comes later.

FAULTY	20% of the country's wealth is held by 5% of its people.
REVISED	Twenty percent of the country's wealth is held by five percent of its people.
REVISED	In this country, 20% of the wealth is held by 5% of the people.

31g | Use figures in sentences according to convention.

Numbers longer than two words: 5,479,354

Units of measure: 45 mph, 75° F, 4 1/2 ft., 135 lbs.

Money: $35.00, $2.5 billion (Amounts that can be written in a few words can be spelled out: thirty-five dollars, two and a half billion dollars.)

Scores, Statistics, Ratios: a 7-1 loss, a 30% chance of rain, odds of 15-1

Addresses: 704 Howser Street, 24th Avenue

Phone numbers: 705-555-7996

Volume, page, and line references: Volume 2, pages 7-25, line 73

Military units: the 4077th MASH unit

Dates and times: January 5, 1973, 350 B.C., 1940-45, 6:00 p.m. (*but* six o'clock in the evening)

31h | Edit to eliminate numbers and figures mixed together in one sentence, unless these have different references.

FAULTY — Yesterday the temperature rose to one hundred two degrees, and 16 people had to be rushed to the hospital with heat exhaustion.

REVISED — Yesterday the temperature rose to 102°, and 16 people had to be rushed to the hospital with heat exhaustion.

ACCEPTABLE — On Thursday the temperature was 97°, and on Friday it rose to 102°; in the two-day period twenty-two people had to be rushed to the hospital with heat exhaustion. [Both numbers referring to temperature are presented as figures; the number referring to people is written out.]

EXERCISE 31-1 **Using abbreviations**

In the following sentences, correct the use of abbreviations. Circle the number of any correct sentences.

EXAMPLE   The DEA (United States Drug Enforcement Agency) considers the city of Cali to be the new center of drug activity in Colombia.

The United States Drug Enforcement Agency (DEA) considers the city of Cali to be the new center of drug activity in Colombia.

1. According to DEA officials, members of the Cali cartel have connections in NYC, L.A., and many other cities in N. America.
2. One DEA official calls the leader of the Cali cartel "my Prof. Moriarty," referring to the arch-enemy of Mister S. Holmes.
3. The United States Justice Dept. has been trying to extradite members of the cartel for years, according to Atty. Gen. Dick Thornburgh.
4. The FBI uncovered a New York Department of Motor Vehicles operation in which cartel members were issued drivers' licenses and car registrations.
5. The Cali cartel is run like a major corp., complete with CPAs and other managers.
6. One would have trouble picking out a cartel operative on the st., even though the car he is driving might contain hundreds of kgs. of cocaine.
7. In Apr. 1988, U.S. Customs inspectors seized a freighter in Fla., and found cocaine hidden in wooden planks; but less than ten percent of the planks had cocaine in them.
8. Care and ingenuity allow the cartel to bypass customs; e.g., they once transported cocaine in toxic chem. drums.
9. In addition to its U.S. operations, the cartel also ships cocaine to W. Europe and Japan.
10. The Cali cartel is worth billions of $; it will take millions to shut it down.

EXERCISE 31-2   Using numbers

In the following sentences, correct the use of numbers. Circle the number of any correct sentences.

EXAMPLE   40% of lawns in this country are subject to chemical treatment.

Forty percent of lawns in this country are subject to chemical treatment.

Of the lawns in this country, 40% are subject to chemical treatment.

1. People spend 100's of dollars on their lawns, sometimes more than they spend on their children's schooling.
2. In the nineteen sixties, people didn't seem to be so obsessed with lawns.
3. Now private lawns receive up to 5 times as much pesticide per acre as do farms.
4. On May seventeenth, nineteen eighty-nine, a young mother in New Jersey began to feel dizzy and to vomit within hours after her neighbors had sprayed their lawn.
5. Professional services aren't the only culprits; four times as many individuals buy their own pesticides than subscribe to lawn services.
6. American lawns take up twenty-five to 30 million acres; if all of that area is sprayed with pesticides, then a good deal of environmental damage is being done.
7. Over 6,000,000,000 dollars are spent every year on lawn care.
8. Some experts say that the chances of becoming ill from lawn care products are ten percent higher than those of becoming ill from toxic waste dumps.
9. Of all the pesticides used on lawns, the EPA has declared only 2 safe.
10. 29 of the 34 most popular chemicals are known to cause rashes.

EXERCISE 31-3   Review

Correct the use of abbreviations and numbers in the following paragraph.

Washington, District of Columbia is the home of many important organizations. Most federal govt. organizations—the Treasury, the Mint, the F.B.I., etc.—have their headquarters in Washington. But there are also a number of private organizations, among them 70 think tanks, i.e., organizations devoted to studying issues in depth. On May sixth, nineteen sixteen, the oldest and most prestigious of Washington's think tanks was born. The Brookings Institute was known throughout much of the century as a liberal organization, but in the early '70s it made a conscious effort to move toward a more central political position. Some people in the capital praise this move, while others, such as those at the EPI (Economic Policy Institute) feel that the liberal bent of Brookings balanced such conservative think tanks as The American Enterprise Institute and the Heritage Foundation. Brookings scholars spend their time thinking and writing books, most of which sell fewer than 5000 copies. But their impact these days comes from television exposure. All of the major broadcast news organizations look to Brookings scholars for commentary. Of the seventy think tanks in Washington, only about 15 are very well known or influential. Brookings is at the top of that list.

CHAPTER 32

Hyphens

32a | Using hyphens to make compound words

Compound words are created when two or more words are brought together to create a distinctive meaning and to function grammatically as a single word. Consult a dictionary to determine whether a compound word is spelled as one word (notebook), as separate words (note paper), or as a hyphenated word (note-taking).

1   Form compound adjectives with a hyphen to prevent misreading when they precede the noun being modified.

Only when the compound adjective precedes the noun is hyphenation necessary; when it comes after the noun, there is no chance for misreading.

high-powered executive	The executive is high powered.
sought-after performer	The performer is sought after.
animal-rights activist	The activist works for animal rights.

A compound modifier is not hyphenated when its first word ends with the distinctive suffix of a modifier.

highly charged meeting   clearly articulated argument

2   Form compound nouns and verbs with a hyphen to prevent misreading.

CONFUSING   We were victims of a break in the night before last.

REVISED   We were victims of a break-in the night before last.

3   Use hanging hyphens in a series of compound adjectives.

The pre- and post-game shows were longer than the game itself.

4   Follow conventions in hyphenating numbers, letters, and units.

Hyphenate fractions and the numbers twenty-one through ninety-nine.

Unless the numerator and/or denominator of a fraction is already hyphenated, place a hyphen between the two.

three-fifths   three twenty-fifths   twenty-five

Hyphenate figures and letters joined with words to form nouns or modifiers.

Unless a number is joined with a possessive noun, use a hyphen.

C-student   40-hour week   5 day's pay

Hyphenate units of measure.

kilowatt-hour   light-year

5   **Hyphenate compounds formed by prefixes or suffixes according to convention.**

Use a hyphen with the prefixes *ex, quasi,* and *self* and with the suffix *elect,* and with most uses of *vice.* (Consult a dictionary for specifics.)

ex-husband   quasi-liberal   self-confidence

President-elect   vice-consul

Use a hyphen with the prefixes *pro, anti,* and *pre* only when these are joined with proper nouns.

preheat   pre-Revolutionary War

prochoice   pro-Communist

antimatter   anti-Stalinist

Use a hyphen with a prefix or suffix that doubles a vowel or triples a consonant, except with some short prefixes that double words. (Consult a dictionary for current usage.)

reconvene   re-evaluate

childlike   shell-like

reentry   *or*   re-entry

6 Hyphenate to avoid misreading.

re-form (to form an object again)

reform (to update)

32b Using hyphens to divide a word at the end of a line

Although you should avoid dividing words at the end of a line, if you must do so, consult a dictionary and follow convention.

Divide compound words at the hyphen marking the compound.

CONFUSING   The two families met every year at the annual sheep-shear-
            ing festival.

REVISED   The two families met every year at the annual sheep-
            shearing festival.

Divide words at a prefix or suffix.

ex-traordinary   inter-active   accept-able

For prefixes and suffixes that require a hyphen (anti-American, governor-elect), always divide at the hyphen and nowhere else.

Eliminate hyphenations that hang a single letter at the beginning or end of a line.

CONFUSING   At the festival, judges spend a good deal of time e-
            valuating the techniques of herding sheep.

REVISED   At the festival, judges spend a good deal of time eval-
            uating the techniques of herding sheep.

Eliminate misleading hyphenations.

If the first syllable of a word is itself a word (human-itarian, long-itude), divide the word so as to avoid confusion.

CONFUSING   The festival is held at the old center of town, near the cross-
            roads.

REVISED   The festival is held at the old center of town, near the
            crossroads.

Single-syllable words are never hyphenated.

Do not divide any single-syllable words (such as *creased, thought, swathed*).

Abbreviations, contractions, or multiple-digit numbers are not hyphenated.

Since abbreviations and contractions are already shortened forms, hyphenating them only causes confusion. Similarly, multiple-digit numbers are only meaningful if they are read at once.

EXERCISE 32-1   Using hyphens to make compound words

In the following sentences use hyphens where necessary to form compound adjectives; to mark prefixes or suffixes; to note fractions, numbers less than one hundred, or words formed with figures; and to prevent misreading. Circle the number of any correct sentences.

EXAMPLE   In the early sixties we witnessed the color television revolution.

In the early sixties we witnessed the color-television revolution.

1. In the post color TV era, the videocassette recorder took the country by storm.
2. By the early eighties, the computer literate population had mushroomed.
3. Young people also used video games such as Nintendo for recreation.
4. A computer generated survey in 1985 indicated that fully one half of the pre teen population knew how to use video games.
5. The video game craze has ebbed a bit, but older people have found their own new toy in the compact disc player.
6. Twenty years ago nobody could have imagined that we could hear concert hall quality sound on our stereos.
7. The technology that produced color TV, VCRs, computers, and CD players has come up with "interactive multimedia," a TV CD computer combination.
8. With interactive multimedia, consumers can tune in to more than just a television show; they can become self taught experts in many fields.
9. Viewers will be able to consult travel guide programs, get involved in role playing games, and examine pre and post game statistics in sports.
10. Best of all, the ex couch potato will, with the help of interactive multimedia, find him or herself an active participant in the electronics revolution.

EXERCISE 32-2   Using hyphens to divide words

Rewrite the following words, indicating with a hyphen where the words could be divided at the end of a line. For words that can be divided in more than one place, choose the most appropriate place. Write out in full words that should not be divided.

EXAMPLE   interdenominational   _inter-denominational_

1. vice-chancellor   _____

2. intrastate   _____

3. fraught   _____

4. Postimpressionism   _____

5. haven't   _____

6. runner-up   _____

7. even   _____

8. commencement   _____

9. reiterate   _____

10. onstage   _____

CHAPTER ESL-45

Using English Nouns, Pronouns, and Articles

ESL

45a Using the different classes of English nouns

English nouns name things or people that are considered either countable or not countable in English. English also distinguishes whether a noun names a person or thing that is specific, or something that is generic.

1 Identifying and using count nouns

In English, **count nouns** name things or people that are considered countable. They identify one of many possible individuals or things in the category named. Count nouns have three important characteristics.

- Singular count nouns can be preceded by *one*, or by *a/an*—the indefinite articles that convey the meaning "one (of many)."

  one car   a rowboat   a truck   an ambulance

  Singular count nouns can also be preceded by demonstrative pronouns (*this*, *that*), by possessive pronouns (*my, your, their*), and often by the definite article (*the*).

- Plural count nouns can be preceded by expressions of quantity (*two, three, some, many, a few*) and can use a plural form.

  two cars   some rowboats   many trucks   a few ambulances

- A count noun used as a singular or plural subject must be made to agree with a singular or plural verb form.

  This *car stops* quickly. [A singular subject and verb agree.]
  Other *cars stop* slowly. [A plural subject and verb agree.]

  (See 10a for guidelines on subject-verb agreement.)

2 Forming plurals with count nouns

Plural count nouns are either regular or irregular. Regular nouns form the plural with -s or -es. Irregular plural forms—such as *man/men, tooth/teeth, wolf/wolves, medium/media*—follow the models shown in 23e. (See rules for plural forms in 10a and in the spelling sections in 23e-1, 3, and 5.)

3 Identifying and using noncount (mass) nouns

In English; **noncount (mass) nouns** name things that are being considered as a whole, undivided group or category that is not being counted. Noncount (mass) nouns name various kinds of individuals or things that are considered as group categories in English, such as:

> **abstractions:** courage, grammar
>
> **fields of activity:** chemistry, tennis
>
> **natural phenomena:** weather, dew, rain
>
> **whole groups of objects:** rice, sand, oxygen, wood, oil

Objects considered too numerous or shapeless to count are often treated as noncount nouns, as with the word *rock* in this sentence.

> We mined dense *rock* in this mountain.

As such objects become individually identifiable, the same word may be used as count noun.

> Four <u>rocks</u> fell across the road.

Some nouns name things that can be considered either countable or noncountable in English, depending on whether they name something specific or something generic.

Countable (and specific)	A *chicken* or two ran off. A *straw* or two flew up.
Noncountable (and generic)	*Chicken* needs a lot of cooking. *Straw* can be very dry.

Nouns that name generalized or generic things often occur in noncountable form, but may also occur in singular form in scientific usage (see ESL-45a-5).

Three characteristics distinguish noncount (mass) nouns:

- Noncount nouns never use the indefinite article *a/an* (or *one*). (Articles are discussed in detail in ESL-45b.)

- Noncount nouns are never used in a plural form.

- Noncount nouns always take singular verbs. (See 10a for guidelines on subject-verb agreement.)

 4 Using expressions of quantity with count and noncount nouns

Expressions of quantity—such as *many, few, much, little, some, plenty*—are typically used to modify nouns. Some expressions are used to quantify count nouns; some are used with noncount nouns; and others are used with both kinds of nouns.

Count Nouns	Noncount Nouns	Both Count and Noncount Nouns
many potatoes	*much* rice	*lots of* potatoes and rice
few potatoes	*little* rice	*plenty of* potatoes and rice
		some, any potatoes and rice

When the context is very clear, these expressions can also be used alone as pronouns.

Do you have *any* potatoes or rice?
I have *plenty* if you need *some*.

5 Using nouns in specific and generic senses

English nouns show differences in usage between nouns that name specific things or people and nouns that name generalized or generic things.

A DEFINITE NOUN	The whale migrated thousands of miles. The whales migrated thousands of miles. [When a noun names something very specific, either singular or plural, it is preceded by the **definite article** (or by demonstrative pronouns *this/that*).]
AN INDEFINITE NOUN	A whale surfaced nearby; then several whales surfaced. [When a noun names something indefinite but countable, the **indefinite article** is used.]

GENERIC USAGE	Whales are migratory animals. A whale is a migratory animal. [When the reference is to a general group, nouns often use either the **plural with no article** or the **singular with an indefinite article.**]
SCIENTIFIC USAGE	The whale is a migratory animal. The whales are migratory animals. [A generic noun may also be singular or plural with a definite article (see ESL-45b-3).]

6   Distinguishing pronouns in specific and indefinite or generic uses

Most pronouns, including personal pronouns, rename and refer to a noun located elsewhere that names a specific individual or thing. However, indefinite pronouns, such as *some, any, one, someone,* or *anyone,* may refer to a noun in an indefinite or generic sense.

PERSONAL PRONOUN	Where are my pencils? I need *them*. [Meaning: I need specific pencils that are mine.]
INDEFINITE PRONOUN	Where are my pencils? I need *some*. [Meaning: I need generic, indefinite pencils; I will use any I can find.]

(The list in 7a-7 gives terms that describe various classes of pronouns.)

ESL

45b   Using articles with nouns

Articles are the most important class of words used in English to show whether nouns are being used as count or noncount nouns, or as specific or generic nouns. There are three articles in English: *a, an,* and *the. Some,* the indefinite pronoun, is occasionally used as if it were an indefinite article.

1   Nouns sometimes take the indefinite articles *a* and *an.*

The indefinite articles *a* and *an* are grammatically the same: they are singular indefinite articles that mean "one (of many)," and they are used only with singular count nouns. Pronunciation determines which to use: *A* precedes a noun beginning with a consonant or a consonant sound (a bottle, a hotel, a youth, a user, a xylophone). *An* precedes a noun beginning with a vowel or vowel sound (an egg, an hour, an undertaker).

A is sometimes used with the quantifiers *little* and *few*. Note the difference in meaning in the following examples.

Example	Meaning
a little, a few a few onions a little oil	a small amount of something
little, few few onions little oil	a less-than-expected amount of something

A and *an* are rarely used with proper nouns, which usually identify a unique individual rather than one of many. The indefinite article occasionally appears with a proper noun in a hypothetical statement about one of many possible persons or things in the category named, as in this sentence.

Dr. King dreamed of *an America* where children of all colors would grow up in harmony. [We may dream of more than one possible "America."]

 2 **Nouns sometimes take the definite article *the*.**

Use *the* with specific singular and plural count nouns and with noncount nouns.

SPECIFIC NOUNS

I need *the tool* and *the rivets*. [one singular and one plural noun]

I need *the equipment*. [a noncount noun]

I need *the tool* on *the top shelf*. [Note the modifiers, clauses, and phrases that make the nouns specific.]

I need *the tools* that are painted orange.

I need *the smallest tool* on *that shelf*.

GENERIC NOUNS

I need tools for that work. [In this case, no article is used.]
(For varieties of usage with generic nouns, see ESL-45a-5.)

Use *the* in a context where a noun has previously been mentioned, or where the writer and the reader both know the particular thing or person being referred to.

I saw a giraffe at the zoo. *The giraffe* was eating leaves from a tree.

I stopped at an intersection. When *the light* turned green, I started to leave. [The sentence assumes the existence of a particular traffic light at the intersection.]

Other uses of the definite article

- Use *the* with items that are to be designated as one of a kind (*the* sun, *the* moon, *the* first, *the* second, *the* last).

- Use *the* with official names of countries when it is needed to give specific meaning to nouns like *union, kingdom, state(s), republic, duchy,* etc. (*the* United States, *the* Republic of Cyprus, *the* Hashemite Kingdom of Jordan). No article is needed with certain other countries (Cyprus, Jordan, Japan, El Salvador).

- Use *the* when a noun identifies institutions or generic activities *other than sports,* and in certain usages for generic groups (see ESL-45a-5).

  We called *the* newspapers, *the* radio, and *the* news services.

  Sergei plays *the* piano, *the* flute, and *the* guitar.

  The whales are migratory animals. *The* birds have feathers.

  Without an article   Nadia plays basketball, hockey, and volleyball.

- Use *the* with names of oceans, seas, rivers, and deserts.

  the Pacific, *the* Amazon, *the* Himalayas, *the* Sahara

  Without an article   Lake Michigan, Mt. Fuji

- Use *the* to give specific meaning to expressions using the noun *language,* but not for the proper name of a language by itself.

  He studied the Sanskrit language, not the Urdu language.

  Without an article   He studied Sanskrit, not Urdu.

- Use *the* with names of colleges and universities containing *of.*

  He studied at *the* University *of* Michigan.

  Without an article (typically)   He studied at Michigan State University.

3   **Nouns sometimes take no article.**

Typically no article is needed with names of unique individuals, as they do not need to be made specific and they are not usually counted as one among many. In addition, nouns naming generalized persons or things in a generic usage commonly use no article: *Managers often work long hours. Whales are migratory animals.* (See ESL-45a-5.)

Some situations in which no article is used are shown in ESL-45b-2. Here are some others.

- Use no article with proper names of continents, states, cities, streets, and with religious place names.

    Europe   Alaska   New York   Main Street   heaven   hell

- Use no article with titles of officials when accompanied by personal names; the title effectively becomes part of the proper noun.

    President Truman   King Juan Carlos   Emperor Napoleon

- Use no article with fields of study.

    Ali studied literature.   Juan studied engineering.

- Use no article with names of diseases.

    He has cancer.   AIDS is a very serious disease.

- Use no article with names of magazines and periodicals, unless the article is part of the formal title.

    Life   Popular Science   Sports Illustrated

    BUT: *The New Yorker* [The article is part of the proper name.]

ESL
45c   Using nouns with prepositions

Some of the complex forms of prepositions in English are determined by their use with nouns. Nouns that follow prepositions are called **objects of prepositions** (see 7a-8 and 8b-1); this grouping forms a modifying **prepositional phrase** (7d-1).

The distinctive function of such modifying phrases often determines which preposition to choose in an English sentence.

1   Using the preposition *of* to show possession.

The preposition *of* is often used to show possession as an alternative to the possessive case form (*I hear a man's voice. I hear the voice of a man*). It is also widely used to show possession for many nouns that do not usually take a possessive form. For example, many inanimate nouns, as well as some nouns naming a large group of people (*crowd, mob, company*) or a location (*place, center*) are not typically used with a possessive case form, and are likely to show possession with the preposition *of*.

FAULTY   I washed the *car's hood*.

CORRECT   I washed the *hood of her car*.

FAULTY   *The Information Center's* location is unknown.

CORRECT   The location *of the Information Center* is unknown.

The preposition *of* is not used with proper nouns.

FAULTY   I washed the *car of Luisa*.

CORRECT   I washed *Luisa's car*.

2   Using prepositions in phrases with nouns or pronouns

The distinctive function of a modifying prepositional phrase often determines which preposition to choose in an English sentence. Here are a few typical functions for prepositional phrases, with distinctive prepositions in use.

Function	Preposition	Example/Explanation
Passive voice (9g)	*by* the cook	He was insulted *by* the cook.
	with a snowball	I was hit *with* a snowball.
Time expressions	*on* January 1	use for specific dates
	on Sundays	use for specific days
	in January	use for months
	in 1984	use for years
	in spring	use for seasons
	at noon, *at* 5 p.m.	use for specific times
	by noon, *by* 5 p.m.	use to indicate *before* a specific hour
	by April 15	use to indicate *before* a specific date

Locations	*at* 301 South Street	use for an address
	in the house	
	on the floor	

Directions	*onto* to floor	
	beside the library	
	through the window	
	into the air	

For information on verbs with prepositions see ESL-46f; for information on adjectives with prepositions see ESL-47b.

EXERCISE ESL-45-1   Identifying count and noncount (mass) nouns

In the blank at the left, identify each of the following nouns as a count or a noncount noun.

EXAMPLE   beauty   _____ *noncount* _____

1. highway   _____
2. telephone   _____
3. dark   _____
4. peace   _____
5. piece   _____
6. hockey   _____
7. sport   _____
8. water   _____
9. snow   _____
10. snowflake   _____

EXERCISE ESL-45-2   Using articles with nouns

For each of the following sentences, fill in the blanks with the appropriate article. If the noun does not call for an article, leave the space blank.

EXAMPLE   Tomorrow is ___*a*___ holiday in ___*the*___ United States.

1. It is _____ Fourth of July, otherwise known as _____ Independence Day.

2. Most people do not have to go to _____ work on this day.

3. I have _____ job at _____ Mercy Hospital, however, and must work.

4. My sister is going to _____ picnic; she loves _____ picnics.

5. When I leave _____ hospital, I hope to see _____ fireworks over _____

    Lake Champlain at _____ University of Vermont.

Name _____ *Section* _____ *Date* _____

EXERCISE ESL-45-3   Using prepositions for time, location, and direction

For each of the following sentences, insert the appropriate preposition.

EXAMPLE   I visited my sister _in_ Pittsburgh _on_ Saturday.

1. I will be _____ your house _____ five o'clock, if I am done working
   _____ that time.
2. The work will be ready _____ a week and will be delivered _____ your
   front door.
3. If you drive _____ my house _____ Saturday, I will be there.
4. She will take grandpa _____ the movies if she can get _____ the theater.
5. _____ the springtime we can no longer cross _____ the ice to the other side
   of the lake.

Using English Verbs

ESL

46a Distinguishing different types of verbs and verb constructions

A verb, the main word in the predicate of an English sentence, asserts the action undertaken by the subject or else the condition in which the subject exists. The four types of verbs include transitive verbs (which take direct objects), intransitive verbs (which do not take direct objects), linking verbs, and helping or auxiliary verbs, (which show tense or mood). Although only transitive verbs can show passive voice, all three types of verbs can show various verb tenses and mood. (See chapter 9 for a discussion of verb usage.)

 1 Transitive and intransitive verbs work differently.

A **transitive verb** can take an object. Examples of transitive verbs include *throw* and *take*.

He throws a pass.	They took the ball.
↑ ↑ ↑	↑ ↑ ↑
[subject] [verb] [object]	[subject] [verb] [object]

Because transitive verbs can take an object, most of them can operate in both the active and passive voices.* The active and the passive forms of the verb may be similar in meaning, but the emphasis changes with the rearrangement of the subject and object, as well as with changes in the verb form (to the past participle with *be*).

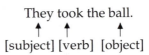

active voice	passive voice
Workers in Ohio make Hondas.	Hondas are made (by workers) in Ohio
↑ ↑ ↑	↑ ↑ ↑
[subject] [verb] [object]	[subject] [verb] [modifiers]

Notice how the active-voice object *Hondas* in the first sentence becomes the passive-voice subject in the second. In a passive-voice sentence the original

---

Exceptions: Transitive verbs *have, get, want, like,* and *hate* are seldom used in passive voice.

performer of the action (*workers* in the example) is not emphasized and may even be omitted. (See 9g on the uses of passive constructions.)

By contrast, an **intransitive verb** never takes an object and can never be used in the passive voice. Examples of intransitive verbs include *smile* and *go.*

The politician smiled.   He went into the crowd.
   ↑   ↑   ↑   ↑
[subject] [verb]   [subject] [verb]

2 | Linking verbs are used in distinctive patterns.

Linking verbs, the most common example of which is *be,* serve in sentences as "equals signs" to link a subject with an equivalent noun or adjective. Some other linking verbs are *appear, become,* and *seem.* (See 11d for a full list and description of linking verbs; see also 7b, Pattern 5.)

Things *seem* unsettled. Shall I *become* a doctor?

Expletives

Linking verbs also serve in a distinctive English construction that uses changed word order with an **expletive** word, *there* or *it.* Expletives are used only with linking verbs, as in these sentences.

It *is* important to leave now. It *appears* unnecessary to do that.
There *seems* to be a problem. It *seems* important.

There or *it* form "dummy subjects" or filler words that occupy the position of the subject in a normal sentence; the true subject is elsewhere in the sentence, and the verb agrees with the true subject (see 10a-8).

Expletive in Subject Position	True Subject
There is a cat in that tree.	*A cat* is in that tree.
There are some cats in the tree.	*Some cats* are in the tree.
It is convenient to use the train.	*To use the train* is convenient.

The expletive *it* also has a unique role in expressing length of time with *take* followed by an infinitive.

It takes an hour to get home by car. *It took* us forever.

Expletive constructions are important and useful for length-of-time expressions and for short or emphatic statements.

It is a tale of great sorrow. There were no survivors.

However, in complex and formal English sentences, the "dummy subject" expletive becomes an unnecessary word obscuring the true subject. The expletive also encourages using linking verbs instead of more direct, active verbs—transitive or intransitive verbs. To eliminate wordiness and promote the clear, direct style that is preferred in English academic prose, try to avoid expletives; revise sentences to restore normal word order (see 17a-3).

ESL

46b Changing verb forms

Verb forms express *tense,* an indication of when an action or state of being occurs. The three basic tenses in English are the past, the present, and the future. (See 9a for a discussion of the forms of English verbs, and 9e-1, 2 for a basic discussion of tenses.)

1 Not all verbs use progressive tense forms.

Each of the three basic tenses has a progressive form, made up of *be* and the present participle (the *-ing* form of the verb). The progressive tense emphasizes the *process* of doing whatever action the verb asserts. The tense is indicated by a form of *be:* present progressive (I *am going*), past progressive (I *was going*), past perfect progressive (I *had been going*), future progressive (I *will be going*). For examples, see 9e and 9f.

Certain verbs are generally *not* used in the progressive form; others have a progressive use only for process-oriented or ongoing meanings of the verb.

Words that are rarely seen in a progressive form

Think (in the sense of "believe"): "I think not."

EXCEPTION: The progressive form can be used for a process of considering something.

FAULTY	I *am thinking* it is wrong.
CORRECT	I *am thinking* about changing jobs. [considering]

Believe, understanding, recognize, realize, remember: "You believe it."

EXCEPTION: The last four can sometimes use the progressive form if a process of recognition or recollection is meant: "He is slowly realizing the truth." "He is gradually remembering what happened."

Belong, possess, own, want, need: "We want some." "We once owned it."
Have: "You have what you need."

EXCEPTION: The progressive form can be used in the sense of "experiencing."

FAULTY	Maria *is having* a car.
CORRECT	Mary *is having* a baby. [experiencing childbirth]
	Maria *is having* success in her project.

Be, exist, seem: "This seems acceptable."

EXCEPTION: The progressive form is used only with an abstract emphasis on a process of "being" or "seeming": "Just existing from day to day is enough."

Smell, sound, and **taste** as intransitive verbs, as in "It smells good"; "it sounds funny"; "it tastes bad."
Appear in the sense of "seem": "It appeared to be the right time."

EXCEPTION: Sometimes the progressive form is used in the sense of presenting itself/oneself over a time period. "She's appearing nightly as the star actress."

See: "I can never see why you do it."

EXCEPTION: The progressive form is used in the sense of interviewing someone or witnessing or experiencing something.

FAULTY	I *am seeing* an airplane now.
REVISED	I *am seeing* a new patient. [interviewing]

Surprise, hate, love, like: "It surprises me"; I absolutely hate it."

2 | Using the perfect forms

The perfect tense is made up of *have* and the past participle (the *-ed* form of the verb). The form of *have* indicates the tense: present perfect (*has* worked), past perfect (*had* worked), and future perfect (*will have* worked). (See 9e and 9f, also 9b.)

Sometimes students confuse the use of the simple past with the use of the present perfect. The present perfect is used when an action or state of being that began in the past continues to the present; it is also used to express an action or state of being that happened at an indefinite time in the past.

PRESENT PERFECT	Linda has worked in Mexico since 1987.
PRESENT PERFECT	Ann has worked in Mexico. [The time is unspecified.]

By contrast, the simple past is used when an action or state of being began *and ended* in the past.

SIMPLE PAST	Linda worked in Mexico last year. [She no longer works there.]

Using *since* with perfect tenses in prepositional phrases of time

A phrase with *since* requires using the present perfect (*has worked*) or past perfect tenses (*had worked*); it indicates action beginning at *a single point in time* and still continuing at the time shown by the verb tense.

> She [has/had worked] *since* noon
> > > *since* July
> > > *since* 1991
> > > *since* the end of the school year
> > > *since* the last storm
> > > *since* the baby was born

A time phrase with *since* cannot have a noun object that shows plural time; *since* phrases must indicate a single point in time.

FAULTY	He lived here since three months.
	I am here since May.
REVISED	He has lived here *for* three months.
	I have been here since May.

Also, a time phrase with *since* cannot modify a simple past tense or any present tense.

FAULTY	He lived here since three months.
	I am here since May.
REVISED	He *had lived* here since February.
	I *have been* here since May.

The perfect tenses can have a time modifier with a prepositional phrase formed either with *since* or *for*.

He has worked since noon.
He had worked for a month.

A modifying phrase with *for* indicates action *through a duration of time.*

> He [has/had worked] *for* three hours
> > > *for* a month and a half
> > > *for* two years
> > > *for* a few weeks

When a phrase uses a plural noun, thus showing duration of time, this signals that the preposition in the modifier must be *for,* not *since.*

FAULTY   I had worked on it since many years.
REVISED   I had worked on it for many years.

 Using the varied forms of English future tenses

The following list shows different ways of expressing the future.

Verb Form	Explanation
She *will call* us soon. She *is going to* call us soon.	These examples have the same meaning.
The movie *arrives* in town tomorrow. The next bus *leaves* in five minutes. The bus *is leaving* very soon.	The simple present and the present progressive are used to express definite future plans, as from a schedule.
Your flight *is taking off* at 6:55. The doctor *is operating* at once. I *am calling* them right now.	The present progressive is sometimes used to make strong statements about the future.
Hurry! The movie *is about to* begin. Finish up! The bell *is about to* ring.	The "near" future is expressed by some form of *be* plus *about to* and a verb.
It's cold. *I'm going to* get a sweater.	This suggests a plan.
It's cold. *I'll lend* you a sweater.	This suggests a willingness.

Verbs expressing thoughts about future actions, such as *intend* and *hope,* are not used in any future tense, and the verb *plan* uses a future tense only in the idiomatic *plan on* (to make or follow a plan).

FAULTY   I will intend to meet my friends tomorrow.
REVISED   I intend to meet my friends tomorrow.
                 I plan to attend college.

See ESL-46b-5 for guidelines on expressing future time in conditional sentences.

 Using verb tenses in sentences with a sequence of actions

In complex sentences that have more than one verb it is important to adjust the sequence of verb tenses to avoid confusion. See the discussion on verb tense combinations in 9f.

Verb tenses with reported speech

Reported speech, or indirect discourse, is very different from directly quoted speech, which gives the exact verb tense of the original.

Direct Speech   Ellie said, "He is taking a picture of my boat."

Indirectly quoted speech may occasionally be reported immediately.

Reported Speech   Ellie just said [that] he is taking a picture of her boat.

Some kinds of reported speech can be summarized with verbs like *tell, ask, remind,* or *urge* followed by an infinitive:

Reported Speech   Ellie asked him to take a picture of her boat.

Most often, however, reported speech has occurred some time before the time of the main verb reporting it. In English, the indirect quotation then requires changes in verb tense and pronouns.

Reported Speech   She said [that] he had taken a picture of her boat.

In this situation, the reported speech itself takes the form of a *that* noun clause (although the word *that* is often omitted); its verb tense shifts to past tense, following the guidelines shown in 9f-1 for tense sequences.

The following table shows the patterns for changing verb tenses, verb forms, and modal auxiliaries in reported speech or indirect discourse.

Direct Speech		*Reported Speech*
Tenses:		
present	———→	**past**
Ellie said, "I like horses."		Ellie said [that] she liked horses.
past	———→	**past perfect**
Ellie said, "I rode the horse."		Ellie said [that] she had ridden the horse.
present progressive	———→	**past progressive**
Ellie said, "I'm going riding."		Ellie said [that] she was going riding.
present perfect	———→	**past perfect**
Ellie said, "I have ridden there."		Ellie said [that] she had ridden there.

past progressive	———→	past perfect progressive
She said, "I was out riding."		She said [that] she had been out riding.
*past perfect	———→	past perfect
She said, "I had ridden there."		She said [that] she had ridden there.

Auxiliary verbs:

can	———→	could
She said, "I can show him."		She said [that] she could show him.
will	———→	would
She said, "I will ride again."		She said [that] she would ride again.
*could	———→	could
She said, "I could ride."		She said [that] she could ride.
*would	———→	would
She said, "I would go."		She said [that] she would go.

Note: The asterisked verbs do not change form as they undergo tense shifts.

Conventions for maintaining consistency with direct and indirect discourse in English are discussed in 16d; punctuation is discussed in 28a-1.

5 Using verb tenses in conditional and subjunctive sentences

Conditional sentences talk about situations that are either possible in the future or else unreal or hypothetical (contrary to fact) in the present or past. Conditional sentences typically contain the conjunction *if* or a related conditional term (*unless, provided that, only if, (only) after, (only) when,* etc. The following are guidelines for using verb forms in conditional sentences.

Possible or real statements about the future

Use the present tense to express the condition in possible statements about the future; in the same sentence, use the future to express the result of that condition.

	conditional + present	—	**future (*will* + base form)**
REAL STATEMENT	*If I have* enough money,		*I will go* next week.
	When I get enough money,		*I will go.* [**Meaning:** The speaker may have enough money.]

Hypothetical or unreal statements about the future

Use the past subjunctive form (which looks like a past tense) with sentences that make "unreal" or hypothetical statements about the future; in the same sentence, use the past form of a modal auxiliary (usually *would, could,* or *might*) to express an unreal result of that stated condition.

	If + past —	past form of modal (*would*)
UNREAL STATEMENT	*If you found* the money,	*you would go* next week. [**Meaning:** The speaker now is fairly sure you will not have the money.]

Hypothetical or unreal statements about the past

Use the subjunctive with appropriate perfect tense verb forms with sentences that make hypothetical or unreal statements about the past. Use the past perfect tense for the unreal statement about the past. In the same sentence, use the past form of the modal auxiliary plus the present perfect to express the unreal result.

	If + past perfect —	past modal + present perfect
	(had made)	*(would)* *(have gone)*
UNREAL STATEMENT	*If I had made* money,	*I would have gone* last week. [**Meaning:** At that time the speaker didn't have the money.]

For more on the subjunctive, see 9h-1; for more on modal auxiliaries, see ESL-46d.

---

6 Expressing a wish or suggestion for a hypothetical event

In stating a wish in the present that might hypothetically occur, use the **past subjunctive** (which looks like the past tense) in the clause expressing the wish. (The object of the wish takes the form of a *that-* clause, although the word *that* is often omitted.)

present	[*that*]	past subjunctive (like past tense)
He *wishes*	[that]	she *had* a holiday.
I *wish*	[that]	I *were* on vacation.

The auxiliaries *would* or *could* (which have the same form in the present and past tenses) are often used to express the object of a wish.

present	[that]	*would/could* + **base form**
I *wish*	[that]	she *would stay*.
We *wish*	[that]	we *could take* a vacation day.

In stating a wish made in the past or present for something that hypothetically might have occurred in the past, use the past perfect in the *that* clause. (The verb *wish* may be expressed either in the past or in the present tense.)

present OR past	**[that]**	**past perfect [*had worked*]**
I wished	[that]	I *had* not *worked* yesterday.
I wish	[that]	it *had been* a holiday.

See 9h-4 for usage guidelines on using the subjunctive mood with *that* clauses.

Expressing a recommendation, suggestion, or urgent request

In stating a suggestion, recommendation, or urgent request, use the **present subjunctive**—the base form of the verb (*be, do*)—in the *that* clause (see 9h).

present	[that]	**present subjunctive = base form**
We *suggest*	[that]	he *find* the money
We *advise*	[that]	you *be* there on time.

(See 9h-5 for comments on the subjunctive in this form.)

ESL

46c | Changing word order with verbs

1 | Invert the subject and all or part of the verb to form questions.

The subject and verb are inverted from normal order to form questions. The following patterns are used with the verb *be,* with modal auxiliaries, with progressive forms, and with perfect forms.

	Normal Statement Form	Question Form
Be	He *is* sick today.	*Is he* sick today?
Modals	She *can* help us.	*Can she* help us?
Progressive	They *are* studying here.	*Are they* studying here?
Perfect	It *has made* this sound before.	*Has it* made this sound before?

Questions (and negatives) with the auxiliary *do/does*

Verbs other than those shown above use the auxiliary verbs *do/does* to form questions, and also to form negatives with *not*. In this form, when the auxiliary verbs *do/does* are added, the verb changes to the base form (the dictionary form). Use this pattern for the simple present and simple past.

Statement Form—Question Form/Negative Form: Do + Base Form

He *gets on* this bus.

Question	*Does he get on* this bus?
Negative	He *does not get on* this bus.
AVOID	Does he *gets on* this bus?
	[Needs a base form.]

She *finishes* at noon.

Question	*Does* she *finish* at noon?
Negative	She *does not finish*.
AVOID	Does she *finishes* at noon?
	[Needs a base form.]

It *ran* better yesterday.

Question	*Did* it *run* better yesterday?
Negative	It *did not run* better.
AVOID	Did it *ran* better yesterday?
	[Needs a base form.]

They *arrived* at noon.

Question	When *did* they *arrive?*
Negative	They *did not arrive*.
AVOID	When do they *arrived?*
	[Needs a base form.]

For more on auxiliary verbs, see the listings in 9c and in ESL-46d.

---

2 **Invert the subject and verb in some emphatic statements.**

The question form is also used with auxiliaries or expletives in some emphatic statements that begin with adverbs such as *never, rarely,* and *hardly,* producing a negative meaning.

Normal	**Emphatic**
There is never an easy answer.	Never *is there* an easy answer to that.
They have rarely come to check.	Rarely *have they* come to check the work.

ESL

 46d Using the helping verbs: Auxiliaries and modal auxiliaries

 Auxiliary verbs, or helping verbs, are part of basic grammar.

The basic auxiliary verbs (*be, will, have, do*) are used to show tense, to form questions, to show emphasis, and to show negation.

To show tense, or aspect (*be, will, have*): He is driving. She has driven.
To form questions (*do/does*): Do they drive? Why do you drive?
To show negation (*do/does + not*): I do not drive there.
To show emphasis (*do/does*): She does drive sometimes.

2 Use modal auxiliaries for a wide range of meanings.

Modal auxiliaries include *can, could, may, might, should, would,* and *must,* as well as four modals that always appear with the particle *to: ought to, have to, able to,* and *have got to.* The base form of the verb (the dictionary form) is always used with a modal auxiliary, whether the time reference is to the future, present, or past. For a past time reference, use the modal plus the past perfect (*have* + the past participle).

Meaning Expressed	Present Time or Past Time	Modal + Past Perfect
ability and permission	She can drive. She could drive.	She could have driven.
possibility	She may drive. She might drive.	She might have driven.
advisability	She should drive. She ought to drive. She had better drive.	She should have driven. She ought to have driven.
necessity	She must drive. She has to drive.	She had to drive.
negative necessity	She does not have to drive. [she need not]	
versus prohibition*	She must not drive. [she is not allowed]	

*****NOTE:** The two negatives above have very different meanings.

Some idiomatic expressions with modals

Some other idiomatic expressions with modals are expressed in the following list.

Example	Meaning
I *would rather* drive than fly.	I prefer driving to flying.
We *would talk* for hours.	We always talked for hours then.
She has car keys, so she *must* drive.	[must = probably does]
Shall we dance again?	I'm inviting you to dance again.
Would you mind turning the heat up?	[would you mind = would you object to]
Do you mind turning it off?	Please turn it off.

ESL

46e   Choosing gerunds and infinitives with verbs

There are three types of verbals: infinitives, gerunds, and participles (see 7a-4).

1   Using infinitives and gerunds as nouns

Use an infinitive or a gerund to function either as a subject or as an object.

As Subjects   *To be one of the leaders here* is not really what I want.
              His being one of the leaders here is unacceptable.

As Objects   I don't really want *to be one of the leaders here.*
              I don't accept *his being one of the leaders here.*

NOTE: The possessive case is used with gerunds; see 8c-2.

(See 7a-4 and 7d-2, 3 for basic definitions and examples of verbals. See ESL-47a-1 for participles which function as modifiers, and ESL-46b-1 for participles in the progressive form of English verbs.)

2   Learning idiomatic uses of verb/verbal sequences

Sometimes it is different to determine which verbs are followed by a gerund, which are followed by an infinitive, and which can be followed by either verbal. This usage is idiomatic and must be memorized; there are no rules to govern these forms. Note in the following examples that verb tense does not affect a verbal.

Verb + Gerund	*Verb + Infinitive*	*Verb + Either Verbal*
enjoy	**want**	**begin**
I enjoy swimming.	I want to swim now.	Today I begin swimming.
		Today I begin to swim.

go	**agree**	**continue**
I went swimming	I agreed to swim.	I continued swimming.
		I continued to swim.
enjoy + gerund	want + infinitive	begin + either verbal
go + gerund	agree + infinitive	continue + either verbal
finish + gerund	decide + infinitive	like + either verbal
recommend + gerund	need + infinitive	prefer + either verbal
risk + gerund	plan + infinitive	start + either verbal
suggest + gerund	seem + infinitive	love + either verbal
consider + gerund	expect + infinitive	hate + either verbal
postpone + gerund	fail + infinitive	can't bear + either verbal
practice + gerund	pretend + infinitive	can't stand + either verbal

NOTE: There is no difference in meaning between I begin to swim and I begin swimming. However, sentences with other verbs differ in meaning depending on whether a gerund or an infinitive follows the verb. This difference in meaning is a function of certain verbs. See the following examples.

Example	**Meaning**
I always remember *to lock* the car.	I always remember to do this.
I remember *locking* the car.	I remember that I did this.
They stop *to drink* some water.	They stopped in order to drink.
They stopped *drinking* water.	They didn't drink anymore.

Information on idiomatic usage is provided in ESL dictionaries such as the *Longman Dictionary of American English: A Dictionary for Learners of English*, 1983.

ESL 46f Using two- and three-word verbs, or phrasal verbs, with particles

Phrasal verbs consist of a verb and a **particle.** Note that a particle can be one or more prepositions (off, up, with) or an adverb (away, back). English has many phrasal verbs, often built on verbs that have one basic meaning in their simple one-word form, but different meanings when particles are added.

> The coach *called off* the game because of the storm.
> He *left out* some important details.

The meaning of a phrasal verb is idiomatic; that is, the words as a group have a different meaning than each of the words separately. Most of these varied meanings are found in a standard English dictionary. Here are some examples of sentences with two-word and three-word verbs.

> I *got ready* for work.
> She didn't go to the party because she didn't *feel up to* it.
> The doctor told him to *cut down on* red meat.
> They *did without* a television for a few years.

1   **Some phrasal verbs are separable.**

With separable phrasal verbs, a noun object can either separate a verb and particle, or it can follow the particle.

	noun object	**noun object**
CORRECT	I *made out a check* to the IRS.	I *made a check out* to the IRS.

However, a pronoun object always separates the verb and the particle. A pronoun never follows the particle.

	pronoun object
FAULTY	I *made out it* to the IRS.
REVISED	I *made it out* to the IRS.

Other separable phrasal verbs include the following:

call off	hand out	put back	start over, up
check out	hang out, up	put off	take on
divide up	[suspend: trans.]	put over [present	throw out
fill in	leave in, out	deceptively]	turn on, off, up,
find out	look up [research]	put up to [promote]	down
fit in	pick up	set up	wake up
give back, up	prevent from	sign on, up	write down

2   **Some phrasal verbs are nonseparable.**

With nonseparable phrasal verbs, a noun or pronoun object always follows the particle. For these verbs it is not possible to separate the verb and its particle with a noun or pronoun object.

	noun object		**pronoun object**
FAULTY	I ran Mary into.	FAULTY	I ran her into.
REVISED	I ran into Mary.	REVISED	I ran into her.

Other nonseparable phrasal verbs include the following:

bump into	call on	do without
get into	get over	get through
keep on	keep up with	hang out [= stay]
refer to	stop by	see about

Several verbs in their basic form are intransitive, but can become transitive phrasal verbs when a nonseparable prepositional particle is added to them.

| INTRANSITIVE | The politician *smiled* sheepishly, then quickly *apologized.* |
| TRANSITIVE | He *smiled at* me sheepishly, then *apologized* quickly *for* being late. |

Other examples of this kind of verb include:

insist on	object to	run into
complain about	participate in	laugh at
walk around, down, up, into, etc.		feel up to
look at, into		

NOTE: An adverb, but not a noun or pronoun, may separate the verb from its particle.

He *apologized* quickly *for* being late.

The following are nonseparable two-word verbs that are intransitive, but that can be made transitive if still another particle is added to them:

run around with	*get ready* for	*get by* with
get away with	*drop out* of	*look out* for
read up on		

3 **Some phrasal verbs can be either separable or nonseparable.**

Some phrasal verbs can be either separable or nonseparable. The meaning of a phrasal verb will change, depending on whether or not the phrase is separated by an object. Note the difference in meaning that appears with the placement of the object in the similar verbs below.

Examples	**Meaning**
I *saw through* it. [nonsep.]	I found it transparent.
I *saw* it *through.* [sep.]	I persisted.
She *looked over* the wall. [nonsep.]	She looked over the top of it.
She *looked* the wall *over.* [sep.]	She examined or studied it.
I *turned on* him. [nonsep]	I turned to attack him.
I *turned* it *on.* [sep.]	I flipped a switch.
I *turned* him *on.* [sep.]	I aroused his passion.
They *talked to* us. [nonsep.]	They spoke to us.
They *talked* us *into* something. [sep]	They convinced us to do something.

NOTE: Standard dictionaries usually list verbs with the meanings of most particles (indicating whether or not they are transitive), but they usually do not indicate whether a phrasal verb is separable or nonseparable. However, this information is provided in ESL dictionaries such as the Longman Dictionary of American English: A Dictionary for Learners of English, 1983.

EXERCISE ESL-46-1   Identifying verb types

For each of the following sentences, identify the underlined verb as **transitive,**
intransitive, or **linking.**

EXAMPLE   Edward T. Hall <u>is</u> a cultural anthropologist.   ____linking____

1. Hall once <u>worked</u> for the United States Department of State.   _____

2. Hall <u>married</u> Mildred Reed in 1946.   _____

3. The Halls <u>have written</u> many books and articles.   _____

4. The Halls <u>write</u> about culture.   _____

5. Edward Hall <u>has been</u> a university professor.   _____

6. The Halls' first book together <u>was</u> *The Fourth Dimension in*
    Architecture: The Impact of Building on Man's Behavior, published
    in 1975.   _____

7. Edward Hall <u>wrote</u> *The Hidden Dimension* in 1966.   _____

8. The Halls <u>travel</u> all over the world.   _____

9. Edward Hall <u>conducts</u> field research.   _____

10. Cultural anthropologists <u>speak</u> highly of the Halls' work.   _____

EXERCISE ESL-46-2   Active and passive verbs

Underline the verbs in the following sentences and identify them as **active** or
passive. Then revise each passive-verb sentence to make it active, and each active-
verb sentence to make it passive. (If necessary, provide a performer of the action.)

EXAMPLE   The University Ballet Company <u>performed</u> *Sleeping*
           Beauty last month.   ____active____
           Sleeping Beauty was performed by the University
           Ballet Company last month.

1. The music was provided by the Alumni Philharmonic.   _____

2. Marita Colon danced the lead.   _____

3. When she was a child, she was always annoyed by dance
    lessons.   _____

4. The audience was mesmerized by her performance.   _____

5. On closing night, a party was given in her honor.   _____

EXERCISE ESL-46-3   Knowing when to use progressive forms

For each of the following sentences, determine whether or not the progressive form is called for, and circle the appropriate form.

EXAMPLE   While I (clean, am cleaning) the bathroom, you can (sweep, be sweeping) the kitchen floor.

1. This whole house (needs, is needing) a good scrubbing.

2. If you (think, are thinking) about going out today, then you should (change, be changing) your mind.

3. As your clothes accumulate, it (becomes, is becoming) impossible to find the floor of your room.

4. Tomorrow you should (throw, be throwing) out all of the trash on the floor.

5. For weeks I (have told, have been telling) you to clean your room.

EXERCISE ESL-46-4   Distinguishing simple past from present perfect

In each of the following sentences, fill in the blank with the appropriate form of either simple past or present perfect for the verb in parentheses.

EXAMPLE   The court (be) *has been* in session since nine o'clock.

1. By now the judge (hear) _____ these arguments many times.

2. We (watch) _____ the case on television this morning.

3. Most people (expect) _____ to hear a verdict by now.

4. The defense attorney (ask) _____ for a recess a moment ago.

5. In the past week the jury (listen) _____ to hours of testimony.

EXERCISE ESL-46-5   Recording reported speech

Rewrite each of the following sentences, changing direct speech to reported speech. Make the appropriate changes in verb tenses.

EXAMPLE   Sylvia Porter once said, "I've always been independent, and I don't see how it conflicts with femininity."

Sylvia Porter once said that she had always been independent, and she didn't see how it conflicted with femininity.

1. Mary Wollstonecraft wrote, "I do not wish women to have power over men; but over themselves."

2. Marlene Dietrich told a friend, "It is the friends that you can call at 4 a.m. that matter."

3. Representative Mary Norton said, "I'm no lady; I'm a member of Congress, and I'll proceed on that basis."

4. Elisabeth Kubler-Ross wrote, "If we make our goal to live a life of compassion and unconditional love, then the world will indeed become a garden where all kinds of flowers can bloom and grow."

5. May Sarton said, "I have a great responsibility because I can afford to be honest."

EXERCISE ESL-46-6 **Using verb tenses in conditional and subjunctive sentences**

Fill in the blanks in the following sentences with the appropriate form of the verb in parentheses. Use the guidelines in ESL-46b-5 and 6 to determine whether or not the subjunctive mood should be used.

EXAMPLE   If I (be) _were_ President, I (meet) _would meet_ with the press regularly.

1. If the President (have) _____ the time, he (hold) _____ a press conference tomorrow.

2. If he (speak) _____ to the press last week, he (have, not) _____ so many problems now.

3. I wish that the President (listen) _____ to his advisers during these difficult times.

4. During the campaign, he said, "If I (become) _____ your President, I (talk) _____ weekly with the press."

5. When he (become) _____ President, he (stop) _____ talking to anyone.

6. If only two Senators (change) _____ their votes tomorrow, the bill (pass) _____.

7. If three Representatives (change) _____ their votes last week, the bill (fail) _____.

8. One Senator was overheard warning another, "I suggest that you (be) _____ present at the vote."

9. A Representative said of the President, "I advise that he (address) _____ the Congress soon."

10. The President retorted, "If you (be) _____ President, you (give, not) _____ advice so freely."

EXERCISE ESL-46-7   Changing word order with verbs

Rewrite the following sentences first as a question, and then as a negative, inverting word order as necessary.

EXAMPLE   Amy Tan wrote *The Joy Luck Club.*
            Question: Did Amy Tan write *The Joy Luck Club?*
            Negative: Amy Tan did not write *The Joy Luck Club.*

1. You read the book last week.
    Question:

    Negative:

2. You liked the book very much.
    Question:

    Negative:

3. Elena found the book confusing.
    Question:

    Negative:

4. I liked her second book, *The Kitchen God's Wife*, better.
    Question:

    Negative:

5. Tan also wrote a children's book called *The Moon Lady.*
    Question:

    Negative:

EXERCISE ESL-46-8   Using gerunds and infinitives with verbs

For each of the following verbs, create a sentence using either a gerund or an infinitive to complete the sentence. If the verb can take either, write two sentences. (You can refer to the list in ESL-46e-2 for help.)

EXAMPLE   love   My sister loves **to make** trouble.
                        My sister loves **making** trouble.

1. hate

2. expect

3. start

4. practice

5. suggest

6. need

7. prefer

8. fail

9. recommend

10. consider

EXERCISE ESL-46-9   Using phrasal verbs with particles

Create a sentence using each of the following phrasal verbs. If the phrasal verb is separable, separate the verb and particle in your sentence. If the phrasal verb can be either separable or nonseparable, write one sentence for each.

EXAMPLE   look over   Lester **looked over** the stack of boxes to see what was
                       behind it.
                       Regina **looked** the stack of boxes **over** to see if it would fall.

1. hand out

2. turn up

3. do without

4. participate in

5. see through

6. look up (research)

7. get over

8. drop out of

9. insist on

10. leave out

Using Modifiers and Connectors in English Sentences

Modifiers expand sentences in a variety of ways. The two types of modifiers are adjectives and adverbs, as well as phrases and clauses that function as adjectives or adverbs. There are two types of adverbs, descriptive and conjunctive. For basic discussions of the types of modifiers, how they function, and how they are placed or located in sentences, see 7a-5 and 6, and 7c. (For more on adjectives, see 11a-1 and 11e. For more on descriptive adverbs, see 11e and f. For more on conjunctive adverbs, see 19a-3.)

ESL

47a Using single-word adjectives and nouns as modifiers of nouns

A modifier of a noun must be placed as close to the noun modified as possible (11a-1; 15a). Single-word adjective modifiers are normally placed before a noun or after a linking verb.

BEFORE A NOUN   The *bored student* slept through the *boring lecture.*

AFTER A LINKING VERB   Jack *is bored.* The lecture he heard *was boring.*

1 Using the present and past participle forms of verbs as adjectives

The present participle and the past participle forms of verbs are often used as single-word adjectives. The choice of form has an important impact on meaning. In the following examples, notice that these forms can be very different—almost opposite—in meaning.

Past Participle	Meaning
a tired student	Something tired this student.
damaged buildings	Something damaged these buildings.

a frightened passenger	Something frightened this passenger.
excited tourists	Something excited the tourists.
an accredited school	Some group accredited the school.
Present Participle	*Meaning*
a tiring lecture	The lecture causes a feeling of being tired.
a damaging explosion	The explosion caused the damage.
a frightening storm	The storm causes the fright.
an exciting tour	The tour caused excitement.
an accrediting board	This group gives accrediting status.

2 Using nouns as modifiers

When two nouns are combined in sequence, the last is considered to be the noun modified; the first is the modifier. (This follows the pattern for single-word adjectives mentioned earlier.) The importance of sequence is evident in the following examples, where the same nouns are combined in different order to produce quite different meanings.

Modifier	+ Noun Modified	Meaning
a car	company	a company whose business involves cars
a company	car	a car provided to someone by the business
a light	truck	a small truck
a truck	light	a light attached to a truck
a game	parlor	a place where indoor games are played
a parlor	game	a type of game, like chess, played indoors

When more than two nouns are combined in sequence, it is increasingly difficult to determine which noun is modified and which is a modifier; see ESL-47f-2. For this reason, it is best to avoid overusing nouns as modifiers (see 11g).

ESL

47b Using adjectival modifiers with linking verbs and prepositions

Adjectives and past participle adjectives are often followed by a modifying prepositional phrase.

We are *ready.* We are *ready for* the next phase of training.
Jenny seems an *involved* person. She is *involved with* a boyfriend.

The preposition to be used in such phrases is determined by the adjective or participle adjective. With each such adjective, the choice of preposition is idiomatic, not logical; therefore, adjective/preposition combinations must be memorized. Sometimes the same adjective will change its meaning with different prepositions, as in this example.

Jenny was *involved in* planning from the start. Meanwhile, she was *involved with* a new boyfriend.

Past-participle adjective examples include the following:

excited about	acquainted with	divorced from
composed of	opposed to	scared of/by
involved in	interested in	cautioned to/against
exhausted from	done with	angry at/with

Single-word adjective examples include the following:

absent from	afraid of	mad at
bad for	clear to	sure of
crazy about	familiar with	cruel to
excited about	capable of	accustomed to
guilty of	responsible for	

NOTE: Standard dictionaries may not indicate which preposition is typically used with a given adjective. However, this information is provided in ESL dictionaries such as the *Longman Dictionary of American English: A Dictionary for Learners of English,* 1983.

ESL

47c Positioning adverbial modifiers

1 Observe typical locations for adverbs in English sentences.

Adverbs have typical or standard locations in English sentences, although these patterns can be varied for special emphasis. Adverbs are typically located immediately before a transitive or intransitive verb:

FAULTY   She finishes always her homework.

REVISED   She always finishes her homework.

EMPHATIC   She finishes her homework—always!

Adverbs typically are placed after the verb *be* and helping verbs in normal sentences.

He was frequently at the gym on Fridays.
She may often discuss politics.

However, when sentences are inverted for questions or negatives, the adverb is usually placed before the helping verb.

| FAULTY | They don't frequently talk. It doesn't sometimes matter. Ever did you hear from them again? |
| REVISED | They frequently don't talk. It sometimes doesn't matter. Did you ever hear from them again? |

2 Limiting modifiers cannot move without changing meaning.

Although many adverbs can be located at a number of different places in a sentence without changing the meaning, positioning is quite critical with certain **limiting modifiers** such as *only, almost, just, nearly, even, simply* (see 15b).

No Change in Meaning	*Significant Change in Meaning*
Generally it rains a lot in April.	*Only* Leonid sings those songs.
It *generally* rains a lot in April.	Leonid *only* sings those songs.
It rains a lot in April, *generally*.	Leonid sings *only* those songs. [OR . . . sings those songs *only*.]

See 15a–g and ESL-47d-3 for more on positioning modifiers. See also ESL-46c-2 for inverted word order with adverbs—such as *rarely, never, seldom*—located at the beginning of a sentence.

ESL

47d Using phrases and clauses to modify nouns and pronouns

See the guidelines for modifier placement in 15a–h.

1 Positioning adjective phrases and clauses

Unlike single-word adjective modifiers (which are placed before a noun and after a linking verb; ESL-47a), a phrase or clause functioning as an adjective must immediately *follow* the noun or pronoun it modifies in order to avoid confusion with adverbial modifiers in the sentence.

FAULTY	I brought the tire to the garage *with the puncture.*
	I brought the tire to the garage *which had a puncture.*
	[The modifier next to *garage* is very confusing.]
REVISED	I brought the tire *with the puncture* to the garage.
	I brought the tire *which had a puncture* to the garage.

If two or more adjective phrases or clauses modify the same noun, typical patterns of sequence operate, as shown in ESL-47f-1. (See 25d-1–3 for rules on punctuating adjective clauses.)

2 Avoid adding unnecessary pronouns after adjective clauses.

The subject in an English sentence can be stated only once; pronouns in the sentence refer to the subject (or to other nouns) but they do not repeat it. When a lengthy adjective clause follows the subject as a modifier, it is important not to repeat the subject with an unnecessary pronoun before the verb.

FAULTY	The *person* who works in office #382 *she* decides. [The subject is repeated with an unnecessary pronoun.]
REVISED	The person who works in office #382 decides.

This error is likely to occur because of a failure to observe the steps in forming a dependent clause. Here is the process for forming an adjective clause, using *who, which,* or *that* to replace the noun or pronoun of the dependent clause:

TWO SENTENCES	The person decides. *She* works in office #382.
TRANSFORM TO A CLAUSE	[*she = who*] *who* works in office #382
PLACE THE CLAUSE	The person <u>*who works in office #382*</u> decides.

The correct form for the relative pronouns *who* or *whom* in a dependent clause is discussed in 8f-2.

3 Use the relative pronoun *whose* for a clause showing possession.

An adjective clause is often constructed with the relative pronoun *whose* to show possession by the person or thing modified. Students sometimes omit a step in transforming a separate possessive statement into an adjective clause with *whose.*

FAULTY   The person whom her office was locked called security.

REVISED   The person whose office was locked called security.

Here is the pattern for transforming a sentence showing possession to a relative clause showing possession, using *whose* to replace the possessive noun or pronoun.

TWO SENTENCES   The person called security
                                                   Her office was locked.

REPLACE POSSESSIVE SUBJECT WITH *WHOSE*   *whose* office was locked
                                                   [*Her = whose*]

PLACE THE CLAUSE   The person *whose office was
                                                   locked* called security.

The same process is used for a clause showing possession of a thing.

TWO SENTENCES   The government made a protest. *Its* ambassador was
                     insulted.

TRANSFORM: Replace with *whose* [*its = whose*] whose ambassador was insulted.

PLACE THE CLAUSE   The government *whose ambassador was insulted* made a
                     protest.

ESL

| 47e | Combining phrases and clauses with connecting words

As writers combine phrases and clauses, they choose between two basic relationships: a coordinate or a subordinate connection. Elements that have a **coordinate** connection emphasize a balance or equality between elements. (See 19a for a discussion of coordinate relationships.) Elements can also have a **subordinate** or **dependent** connection which emphasizes that the elements are unequal, with one having a dependent link to another. (See 7e and 19b for a discussion of subordinate relationships.)

Phrases and clauses are often logically linked with connecting words, **conjunctions** and **conjunctive adverbs**, that require careful consideration of the kind of connection students wish to establish.

1   **Choose the right connecting word for coordinate structures.**

Connecting words for a coordinate, or balanced relationship include **coordinating conjunctions** (*and, but, or, nor, so, for, yet*), **correlative conjunctions**

(*either/or, neither/nor, both/and, not only/but, whether/or, not only/but also*) and many
conjunctive adverbs (*however, nevertheless, accordingly, also, besides, afterward, then,
indeed, otherwise*). These words show relationships of contrast, consequence,
sequence, and emphasis; they are discussed in 19a-1, 2, 3.

After deciding on the desired relationship among sentence parts, select a *single
set of connecting words*. Avoid a mixture of words that may cancel out the meaning.

MIXED   They were *both* competitive, *but however* they were well
                  matched. [The mixed connecting words show similarity and
                  contrast at the same time.]

BALANCED   They were *both* competitive, *and* they were well matched.
                  They were competitive; *however,* they were well matched.

See 25a-1 and 25f-1 for appropriate rules on punctuation.

2   **Choose the subordinating conjunction that establishes the desired dependent
relationship.**

Subordinating conjunctions establish different relationships including
conditional relationships and relationships of contrast, cause and effect, time and
place, purpose, and outcome (see chapter 19). In your writing, choose a single
subordinating conjunction, and avoid combinations that are contradictory or
confusing.

MIXED   *Because* she was sick, *so* she went to the clinic. [A relation of
                  cause and effect is confusingly combined with one of purpose
                  or outcome.]

CLEAR   *Because* she was sick, she went to the clinic. [cause/effect]
                  She was sick, *so* she went to the clinic. [outcome]

See 19b for a full discussion on establishing clear subordinate relationships
among sentence parts. See 25a-1 and 25f-1 for rules on punctuation.

ESL

47f   Arranging cumulative modifiers

1   **Observing typical order of cumulative adjectives**

Single-word adjective modifiers are placed close to a noun, immediately before
a noun, or after a linking verb (ESL-47a).

Cumulative adjectives are groups of adjectives that modify the same noun. There is a typical order of modifiers and cumulative adjectives in an English sentence. A major disruption of typical order can be confusing.

| FAULTY | a beach French gorgeous tent | red light my small bulb |
| REVISED | a gorgeous French beach tent | my small red light bulb |

Although some stylistic variations from typical order in the location of cumulative adjectives are possible for emphasis, typical locations in an English sentence provide a very strong normal pattern. Here are some guidelines.

Possessives precede numbers. Ordinal numbers precede cardinal numbers.

Jill's first car   my first nine drafts

The typical order of descriptive adjectives is shown below:

(1) Opinion	(2) Size	(3) Shape	(4) Condition	(5) Age	(6) Color	(7) Origin	(8) Noun
ugly		round			green		fenders
	huge		muddy				spots
lovely				old	red	Turkish	slippers
comfortable			sunny				room

---

2   Arranging cumulative phrases, clauses, or noun modifiers[*]

A single phrase or clause functioning as an adjective immediately follows the noun or pronoun it modifies to avoid confusion with any adverbial phrases in the same sentence (ESL-47b).

When accumulated adjective phrases or clauses modify the same noun, their flexible emphasis creates an extremely varied sequence, especially for issues of opinion. In a neutral context some of the same typical sequences may be observed as for single-word adjectives (above), except that the modifying phrases follow the noun:

I found *spots* which are *huge* and which are also very *muddy*.
We saw that the *rooms* were very *narrow* and yet they seemed *bright*.

---

[*]We owe this discussion on order of modifiers to Jean Praninskas, *Rapid Review of English Grammar* (Englewood Cliffs, NJ: Prentice-Hall, 1975).

When two adverbial phrases or clauses are accumulated, place phrases typically precede time phrases.

NOT TYPICAL	They lived in the 1970s in Japan.
TYPICAL	They lived in Japan in the 1970s.

Two-word modifiers of nouns

Three nouns are often combined, with the first two forming a two-word modifier for the last noun. When this happens, nouns fall into a typical arrangement somewhat comparable with that of adjectives.

NOT TYPICAL	a file steel cabinet
TYPICAL	a steel file cabinet

The sequence of two nouns used to modify a third noun may be classified and arranged in this sequence.

Material, Number, or Location	Origin, Purpose, or Type	Noun Modified
chapter	review	questions
two-word	noun	modifier
slate	roofing	tile
steel	file	cabinet

However, the categories of meaning for nouns are less clear than for adjectives and the opportunity for confusion is much greater. Students are therefore advised to avoid accumulating noun modifiers beyond this limit, and to rewrite combinations as phrases and clauses (see 11g).

EXERCISE ESL-47-1   Identifying single-word modifiers

Underline the single-word modifiers in each of the following sentences; then, above the modifiers, identify them as adjectives, present participles, past participles, or nouns.

EXAMPLE   *adjective*   *pres. participle*   *past participle*
        Central Asia contains a struggling democracy and a ravaged republic.

1. In Kyrgyzstan, a scientist president presides over a country with simmering

   tensions between the Kyrgyz majority and ethnic minorities.

2. In nearby Tajikistan, a civil war is raging, while embattled citizens try to live

   peacefully amid mounting chaos.

3. Muslim forces in Tajikistan have joined with democrats and nationalists to oppose

   the corrupt Communist government of the dreaded Rakhmon Nabiyev.

4. Filmmaker Davlat Khudonazarov lost to Nabiyev in a rigged election in 1991, but

   still traveled the country hoping to secure a lasting peace.

5. Compared with Tajikistan, troubled Kyrgyzstan seems a peaceful place, but it too

   faces a rising tide of ethnic violence.

EXERCISE ESL-47-2   **Using adjectival modifiers with linking verbs and prepositions**

For each of the following modifiers with prepositional phrases, create a sentence.

EXAMPLE   afraid of   Jon seemed **afraid of** the Nguyen's new dog.

1. excited about

2. interested in

3. accustomed to

4. cautioned against

5. familiar with

6. guilty of

7. involved in

8. sure of

9. opposed to

10. responsible for

EXERCISE ESL-47-3   Positioning adverbial modifiers

Each of the following sentences is followed by a modifier in parentheses. Rewrite each sentence, placing the modifier in the appropriate position.

EXAMPLE   Rebecca Ann Felton helped her husband in his political campaigns. (always)

Rebecca Ann Felton **always** helped her husband in his political campaigns.

1. She worked on behalf of the Woman's Christian Temperance Union at the turn of the century. (tirelessly)

2. Did Felton support women's rights? (strongly)

3. Yes, but she didn't overcome her prejudice against Catholics, Jews, and African Americans. (ever)

4. When Georgia Senator Thomas E. Watson died in 1922, the Governor appointed Felton to fill the seat for one day. (cynically)

5. The appointment was made to win favor with women's groups. (clearly)

EXERCISE ESL-47-4   **Using the relative pronoun** *whose* **in clauses showing possession**

Combine the following pairs of sentences, turning the second sentence into a relative clause showing possession.

EXAMPLE   Eugene McCarthy ran for president in 1968.
McCarthy's opposition to the Vietnam war was well known.

Eugene McCarthy, whose opposition to the Vietnam war was well known, ran for president in 1968.

1. President Lyndon Johnson chose not to run for reelection in 1968.
Johnson's policies were widely criticized.

2. When Johnson announced his retirement, Robert Kennedy chose to run.
Kennedy's brother John had been assassinated five years earlier.

3. Robert Kennedy was himself assassinated in June of 1968.
Kennedy's chances for winning the election seemed better than those of any other Democrat.

4. McCarthy tried to gain the nomination at the Chicago convention.
McCarthy's politics most closely resembled Kennedy's.

5. The convention chose instead Vice President Hubert Humphrey.
Humphrey's association with Johnson would surely hurt his chances for ele

EXERCISE ESL-47-5   Arranging cumulative modifiers

For each of the following nouns, arrange the modifiers in the appropriate order.

EXAMPLE   computer   (old, Nancy's, from the 1980s, personal)

Nancy's old personal computer from the 1980s

1. elephant   (Indian, six-hundred-pound, baby, the zoo's, new, cute)

2. ring   (antique, gaudy, sapphire, tarnished, in the drawer)

3. bushes   (rose, three, of the summer, flowering, first)

4. dancer   (from the Royal Company, young, beautiful, ballet)

5. waves   (white-capped, choppy, on the lake, hundreds of, frightening)